Taxation of Small Businesses 2021/22

Malcolm James
Cardiff Metropolitan University

First published October 2008

This (fourteenth) edition published September 2021
by Spiramus Press Ltd
102 Blandford Street
London W1U 8AG
www.spiramus.com

ISBN

9781913507152	Paperback
9781913507169	Ebook

British Library Cataloguing-in-Publication Data.

A catalogue record for this book is available from the British Library.

Printed and bound in Great Britain by Grosvenor Group (Print Services) Ltd

Preface

This book is intended for advisors to small businesses, whether they are sole traders, partnerships or small companies. Whilst such businesses may vary greatly, their affairs will generally be handled by sole practitioners and small partnerships. This book has therefore been written with their needs in mind and covers the situations which they are likely to encounter in practice, but is necessarily not exhaustive. It also recognizes that such practices have limited resources for reference books and that it is therefore necessary to cover situations which may be encountered more rarely, but where guidance may be all the more necessary due to the infrequency with which they occur. For example, the CGT treatment of assets held at 6 April 1965 and 31 March 1982 is not now relevant to individuals and unincorporated businesses. However, many small companies may own assets, particularly land and buildings which were acquired before those dates, therefore these topics have been included in the book. The book has also attempted not just to set out the law in a particular area, but also, where appropriate, the practice of HM Revenue & Customs as set out in their manuals. Whilst such practice may not be a definitive statement of the law it will generally be prohibitively expensive to challenge it through the courts and it is advisable to be forewarned of HMRC's stance in a particular situation.

I would like to thank everyone at Spiramus Press for their assistance and comments in the writing of this book and also Wyn Derbyshire for his advice on Chapter 12 (Pensions).

If any reader has comments for corrections or improvements to the book, please contact the publisher, and I will delighted to incorporate them into future editions.

The book reflects the law as at 15 July 2021.

About the author

Malcolm James is the Head of Department of the Accounting, Economics and Finance Department at Cardiff Metropolitan University and has lectured widely on the subject of taxation on both professional and undergraduate courses. Before becoming a lecturer he worked for several large firms of accountants and also in industry.

Contents

List of abbreviations

Statute is a major, but by no means dominant, part of UK taxation law and consists of the following major acts:

CA 2006	Companies Act 2006
CAA 2001	Capital Allowances Act 2001
CTA 2009	Corporation Tax Act 2009
CTA 2010	Corporation Tax Act 2010
FA 2021 etc.	Finance Acts
ITA 2007	Income Tax Act 2007
ITEPA 2003	Income Tax (Earnings and Pensions) Act 2003
ITTOIA 2005	Income Tax (Trading and Other Income) Act 2005
SSCBA 1992	Social Security Contributions and Benefits Act 1992
SSCR 2001	Social Security (Contributions) Regulations 2001 (SI 2001/1004)
TCGA 1992	Taxation of Chargeable Gains Act 1992
TIOPA 2010	Taxation (International and Other Provisions) Act 2010
TMA 1970	Taxes Management Act 1970
VATA 1994	Value Added Tax Act 1994

Tables of authorities

Cases

Statutes

Income Tax (Earnings and Pensions) Act 2003

Taxation of Chargeable Gains Act 1992

Regulations

Chapter 1. Income Tax Computation

1.1. Aggregation of Taxpayer's Income

A taxpayer's income from all sources must be aggregated in the tax computation, although each type of income should be shown separately (see comprehensive example in section **1.9**). The income must be analysed between:

1. Non-savings income;
2. Savings income, other than dividends. This includes:

- interest chargeable under ITTOIA 2005 Part 4, Chapter 2. This includes building society dividends, distributions from authorised unit trust and open-ended investment companies and payments from industrial and provident societies;
- income element of purchased life annuities chargeable under ITTOIA 2005 Part 4, Chapter 7. This excludes certain securities defined in ITTOIA 2005 s.718(2);
- profits from deeply discounted securities chargeable under ITTOIA 2005 Part 4, Chapter 8;
- income taxable under the accrued income scheme chargeable under ITA 2007 Part 12, Chapter 2;
- gains from life insurance contracts chargeable under ITTOIA 2005 Part 4, Chapter 9, where an individual or personal representative meets the conditions in ITTOIA 2005 ss.465 & 466.

  (ITA 2007 ss.12, 18)

  Savings income excludes relevant foreign income taxed on the remittance basis *(ITA 2007 s.18(2)(b))*.

3. Dividends. These include:

- dividends from UK resident companies chargeable under ITTOIA 2005 Part 4, Chapter 3;
- dividends from non-UK resident companies chargeable under ITTOIA 2005 Part 4, Chapter 4;
- stock dividends from UK-resident companies chargeable under ITTOIA 2005 Part 4, Chapter 5;
- releases of loans to participators in close companies chargeable under ITTOIA 2005 Part 4, Chapter 6; and
- relevant foreign distributions chargeable under ITTOIA 2005 Part 5, Chapter 8.

Relevant foreign income taxed on the remittance basis falling in the basic rate band does not qualify as dividend income *(ITA 2007 s.13(1)(c))*. However, such income falling in the higher rate band does qualify.

Income is classified broadly as would be expected, although it should be noted that property income is classified as non-savings income. Certain sources of income are exempt. These include:

- annual payments under an insurance policy if the payment is a benefit provided under so much of the policy as insures against a health or employment risk e.g. a physical or mental illness or disability or deterioration in such a condition so that the taxpayer ceases to be employed or carry on a trade, profession or vocation *(ITTOIA 2005 ss.735 & 736)*;
- betting and gaming winnings;
- social security benefits listed in ITEPA 2003 s.677(1);
- gifts;
- damages and compensation for personal injury *(ITTOIA 2005 s.751)*;
- interest on National Savings Certificates and ISAs;
- repayment supplements from HM Revenue & Customs;
- statutory redundancy payments and certain *ex gratia* payments on the termination of employment.

1.2. Interest

Interest on the following categories of loans qualifies for tax relief and is deducted from total income (the interest is paid gross):

- loan to purchase plant and machinery used in the business by a partner or employee. Relief is available for a period of three years from the end of the tax year in which the loan is taken out. If there is an element of private use, only the business proportion of any interest is allowable *(ITA 2007 ss.388-391)*;
- loan to purchase interest in close company other than a close investment-holding company. This includes a company which is resident in an EEA state other than the UK and which would be a close company if it were resident in the UK *(ITA 2007 s.392-395)*;
- loan to purchase interest in employee-controlled company resident in the UK or another EEA state and is not resident outside the EEA *(ITA 2007 ss.396& 397)*;
- loan to purchase an interest in a partnership or to contribute to partnership capital. This relief is not available to limited partners in a limited partnership or members of an investment LLP. In order to qualify the individual must have been a member of the partnership from the date the loan was made until the date the interest is paid. During that period they must not have recovered any capital from the partnership, other than capital representing repayment of the loan *(ITA 2007 ss.398 & 399)*. If the partnership which made the loan is dissolved and a new partnership is formed to carry on the whole or part of the business of previous

partnership, the two partnerships are treated as the same partnership *(ITA 2007 s.409)*; and

- investment in a co-operative. This applies to both shares in and loans to the co-operative *(ITA 2007 ss.401 & 402)*.

If only part of a loan is used for a qualifying purpose, a deduction may only be claimed for the interest on the portion of the loan used for a qualifying purpose *(ITA 2007 s.386)*. Interest for which a deduction is claimed under these sections is not allowable for any other income tax purposes and, similarly, no deduction may be claimed under these sections where the interest is taken into account in calculating the profits of any trade, profession or vocation or any UK or overseas property business *(ITA 2007 s.387(1), (2))*.

1.3. Limit on Deductions from Adjusted Net Income

The total deductions which a taxpayer may claim against their adjusted net income is limited to the lower of:

A. The total reliefs under the following headings:

(i) Trading loss relief against total income (see section **6.4**) *(ITA 2007 s.64);*
(ii) Relief for trading losses in early years (see section **6.6**) *(ITA 2007 s.72);*
(iii) Post-cessation trade relief (see section **2.45**) *(ITA 2007 s.96);*
(iv) Property loss relief against general income (see section **7.10**) *(ITA 2007 s.120);*
(v) Post-cessation property relief *(ITA 2007 s.125);*
(vi) Employment loss relief against general income *(ITA 2007 s.128);*
(vii) Share loss relief *(ITA 2007 pt 4 ch. 6);*
(viii) Interest payments (see section 1.2) *(ITA 2007 pt 8 ch. 1);*
(ix) Liabilities relating to former employment *(ITEPA 2003 s.555);*
(x) Strips of government securities, relief for losses *(ITTOIA 2005 s.446);*
(xi) Listed securities held since 26 March 2003, relief for losses *(ITTOIA 2005 s.454(4))*.

Any deductions relating to the following may be disregarded:

- Business premises renovation allowances (see section **1.1**) *(CAA 2001 pt 3AA);*
- Deduction under headings (i) to (v) above, insofar as they are made against profits of the trade or business to which the relief in question relates;
- Deductions under headings (i) or (ii) above, insofar as they relate to relief for overlap profits on cessation or change of accounting date (see sections **5.3** & **5.8**);
- Deductions under heading (vii) above to which EIS relief or seed enterprise investment scheme are attributable.

And

B. The higher of £50,000 and 25% of adjusted total income.
(ITA 2007 s.24A)

Adjusted total income is defined as total income;

(i) plus any deduction under the payroll giving scheme (*ITEPA 2003 pt 12*);

(ii) less relief at source for pension contributions under FA 2004 ss.192, 193(4) or 194(1) (see section **12.6.1**). The amount to be deducted is the gross contribution.

1.4. Payments to Charities

1.4.1. Gift Aid scheme

Any gift of money to a registered charity qualifies for relief, provided that:

- it is not subject to any condition of repayment;
- the payment does not fall within the payroll deduction scheme and is not deductible in calculating the individual's income from any source;
- the payment is not conditional on, associated with, or part of any arrangement involving the acquisition of property by the charity from the individual; and
- a gift aid declaration is made.

The payment must be a gift and the payer must not receive valuable consideration in return. There are, however, a couple of exceptions:

- free or reduced entry to properties preserved, maintained, kept or created by a charity for its charitable purposes is permitted, provided that *either* the public can obtain admission at all times during a 12-month period *or* the gift is at least 10% greater than the admission price granting similar rights that would otherwise be payable. A subscription to the National Trust will, therefore, fall within the gift aid scheme *(ITA 2007 s.420(1),(3))*. The condition that the property must be open to the public at all times in a 12-month period may exclude up to five days per year when special events are held *(ITA 2007 s.421)*;
- the value of any benefits obtained in return is ignored if they do not exceed the following amounts *(ITA 2007 s.418(2))*. These limits apply to the value of the benefits to the recipient, not to the cost to the organisation of providing them:

Amount of Gross Donation	**Permissible Benefit**
£1 - £100	25%
Over £100	£25 plus 5% of the excess

- the total value of the benefits associated with the gift and any other qualifying gifts in the tax year must not exceed £2,500 *(ITA 2007 s.418(3))*.

Tax relief may be withdrawn if a donation is a 'tainted' donation *(ITA 2007 s.809ZH; CTA 2010 pt 21C)*. A donation is tainted if the following conditions are met:

1. the donor, or a person connected with the donor, enters into arrangement, either before or after the donation is made and it is reasonable to assume that the donation would not have been made if the arrangement had not been made; and
2. the main purpose, or one of the main purposes, of entering into the arrangements is that the donor, or connected person, will obtain a financial advantage; and
3. the donor is not a qualifying charity-owned company or a relevant housing provider linked with the charity to which the donation is made.

(ITA 2007 s.809ZJ(1)-(6))

There are certain situations where the financial advantage is ignored, for example where the donation is solely for the advantage of charitable purposes *(ITA 2007 s.809ZL)*.

Care must, therefore, be taken when paying a subscription to, for example, an educational charity, because the value of a regular magazine, reduced entry to conferences or the right to tuition may well exceed the relevant limit.

A charitable donation may be carried back to the previous tax year if an election is made by 31 January following the end of the tax year in which the donation was made *(ITA 2007 s.426)*.

Relief for gifts to charities is given through the extension of the basic rate band.

1.4.2. Gifts of land and buildings or shares

A gift of land and buildings or shares and securities to a charity will be a charge on income *(ITA 2007 ss.431-436)*. A qualifying investment is:

- shares or securities which are listed or dealt on a recognised Stock Exchange;
- units in an authorised unit trust;
- shares in an Open-ended Investment Company;
- an interest in an offshore fund; or
- a qualifying interest in land, i.e. a freehold or leasehold interest.

(ITA 2007 s.432)

The amount of the tax relief is the difference between the market value and the amount of consideration received *(ITA 2007 s.434)*. The market value is established in the same manner as for CGT, except in the case of an interest in offshore funds where it is calculated in accordance with TCGA 1992 s.272(5) *(ITA 2007 s.438 (1), (2))*.

1.5. Personal Allowances Deducted from Net Income

1.5.1. Introduction

There are two types of personal allowances, namely those deducted from a taxpayer's net income and tax reducers (see section **1.7**). There are two types of personal allowances which are deducted from the net income to arrive at a taxpayer's taxable income:

1. Personal Allowance *(ITA 2007 s.35)*; and
2. Blind Person's Allowance *(ITA 2007 s.38)*.

1.5.2. Personal allowance

This allowance (2021/22 £12,570) is available to all taxpayers.

The personal allowance is withdrawn from taxpayers whose adjusted net income exceeds a threshold level (2021/22 £100,000) at a rate of half of the excess *(FA 2009 s.4)*. Adjusted net income is defined as:

Net income	X
Less:	
Gross gift aid donations under ITA 2007 s.426	(X)
Plus:	
Payments to trade unions or police organisations under ITA 2007 ss. 457 & 458	X
Adjusted net income	X

(ITA 2007 s.58)

Example

Sally has net income of £105,000 in 2021/22 and paid gift aid donations amounting to £800 during the year. The allowance to which Sally is entitled is:

	Income
	£
Net income	105,000
Gift aid donations £800 x 100/80	(1,000)
Adjusted net income	£104,000
Standard personal allowance	12,570
Reduction (£104,000 - £100,000) x ½	(2,000)
Personal allowance due to Sally	£10,570

1.5.3. Transfer of Personal Allowance

An individual may elect to transfer 10% of their personal allowance (2021/22 £1,257) to their spouse or civil partner, provided that:

1. the transferee spouse or civil partner is only liable to tax at the basic rate, dividend ordinary rate and starting rate for savings; and
2. the transferee spouse or civil partner is resident in the UK for tax purposes in the tax year; and

3. after taking into account the reduced personal allowance, the transferor spouse or civil partner is only liable to tax at the basic rate, dividend ordinary rate and starting rate for savings; and
4. neither spouse or civil partner has made an election under ITA s.45 or 46 to transfer 10% of the married couples' allowance (see section **1.7.2**). *(ITA 2007 s.55B(2))*

A claim to make the transfer must be made by four years from the end of the tax year to which the claim relates and, if it is made within the tax year, it will continue in force until it is withdrawn or the election is ineffective due to a condition not being satisfied *(ITA 2007 s.55D(1),(2)&(5))*.

1.5.4. Blind person's allowance

Blind person's allowance (2021/22 £2,520) is given to a taxpayer who is registered blind under the *National Assistance Act 1948 s.29* if they are resident in England or Wales *(ITA 2007 s.38(2)*, or who is unable to do any work for which eyesight is essential if they are resident in Scotland or Northern Ireland *(ITA 2007 s.38(3))*. When a taxpayer first claims the allowance, they may also claim it for the previous tax year provided that they can show that they were also blind in that tax year *(ITA s.38(4))*. If a taxpayer claiming the allowance has insufficient income to make use of the allowance, the excess may be transferred to the spouse or civil partner, provided that the spouse or civil partner is either resident in the UK for the tax year or falls within one of the categories in ITA 2007 s.56(3) and an irrevocable election is made in writing by 31 January in the sixth year following the year of assessment to which the election relates *(ITA 2007 s.39)*.

1.5.5. Trading allowance

An allowance of £1,000 may available to be offset against the income of a relevant trade and/or miscellaneous income, i.e. before any deductions such as expenses, chargeable under ITTOIA 2005 Pt 5 Ch. 8. The aim of this relief is to take very small sources of income from the provision of goods, services or other assets out of the charge to tax *(ITTOIA 2005 Pt 6A Ch.1)*.

Full relief is available if:

1. the taxpayer's income from these sources does not exceed £1,000 and the taxpayer has not made an election not to be given full relief for the year.
2. the taxpayer's total income from all relevant sources exceeds £1,000 and;
   (a) they are eligible to elect for the cash basis to be used; and
   (b) no election has been made to use the cash basis and the income would not have exceeded £1,000 if such an election had been in force; and

(c) if the trade was carried on in the previous tax year, an election to use the cash basis was in force in that year or they were eligible to make such an election.

(ITTOIA 2005 s.783AE)

Where a taxpayer's relevant income exceeds £1,000, a taxpayer may elect to offset the allowance against the income as an alternative to offsetting actual expenses incurred. Where a taxpayer has both trading income and miscellaneous income they may choose how to split the allowance between the two, although the allowance must not create a loss *(ITTOIA 2005 ss.783AH-AK)*. Where a taxpayer carries on more than one trade the receipts of all trades must be aggregated.

Where full relief is available it is given automatically, unless the taxpayer makes an election to receive a lower amount. Where a taxpayer qualifies for partial relief, they must make an election to receive this allowance. Both elections must be made by 31 January in the second tax year following the year to which it relates *(ITTOIA 2005 ss.783AL&AM)*.

There are a number of exclusions from this relief:

1. income from a trade carried on in partnership;
2. income qualifying for rent-a-room relief where either:
   (a) the income so qualifying does not exceed the limit for the year and no election has been made to disapply full rent-a-room relief for the year; or
   (b) the income so qualifying exceeds the limit for the year and no election has been made to apply the alternative basis.
3. the income includes any receipts from an employer or the employer of a spouse or civil partner;
4. the income includes any receipts from a partnership at a time when the taxpayer was either a partner or connected with a partner;
5. the income includes receipts from a close company at a time when the taxpayer was a participator in the company or an associate of a participator.

(ITTOIA 2005 ss.783AO-AQ)

1.5.6. Property allowance

An allowance of £1,000 is available for offset against a taxpayer's property income, other than receipts to which rent-a-room relief applies or non-relievable balancing charges *(ITTOIA 2005 Pt 6A Ch. 2)*. The conditions mirror those which apply for the trading allowance (see 1.5.6), apart from the fact that references to the cash basis do not apply.

1.6. Computation of Tax

1.6.1. Tax rates

There are three different sets of tax rates, one for non-savings income, one for savings income and one for dividend income *(ITA 2007 ss.6-8)*. These are:

	Non-savings income	**Savings income**[1]	**Dividends**[2]
Starting rate (first £5,000)	20%	0%	7.5%
Basic rate (next £32, 00)	20%	20%	7.5%
Higher rate (next £112,300)	40%	40%	32.5%
Additional rate (over £150,000)	45%	45%	38.1%

[1] Savings nil rate band applies to to first £500/£1,000.
[2] Dividend nil rate band applies to first £2,000.

The bands are allocated to the categories of income in the following order:

- non-savings income;
- savings income;
- dividends.

(ITA 2007 s.16)

If a taxpayer's non-savings income exceeds the basic rate band or the higher rate band, saving income immediately becomes taxable at the higher rate or additional rate respectively.

1.6.2. Scottish and Welsh rates of income tax

The following rates of tax apply in Scotland to non-savings income.

Starting rate (first £2,097)	19%
Basic rate (next £10,629)	20%
Intermediate rate (next £18,366)	21%
Higher rate (next £118,908)	41%
Additional rate (over £150,000)	46%

The Welsh government now also has the power to vary income tax, but it has not done so, therefore the rates applicable in Wales are the same as in England and Northern Ireland.

1.6.3. Extension of basic rate band

The basic rate band is extended by the grossed up amount of charitable gift aid donations and pension contributions *(ITA 2007 s.414(2)(b))*. Therefore, a charitable donation of £400 will lead to an extension of the basic rate band by £500 (£400 x 100/80) to £38,000.

1.6.4. Savings allowance

This is an additional allowance for savings, which is in addition to any part of the personal allowance which might be available for offset against it. This allowance is available to all taxpayers and is in addition to the starting rate band of £5,000, which is available where a taxpayer has no, or only a small amount of, non-savings income *(ITA 2007 s.12A).*

The savings allowance is £1,000 if no income is taxable at the higher rate or dividend upper rate and £500 if any income is taxable at the higher rate or dividend upper rate. No allowance is available where any income is taxable at the additional rate *(ITA 2007 s.12B).*

This is a nil rate band, rather than an allowance, means that if some of the savings income exempted by the nil rate band would otherwise have been taxable at the basic rate and some would have been taxable at the higher rate (or some would have been taxable at the higher rate and some would have been taxable at the additional rate), income in excess of the nil rate band are immediately taxable at the higher rate *(ITA 2007s.13A).*

Example

In 2021/22 Adam has non-savings income of £47,270 and savings income of £3,000, whilst Sophie has non-savings income of £47,370 and savings income of £3,000. The savings allowances to which they are entitled are:

Adam

	Non-savings	Savings	Total
	£	£	£
Non-savings income	47,270		47,270
Savings income		3,000	3,000
	47,270	3,000	50,270
Personal allowance	(12,570)		(12,570)
Taxable income	£34,700	£3,000	£37,700
Non-savings			
£34,700 @ 20%	6,940.00		
Savings			
£1,000 @ 0%	0.00		
£2,000 @ 20%	400.00		
	£7,340.00		

Sophie

	Non-savings	Savings	Total
	£	£	£
Non-savings income	47,370		47,370
Savings income		3,000	3,000
	47,370	3,000	50,370
Personal allowance	(12,570)		(12,570)
Taxable income	£34,800	£3,000	£37,800

Non-savings	
£34,800 @ 20%	6,960.00
Savings	
£500 @ 0%	0.00
£2,400 @ 20%	480.00
£100 @ 40%	40.00
	£7,480.00

The tax on the additional £100 of income is therefore £140, giving an effective marginal rate of 140%. However, this assumes that Sophie's basic rate band has not been extended and, if she is aware of the situation, she can make a gift aid donation to extend the band to £37,800.

1.6.5. Dividends Nil Rate Band

In 2021/22 there is a dividend nil rate band of £2,000. This is similarly a nil rate band, rather than an allowance, means that if some of the dividends exempted by the nil rate band would otherwise have been taxable at the ordinary rate of 7.5% and some would have been taxable at the upper rate of 32.5% (or some would have been taxable at the upper rate and some would have been taxable at the additional rate of 38.1%), dividends in excess of the nil rate band are immediately taxable at the higher rate *(ITA 2007s.13A)*.

Example

In 2021/22 Kate has non-savings income of £43,650 and dividend income of £12,000. Her tax payable is:

	Non-savings	**Dividends**
	£	**£**
Non-savings income	43,650	
Dividends		12,000
	43,650	12,000
Personal allowance	(12,570)	
	£31,080	£12,000
Tax – non-savings		
£31,080 @ 20%	6,216.00	
Dividends		
£2,000 @ 0%	0.00	
£4,620 @ 7.5%	346.50	
£5,380 @ 32.5%	1,748.50	
	£8,311.00	

1.7. Tax Reducers

1.7.1. Categories of tax reducers

The following allowances may reduce the tax liability calculated in the previous stage, but can only reduce a tax liability to nil and cannot give rise to a repayment:

- spreading of patent royalty receipts *(ITA 2007 s.461);*
- top slicing relief *(ITTOIA 2005 s.535);*
- relief for deficiencies *(ITTOIA 2005 s.539);*
- investment in Venture Capital Trusts (VCT) *(ITA 2007 ss.261-265);*
- community investment tax relief (CITR) *(ITA 2007 ss.333-339);*
- relief for interest on loan to buy life annuity *(ICTA 1988 s.353 (1A));*
- qualifying maintenance payments *(ITA 2007 ss.453-455);*
- payments for benefit of family members *(ITA 2007 s.459);*
- Married Couples' Age Allowance (including civil partners) (MCAA) *(ITA 2007 pt. 3 ch. 5);*
- double tax relief – treaty relief *(TIOPA 2010 s.18);*
- double tax relief – unilateral relief *(TIOPA 2010 s.18);*
- qualifying distribution after linked non-qualifying distribution *(ITTOIA 2005 s.401);*
- relief where foreign estates have borne income *(ITTOIA 2005 ss.677 & 678).*

Investments in VCTs give a tax reduction of 30% *(ITA 2007 ss.158(2), 263(2))* and the others give a tax reduction at 10%, e.g. the married couple's age allowance is £8,915 and this translates into a tax reduction of £892.

Where a taxpayer is entitled to a tax reduction under more than one of the above sections, the reductions are to be deducted in the order which will result in the greatest reduction in the tax liability *(ITA 2007 s.27(2))*, subject to the following restrictions:

- if the taxpayer is entitled to a tax reduction under more than one of the following sections, a tax reduction under a provision mentioned earlier in the list must be deducted before a reduction under a provision mentioned later in the list *(ITA 2007 s.27(4),(5))*:
  1. investment in Venture Capital Trusts (VCT) *(ITA 2007 ss.261-265);*
  2. community investment tax relief (CITR) *(ITA 2007 ss.333-339);*
  3. relief for interest on loan to buy life annuity *(ICTA 1988 s.353(1A));*
  4. qualifying maintenance payments *(ITA 2007 ss.453-455);*
  5. payments for benefit of family members *(ITA 2007 s.459);*
  6. married couples' age allowance (including civil partners) (MCAA) *(ITA 2007 pt. 3 ch. 5);*

- tax reductions under the following sections (double tax relief) must be deducted after any other deductions to which the taxpayer may be entitled *(ITA 2007 s.27(6))*:
  1. double tax relief – treaty relief *(TIOPA 2010 s.18);*
  2. double tax relief – unilateral relief *(TIOPA 2010 s.18).*

  (ITA 2007 s.27(5), (6))

1.7.2. Married couple's age allowance (MCAA)

The married couple's age allowance is now only available to couples where at least one spouse was born before 6 April 1935. The allowance available is determined by the age of the older spouse and the allowance given in 2021/22 is 10% of £9,125 *(ITA 2007 ss.4 5& 46)*. All references to the MCAA include civil partners in partnerships registered on or after 5 December 2005.

1.7.3. Reduction in MCAA

The CAA is withdrawn from taxpayers whose adjusted net income (defined as in section **1.5.2**) exceeds a threshold level (2021/22 £30,400) at a rate of half of the excess.

(ITA 2007 s.45(4) & 46(4))

This restriction only applies to the husband, in the case of married couples who married before 5 December 2005 and who have not elected by the start of the tax year for ITA 2007 s.46(2) to take effect (see below) *(ITA 2007 s.45(2)(e))*. The restriction applies to the spouse or civil partner with the higher income, where a marriage took place or a civil partnership is formed on or after 5 December 2005, or where a couple have elected before the start of the tax year for this to take effect *(ITA 2007 s.46(2)(e))*. If both spouses or civil partners have the same income the reduction is made to the income of the spouse or civil partner specified in an election (ITA 2007 s.46(2)(e)). The MCAA cannot, however, fall below £3,530 (this is a notional figure which equates to the married couples' allowance which would have been available to married taxpayers in general if the allowance had not been abolished except for older couples) *(ITA 2007 ss.45(5) & 46 (5))*.

1.7.4. Marriage during tax year

Where a couple qualifying for the MCAA marry during a tax year, the allowance is reduced by 1/12 for every complete tax month which has elapsed before the wedding (a tax month runs from the 6th of a month to the 5th of the following month) *(ITA 2007 s.54 (6))*.

1.7.5. Transfer of MCAA

The MCAA is given to the husband in the first instance, but his wife can make a unilateral election to receive £1,765 of the MCAA, i.e. half of the notional MCAA which would have available to all married taxpayers *(ITA 2007 s.47)*.

A joint election may be made for his wife to receive £3,530 of the MCAA *(ITA 2007 s.48)*. This election must normally be made before the start of the tax year for which it is first to take effect and remains in force until it is withdrawn *(ITA 2007 s.50(2))*, but an election may be made during the tax year in the year of marriage or formation of a civil partnership *(ITA 2007 s.50(3)(a))* or in the first 30 days of the tax year for which it is first to take effect, if appropriate notice of the intention to make an election is given to HM Revenue & Customs before the start of the tax year *(ITA 2007 s.50(3)(b))*. Where either spouse has insufficient income to use the MCAA in full, any unused portion may be transferred to the other spouse by making an election by 31 January in the sixth year after the end of the tax year concerned *(ITA 2007 s.51)*. The MCAA may only be transferred if the transferee spouse or civil partner is either resident in the UK for the tax year or falls within one of the categories in ITA 2007 s.56(3) *(ITA 2007 ss.47(2)(c), 48(2)(c), 51(4)(c))*.

1.7.6. Maintenance payments

Maintenance payments only qualify for tax relief if the taxpayer was born before 6 April 1935. Relief is given at 10% on the lower of £3,530 and payments made in the tax year *(ITA 2007 ss.454 & 455)*.

The payments must be made to the ex-spouse or partner and not directly to the child. By concession, relief will be available where school fees are paid direct to the school.

1.8. Tax Retained on Interest, Royalties and Gift Aid donations

In addition to tax on his own income, the taxpayer is also liable to pay tax retained on payments made net of tax. In doing this the taxpayer is acting as a tax collector for HM Revenue & Customs, and is paying the payee's basic rate liability on the income in the same way as a bank or building society acts as a tax collector for the investors' tax liability on interest. A taxpayer is therefore obliged to pay over the tax retained, even if his income, ignoring the payment, would be less than his personal allowance, and payment has not therefore given him any tax reduction *(ITA 2007 ss.963 & 964)*.

Where a taxpayer makes a gift aid donation, but does not pay tax at the basic rate on his income and/or his capital gains, the following allowances will be restricted to ensure that the tax retained on the donation is collected *(ITA 2007 s.423)*:

- personal allowance;
- blind person's allowance;
- MCAA;
- payments for benefits of family members;

- payments to trade unions and political organisations.

If this still does not achieve the right result, e.g. a taxpayer has no income or capital gains during a tax year, an assessment will be raised *(ITA 2007 s.424)*.

1.9. Comprehensive Example

Mr Jones has the following income in 2021/22:

Income Tax Computation

	Non-savings income	Non-dividend income	Dividends	Total
	£	£	£	£
Trading income	42,370			42,370
Rental income	4,500			4,500
Building Society Interest		1,500		1,500
Dividends			7,000	7,000
Total income	46,870	1,500	7,000	55,370
Interest	(600)			(600)
Net income	46,270	1,500	7,000	54,770
Personal Allowance	(12,570)			(12,570)
Taxable Income	£33,700	£1,500	£7,000	£42,200

Mr Jones also made gift aid donations totalling £400 (net) during 2021/22.

Mr Jones' basic rate band will be extended to:

	£
Basic rate band	37,700
Gift aid donations £400 x 100/80	500
	£38,200

Tax Payable

Non-savings Income	£
£33,700 @ 20%	6,740.00
Savings income	
£500 @ 0%	0.00
£1,000 @ 20%	200.00
Dividends	
£2,000 @ 0%	0.00
£1,000 @ 7.5%	75.00
£4,000 @ 32.5%	1,300.00
Tax payable	£8,315.00

1.10. Death and Separation

1.10.1. Death

A taxpayer will receive any allowances to which they are entitled in full, even if they die during the tax year *(ITA 2007 s.41(1))*.

1.10.2. Divorce and separation

For tax purposes the relevant date is the date of separation rather than the date of divorce. This will be the date of the court deed of separation or the date the couple separate in circumstances which are likely to be permanent. This does not necessarily mean that the couple are living under separate roofs *(Holmes v Mitchell (HMIT)(1991)(BTC 28))*. Spouses or civil partners are treated as single people from the date of separation, but in the tax year of separation the husband, or the civil partner receiving the MCAA will still receive the MCAA (if appropriate) *(ITA 2007 ss.45(2)(a)&46 (2)(a))* and half or all of the minimum MCAA may be transferred to his wife or other civil partner.

Where a couple separate in one tax year and are reconciled in a later tax year, in the tax year of reconciliation the husband or civil partner will receive the full MCAA (if appropriate), whenever the reconciliation takes place in the tax year. If a couple are separated and reconciled within the same tax year the separation is ignored.

1.11. Married Couples – Joint Property

Where a married couple jointly own an income-bearing asset such as property or shares, HM Revenue & Customs will normally assume that they own equal shares and apportion half the income to each partner *(ITA 2007 s.836)*. This does not apply to certain types of income, the most important being partnership income and income from furnished holiday letting *(ITA 2007 s.836(3))*. A couple may, however, elect for the income to be apportioned in some other manner *(ITA 2007 s.837 (1),(2))* and this is a means by which a non-working spouse may use his personal allowance.

Any election must, however, reflect the facts and if one spouse wishes to transfer some or all of the income to the other spouse they must make an outright and irrevocable gift of the underlying asset. For example, where an attempt is made to transfer dividend income to the other spouse whilst retaining ownership of the underlying capital, HMRC will invoke anti-avoidance settlement rules under ITTOIA 2005 ss.624-627.

1.12. Minor Children

Minor children are taxable persons and are entitled to a personal allowance, but most children simply do not have sufficient income to pay any tax.

Under ITTOIA 2005 s.629(1),(2) any income which has arisen from capital gifted from a child's parents is taxable on the parents. This, however, does not apply if:

- the amount of income arising in the tax year does not exceed £100, which covers items such as birthday and Christmas gifts *(ITTOIA 2005 s.629 (3)(4));*
- the child is employed in the parent's trade and the payment represents reasonable remuneration.

These provisions do not cover gifts by other family members such as grandparents, and the gifting of capital by grandparents directly to grandchildren is a common and effective tax planning strategy.

1.13. High Income Child Benefit Charge

1. A high income benefit charge applies where a taxpayer has an adjusted net income (see section **1.5.2**) in excess of £50,000 and the taxpayer, or taxpayer's partner, is entitled to receive child benefit for a week (defined as an period of seven days commencing on a Monday beginning in the tax year) in the tax year; and
2. during that week the taxpayer does not have a partner or has a partner whose adjusted net income does not exceed that of the taxpayer.

(ITEPA 2003 s.681B)

The amount of the charge will be 1% of the child benefit received by the taxpayer and/or their partner for every £100 by which the adjusted net income exceeds £50,000, up to a maximum of 100% of the amount of the benefit *(ITEPA 2003 s.681C).*

Example

Lisa does not have a partner and has an adjusted net income of £52,000. During 2021/22 she receives child benefit of £150 per week.

Lisa receives child benefit of £7,800 (£150 x 52) in 2021/22. The charge will therefore be:

$$\frac{£52{,}000 - £50{,}000}{£100} \times 1\% \times £7{,}800 = £1{,}560$$

A partner is defined as a person of the same or opposite gender to whom the taxpayer is married or with whom they have entered into a civil partnership, provided that they are not separated under circumstances which are likely to be permanent, or who are living together as husband and wife or as civil partners *(ITEPA 2003 s.681G).*

If neither the taxpayer is entitled to child benefit during a week, and neither the taxpayer nor any partner of the taxpayer, is liable for the charge, but the child in respect of whom the benefit is claimed is living with another person, the person with whom the child is living may be liable for the charge, if they satisfy the conditons set out in ITEPA 2003 s.681B. Where there is more than one such person with whom the child is living, the charge will apply to the person with the highest adjusted net income *(ITEPA 2003 s.681D)*.

A taxpayer may make an election not to receive child benefit to which they are entitled, where they reasonably expect to be subject to the charge. The election may be back-dated by up to three months. The election may be revoked from the week commencing after the date of the revocation *(Social Security Administration Act 1992 s.13A(1)-(6))*. If a taxpayer makes an election and it subsequently transpires that no charge would have arisen on the payments forgone, the election may be revoked in relation to these payments within two years from the end of the tax year to which they relate *(Social Security Administration Act 1992 s.13A(7))*.

Chapter 2. Taxation of Trading Income

Note: Most of this chapter applies equally to companies and unincorporated businesses. However, for economy of space only references to ITTOIA 2005 are cited in this chapter. For aspects of the taxation of trading income relating solely to companies, see Chapter 1.

2.1. Introduction

By definition, only income of a trading nature is assessable under this heading. It is, therefore, necessary first to ascertain whether a taxpayer is trading, and if they are held to be trading, to distinguish trading income from:

- income of a capital nature;
- income arising otherwise than from the trade;
- income received as an employee of a business rather than as a self-employed sub-contractor (this is covered in more detail in **Chapter 1**).

Similarly, in order for an expense to be deductible from trading profits, it must be:

- revenue, as opposed to capital, in nature. There are a number of exceptions where expenditure of a capital nature is expressly deductible by statute;
- incurred in the course of the business, i.e. it is a proper debit under the principles of commercial accounting; and
- not otherwise disallowed by statute.

Accounts should be drawn up so as to show a 'true and fair view' and in accordance with GAAP, unless an election has been made under ITTOIA 2005 s.25A to use the cash basis (see section **2.10**) and, in general, the taxation treatment will follow the accounting treatment *(Gallagher v Jones (1993) & Threlfall v Jones (1993) (BTC 310); Herbert Smith (A Firm) v Honour (1999) (72 TC 130) (BTC 44)).* Where a receipt is not in the form of money, the amount brought into account must be the full money's worth *(ITTOIA 2005 s.28A).*

In certain cases this may be challenged if it is felt that the accounts take too conservative a view and, in establishing this, an Officer of HM Revenue & Customs will look at whether the accounting treatment followed is generally acceptable and whether there are alternative generally accepted accounting practices which could be justified in the circumstances. Where a change in accounting treatment is made from one valid basis to another, an adjustment will be made to the accounts. Where a change in accounting treatment is made from an invalid to a valid basis, both the opening and closing figures are calculated using the new valid basis. In addition, where a change has been made from an invalid to a valid basis, it may be possible for the Officer to reopen earlier years by making a discovery assessment if they feel that the change constitutes new information.

2.2. Statutory Definitions of Trading

The legislation, unfortunately, gives very little guidance as to whether a particular activity constitutes trading. The definition states that a trade 'includes any venture in the nature of a trade' *(ITA 2007 s.989)*, which merely means that whether an activity is a trade depends on the substance of what is being carried on and how it is being carried on, rather than the description given to it by an individual, and does not necessarily need to have all the attributes associated with a trade in order to be chargeable. It has, therefore, fallen to case law to provide more specific guidance.

2.3. Statutory Trades

There are a number of statutory trades, the profits from which were taxable as trading income, i.e. activities which are deemed to be a trade, such as farming, market gardening and the occupation of land managed on a commercial basis with a view to realising profits (other than woodlands). Profits from the occupation of woodlands are outside the scope of tax, but the occupier may be taxable on activities which constitute an actual trade e.g. the sale of timber.

2.4. Case Law

2.4.1. Badges of trade

Where a business is not a statutory trade, case law has developed numerous tests, known as the 'badges of trade' to determine whether a particular activity constitutes trading. A leading case in this area is *American Leaf Blending Co SDN BHD v Director-General of Inland Revenue (1979) (AC676)* in which Lord Diplock held that:

> *'in the case of a company incorporated for the purpose of making profits for its shareholders any gainful use to which it puts any of its assets prima facie amounts to the carrying on of a business.'*

It must be emphasised that these are merely indications, not hard and fast rules which are applicable in all situations, and all cases must be judged according to their individual circumstances. The decision will depend on the overall impression and the weight given to the different factors may vary in different cases.

2.4.2. Trading or investment

Where an asset is held as an investment, either because it is income-producing or has the potential for capital appreciation, or for personal enjoyment any profit on sale is unlikely to be treated as a trading profit. If the acquisition of the asset has been funded by a loan, so that the interest may largely offset any income gained, the income-bearing motive becomes less important. If property originally purchased as an investment is later appropriated as trading stock, a sale may be treated as trading depending on the circumstances. In the case of *Wisdom v Chamberlain (1968) (45 TC 103),* the actor Norman Wisdom purchased silver bullion as a hedge against devaluation and sold it at a loss. He then purchased more bullion which was sold at a profit. The profit on the second transaction was held to be a trading profit because the bullion was not income producing and was bought for short-term profit. In *Rellimi Ltd v Wise (1951) (32 TC 254)* a builder constructed houses which they either sold or let. He stopped building in 1941, but it was held that the completed houses were still his stock in trade and that a profit on the sale of a house sold in 1947 was a trading profit. An isolated land transaction was not held to be trading in *Marson v Morton (1986) (BTC 377),* where four wholesale potato merchants bought three acres of land on the recommendation of an estate agent. They argued that they had not purchased the land as a medium or long-term investment, rather to use it or develop it or receive income from it.

2.4.3. Profit motive

If the motive for the transaction was to earn a profit this will normally show that a trade is being carried on. This will again depend on the other circumstances. So, the presence of a profit motive will not necessarily be taken as an indication of trading, and nor will the absence of a profit motive necessarily preclude an individual from being treated as trading if the facts of the case indicate this. In *Overseas Containers (Finance) Ltd v Stoker (HMIT) (1989) (BTC 153)* the taxpayer company was a subsidiary, which had been formed largely for tax reasons. The parent company wanted to borrow Deutschmarks, but was concerned that in the likely event of a devaluation of sterling against the Deutschmark, the resulting loss would be on capital account. It hoped that by setting up a finance subsidiary to borrow the currency, the loss would be turned into a trading loss and thus available for group relief. It was held that the resulting loss was not a trading loss, since the company had been formed for tax reasons and did not have a commercial purpose. This can be contrasted with *Ensign Tankers (Leasing) Ltd v Stokes (HMIT) (1992) (BTC 110).* The Court of Appeal, overturning a decision by the Special Commissioners, ruled that capital expenditure under a film scheme was of a trading nature because it was entered into for a commercial purpose, even though the transaction had been deliberately structured to secure a tax advantage. The case was referred to the House of Lords, which agreed that the transaction was of a trading nature and that first year allowances were therefore available, even though the overall purpose of the transaction was fiscal. The rules governing the tax treatment for reinvestment in films have since been substantially revised.

2.4.4. Subject matter

The nature of the goods being bought and sold may sometimes indicate whether a trade is being carried on. In the case of *Rutledge v CIR 1929 (14 TC 490),* one million rolls of toilet paper were purchased and resold at a profit. This was held to be a trading transaction, even though there was only a single transaction, since the court understandably considered that the only possible motive for acquiring the toilet rolls was to resell them, at a profit. Similarly in *CIR v Fraser 1942 (24 TC 498),* the purchase and sale of whisky was held to be a trading transaction since the quantity was far in excess of any amount required for personal enjoyment. This can be contrasted with income-producing assets, or assets which may be purchased for personal enjoyment, where it will be necessary to make frequent purchases and sales in order to be regarded as trading. In the case of *IRC v Reinhold (1953) (34 TC 389),* a company director bought four houses and sold them at a profit. This was not held to be trading because the houses were *prima facie* purchased as an investment and not for short-term gain.

2.4.5. Frequency of transactions

Trading, by its nature, generally involves frequent transactions; therefore transactions which in isolation may be considered to be of a capital nature may be considered to be trading if they are carried out regularly. In the case of *Leach v Pogson (1962) (40 TC 585),* the plaintiff set up and subsequently sold a number of driving schools. If they had stopped after the first transaction, the profit on the sale would probably have been considered to be a capital transaction, but taken together it was held that they were carrying on a trade and this finding coloured all the transactions including the first one. The presumption of trading will be greater if there is a regular pattern to the transactions or there are a number of related transactions over a reasonably short period of time. In the case of *Salt v Chamberlain (1979) (53 TC 143),* it was held that individuals who deal in stocks and shares on a regular basis are not trading and that any profits will therefore be subject to capital gains tax rather than income tax, no matter how frequent the transactions. This presumption is now weaker in the light of the decision in *Wannell v Rothwell (1996) (68 TC 719)* (see section **2.7**). This also means that losses incurred in playing the market cannot be treated as trading losses.

2.4.6. Length of ownership

If goods are being traded, the trader would normally only own them for a short period, whereas items purchased as an investment would normally be retained for a longer period of time. In *Johnston v Heath (1970) (46 TC 463),* a purchaser for a property had been found before it was acquired by the taxpayer. This was therefore held to be trading.

2.4.7. Supplementary work

Carrying out further work on goods before they are resold will not in itself be indicative of trading. In the case of *IRC v Old Bushmill Distillery Co. Ltd (1928) (12 TC 1148)* a liquidator purchased whisky for blending and casks and bottles for bottling. The whisky was not saleable in its original state, and therefore had to be blended and bottled. It was held that the liquidator was merely putting the spirits into a saleable form in order to enhance their value. This can be contrasted with the case of *Cape Brandy Syndicate v CIR (1921) (12 TC 358),* where three individuals in the wine trade purchased, re-casked and blended brandy before reselling it. This was held to be a trading transaction because the individuals were experts and had bought the brandy with a view to resale at a profit.

2.4.8. Manner in which assets are acquired and circumstances surrounding sale

When goods are being traded the purchase and sale of these goods are deliberate acts. If a person acquires the goods, for example, by gift or inheritance, it is unlikely that any profit arising on a subsequent sale will be held to be a trading profit. A contrary indication would be where a purchase is funded by a loan, and the loan can only be repaid from the proceeds of sale of the asset, or where the purchase is funded from an existing trade. Similarly, if the goods are sold through financial necessity any profit is likely to be a capital profit. In the case of *Taylor v Good (1974) (49 TC 294),* a grocer bought a large house for sentimental reasons, but decided that it was not practical to live in it. So, he obtained planning permission and sold it at a profit. This was not held to be trading since the enhancement of a property before sale was considered to be common sense rather than an indicator of trading. A further test is whether the business is conducted in the same manner as a business which is indisputably trading.

2.5. Gambling and Speculation

A gambler is not liable to tax on thier winnings, even if a professional tipster, unless the winnings are ancillary to a taxable trade or vocation e.g. a club owner who regularly won playing cards with other members *(Burdge v Pyne (1968) (45 TC 320)).* Gains from speculation by individuals in shares and commodities are in general not considered to be taxable.

2.6. Illegal Activities

An activity can still be considered to be a trade and any profits may be taxed, even if the activity is illegal. The case of *IRC v Aken (1990) (BTC 352)* held that the earnings of a prostitute were taxable.

2.7. Individuals Trading in Shares

HM Revenue & Customs have generally been very reluctant to treat an individual dealing in shares as carrying on a trade, although the strength of this presumption is weaker than it was. In *Wannell v Rothwell (1996) (68 TC 719)* the taxpayer was held to be carrying on a trade of dealing in shares and commodity futures, although loss relief was denied because the taxpayer was not held to be carrying on the trade on a commercial basis. The factors which might indicate that a taxpayer is carrying on a trade include:

1. the business background of the taxpayer. In the above case the taxpayer was formerly a salaried commodities dealer;
2. the reason for the decision to trade in shares and commodities;
3. types of shares dealt in and in particular whether the shares have a history of paying dividends;
4. whether the taxpayer uses brokers and/or advisers and, in particular, whether the brokers or advisers have authority to purchase shares or not. If they do not, and all decisions are taken by the taxpayer, this will be more indicative of trading;
5. what types of research are carried out before acquiring shares and how the decision to acquire particular shares is taken;
6. how long the taxpayer intends to hold the shares;
7. how a decision to dispose of shares is taken;
8. the financing arrangements, e.g. whether credit is used or there are arrangements for deferred payment, so that shares do not have to be paid for until they are sold;
9. a description of the taxpayer's typical trading day, e.g. hours and location, number of calls to brokers;
10. volume of trading;
11. evidence of profit motive.

2.8. Definition of Trading – National Insurance

A person is largely defined as self-employed by default, i.e. if they do not satisfy the tests for being an employed earner. A person will be self-employed if they hold themself out as being ready to be gainfully employed, although no liability arises until they are gainfully employed. A liability may arise wherever a gain arises, even if the making of the gain was not the motive for entering into the arrangements e.g. payments to foster-parents in excess of expenses. A sleeping partner, or a non-working name at Lloyd's, does not incur a liability, provided that they do not actually perform any work for the partnership. No liability will therefore arise whilst they are undertaking preparatory activities, such as advertising, printing stationery etc. but self-employment does not cease simply because of a short period of inactivity. In *Secretary of State's Decision M37 (1953)* it was held that a theatre producer who mainly produced pantomime and summer shows, but who was also willing to accept and actually accepted offers of work at other times of the year, remained self-employed throughout the year. This is in contrast to a cricket umpire *(Decision M38 (1954))*, where no employment opportunities existed outside a certain period of the year. In *Decision M36 (1953)* it was held that a boarding house owner, whose house was only fully occupied during part of the year, remained self-employed throughout the year, since the work undertaken out of season, such as cleaning and refurbishment, was held to be an integral part of the trade.

2.9. Mutual Trading

See section **16.17.1** (Profits from mutual trading).

2.10. Election to Use Cash Basis

2.10.1. Conditions for making election

An unincorporated business may make an election to be assessed on a cash basis if the aggregate cash receipts for a tax year from all trades, professions or vocations carried on during the tax year by the taxpayer and any company controlled by them do not exceed the VAT registration threshold for the tax year (or twice the registration threshold where the taxpayer is a universal credit claimant) and the aggregate receipts for the previous tax year did not exceed twice the VAT registration threshold for the previous tax year *(ITTOIA 2005 ss. 31A&31B)*. Once an election has been made it will remain in force until:

(i) the aggregate receipts from trades, professions and vocations carried on by the taxpayer and companies controlled by them exceed the VAT registration threshold for that year; or

(ii) there is a change in circumstances which make it more appropriate for the profits of the trade, profession or vocation to be calculated in accordance with GAAP in subsequent tax years; or

(iii) the taxpayer elects for the election to cease to have effect.

(ITTOIA 2005 s.31D(1)-(3))

Certain taxpayers may not make an election under ITTOIA 2005 s.31A. These include:

(i) taxpayers who have been a Lloyd's underwriter at any time during the tax year;

(ii) taxpayers who have made an election for the herd basis to apply (see section **16.2.8**);

(iii) taxpayers who have made an election for the averaging of fluctuating profits (see section **16.2.2**);

(iv) taxpayers who have received business premises renovation allowances at any time with the seven years preceding the start of the basis period for the tax year (see section **1.1**).

(ITTOIA 2005 s.31D)

2.10.2. Amendments to rules relating to computation of profits

Where an election has been made for the cash basis to apply no deduction may be claimed for bad debts (see section **2.22**) or unpaid remuneration (see section **2.24**) *(ITTOIA 2005 s.32A)*. A deduction for capital expenditure may be claimed on a cash basis, provided it is of a type which would otherwise qualify as plant and machinery and is not expenditure on or in connection with:

- the acquisition or disposal of a business, or part of a business;
- an item of a capital nature to be used for the purpose of education or training;
- an asset which is not a depreciating asset (an asset with an expected useful life of less than 20 year or which is expected to lose at least 90% of its value in that period);
- any asset not acquired or created for use on a continuing basis in the trade;
- a car;
- land;
- an intangible asset, unless it must cease to exist within 20 years, or where the trader has granted a licence or any other right to another person in respect of it;
- a financial instrument or arrangement which is capable of producing a return that is economically equivalent to a financial instrument.

A deduction is available for expenditure on a depreciating asset, where it is installed or is otherwise fixed to land, so as to become, in law, part of the land, an is not:

- a building;
- a wall, floor, ceiling, door, gate, shutter, window or stairs;
- a waste disposal system;
- a sewerage or drainage system;
- a shaft or other structure in which a lift, hoist, escalator or moving walkway may be installed.

(ITTOIA 2005 s.33A).

Where disposal proceeds or a capital refund are received in respect of an asset acquired before the trader made an election to use the cash basis, but which would have been deductible if the cash basis had been in effect, these are brought into account as a receipt in calculating the profits of the trade *(ITTOIA 2005 s.96A(3), (3A) & (3I))*.

Where disposal proceeds or a capital refund are received in a tax year after an election to use the cash basis has lapsed in respect of an asset:

- for which a deduction was obtained on the cash basis, but would not have been qualifying expenditure if the election to use the cash basis had not been in force; or
- acquired in a period before the tax year in which the cash basis had effect;

the proceeds are brought into account as a receipt in calculating the profits of the trade *(ITTOIA 2005 s.96A(3C), (3D) & (3I))*.

A deduction may be claimed for interest, but is restricted to a maximum of £500 (including deductions for incidental costs of obtaining loan finance) *(ITTOIA 2005 s.57B)*.

Where a taxpayers has made an election and subsequently ceases to trade, a sum received after cessation is only treated as a post-cessation receipt (see section **2.13.7**) if it would have been treated as a receipt if it had been received before cessation *(ITTOIA 2005 s.246(2A))* and a deduction from post-cessation receipts is only allowable if it would have been deductible if it had been made before cessation *(ITTOIA 2005 s.254(2A))*.

Where a taxpayers has made an election and subsequently ceases to trade the value of stock and work-in-progress at cessation is treated as a receipt of the final period of trading *(ITTOIA 2005 ss. 97A&97B)*.

2.10.3. Transitional provisions – unrelieved capital expenditure

Where an election is made any unrelieved capital expenditure may be claimed as a deduction in the first period that the election applies *(ITTOIA 2005 s.240C)*. If the taxpayer has not fully paid for an asset, the deduction is restricted to the proportion of the amount upon which allowances were being claimed that has actually been paid *(ITTOIA 2005 s.240D)*. Where there is a transfer of trade, an election under CAA 2001 s.266 has been made to transfer assets at tax written down value and the successor has made an election to use the cash basis, these provisions will apply to assets acquired from the predecessor and any amount actually paid for the assets by the successor is ignored in any computation of trading profits *(ITTOIA 2005 s.240E)*.

2.10.4. Spreading of adjustment income

Any adjustment income arising when leaving the cash basis is spread over a period of six years, but an election to be made to accelerate some or all of the outstanding adjustment expenditure by the first anniversary of the filing date for the tax year to which it relates. The amount of adjustment income to be spread over the remaining years is adjusted accordingly *(ITTOIA 2005 s.239A&B)*.

Example

Tom left the cash basis in 2018/19 and this gave rise to adjustment income of £30,000. £5,000 of this amount was therefore charged in each of 2018/19 to 2023/24, but Tom elected to accelerate £6,000 of this charge in 2021/22, i.e. a total of £11,000 is to be charged in that year. This leaves a further £4,000 outstanding and £2,000 will therefore be charged in each of 2022/23 and 2023/24, subject to any further claims under this section.

2.11. Capital and Revenue Receipts

2.11.1. General principles

In general, the taxation treatment of transactions will follow the accounting treatment, i.e. if a receipt or expense is included in the profit and loss account of a business, it will be treated as a revenue item and if it is treated as a capital receipt in the accounts it will be so treated for taxation purposes. The accounting treatment is, however, not conclusive. Whilst the great majority of receipts and payments will clearly fall into one or other of these categories, the distinction will sometimes be an extremely fine one.

2.11.2. Compensation for loss or sterilisation of profit-making apparatus

A receipt which compensates for the loss or sterilisation of a traders' profit-making apparatus is a capital receipt.

In *Glenboig Union Fireclay Co v IRC (1921) (12 TC 427 HL),* the company was paid a sum by a railway company in return for agreeing not to work a bed of fireclay which it owned under a railway.

A receipt in return for entering into a restrictive covenant will generally be capital. In *Higgs v Olivier (1952) (33 TC 136),* Sir Laurence (later Lord) Olivier was paid a sum of £15,000 in return for an agreement that he should not, for a period of 18 months, appear in a film made by any company other than the company for which he had just made 'Henry V'. It was held that this receipt was *capital* since it did not arise from Olivier pursuing his acting vocation, but from an agreement not to do so. In some circumstance a receipt in return for agreeing to restrict operations in a particular area may be treated as revenue if it is intended to replace profits which would otherwise have been made *(Thompson v Magnesium Elektron Ltd (1943) (26 TC 1)).*

Similarly the receipt by ICI Ltd of lump sums in return for agreeing not to manufacture terylene in countries where it had granted licences to overseas companies *(Murray v Imperial Chemical Industries Ltd (1967) (44 TC 175))* was held to be capital.

The above cases can be contrasted with the following in which the receipt was held to be of a revenue nature.

In *Croydon Hotel & Leisure Co v Bowen (HMIT) (1996) (SpC 101),* a hotel owned by the taxpayer was managed by Holiday Inns as agents. A payment to Holiday Inns to terminate this agreement was not a capital receipt since it did not alter the structure of the operations, but simply allowed the hotel to be run more efficiently.

Payments under an agreement under which an oil company agreed to supply petrol to a garage proprietor and to pay sums towards promotion costs, in return for the proprietor agreeing to buy petrol exclusively from that oil company and giving them first refusal if he should decide to sell, were not held to be capital since the agreement was essentially one for the long-term supply of petrol *(Evans v Wheatley (1958) (38 TC 216)).* In such cases the terms of the agreement are important and if the receipt is paid as a lump sum or is made for, and the money is actually spent for a specific capital purpose, the receipt will be capital. Where it is in the nature of income, or is a re-imbursement of capital expenditure, it will be treated as revenue. Where the agreement is silent, further evidence as to the nature of the receipt will be sought.

2.11.3. Compensation for loss of profit

Compensation will be treated as a revenue receipt where the payment is in lieu of trading receipts, profit lost or forgone or trading stock lost, destroyed *(London Investment & Mortgage Co v IRC, London Investment & Mortgage Co v Worthington (1958) (38 TC 86)* or expropriated *(IRC v Newcastle Breweries Ltd (1927) (12 TC 927)).*

- A payment for the compulsory hiring of a ship by the Admiralty was held to be a revenue receipt, on the grounds that it compensated for the loss of income and profit from that ship during the period of the hire *(Sutherland v IRC (1918) (12 TC 63)).*
- A compensation payment made by an agent where they had negligently failed to object to a rent increase, resulting in the taxpayer paying rent in excess of what he claimed was a market rent, was a revenue receipt since it compensated for increased revenue expenditure *(Donald Fisher (Ealing) Ltd v Spencer (HMIT) (1989) (BTC 112).*
- In *Roberts v WS Electronics (1967) (44 TC 525)* a company sued two directors, claiming that they had diverted profit to companies in which they had a personal interest. Of the compensation awarded of £19,000, £11,000 was to compensate for the alleged loss of goodwill, but the £11,000 was held to be a revenue receipt for the loss of profit.
- A guaranteed profit payment to increase profits to a guaranteed 'mill standard' and to guarantee that they remained in business was held to be a revenue receipt *(Charles Brown & Co v IRC (1930) (12 TC 1256)).*

2.11.4. Compensation for loss of or damage to fixed assets

Compensation for the destruction or permanent non-use of a capital asset has been considered to be a capital receipt. However, compensation for damage to a capital asset will reduce deductible expenditure on the repair of the asset, and compensation for the temporary loss of use of property may be compensation for loss of profits.

- Compensation for salt water damage to pasture land was held to be capital since the payment was made to enable the farmer to return the land to its former level of productivity rather than for any loss of profits *(Watson v Samson Bros (1959) (38 TC 346)).*
- Where payments for a capital asset are made in regular instalments the payments will be treated as capital *(Boyce v Whitwick Colliery Co Ltd (1934) (18 TC 655)).* This will be the case even where the amount of those instalments is calculated by reference to their income-producing potential, such as in the case of *Legge v Flettons Ltd (1939) (22 TC 455)* where the annual instalments for the purchase of railway sidings by a railway company were calculated by reference to the volume of freight traffic.

2.11.5. Compensation and liability to tax

Many types of compensation, such as compensation for wrongful dismissal or personal injury, are not liable to income tax. In cases where the receipts or profits which are being replaced would themselves have been liable to tax, e.g. lost earnings, the amount of compensation awarded should be calculated by reference to the post-tax profits lost *(British Transport Commission v Gourlay (1956) (AC 185)).* This principle will not apply where the compensation payment is taxable or the tax position is uncertain *(Pennine Raceway Ltd v Kirklees Metropolitan Borough Council (No. 2) (1989) (BTC 42)).*

2.11.6. Know-how

Know-how is defined as 'any industrial information and techniques likely to assist in the manufacture or processing of goods or materials or in the working of a mine, oil-well or other source of mineral deposits (including the searching for, discovery, or testing of deposits or the winning of access thereto), or in the carrying out of any agricultural, forestry or fishing operations' *(ITTOIA 2005 s.583 (2),(5)).* A receipt from the disposal of know-how may be treated as either a capital or a revenue receipt depending on the circumstances. The treatment can be summarised as follows:

- where a trader disposes of know-how, or agrees to restrict activity in return for a fee, and continues in the same trade the receipt will be treated as revenue *(ITTOIA 2005 s.192(3),(4));*
- where a trader disposes of know-how, or agrees to restrict activity along with, or as part of their trade, the receipt will be treated as capital *(ITTOIA*

2005 s.194 (1)-(3)), unless the trade was carried on wholly outside the UK *(ITTOIA 2005 s.194(4))*. The vendor and purchaser may, however, make a joint election under ITTOIA 2005 s.194(5) for this section not to apply;

- where the seller and purchaser are connected the receipt will be treated as capital *(ITTOIA 2005 s.195)*;
- where none of the above circumstances applies, the receipt will be treated as revenue.

2.11.7. Foreign currency transactions

After the decision in the case of *Pattison (HMIT) v Marine Midland Ltd (1983) (57 TC 219),* HM Revenue & Customs issued SP1/87 setting out the treatment of foreign exchange gains and losses. This statement has now been superseded by SP2/02. The treatment can be summarised as follows:

- where a business owes or is owed a trade debt denominated in a foreign currency, any exchange gain or loss will be treated as a trading gain or loss;
- where there is an exchange loss on capital items and an overall exchange loss charged to the profit and loss account, the smaller of the two losses must be disallowed. Conversely, where there is an exchange gain on capital items and an overall exchange gain in the profit and loss account, the smaller of the two gains must be deducted.

Example

A trader borrows €1,100,000 on capital account, purchases current assets with a value of €550,000 and converts the remaining €550,000 into sterling when the exchange rate was £1 = €1.25. The loan is translated in the balance sheet at £880,000 and €550,000 is converted into cash of £440,000. At the balance sheet date, the rate is £1 = €1.10. The loan is revalued to £1,000,000 and the current assets to £500,000. There is therefore an exchange loss of £120,000 on the loan, and an exchange gain of £60,000 on the current assets, giving a net loss of £60,000 charged to the profit and loss account. Although the loss of £120,000 is on a capital item, £60,000 of the loss can be matched with the gain on the assets and only the balance of the loss of £60,000 is disallowed.

Where there is a net exchange loss on capital items, but a net exchange gain on trading items, or vice versa, no adjustment is necessary.

Example

A trader borrows €1,100,000 on capital account and borrows a further £440,000, also on capital account. The sterling is converted into €550,000 at £1 = €1.25, making total cash raised of €1,650,000. He makes a loan (not in the course of the trade) of €825,000 and retains the balance of €825,000 as a current asset. At the balance sheet date the exchange rate is £1 = €1.10. The books will show:

	£		£
Capital assets (€825,000)	750,000	Capital loan (€1,100,000)	1,000,000
Current assets (€825,000)	750,000	Capital loan	440,000
		Exchange gain	60,000
	£1,500,000		£1,500,000

The gain of £60,000 can be analysed as an exchange gain on the capital assets of £90,000, an exchange gain of £90,000 on the current assets and an exchange loss of £120,000 on the capital loan. There is, therefore, an overall capital loss of £30,000 and a gain of £90,000 on the current assets. The capital loss can be matched against £30,000 of the gain on the current assets and the remaining £60,000 of the gain is treated as revenue. No adjustment is therefore required.

Where there is more than one currency involved, the gains and losses on each currency must be calculated separately.

In considering whether a trader is matched in a particular currency, forward exchange contracts and currency futures entered into for hedging purposes may be taken into account, provided that the hedging is reflected in the accounts on a consistent basis and is in accordance with accepted accounting practice.

2.11.8. Grants

The taxation of grant income is subject to the normal rules and will depend on whether the grant is revenue or capital in nature. Grants which meet revenue expenditure are normally treated as trading receipts, whilst grants which are capital in nature, e.g. to acquire capital assets or to facilitate the cessation of a trade or part of a trade are not treated as a trading receipt, but may reduce the qualifying capital expenditure. Where a grant is undifferentiated, i.e. it is not given for any specific purpose, it should be treated as a trading receipt *(Poulter v Gayjon Processes Ltd (1985) (58 TC 350))*.

Grants from the government, local authorities or the EU follow normal principles.

A grant received in respect of non-trading activities is not taxable.

2.12. Receipts not Received in Course of Trade

2.12.1. Non-contractual receipts

Where a trader receives an amount which the payer has no contractual obligation to make, it will not be taxable provided:

- the payment is unsolicited;
- any business connection has ceased before the payment is made;
- the payment is not for past services and there should be no suggestion that fees charged by the recipient in the past were less than the market rate;
- the payment is not an advance payment or retainer for future services;

- the payment is not compensation for loss of business.

(Simpson v John Reynolds & Co (Insurances) Ltd (1975) (49 TC 693))

The factor determining the treatment of the receipt is its nature in the hands of the recipient, rather than the motive of the payer *(Murray v Goodhews (1978) (52 TC 86)).*

2.12.2. Unclaimed money

Where a trader receives money which they are supposed to repay, but which is never claimed, the money does not constitute a trading receipt *(Morley v Tattersall (1938) (22 TC 51))* unless the money becomes the property of the trader by operation of law *(Jay's the Jewellers Ltd v IRC (1947) (29 TC 274)).*

2.12.3. Commission, discounts and cashback

HM Revenue & Customs have set out in SP4/97 the circumstances in which commission, discounts and cashback received by a trader are taxable. Where a taxpayer has an entitlement to a receipt the commission, cashback or a discount will be treated as trading income where they are:

- received by the trader; or
- netted off against a payment made by the trader; or
- invested or applied by the purchaser in any way for the benefit of the trader;

and the services which gave rise to the receipt are provided 'on a sufficiently commercial, regular and organised basis to amount to a trade or profession'.

A discount will be taxable in similar circumstances where a discounted purchase price is paid or extra value is added to the goods or services, e.g. allocation of bonus units in an investment. Where there is no entitlement to the commission or cashback they will only be taxable where it is actually received. Self-employed insurance agents and travel agents are two professions where SP4/97 envisages that receipts would be taxable. The receipt will also be taxable where it is incidental to the carrying on of a trade or profession. The Statement of Practice gives the examples of an accountant receiving commission in the course of business, a grocer receiving commission as a result of taking out insurance contracts or a cashback being received on the purchase of an asset such as a car. In the latter situation the receipt will reduce the capital allowances available. If part of the commission is received by the customer, the full amount is still taxable on the trader, whether the trader passes on the commission or the commission is paid directly to the customer, but the amount passed on to the customer may be deducted if this payment satisfies the 'wholly and exclusively' rule (see section **2.15**).

Where commission is passed on to a customer by a separate payment, the gross commission must be shown as a receipt in the accounts and the payment to the customer shown separately. Where the commission is passed directly to the customer only a net amount need be shown, if either the customer required the commission to be passed on as a condition for entering into the business, or the transaction was between independent parties acting at arm's length.

Where commission is receivable as consideration for introducing business to another person, but the receipt is not taxable as trading income, it may be taxable if an enforceable contract exists. A sum received by an ordinary retail customer, however described, will not be taxable. Where part of the commission is passed on to a customer, a deduction is available if either the customer required the commission to be passed on as a condition for entering into the business, or it is otherwise necessary to pass on the commission in order to earn the commission.

2.12.4. Sponsorship

Where a sportsman is treated as being self-employed, e.g. golfers and snooker players in contrast to footballers and cricketers who are employees of their clubs, sponsorship payments will be taxable unless it can be argued that they have been paid on the grounds of their personal qualities *(Seymour v Reed (1927) (11 TC 625))*. Since such payments are generally negotiated in advance this exception will only very rarely apply.

2.13. Other Receipts

2.13.1. Rebates, insurance receipts, damages, statutory payments and interest

Rebates on the purchase cost of goods, insurance receipts for loss of trading receipts or additional trading costs and damages for acts such as negligence will be trading receipts. Where a trader deals in money, interest earned will also be a taxable trading receipt.

Where a deduction has been allowed for a loss or expense and a sum is recovered under an insurance policy or contract of indemnity, which is of a capital nature, the sum is treated as a revenue receipt up to the amount of the deduction *(ITTOIA 2005 s.106)*.

Interest receivable on overdue debts under the *Late Payment of Commercial Debts (Interest) Act 1998* is treated as trading income where the debt arose through an activity forming an integral part of a trade. The period in which the interest is assessable is determined by normal accounting principles.

2.13.2. Release from debts

Where a trader is released from the obligation to pay a debt, the amount of the debt released is treated as a trading receipt in the period in which the release is made *(ITTOIA 2005 s.97)*. The mere failure to pay a debt, whether due to bankruptcy or other reasons, will not give rise to a trading receipt.

2.13.3. Directors' fees and professional appointments

Where a professional in practice on his own account is appointed as a director or a consultant by another business it will generally be treated as an employment, although directors' fees will be treated as income of the business in the following circumstances:

- the directorship is a normal incident of the profession and the particular practice; and
- the fees are only a small part of the profits; and
- under the partnership agreement the fees are pooled for division amongst the partners.

(ITTOIA 2005 s.16B)

Partnerships seeking this treatment must give HM Revenue & Customs a written undertaking that such fees will be included in full in the gross income of the basis period, regardless of whether the directorship is still held or the partner concerned is still a partner in the year of assessment *(ESC A37 para. 1)*. Doctors and dentists will be taxable in respect of fees from private and NHS payments, but receipts in respect of hospital appointments are taxable as employment income.

2.13.4. Rent receivable

Rental income is normally treated as property income, but will be treated as trading income in the following cases:

- rent receivable in respect of tied premises where the landlord conducts a trade in letting them *(ITTOIA 2005 s.19)*;
- rent receivable in respect of business premises which are temporarily surplus to requirements;
- the portion of rent applicable to the provision of trading services by the landlord, unless the lease specifies that the services are to be provided for no separate cost *(Salisbury House Estate Ltd v Fry (1926) (15 TC 266))*.

2.13.5. Casual receipts

The proceeds of a single adventure in the nature of a trade may be treated as trading income, but casual receipts which would be treated as arising from a profession if the person were carrying on a profession or vocation are treated as other income. These may include:

- commission paid by a company to a director for personally guaranteeing a loan *(Ryall (HMIT) v Hoare (1923) (8 TC 521))*;

- commission paid by a syndicate to a company director in return for underwriting shares in a new company *(Lyons v Cowcher (HMIT) (1926) (10 TC 438);*
- commission received in instalments and partly in shares for negotiating the sale of shares *(Grey v Tiley (1932) (16 TC 414));*
- architect's share of profit on the purchase and re-sale of a company *(Brocklesby v Merricks (1934) (18 TC 576));*
- receipts for the sale of nominations to a stallion *(Benson v Counsell (1942) (24 TC 178));*
- sale of material to write life story *(Hobbs v Hussey (HMIT) (1942) (24 TC 153));*
- prizes from a recreational activity, e.g. share of winnings paid to racehorse breeder, where these arise from business-like activities *(Norman v Evans (1965) (42 TC 188)).*

SP 4/97 states that where services are remunerated on a sufficiently commercial, regular and organised basis they may be treated as trading income.

Other income not charged to tax under any specific statutory provisions ("other income") is taxable on an actual basis *(ITTOIA 2005 s.688(1)).* Where the receipts derive from business-like activities, deductions are allowable provided that they satisfy the 'wholly and exclusively' test and are not disallowed by any other provisions. Where a loss arises, this can be offset against income from other sources in the same year which it is treated as other income. Unrelieved losses may be carried forward and offset income treated as other income of subsequent years.

Where a taxpayer exploits his earning capacity by exchanging the right to earnings for a capital sum (whether in money or money's worth) the sum is treated as other income if the main, or one of the main, objects was the avoidance of tax *(ITA 2007 ss.777-779).* A similar liability may arise where a capital sum is derived by an individual or another person in respect of the individual's activities *(ITA 2007 s.777(5)).*

Other receipts treated as other income are:

- rents from mines, quarries and electric line wayleaves *(ITTOIA 2005 s.12(4), 22(1)).* Where the receipt of electric line wayleaves is to a person running a property business, which includes the land in respect of the wayleaves are paid, it is treated as property income *(ITTOIA 2005 s.346(1)&(2));*
- capital gains from the disposal of land or buildings or any property deriving its value from land, which were acquired with a view to realising

a gain from resale, or which were developed with a view to realising a gain on disposal *(ITA 2007 Pt 13 Ch. 2)*;

- profits from the sale of patent rights wholly, or partly, for a capital sum. The sum is taxed in six equal instalments, starting in the tax year of the disposal, but an election may be made by 31 January in the second tax year following the year of the disposal for the entire sum to be taxed in the year of the disposal *(ITTOIA 2005 s.590)*. If the person receiving the proceeds is non-resident, and does not receive the proceeds in instalments, the proceeds are taxed in the year of the disposal unless an election is made by 31 January in the second tax year following the year of the disposal for the sum to be taxed in six equal instalments, starting in the tax year of the disposal *(ITTOIA 2005 s.591)*. Tax at 20% must be deducted on payments to non-residents *(ITTOIA 2005 s.595 (2))*; and
- non-trading investors in theatrical productions ('theatre angels') may offset losses against profits from investments in successful productions *(ESC A94)*. Strictly, profits and losses are subject to CGT rules, but the concession permits profits and losses to be treated as other income. Tax need not be deducted at source where the backer is resident in the UK.

2.13.6. Receipts in kind

Where a trader is paid in kind the value of the receipt must be brought into the accounts. If it is difficult to value the item a trader may wait until the item has been valued, or if necessary sold, before including it in a computation. In the case of exchange and trading schemes HM Revenue & Customs' approach will generally be based on a combination of *Gold Coast Selection Trust v Humphrey (1948) (AC 459)*, where goods had to be credited at market value and *Sharkey v Wernher (1955) (36 TC 275)*, where it was also necessary to add back the profit forgone.

2.13.7. Post-cessation receipts

Receipts arising after the cessation of trade are generally taxed as trading income *(ITTOIA 2005 s.242(1))*. An election may be made under ITTOIA 2005 s.257(1),(2)&(4) for the receipt to be treated as having arisen in the year of cessation. Such a claim must be made by 31 January in the second tax year following the end of the tax year in which the receipt arose. Such a claim will be advantageous where the taxpayer has losses or is paying a low marginal rate of tax in the year of cessation. Where a claim is made any extra tax due is calculated by reference to the year of cessation, but the tax is actually payable in the year the receipt arose, and no interest will be payable *(TMA 1970 Sch. 1B para. 5)*.

2.13.8. Coronavirus Support Payments

These provisions apply to payments received by businesses under:

1. the coronavirus job retention scheme; or
2. the self-employment income support scheme; or
3. a coronavirus business support grant scheme; or
4. Test and Trace Support Payment Scheme (in England); or
5. Self-isolation Support Grant (in Scotland); or
6. Self-isolation Support Scheme (in Wales); or
7. any other scheme specified by either *Coronavirus Act 2020 s. 76* or regulations made by the Treasury.

The payments may be received either before or after the passing of the *Finance Act 2020. (Finance Act 2020 s.106)*

Payments are taxable as a receipt of the business if they are referable to a business which is carried on either alone or in partnership *(Finance Act 2020 Sch. 16 para. 1)*. Where the business is no longer being carried on by the recipient and the amount is not referable to activities of the business undertaken at a time when it was being carried on by the recipient, the recipient will be treated as still carrying on the business and the payment will still be treated as being referable to the business, unless the payment is taxable as a post-cessation receipt. Where a payment is referable to more than one business it must be apportioned between them on a just and reasonable basis *(Finance Act 2020 Sch. 16 para. 1(4))*.

Any expenses incurred may be deducted from the payment where they are referable to the payment and are deductible as an expense of the business, unless they arise directly or indirectly from the cessation of the business *(Finance Act 2020 Sch. 16 para. 2)*. Pre-trading employment costs do not qualify as pre-trading expenses under ITTOIA 2005 s.57, insofar as they are covered by a payment under the coronavirus job retention scheme *(Finance Act 2020 Sch. 16 para. 4(6))*.

A payment under the job retention scheme is referable to the business of the person who is entitled to it as an employer, even if they are not treated as the employer of the employees to which it relates for other purposes. The payment will not, therefore, be referable to any other business and no expense incurred by these other businesses may be deducted *(Finance Act 2020 Sch. 16 para. 3(1))*.

A payment under the self-employment income support scheme is referable to the business of the self-employed person to whom the payment relates *(Finance Act 2020 Sch. 16 para. 3(2))*. Any payment under the self-employment income support scheme is taxable in full in the tax year in which it is received *(Finance Act 2020 Sch. 16 para. 3(3))*. Where a payment is made to a partner of a partnership and the partner retains the payment, the payment is taxable on the partner individually, rather than on the partnerships *(Finance Act 2020 Sch. 16 para. 3(4)).*

A coronavirus support payment is not taxable where it relates only to mutual activities of a business carrying on a mutual trade and the payment is to be ignored in calculating:

i) the income resources limit for charities or charitable companies under ITA 2007 s.528(1) or CTA 2010 s.482(1);

ii) the income condition for community amateur sports club under CTA 2010 s. 661CA(1);

iii) the exemption from corporation tax for UK trading income of community amateur sports clubs under CTA 2010 s.662(2) or exemption from corporation tax for UK property income community amateur sports clubs under CTA 2010 s.663(2) *(Finance Act 2020 Sch. 16 para. 4).*

Trading and property allowances may not be deducted from payments made under the schemes and they are ignored for the purpose of calculating an individual's relevant income or relevant property income for the year *(Finance Act 2020 Sch. 16 para. 4(4)&(5)).*

Payments under the coronavirus job retention scheme will be taxable in full where they are treated as neither a receipt of the business nor as a post-cessation receipt, and where expenses incurred by another person in respect of the same employment costs are deductible from the profits of a business of that other person *(Finance Act 2020 Sch. 16 para. 5).*

A coronavirus support payment, other than a payment under the coronavirus job retention scheme or the self-employment income support scheme, is taxable even where it is not treated as a receipt of a business or a post-cessation receipt and the person receiving the payment did not carry on a business to which the payment is referable *(Finance Act 2020 Sch. 16 para. 6).*

If a person receives a payment under the scheme, or the self-employment income support scheme, to which they are not entitled is liable to income tax on the payment. This may arise where the person ceases to be entitled to the payment due to a change in circumstances or, in the case of a payment made under the coronavirus job retention scheme, the person has not used the amount to pay the costs it was intended to reimburse within a reasonable period of time *(Finance Act 2020 Sch. 16 para. 8).* In the former case the liability arises at the time of the change of circumstances and, in the latter case on the date the payment was received. The amount of the payment on which tax is due is the amount to which the person is not entitled and which has not been repaid. No loss, expense or allowance may be offset against the payment.

2.14. Capital and Revenue Payments

The courts have formulated several tests to determine whether a payment represents capital or revenue expenditure, notwithstanding the accounting treatment.

- Expenditure on fixed capital, i.e. assets such as factory machinery which are held for the long term in order that they may generate profit, will be capital expenditure.
- Expenditure on circulating capital, i.e. assets such as trading stock which will be sold in the short term in order to generate profit, will be revenue expenditure.
- Where expenditure brings about an enduring benefit, often by bringing a new asset into existence, the expenditure will generally be considered to be capital. An initial payment made by the company to set up a pension fund was ruled to be capital. However, subsequent annual payments into the pension fund were treated as revenue, since they were merely maintaining an existing asset *(British Insulated & Helsby Cables Ltd v Atherton (1926) (10 TC 155))*.
- A payment to secure the closure of a rival business was held to be capital, since it secured a permanent advantage for the company *(Walker v Joint Credit Card Co Ltd (1982) (55 TC 617))*. Similarly, a payment to bind an employee under a restrictive covenant not to compete in the same business was held to be capital *(Associated Portland Cement Manufacturers v Kerr (1945 (27 TC 103))*.
- The acquisition of an asset which is used in the trade process may cause difficulties. In *Hood Barr v IRC (No. 2) (1957) (37 TC 188)* the acquisition of woodland was held to be capital and the trees only became stock-in-trade when they were felled. Similarly the acquisition of an oil well was held to be capital in *Hughes v British Burma Petroleum Co Ltd (1932) (17 TC 286)*. However, in *Golden Horse Shoe (New) Ltd v Thurgood (1933) (18 TC 280)* the purchase of mine dumps was held to be revenue. Following the judgment in *Rolfe v Wimpey Waste Management Ltd (1989) (62 TC 399)*, expenditure on waste disposal sites which does not qualify for capital allowances is statutorily allowed as a revenue deduction.
- The purchase of a business for an initial franchise fee will be treated in principle as capital, but any part of the fee representing payment for revenue items, such as stock, will be revenue.
- HM Revenue & Customs will regard the cost of training courses undertaken by a proprietor as capital if they acquire new skills or expertise, but as revenue if they are simply updating or refreshing existing skills.

- The cost of tangible assets with a useful life of less than one year will be treated as being revenue.

Other examples of the distinction between capital and revenue payments will be discussed under the appropriate headings.

A deduction for certain types of capital expenditure is expressly permitted by statute. These include:

- incidental costs of obtaining loan finance *(ITTOIA 2005 s.58);*
- cost of obtaining, obtaining the extension of, or registering patents, design registrations or registered trade or service mark *(ITTOIA 2005 ss.89 & 90).* The costs of abortive or abandoned applications are also deductible;
- gifts to charities and educational establishments *(ITTOIA 2005 ss.107-110);*
- taxable premiums *(ITTOIA 2005 ss.60&61);*
- redundancy payments *(ITTOIA 2005 s.79);*
- payments for restrictive undertakings;
- payments by traders liable to pool betting duty towards capital expenditure on safety or comfort at sports grounds;
- payments to trusts mainly for the support of athletic sports, but with the power to support the arts.

2.15. Expenditure Incurred in the Course of a Trade

One of the most important principles is that expenditure must be wholly and exclusively incurred for the purposes of the trade. Whilst in the majority of cases the distinction between a trader's business and private expenditure is clear, guidance in the more contentious cases is once again provided by case law.

- A customer was injured by a falling chimney whilst sleeping in an inn owned by the brewery and claimed compensation. The compensation was held to be not deductible since it did not arise out of its capacity as a trader, but as a householder *(Strong and Co. of Romsey Ltd v Woodifield (1906) (5 TC 215)).* The argument put forward by Lord Davey in the House of Lords was that:

  > 'It is not enough that the disbursement is made in the course of, or arises out of, or is connected with the trade or is made out of the profits of the trade. It must be made for the purpose of earning the profits.'

  This argument has been widely criticised, and in practice compensation payments for personal injury or wrongful dismissal are invariably allowed on the grounds that they are an involuntary outgoing incurred in the course of the trade. Lord Davey's words cannot be entirely disregarded since they have been used as guidance in certain later cases such as *Mallalieu v Drummond (1983) (2 AC 386, BTC 380)* (see section **2.16.3**). In *McKnight v*

Sheppard (1999) (BTC 236) it was held that the *motive* for the payment rather than merely its *effect* must be considered. In *AB (a firm) v HMRC (2006) (SpC 5723)* a partnership agreed to pay the costs of the opponents of Mr A, one of its partners, which had been incurred as a result of unsuccessful litigation undertaken by Mr A in a personal capacity, for which he had engaged the services of AB. The agreement was reached because there was a danger that, if Mr A did not pay the costs personally, the opponents would seek payment from the firm under a wasted costs order. The firm claimed a deduction for this payment, even though the costs would not have been deductible if they had been incurred by Mr A personally. It was held that the payment was not deductible, since the liability to pay had always been Mr A's and there was never any likelihood that the firm would become liable. It was also held that the arrangement was a scheme to convert a non-deductible payment into a deductible one.

- A director defrauded the company of £15,000 and this loss was held not to be deductible since it did not arise in the course of trading *(Bamford v ATA Advertising Ltd (1972) (48 TC 359))*. Loss arising from fraud by a junior employee is considered to be incurred in the course of the business and is deductible.
- The costs of filing a tax appeal are not deductible since they arise in an individual's capacity as a taxpayer rather than as a trader, although the annual costs of preparing a tax return are deductible.

A payment is deductible even if the benefit to the business will not arise until some time in the future *(Vallambrosa Rubber Co Ltd v Farmer (1910) (5 TC 529))*. In this case the expenditure related to the care of rubber trees, from which no profit would be derived for another six years or so. In this case the expenditure was for services received in the current year. However, in *Stephenson v Payne, Stone and Frazer and Co (1967) (44 TC 507)*, a payment of £47,000 was made in respect of services received in the current year and the following two years, and the deduction was limited to £32,000, the amount relating to services received in the current year. It is normal accounting practice to spread payments over the period during which services are to be received and in this case a deduction will be permissible. A payment to preserve a taxpayer's business was held to be deductible in *Lawson v Johnson Matthey plc (1992) (BTC 324)* where the company paid £50m to support its insolvent banking subsidiary.

2.16. Duality of Purpose

2.16.1. General principles

Some types of expense can have a dual purpose, part of the expenditure being attributable to trading and part being private expenditure:

- a businessman who makes calls from his home may deduct the cost of business calls, but it is not possible to apportion the line rental charge, which is disallowable;
- if a car is used for both business and private motoring, the business motoring expenses will be deductible. It is necessary to keep a record of business and private motoring to support the apportionment;
- where part of a trader's residence is used as an office, an appropriate proportion of household expenses such as heating and mortgage interest will be deductible, but the trader should be aware that principal private residence relief will not be available on this proportion of any gain on the disposal of the property.

Sometimes expenditure will have a dual purpose, but is not capable of being analysed between business and private use and in this case the expenditure is not deductible.

2.16.2. Expenditure on meals

The additional cost of purchasing food whilst away from home on business is not deductible. The courts have held that eating is a fundamental human necessity and is not connected with the trade. It is, therefore, not possible to divide the cost of food between the need for basic sustenance and expenditure incurred in the course of the trade *(Cailebotte v Quinn (1975) (50 TC 222))*. In practice, HM Revenue & Customs may allow a modest deduction for meals consumed in the course of an occupation which is by its nature itinerant or for an occasional business journey which is outside the normal pattern.

It is also the practice of HM Revenue & Customs to allow the cost of accommodation and food and drink incurred by a UK resident trader, if the business necessitates spending one or more nights away from home. For trips abroad relief is specifically granted by ITTOIA 2005 s.92. Private expenditure e.g. a holiday taken abroad at the same time and costs relating to the trader's spouse and dependants is, however, disallowable.

2.16.3. Business clothing

It is not, in general, possible to claim a deduction for the cost of business clothing. The courts have held that clothing is necessary for warmth and decency and that this element cannot be separated from the need to portray a suitable, professional image *(Mallalieu v Drummond (1983) (2 AC 386, BTC 380))*. This principle is, however, not taken to unreasonable lengths and the cost of specialist clothing, e.g. protective clothing or a clown's outfit, will be deductible.

2.16.4. Travel and motoring expenses

Travel expenses are deductible provided that they satisfy the 'wholly and exclusively' rule e.g. the trader is travelling between two places of work. Where there is a duality of purpose, HM Revenue & Customs will usually allow a proportion of the cost. The cost of travelling from home to work is not deductible *(Newsom v Robertson (1952) (33 TC 452))*, unless the work is considered to have commenced at home *(Horton v Young (1971) (47 TC 60))*. In the former case the home of a barrister was not held to be a place of work, despite the fact that he carried out much of his work there. In the latter case, the home of a self-employed bricklayer was held to be a place of work on the grounds that he kept his books and tools there. In *Jackman (HMIT) v Powell (2004) (STC 645)* a milkman was denied relief for the cost of travel between his home and the franchisor's depot at which his milk float was stored under the terms of the franchise agreement, even though he undertook certain aspects of his business, such as issuing invoices from his home. The taxpayer had originally been granted relief for the expenditure by the Special Commissioners on the grounds that his home was his base, since it was the area from which his trade radiated, but this was overturned in the High Court, which concluded that the Commissioner had erred in law by concluding that it was necessary to determine the base of the trade before applying the statutory test and ruling out the possibility that the territory in which his round was situated could be his base. His situation was compared with that of a commercial traveller, whose area of operation could be distinct from the area in which his home is situated and can be contrasted with situations where the area covered by a business is unpredictable and varied. The costs of attending an overseas conference were held to be deductible in *Edwards v Warmsley Henshall & Co (1968) (44 TC 431)* because, on the facts of the case, the partner went to the USA solely for the purpose of attending the conference, whereas in *Bowden v Russell and Russell (1965) (42 TC 301)* similar expenditure was disallowed because the partner admitted that he also went for the purpose of a holiday and the duality of purpose precluded a deduction.

The costs of business motoring are deductible under general principles. Where a car is used partly for business travel and partly for private travel, an apportionment of motoring expenses may be made and in order to make an accurate apportionment it is necessary to keep detailed records. Businesses may use an alternative basis of claiming a fixed rate per mile on journeys which are wholly and exclusively for business purposes *(ITTOIA 2005 ss.94D-94G)*. However, whichever basis is chosen must be used consistently. In this context, this threshold has been chosen purely for administrative convenience. The mileage rate covers all the normal costs of running a car and other costs such as tolls and parking may be claimed in addition if they relate to a business journey. If the mileage rate basis is used, capital allowances cannot be claimed on the car since the rate contains an allowance for depreciation. The rates currently applicable are:

	Rate per mile
Cars – first 10,000 miles	45p
– over 10,000 miles	25p
Motor cycles	24p
Bicycles	20p

2.16.5. Duality of purpose – other items

A deduction is permitted for some types of expenditure, notwithstanding that the expenditure may have a dual purpose:

- pre-trading expenditure *(ITTOIA 2005 s.57(1)&(2))*;
- contributions to approved local enterprise agencies or to training and enterprise councils and local enterprise companies *(ITTOIA 2005 ss.82 & 84)*;
- intellectual property fees and expenses *(ITTOIA 2005 ss.89 & 90)*;
- expenditure on employees seconded to charities and educational bodies *(ITTOIA 2005 ss.70 & 71)*;
- contributions to payroll giving schemes *(ITTOIA 2005 s.72)*;
- payments to UK Export Finance *(ITTOIA 2005 s.91)*;
- debts which prove to be irrecoverable after events which are treated as discontinuance of the trade *(ITTOIA 2005 s.35(1))*;
- statutory and non-statutory redundancy payments *(ITTOIA 2005 s.79)*;
- payments to employees in respect of restrictive covenants *(ITTOIA 2005 s.69(1)&(2)*;
- reimbursement of employees' training course expenses *(ITTOIA 2005 ss.74 & 75)*;
- counselling services for employees *(ITTOIA 2005 s.73)*;
- contributions to registered pension schemes *(FA 2004 s.196)*;
- expenditure on scientific research *(ITTOIA 2005 s.88)*;
- provision of security assets and services by individuals *(ITTOIA 2005 s.81(4))*.

2.17. Repairs and Maintenance

One of the areas in which the distinction between revenue and capital expenditure is of great importance, and is most likely to be contentious, is the analysis of repairs and maintenance expenditure. A repair essentially restores an asset to its original condition with any improvement due to advances in technology being purely incidental. The case of *Rhodesia Railways Ltd v Collector of Tax of the Bechuanaland Protectorate (1933) (AC 368)* can be contrasted with *Highland Railway Co v Balderston (1889) (2 TC 485)*. In the former case expenditure on replacing part of a railway's running track was held to be revenue expenditure, whereas in the latter the cost of upgrading track to mainline standard was held to be capital. It should be noted in this context that HM Revenue & Customs now accept that the cost of replacing single-glazed windows with double-glazed windows is a revenue expense.

The cost of repairs to a recently acquired asset will generally be disallowable. In *Law Shipping Co Ltd v IRC (1923) (12 TC 621)* the owners of a ship failed to get the cost of initial repairs allowed since the ship was not in a seaworthy condition when it was acquired, and the repairs brought it into such a condition. Where the asset is usable in the condition in which it is purchased and the purchase price has not been substantially reduced on account of the dilapidated state of the asset, but merely reflects normal wear and tear, initial repairs will be allowable e.g. redecoration of new office *(Odeon Associated Theatres v Jones (1972) (48 TC 257)).*

2.18. Replacement of Assets

The replacement of a subsidiary part of an asset is treated as a repair and will therefore be allowable, e.g. a factory chimney *(Samuel Jones and Co (Devondale) Ltd v CIR (1951) (32 TC 513)).* As always, each case needs to be considered on its own facts since in the case of *O'Grady v Bullcroft Main Collieries Ltd (1932) (17 TC 93)* the taxpayer was refused a deduction for £287 of the total cost of erecting a new, improved chimney. It was held that the expenditure had to be looked at in its entirety and on the facts of the case the expenditure was capital. In *Brown v Burnley Football and Athletic Club Ltd (1980)(53 TC 357)* the replacement of a spectator stand by a more modern one was held to be an improvement, since the stand formed a distinct and separate asset, rather than being a subsidiary part of the football ground.

2.19. Depreciation and Amortisation

Depreciation and amortisation charges and losses on the sale of fixed assets are not deductible. Similarly, accounting profits on the sale of fixed assets are not taxable. Tax relief for capital expenditure is provided by the system of capital allowances, which is dealt with in detail in **Chapter 1**. Where depreciation is charged to cost of sales it was held in *HMRC v William Grant and Son (Distillers) Ltd (2007)* and *Small v Mars UK Ltd (2007) (UKHL 15)* that only depreciation charged to the profit and loss account should be added back and that the depreciation charged against fixed assets in a period should be adjusted by the depreciation element of opening and closing stock. Depreciation charged in the accounts will, however, be allowable in respect of a leased asset, since SP3/91 allows the depreciation charge on the asset to be treated as an approximation to the finance charge element of payments under the lease agreement.

2.20. Subscriptions and Donations

The test of 'wholly and exclusively' determines the deductibility of subscriptions and donations. Subscriptions for trading purposes e.g. trade magazines, trade organisations and Chambers of Commerce are allowable. In the case of many organisations, part of the subscription may be disallowable on the grounds that part of the organisation's expenditure would have been disallowable, if it had been made by the taxpayer (*ITTOIA 2005 s.34*). Subscriptions to local enterprise agencies, Training and Enterprise Councils, local enterprise companies or 'business link' organisations are allowable unless the taxpayer receives direct benefit in return (*ITTOIA 2005 ss.82-84*). Strictly speaking, charitable donations not made under Gift Aid[1] are only deductible if they are for the benefit of past or present employees, e.g. a benevolent association run by the industry for retired workers (*ITTOIA 2005 s.45(1),(5)*). In practice, by unpublished concession, small donations to local charities are allowed on the grounds that they generate goodwill in the area from which the organisation draws custom and its employees and are therefore for the benefit of the trade. Thus, a small donation to a local boys' club or hospital appeal would be allowable, whereas a donation of a similar amount to Oxfam, being a national charity, would not be.

Donations to political parties are disallowable.

2.21. Sponsorship

A donation is a payment where no benefit is received in return, and must be distinguished from sponsorship, for example the cost of providing prizes to a raffle or sponsoring a local football team. Such payments will generally be allowable as a form of advertising, but where expenditure is incurred in sponsoring a permanent exhibition or a capital asset, such as a racing car or racehorse, it will be treated as capital.

Where the motive for sponsorship might be seen as being partly a non-business one, the expenditure will be disallowed, e.g. where a business sponsors a relative of the proprietor. In *Executive Network (Consultants) Ltd v O'Connor (HMIT) (1995) (SpC 56)* the company sponsored an equestrian business run by the controlling shareholder's wife. Despite the fact that this sponsorship was commercially profitable there was held to be a duality of purpose and the expenditure was not deductible. Particularly where

---

[1] Donations made under the Gift Aid scheme extend the basic rate band and are not deductible from trading income. These are discussed in section **1.3**

substantial sums are involved it would be prudent to ensure that a formal agreement is entered into, so that it can be shown that the expenditure was incurred exclusively for business purposes.

Where entertainment is provided in connection with the sponsorship of an event, the cost of the entertaining will not be deductible.

2.22. Bad Debts

Losses from bad debts are allowable where the debt has arisen on a trading transaction, e.g. a credit sale *(ITTOIA 2005 s.35)*. A loss arising from the lending of money will be allowable if the purposes of the business include lending money or where the loans are made frequently and are closely related to the business's purposes, even if it is not exclusively in the business of money lending. Losses arising from a loan to ensure supplies or to finance a customer are not deductible *(James Waldie & Sons v IRC (1919) (12 TC 113))*. A deduction is also available if a specific provision is made against a debt or a debt is released as part of a statutory insolvency arrangement.

The judgement as to whether a debt is bad at the balance sheet date must follow accepted accounting practice and HM Revenue & Customs may require evidence to support the judgement.

Relief is only available for the uninsured portion of debts which cannot be discharged in the UK. The trader:

- must have made all reasonable efforts to secure payment and/or to remit the proceeds; and
- must not have used proceeds to finance expenditure outside the UK.

Relief is available for irrecoverable amounts under peer-to-peer loans *(ITTOIA 2005 ss.412A-412J)*. These are loans made through an operator (a person who has permission to operate an electronic system in relation to lending) by:

1. an individual;
2. a partnership consisting of no more than three persons, or which at least one is not a body corporate; or
3. an unincorporated body which is not a partnership and which consists of at least one person who is not a body corporate;

or is a loan made to a recipient falling within one of the above categories which is either no more than £25,000 or is not used wholly or predominantly for the purpose of the recipient's business. The loan must not be part of a scheme or arrangement the main purpose, or one of the main purposes of which, is the avoidance of tax *(ITTOIA 2005 s.412I)*.

Relief is given for irrecoverable amounts against total income *(ITTOIA 2005 s.412I(3))*. Where an amount for which relief has been given is subsequently recovered it is treated as interest of the year in which it is recovered *(ITTOIA 2005 s.412E).*

2.23. Provisions

Provisions appearing in the profit & loss account are deductible provided that they satisfy the following conditions:

- there is a present obligation as a result of past events;
- it is probable that a transfer of economic benefits will be required to satisfy the obligation; and
- a reliable estimate can be made of the amount of the obligation.

(*IAS 37*)

A specific provision against a bad debt will be deductible, but a general provision will not be, since it does not relate to an identifiable past event. In accordance with normal accountancy practice, a provision will be allowable, if, at the balance sheet date, there is no reason to believe that a debt is bad or doubtful, but before the accounts are finalised it transpires that the financial position of the debtor was such that at that date the debt was unlikely to be paid. Where a debtor is habitually a slow payer and there are no grounds for believing that his financial position has deteriorated, a provision against a debt will not be allowable.

Where a claim is made against a business, a prudent estimate of the amount for which the claim is likely to be settled is deductible, but not the cost of estimated future legal costs of contesting the claim. Similarly a provision for the cost of repairs undertaken, but not yet billed, will be allowable, but not a provision for future repairs.

In the case of provisions for claims under guarantees and warranties, where a large number of similar items have been sold, e.g. cars or washing machines, a provision may be calculated using an expected value. So, if past experience has shown that claims are made on 5% of items sold and a claim costs on average £100 to rectify, a provision calculated as £5 for every unit sold will be allowable.

2.24. Payments to Employees & Appropriations of Profit

Payments to employees will be deductible provided that they satisfy the 'wholly and exclusively' tests. Appropriations of profit, i.e. payments to the proprietor or a partner of a business are not deductible. Payments to a proprietor's spouse or children are allowable provided that the payments are commensurate with the duties performed *(Copeman v William Flood and Sons (1940) (24 TC 53))*. See section **2.56.2** for treatment of appropriation of trading stock.

HM Revenue & Customs may contest such payments on the grounds that they do not represent genuine payments to the other party. It is, therefore, necessary to ensure the following:

- there is a contract of employment with the other party;
- payment is actually made i.e. it is not simply a book entry *(Abbott v IRC (1995) (SpC 58))*;
- there is a pattern to the timing and amount of the payments.

Where a proprietor provides services to themself in a personal capacity or to his family, e.g. an accountant preparing his own tax return, the costs of providing this service are disallowable, but no notional profit needs to be added back. This also applies to meals taken by proprietors of restaurants and hotels and their families (*SP A32*).

The following payments on behalf of employees will be deductible:

- private medical insurance provided that the payment satisfies the 'wholly and exclusively' test;
- payments to a nanny in respect of secretarial duties (but not childcare duties) performed;
- payments to approved pension schemes or to trust funds for the benefit of employees. Large payments to pension funds may be spread over a number of years;
- reimbursement of employees' expenses incurred in the course of their employment (except business entertaining expenses). Where a general expense allowance has been given to an employee and part of it has been expended on business entertaining, the whole allowance will be deductible for the business, but the portion used to defray business entertaining expenses will be assessable on the employee;
- payments for the maintenance of leisure facilities for the benefit of employees, although the initial payments to purchase or construct the assets will be capital.

Payments of wages and salaries accrued but not paid at the end of a period of account are deductible, provided that payment is made within nine months of the end of the period of account *(ITTOIA 2005 s.36)*. Otherwise a deduction is only available in the period of actual payment.

If a return is made before the end of the nine-month period, it is assumed that any remuneration not paid by the date of the return will not be paid within the nine-month period. If it is paid within that period the return may be amended *(ITTOIA 2005 s.37)*.

Similarly, employee benefits accrued in the accounts are deductible if they are provided to the employee within nine months of the end of the accounting period *(ITTOIA 2005 s.38)*.

Payments of secondary class 1, 1A and 1B NIC are deductible *(ITTOIA 2005 s.53(3))*.

2.25. Entertainment

Expenditure on entertaining customers or suppliers is not deductible, but expenditure on staff entertainment, such as the Christmas party, is deductible unless it is incidental to the provision of entertainment to others (see section **9.22.8** for details of when such expenditure may be assessable on employees). If the entertaining is merely incidental to an event whose primary purpose is business-related (e.g. a free drink at the start of a business seminar) the cost will be deductible. Costs which are incidental to business entertaining (e.g. the taxi fare to take clients to a restaurant) are also not deductible. The cost of any asset which is used for providing entertainment is not eligible for capital allowances. Legitimate staff entertaining should not be disallowed, as an alternative to reporting it on the form P11D, as is sometimes the practice.

2.26. Gifts to Customers and Samples

The cost of gifts to customers is allowable provided that the following conditions are fulfilled:

- the trade's name is clearly marked on the gift;
- gifts totalling no more than £50 are made to the same recipient during a tax year;
- the gift is not food, drink or tobacco.

A common type of gift which would fall within these provisions is a calendar. The gift of certain assets to local educational, cultural, religious, recreational or benevolent bodies is also deductible *(ITTOIA 2005 s.108)*.

The cost of samples of a trader's own goods given to customers in reasonable quantities is allowable.

2.27. Gifts to Educational Establishments and Charities

Where a trader donates stock or fixed assets to a charity or educational establishment it can claim a deduction for the cost of the item donated without having to impute notional sale proceeds in accordance with ITTOIA 2005 s.172D.

Educational establishments include all UK universities and schools, whether state-run, grant-aided, independent or run by charities. Charities include not only all registered charities, but also bodies listed in ITTOIA 2005 s.108(4). These are:

- The Historic Buildings and Monument Commission for England;
- The National Heritage Memorial Fund;

2.28. Cost of Leasing Cars

The cost of leasing cars is deductible in full provided that one of the following conditions is satisfied:
(1) the vehicle's emissions' rating does not exceed 110g/km;
(2) the vehicle is electrically propelled; or
(3) the vehicle is a qualifying hire car.
(ITTOIA 2005 s.48(1))

Where none of the above conditions are satisfied 15% of the hire charge is disallowed *(ITTOIA 2005 s.48(2))*. The cost of hire of motorcycles is not restricted.

A car is a qualifying hire car if:

1. it is made available to a taxpayer for a period not exceeding 45 consecutive days, or, where there is more than one period of hire, for periods totalling no more than 45 days; or
2. the taxpayer makes the car available to another person (the customer) for no more than 45 consecutive days, or, where it is made available for more than one period, for periods totalling no more than 45 days. The customer must not be an employee of or a person connected with the taxpayer and the customer must not make the car available to an employee of, or a person connected with, the taxpayer under arrangements with the taxpayer, or a person connected with the taxpayer. If this condition is satisfied only for part of a chargeable period, the hire charge must be time-apportioned between the period(s) in which the condition was satisfied and the period(s) in which it was not satisfied.

(ITTOIA 2005 s.50A(2)-(4),(6))

Consecutive periods are amalgamated where the interval between them is no more than 14 days *(ITTOIA 2005 s.50A(7))*. Neither of the above conditions are to be treated as satisfied if the car was made available under arrangement, the purpose, or one of the purposes, of which is to disapply s.48 or otherwise the avoidance of tax *(ITTOIA 2005 s.50A(5))*.

Where two or more connected persons in a chain of lease would otherwise be required to apply the restriction to expenditure incurred on the hiring of the same car for the same period, the restriction only applies to the superior lease *(ITTOIA 2005 s.50B)*.

2.29. Legal and Professional Fees

Legal and professional fees are deductible provided that they have been incurred on trading items. Allowable items would therefore include the following:

- costs of debt collection;
- costs of defending unfair dismissal claims;
- cost of valuation of fixed assets;
- costs of defending title to fixed assets;
- cost of entering architectural competitions or tendering for contracts;
- successful defences of actions for breach of contract;
- cost of preserving a business's reputation, e.g. defending a criminal claim arising from business activities *(Spofforth and Prince v Golder (1945) 26 TC 310))* or an action arising from breach of Stock Exchange rules *(McKnight v Sheppard (1997) (BTC 328));*
- compromising an action for breach of contract;
- costs and damages arising from libel claim in business communication;
- costs of unsuccessful attempt to procure fixed assets, e.g. new licences for public houses *(Southwell v Savill Bros Ltd (1901) (4 TC 430))* or unsuccessful attempts to gain planning permission;
- termination of onerous trading contracts;
- renewal of a short lease, i.e. a lease of 50 years or less;
- costs incurred in obtaining medium or long-term business loans and loan stock, e.g. professional fees and commission, but *not* stamp duty *(ITTOIA 2005 ss.58&59);*
- costs incurred due to a HM Revenue & Customs investigation provided that no adjustments are made which result in more tax becoming payable or adjustments are only made to the year under investigation and these are not due to fraud; and
- cost of registering patents, trademarks and logos (*ITTOIA 2005 ss.89& 90).*

The last three items may appear to be capital, but a deduction for these items is specifically provided for by statute.

The following types of legal and professional fees are not deductible:

- legal or professional fees incurred on the purchase or construction of new assets and the improvement of existing assets. These may qualify for capital allowances under certain circumstances;
- costs of drawing up or varying a partnership agreement; and
- legal and professional fees of appealing against tax assessments. Costs incurred due to an HMRC investigation are not deductible if adjustments are made to previous years or fraud is discovered.

2.30. Fines and Payments Against the Public Interest

Fines for offences such as infringement of health and safety regulations, are generally not allowable. If an employer pays a fine on behalf of an employee the payment will be a taxable emolument in the hands of the employee. Where an employer pays parking fines incurred in the course of business by employees, but not proprietors, these are deductible if the car is owned by the employee or if the penalty notice was actually handed to the employee and the payment of the fine will be a taxable emolument in the hands of the employee. Damages which are punitive in nature must be disallowed, but those which are compensatory in nature are allowable. Bribes and payments in response to threats of blackmail are also not deductible, which is unfortunate for the many businesses which conduct business in parts of the world where such payments are a common feature of business life.

2.31. Interest and Bank Charges

Interest and bank charges on business overdrafts, business loans and business credit cards are deductible. Interest on overdue tax is, however, not deductible. Interest payable to non-residents will only be deductible at a reasonable commercial rate and income tax must be deducted at source and paid to HM Revenue & Customs.

There is no deduction for notional interest on sums which the trader could have invested if they had not been used in the business. No relief is available on interest where a partnership occupies land owned by a partnership if no rent or interest is payable by the partnership. Where interest is paid it will be treated as rent payable to the partner and as rental income in the hands of the partner. Interest paid by the partner may be offset against the rental income.

Where HMRC consider that a trader is using an overdraft on his business account to fund part of his private expenditure, it will seek to disallow a portion of the interest and bank charges. This may occur when funds of the business appear to have been used to purchase a non-business asset which appears in the balance sheet of the business, or when the proprietor appears to have used drawings from the business to reduce his private borrowings. It was held in *I. Dixon (2005) (SpC 511)* that where a mixed-use asset, e.g. shop and adjoining residence, is acquired and financed partly through equity and partly through a loan or mortgage, the interest must be apportioned between the business and private elements of the asset, using the values in the purchase agreement, even if the amount of equity contributed is greater than the cost of the private element.

Interest payable on overdue debts under the Late Payment of Commercial Debts (Interest) Act 1998 is not treated as 'yearly interest' and no income tax should be deducted at source. This does not apply where the interest arose under the terms of the contract.

Interest may not be deducted from trading income if a deduction has been obtained under ITA 2007 s.24(1).

2.32. Pre-trading Expenditure

Expenditure of a trading nature, e.g. rent of premises or purchase of trading stock, incurred in the seven years before the commencement of trading, is treated as a loss arising on the first day of trading *(ITTOIA 2005 s.57).*

2.33. Indirect Taxation

For VAT-registered traders, VAT on the purchase of most items can be reclaimed as input tax. Only the net cost may therefore be claimed for taxation purposes. If a trader is not VAT-registered or the VAT cannot be reclaimed, the full cost including VAT may be claimed.

2.34. Compensation and *ex gratia* Payments to Former Employees

Payments are deductible if they are not capital and are for the benefit of the trade. These will include *ex gratia* redundancy payments and payments to get rid of unsuitable employees and directors, provided that these are made to protect the good name or to maintain the nature and quality of the business, rather than due to a clash of personalities. Such payments may, however, be taxable on the employee (see section **9.7**).

2.35. Redundancy Payments

Statutory redundancy payments within the Employment Rights Act (1996) or the Employment Rights (Northern Ireland) Order 1996 are deductible. Payments made after the cessation of a business are treated as having been made on the last day of the business *(ITTOIA 2005 s.79(5))*. Additional non-statutory payments in excess of the statutory redundancy payments will be deductible provided that they have been made wholly and exclusively for the purpose of the business. In the case of a discontinued business the payment will be deductible, provided that it would have been deductible if the trade had not discontinued, and it is limited to three times the amount of the statutory payment. The payment is treated as having been made on the last day of trading.

A provision for future redundancy payments will be allowable provided that:

- a provision is made in the accounts in accordance with accepted accounting practice;
- a definite decision has been made to proceed with the redundancy programme;

- the provision is calculated using the degree of hindsight permitted by *FRS 21 Events after the Balance Sheet Date;*
- payment is made within nine months of the end of the period of account.

In *IRC v Cosmotron Manufacturing Ltd (1997) (70 TC 292)* it was held that severance payments which the company was legally required to pay to all employees who had been employed on a continuous contract for at least two years on the closure of a factory in Hong Kong were deductible. This was because, although they had been made for the purpose of discharging the employees, rather than the production of profits, the liability had arisen from the terms under which the employees had been employed. The employees had been employed for the purpose of generating profits and the fact that the event which triggered the payments was the closing down of the factory did not preclude a deduction for these costs.

2.36. Removal Expenses to New Business Premises

These will be allowable, provided that the move is not an expansionary one.

2.37. Premiums for Insurance

Motoring and property insurance premiums are deductible, as are premiums for insurance against costs which will arise as a consequence of the death or illness of an employee, provided that:

- the only relationship is that of employer and employee;
- the policy is to insure against loss of profits due to the death or illness of the employee;
- it is an annual or short-term insurance.

Receipts under such policies will be taxable.

Premiums on insurance policies to insure against the death, critical illness, sickness, accident or injury of key personnel are deductible, provided that the sole reason for taking out the policy is the loss of trading income from the loss of service of the key person. In the case of life insurance policies, they are term insurance, providing cover only against the risk that one or more of the lives insured dies within the term of the policy, with no other benefits. The insurance term should not extend beyond the period of the employee's usefulness to the company.

Premiums on policies in favour of a proprietor or partner are in general not deductible, with the exception of premiums on policies to secure locum cover etc.

2.38. Payments to Employees for Restrictive Undertakings

These will be deductible, but the receipt will be taxable in the hands of the employee *(ITTOIA 2005 s.69(1)&(2)).*

2.39. Staff Training and Development

Staff training costs will generally be deductible where the relationship between the employer and the employee does not extend beyond the employment itself, even though the skills being acquired are not relevant to the job which the employee is currently performing and the employee might gain personal enjoyment from the training. Where the employee concerned has a significant proprietary stake in the business, it may be that the expenditure will be partly for the personal benefit of the employee and the expenditure will not be deductible.

Expenditure on retraining courses, whether paid directly or reimbursed to employees, will be deductible provided that:

- the employee commences the retraining whilst still employed by the employer or within one year of leaving;
- the employee must have been employed for two years up to the earlier of the date of starting the course and the date of ceasing employment;
- the course must be full-time or substantially full-time;
- the employee leaves his employment within two years of completing the course;
- the employee is not re-employed by the same employer for two years after leaving;
- the course must be available to all employees or to specified classes of employees.

The course must fulfil the following conditions:

- it must impart knowledge or skills which are relevant to, or which are intended to be used in employment or self-employment and be entirely devoted to the teaching of and practical application of such knowledge and skills;
- it must not exceed one year;
- the course must take place in the UK.

The course must be open on similar terms to all employees, or all employees of a specified class or classes, who satisfy the conditions.
(ITTOIA 2005 ss.74 & 75)

2.40. Counselling Courses in Connection with Termination of Employment

Expenditure on providing, paying or reimbursing employees for fees or travelling expenses in connection 'qualifying counselling services' is deductible. These services must meet the following conditions:

- they must help the employee adjust to the termination of employment or to find alternative employment;

- they must consist wholly of the giving of advice, improving of skills or the provision of office facilities;
- the employee must have been employed for two years up to the earlier of the date of provision of these services or the termination of employment;
- the services must be available to all similar classes of employees on similar terms.

(ITTOIA 2005 s.73)

2.41. Payments to Secure Release from Unprofitable Contracts

Payments to secure release from unprofitable contracts are deductible. In *Anglo-Persian Oil Co Ltd v Dale (1932) (16 TC 253)*, a payment of £300,000 made to secure release from a ten-year contract after nine years was held to be deductible.

2.42. Payments to Political Parties

Payments to political parties or campaigns are not deductible, save in the exceptional case of *Morgan v Tate & Lyle (1954) (35 TC 367)*, where a payment to a political party to fight the potential nationalisation of the company was held to be deductible.

2.43. Preservation of Goodwill

Where a business makes a payment which it is not legally obliged to make, but is made in order to preserve its goodwill, the payment will be deductible. In *Cooke v Quick Shoe Repair Service (1949) (30 TC 460)* the purchaser of the business paid certain debts which the vendor had undertaken to pay, but failed to do so. Failure to have done so would have seriously affected the goodwill of the business, and therefore the payments were held to be deductible.

2.44. Payments on the Cessation of Trade

Payments made on the cessation of trade are disallowable in general law on the grounds that they are not made wholly and exclusively for the purpose of the trade. Redundancy and *ex gratia* payments to employees are deductible under ITTOIA 2005 s.79, but other payments, such as the cost of returning stock to a supplier are not.

2.45. Post-cessation Expenditure

Relief is available for certain types of post-cessation expenditure *(ITA 2007 s.97)*. The types of expenditure for which relief is available are:

- cost of remedying defective work or goods or services supplied in the course of the trade formerly carried on;

- cost of legal and professional expenses incurred in connection with or of insuring against a claim that work performed or goods or services supplied were defective;
- cost of collecting debts outstanding at the cessation of the business;
- debts outstanding at the cessation of the business which prove to be bad. If a debt is subsequently recovered the amount received will be treated as a post-cessation receipt.

The expenditure must be incurred within seven years of the cessation of the business and relief must be claimed within two years of the cessation of the trade. Relief is first given against the taxpayer's income of the year that the payment is made. If a taxpayer's income for the year is insufficient, the payment may be offset against his capital gains for the year *(ITA 2007 Sch. 1, para. 239)* (see section **13.5.2**). Any excess may not, however, be carried forward to be offset against income of future years. No relief is available for payments made as part of an arrangement, the main purpose, or one of the main purposes, of which is the avoidance of tax, unless the payments are made under an unconditional obligation made before that date or for events occurring after that date *(ITA2007 s.98A).*

A claim may be reduced if any expense accrued at the date of cessation of the trade remains unpaid at the end of the tax year in which the post-cessation expenditure arose *(ITA 2007 s.99).* If the expense is subsequently paid, relief will be available for this payment.

Relief may be claimed where a debt is released as part of a statutory insolvency arrangement with creditors under the *Insolvency Act 1986,* the *Bankruptcy (Scotland) Act 1985* or the *Insolvency (Northern Ireland) Order 2002.*

2.46. Rent

Rent payable is deductible under general principles, even if the premises are not currently required for the purpose of the business *(IRC v Falkirk Iron Co Ltd (1933) (17 TC 625))* or are sub-let *(Hyett v Leonard (1940) (23 TC 346)).* Rent paid by a partnership to one of the partners will also be deductible.

Where rent is paid in respect of assets other than land, again only a commercial rent will be deductible, and any excess rent may be carried forward to future years *(ITA 2007 pt 12A ch. 3*). Alternatively, any capital sum received may be taxed as income *(ITA 2007 pt 12A ch. 4).*

A rental guarantee payment to a third party will be deductible.

A provision in the accounts for future rent will be deductible if the inclusion in the accounts is in accordance with accepted accounting principle of prudence *(Herbert Smith (A Firm) v Honour (1999) (72 TC 130) (BTC 44)).* In this case the trader had included a provision for future rental payments in respect of vacant sites which he considered could not be sub-let.

2.47. Lease Premium

If a trader has paid a premium (an initial capital sum in addition to the annual rental) in order to acquire a short lease, part of that premium may deducted each year. This will be the portion of the premium taxable on the lessor spread over the term of the lease *(ITTOIA 2005 s.61)*. The portion taxable on the lessor is given by the formula:

$$\text{Premium} \times \frac{51 - n}{50}$$

where n is the number of years for which the lease has been granted *(ITTOIA 2005 s.277)*.

Example

Keegan granted a 30-year lease to Owen on 1 September 2021 and received a premium of £12,000. Owen has an accounting date of 31 December. The proportion of the premium which is taxable on Keegan in 2021/22 is:

$$\pounds 12{,}000 \times \frac{51 - 30}{50} = \pounds 5{,}040$$

Owen can obtain a deduction of £168 for each of the 30 years. In the year the lease is granted the relief is given *pro rata*, calculated to the nearest month, i.e. in the year ended 31 December 2021, Owen will claim £56 (£168 x 4/12).

For this purpose a lease will be treated as expiring on the earliest date when either the lessor or lessee has an option to terminate the lease which it is likely that they will exercise, e.g. a 20 year lease with an option on either side to terminate after seven years will be treated as a seven year lease. If, but for this rule, the lease would be for a term of more than 50 years, no deduction is available under ITTOIA 2005 s.61 *(ITTOIA 2005 ss.61(5A), 292(4A)-(4C))*.

Where land is sold and then leased back the allowable deduction for rent is limited to a commercial rent *(ITA 2007 s.681AE)*. Where a lease is assigned or surrendered to the landlord, and the lessee enters into a new lease of less than 15 years, the amount of any premium payable which is to be treated as income is:

$$\text{Premium} \times \frac{16 - n}{15}$$

These provisions will also apply where a landlord pays the lessee a capital sum in return for receiving a higher rent in the future.

2.48. Patents and Intellectual Property

The following payments in the course of a trade (but not a profession or vocation) are specifically allowable by statute *(ITTOIA 2005 ss.89-90)*:

- cost of registering or obtaining extension of patent or design registration;
- cost of obtaining or renewing trade mark or service mark;
- costs connected with aborted or failed patent registration.

Royalty payments made for commercial reasons in connection with an individual's trade, profession or vocation are deductible from trading income *(ITA 2007 s.900).*

2.49. Telephone

Telephone expenses are deductible provided that they satisfy the 'wholly and exclusively' rule. Where there is an element of duality, i.e. a phone is used partly for business and partly for private calls, all the expenses may be disallowed *(Lucas v Cattell (HMIT) (1972) (48 TC 353)),* although where calls can be analysed between business and private calls the cost of business calls will be allowable.

2.50. Business Rates and Council Tax

Business rates will be allowable under general principles provided that the payment satisfies the 'wholly and exclusively' rule. Where a property subject only to council tax is used partly for business purposes, e.g. one room of a private residence is used as an office, a portion of the council tax will be deductible. The payment of council tax on behalf of an employee will be deductible, but the payment will be taxed on the employee as a benefit in kind unless the accommodation is job-related *(ITEPA 2003 s.314).*

2.51. Security Expenditure

Expenditure incurred for the purpose of acquiring a 'security asset' (e.g. alarm system or floodlighting) or a 'security service' (e.g. bodyguards) where the threat to a person's security arises wholly or mainly from his trade or vocation, will be deductible. Where it is not intended to use the asset or service wholly to counter this threat, only a proportion of the expenditure will be deductible *(ITTOIA 2005 s.81(4)).* The expenditure is deductible even if the trader's family is also protected and even if the asset becomes the personal property of the trader *(ITTOIA 2005 s.81(3),(5),(6)).*

2.52. Loan Guarantee Payments

Loan guarantee payments will be deductible provided that they are wholly and exclusively for the purpose of the trade and are not capital. The former test is unlikely to be met where there is no trading relation between the two parties.

2.53. Use of Home

HM Revenue & Customs' advice distinguishes between the following types of home-office users:

1. the 'kitchen table' user, who has no distinct office, but carries out office work at the kitchen table;
2. the 'part-time home PC user' who has a computer which is not used exclusively for office work;
3. the 'serious PC user', who has a computer which is used exclusively for office work in a clearly defined space (not necessarily an office);
4. the 'in-home office' where a room may be partly converted into office which is mainly, but not exclusively, used for business, although the room may store domestic or private belongings; and
5. the 'dedicated office', which may be a converted garage, room or lodge in the garden. It may not be used exclusively for business, but private use is likely to be incidental or occasional, possibly limited to the storage of personal records.

Taxpayers falling in types 1 to 3 are unlikely to be able to make high claims for the use of home, but a small claim is unlikely to be challenged. HMRC advice gives a figure of £6 per week, in line with the figure for employees in ITEPA 2003 s.316A. Type 4 or type 5 users will be able to claim a more substantial proportion of household expenses, but any claim will need to be documented. Expenses which may be claimed and the possible methods of apportionment are:

1. light and heat should be apportioned by metered use if possible, or by floor area or the number of rooms otherwise. It may also be appropriate to factor in the percentage use on an hourly basis into the calculation;
2. telephone (including line rental) should be apportioned by call time (incoming and outgoing);
3. rent, council tax, cleaning and re-decoration and internal and external repairs should be apportioned using floor area, or number of rooms and the percentage use;
4. mortgage interest should be apportioned in the same manner as rent, unless part of the mortgage relates specifically to a part of the home used exclusively for business, e.g. a 'top-up mortgage';
5. general household insurance should be apportioned in the same manner as rent. Business-related insurance may be claimed in full;
6. repairs to business equipment must be restricted to the business proportion of use;
7. capital allowances on business equipment must be restricted if there is private use;
8. capital allowances on the cost of fixtures etc. erected for business use; and
9. ISP/Broadband should be apportioned by usage time, or as per telephone costs.

Water rates may not be claimed if there is no business use of water.

The following points should be noted in relation to apportionments:

1. in counting the number of rooms, halls, lavatories, small bathrooms and pantries must be disregarded; and
2. where an apportionment is made on percentage use, HM Revenue & Customs take the view that the proportion of expenses which may be claimed is based on the amount of time for which the room is used for business purposes as a proportion of the *total time*, i.e. including the time when the room is not being used at all. However, it may be argued in the case of, for example, heating that the apportionment should be based on the period during the day that the heating is switched on.

Where a substantial amount of a trade is conducted from home, a fixed-rate deduction may be claimed, the amount depending on the number of hours spent wholly and exclusively on work for the purpose of the trade by the owner or an employee. Where a business is carried on through a partnership the reference to a home includes the home of a partner, although where more than one person does qualifying work on the same premises at the same time, that time may only be counted once.

Number of hours worked	Applicable amount (per month or part of month)
25 or more	£10
51 or more	£18
101 or more	£26

(ITTOIA 2005 s.94H(1)-(4))

If a person has more than one home, all homes are treated as a single home for the purpose of this section *(ITTOIA 2005 s.94H(5)).*

Where premises are used principally for the purpose of a trade, but is also used as a home, in making an apportionment of expenses, the non-business element may be calculated according to the following table:

Number of relevant occupants	Applicable amount (per month or part of month)
1	£350
2	£500
3 or more	£650

(ITTOIA 2005 s.94I(1)-(5))

A relevant occupant is a person who has stayed at the property otherwise than in the course of the trade at any time during the month or part of month *(ITTOIA 2005 s.94I(6)).*

Where a part of the house is used exclusively for business, this will restrict the amount of principal private residence relief which may be claimed on a subsequent disposal.

2.54. Website Expenditure

HM Revenue & Customs take the view that website planning costs will be revenue, but that the initial costs of constructing and designing a website are capital. These will qualify as plant and capital allowances may be claimed and a short-life asset election may be made, where appropriate. The subsequent costs of maintaining and altering the site are revenue.

2.55. Expenses Connected with Foreign Trades

The following reliefs are available where a trade is carried on wholly outside the UK by a person taxed on the arising basis, and who is absent from the UK wholly and exclusively for the purpose of carrying on the trade *(ITTOIA 2005 s.92(1),(4))*:

- travel from any place in the UK to the place where the trade is carried on and the return journey to any place in the UK *(ITTOIA 2005 s.92)*;
- board and lodging incurred for the purpose of performing the duties of the trade *(ITTOIA 2005 s.92)*.

Where more than one trade is carried on wholly overseas and the expenses incurred relate to more than one trade they must be apportioned between the trades on a reasonable basis *(ITTOIA 2005 s.93)*.

Where more than one trade is carried on wholly or partly overseas and at least one of the trades qualifies under ITTOIA 2005 s.92, i.e. it is carried on wholly overseas, a fair and reasonable apportionment of expenses relating to travel between a place where the qualifying trade is being carried on and another place where another trade (which need not qualify) is being carried on must be made *(ITTOIA 2005 s.93(5))*.

Where an employee has more than one employment and the duties are performed partly in the UK and partly outside the UK, it is necessary to apportion travel expenses when they travel to or from a place outside the UK, having performed the duties of one employment in order to perform the duties of the other.

The cost of up to two visits per year by the spouse and children (including step-children, adopted children and illegitimate children) who are under 18 at the time of the outward journey are deductible where the person is absent from the UK for more than 60 days *(ITTOIA 2005 s.94)*.

These provisions apply to trades carried on wholly in Ireland, notwithstanding that the remittance basis (i.e. tax is only payable on income remitted to the UK during a tax year) does not apply to these trades.

2.56. Valuation of Stock

2.56.1. General principles

Stock must be valued using a 'true and fair' basis *(ITTOIA 2005 s.25(1))*.

If goods are sold at less than full market value, a trader will not be taxed on any profit forgone except where:

- stock is sold otherwise than in the course of the trade. The market value of the stock will be brought in as a trading receipt;
- a transaction is with a connected person. The value of the stock used in the transaction will be full market value.

Stock may be valued using any method which is consistent with both accepted accounting principles and the tax statutes. This is termed a 'valid basis'. Where a change is made in the method of stock valuation from one valid basis to another or from a non-valid basis to a valid basis, the opening stock in the year of change must be the same as the closing stock in the previous year. Where a change is made from an invalid basis to a valid basis, both the opening and closing stock must be calculated on the new valid basis. HM Revenue & Customs will not seek to re-open previous years unless there is evidence of fraudulent or negligent conduct.

Stock must be valued at the lower of cost and net realisable value. In general, stock should be valued item by item, but it is permissible to value groups of similar items together and to value these by the use of pre-determined formulae, provided that they are regularly reviewed to ensure that they give a reasonable approximation to net realisable value. This will not necessarily apply to valuations of slow-moving stock since HMRC do not always accept that net realisable value is less than cost price. Any formulae used to calculate provisions will be acceptable provided that they give a realistic estimate of future income from the particular category of stock. Where professional work in progress relates to work undertaken on a 'no win, no fee' basis, an assessment must be made of the chances of winning.

The cost price of stock will normally be the cost calculated using accepted accounting principles. The use of first in first out (FIFO) or average cost is acceptable, but not last in first out (LIFO). In practice, other methods, such as discounted selling price (i.e. full selling price less mark-up) and standard cost (provided that these methods give a good approximation to actual cost) are accepted, but base cost, where a base level of stock is treated as a fixed asset and is valued at historic cost, is not. A mark-to-market method is acceptable provided it is consistent with GAAP and any profits and losses are taken to the profit and loss account rather than reserves.

Work in progress may be valued either including only the direct costs of manufacture or by also including a proportion of indirect costs. In the case of professional work in progress, this will consist of the costs of employees' direct costs and a proportion of indirect costs, but not the costs of partners or proprietors. If detailed time records are not maintained, it may be necessary to value work in progress by using invoices issued after the year-end or statistical techniques.

A problem may arise where raw materials used in production are subject to rapid fluctuation. Where such raw materials form a significant part of the cost of work in progress, it will be acceptable to value the raw materials element of work in progress using the same price as that used for the raw materials stock, irrespective of the price actually paid.

2.56.2. Appropriations of stock

If a proprietor withdraws goods from a sole trader business, the full open market sale price rather than the cost price to the proprietor must be added back. This principle was originally established in *Sharkey v Wernher (1955) (36 TC 275)*, but has been given statutory effect through ITTOIA 2005 s.172B.

Example

Larry Lamb trades as a butcher and during the course of the year he has taken meat for his own consumption which he had purchased for a total sum of £240. The prices are calculated on the basis of a 25% profit on the selling price. No entries have been made in his books in respect of the appropriations. Therefore the accounts show a loss of £240.

	£
Cost (75)%	240
Profit (25% 25/75 x £240)	80
Selling Price (100%)	£320

£320 will therefore be added back in Larry Lamb's taxation computation.

Where trading stock is appropriated by an employee or director of a company this section does not apply, but a benefit in kind will arise under normal principles (see section 10.11).

Where goods belonging to a proprietor which are not trading stock become trading stock of that person's trade, the value brought into account as the cost of the stock must be the open market value of the goods *(ITTOIA 2005 s.172C)*.

SP A32 has not been withdrawn in the following instances where the costs incurred are disallowable, but no notional profit is added back.

1. A trader supplies services to his household, e.g. a plumber making a repair.

2. The cost of meals provided by proprietors of hotels and restaurants for their staff.
3. A trader incurs expenditure on the construction of an asset which is to be used in the business.

2.56.3. Long-term contracts

Where a proportion of a foreseeable loss is recognised on a long-term contract in accordance with FRS 102 (either on the basis of time-apportionment or of expenditure incurred), this will be allowable, provided that profits on other contracts are dealt with similarly. Any further foreseeable loss will only be allowable where a contract has been substantially completed. There may, therefore, be circumstances where a loss calculated in accordance with SSAP 9 may be disallowable. Where there is a change in basis of valuing long-term contracts, the opening stock in the year of change must be the same as the closing stock in the previous year. HM Revenue & Customs will not accept a tax-free uplift of such contracts, but it is permissible to continue to value existing contracts at the date of change on the old basis and only apply the new basis to new contracts.

2.56.4. Discontinuation of trade

Where a trade is discontinued, stock at the date of cessation must be valued at market value, unless the stock is sold to a UK trader who is also liable to income tax. In this case it may be valued at the price paid, if the parties are unconnected *(ITTOIA 2005 ss.175 & 176)*. Where the two parties are connected the price will be the arm's length price *(ITTOIA 2005 s.177)*. The valuation used by the vendor must also be used by the purchaser *(ITTOIA 2005 s.181(2))*. Where this valuation is greater than both the transfer price and the original cost, the two parties may elect for the stock to be valued at the greater of the market value of the stock at the date of discontinuation and the actual price paid *(ITTOIA 2005 s.178(5))*. The election must be made within two years of the end of the chargeable period in which the cessation took place *(ITTOIA 2005 s.178(1)-(4))*.

2.57. Overseas Aspects of Trading

2.57.1. Chargeability of overseas trades

A trade which is carried on wholly or partly in the UK by a taxpayer who is UK-resident is treated as trading income and relief is available for overseas taxes.

Where a trade is carried on wholly outside the UK by a UK resident, the profits are treated as foreign income, with relief available for overseas taxes. A trade carried on wholly outside the UK by a person not resident in the UK is not liable to UK tax.

2.57.2. Computation of profits of overseas trades

The rules relating to the adjustment of profits and basis periods apply also to overseas trades. Where a loss is incurred, relief may be claimed in the same manner as a UK trading loss. Where relief is claimed under ITA 2007 s.64, the income against which the loss may be offset is restricted to overseas trading profits, overseas pensions and foreign earnings taxable as employment income *(ITA 2007 s.95)*.

2.57.3. Traders not resident in the UK

A non-resident is only taxable on profits arising in the UK, i.e. profits from simply trading with the UK are not taxable. Soliciting orders in the UK does not generally by itself constitute trading in the UK *(Grainger & Son v Gough (1896) (3 TC 462))*. Whether a trade is being carried on in the UK is a question of fact and will depend, for example, on where a contract is signed.

The following persons are not treated as UK representatives of a non-resident *(ITA 2007 ss.814(1)-(4); 817(1), 818(1) (FA 1995 s.127(1))*:

- any agent who does not carry on a regular agency for the non-resident;
- any member's agent or syndicate managing agent in respect of the underwriting business of a non-resident member of Lloyd's;
- any broker who:
  a. was in business as a broker at the time of the transaction; and
  b. carried out the transaction in the ordinary course of business; and
  c. was paid for that work at or above the customary rate; and
  d. is not otherwise the non-resident's UK representative;
  e. executed the transaction in the ordinary course of business; and
  f. was paid for that work at or above the customary rate; and
  g. is not otherwise the non-resident's UK representative; and
  h. acted on behalf of the non-resident in an independent capacity; and
  i. has, in a given period, no more than a 20% beneficial interest in the non-resident's income arising from transactions conducted in the UK through brokers or investment managers.

This test is not failed if the failure was outside the manager's control. SP 1/01 *Treatment of Investment Managers and their Overseas Clients* sets out HMRC's position on the interpretation of these rules.

2.57.4. Payments to entertainers and sportsmen

Tax must be deducted at source on payments to non-resident entertainers and sportsmen *(ITTOIA 2005 ss.13 & 14)*. The details are contained in the *Income Tax (Entertainers and Sportsmen) Regulations 1987 (SI 1987/530)* and do not affect any international tax agreements.

These regulations apply to any 'associated payment' made to any person as a result of a 'relevant activity' of a non-resident entertainer or sportsman. The payment need not be in the same tax year as the relevant activity was performed. The regulations cover:

- payments for the activity and also for any activity connected with it, e.g. promotional and sponsorship activities;
- transfers by way of benefits in kind;
- payment by way of loan or temporary use of property;
- payments made indirectly to the entertainer or sportsman concerned, e.g. to an intermediary such as a non-resident trust or company *(ITTOIA 2005 s.13 (5))*.

(Income Tax (Entertainers and Sportsmen) Regulations 1987 (SI 1987/530) regs. 6 & 7)

Tax does not need to be withheld where payments to an entertainer or sportsman do not exceed £1,000 in a tax year. Tax is normally deducted at the basic rate, although under certain circumstances tax may be deducted at a lower rate which more precisely corresponds to the non-resident's actual tax liability. The payment made to the non-resident is the net payment, which must be grossed up by the appropriate rate of tax. If a sportsman wins prize money of £50,000 normally tax of £10,000 will be deducted, giving a net transfer of £40,000, whereas a prize of a car worth £24,000 would give rise to a tax payment of an additional £6,000, i.e. 20/80 x £24,000.

Where tax is required to be deducted the relevant activity will be treated as having been performed in the course of a trade, profession or vocation, even if the payment would not be so treated under general principles *(ITTOIA 2005 s.13(2)-(4))*, unless the payment is taxable on the entertainer or sportsman as employment income. Where payments are treated as being made in the course of a trade, profession or vocation they are taxed on a current year basis *(ITTOIA 2005 s.13(7),(8))*.

The regulations make provision for taxing a 'just and reasonable' proportion of the payment or transfer, for the entertainer or sportsman to deduct expenses incurred by others on his behalf, apportioning profits and gains between different trades, professions and vocations and between different tax years and to treat the deemed UK trade as part of a world-wide trade for the purpose of loss relief. Where tax has been deducted it may be offset against the UK tax liability of the entertainer or sportsman and if the tax deducted exceeds his liability, an 'appropriate part' will be refunded. If there is no tax liability the payment will be refunded in full to the recipient of the payment *(ITA 2007 s.968)*.

Chapter 3. Capital Allowances on Plant and Machinery

3.1. Introduction

Plant and machinery allowances may be claimed on 'qualifying expenditure' incurred in the course of carrying on a 'qualifying activity' *(CAA 2001 s.11(1))*. The following activities are defined as qualifying activities by CAA 2001 s.15(1), provided that the profits and gains derived from them are chargeable to tax:

1. a trade;
2. an ordinary property business (see **Chapter 1**);
3. a furnished holiday lettings business (see section **7.11**);
4. an overseas property business;
5. a profession or vocation;
6. a concern listed in CAA 2001 s.12(4) (mines, transport undertakings etc.);
7. the management of an investment company;
8. special leasing of plant and machinery;
9. an employment or office.

Qualifying expenditure must be capital expenditure incurred on the provision of plant and machinery, and the person incurring the expenditure must own the asset as a result of incurring the expenditure *(CAA 2001 s.11(4))*. Whether expenditure is capital in nature will normally be determined by normal accounting principles (see section **2.11.1**). It is not possible to claim allowances under more than one part of the Capital Allowances Act. Therefore, plant and machinery allowances are not available on expenditure qualifying for allowances under the provisions relating to industrial buildings, dredging, agricultural land and buildings, scientific research, dwelling houses let on assured tenancies, or mineral extraction *(CAA 2001 s.7(1))*.

3.2. Definition of Plant and Machinery

3.2.1. Statutory rules

The definition of plant and machinery for this purpose is far wider than might be expected but, given that this concept is so important, it may be considered surprising that no definition was included in statute before 1994. This definition, now contained in CAA 2001 ss.21-23, distinguishes between expenditure which is treated as being on buildings or structures, and expenditure which is treated as being on plant and machinery.

Examples of items treated as buildings or structures include:

- walls, floors, ceilings, doors, gates, shutters, windows and stairs;

- mains services, and systems of water, electricity and gas;
- waste disposal systems;
- sewerage and drainage systems;
- tunnels, bridges, viaducts, embankments or cuttings;
- pavements, roads, railways or tramways.

(CAA 2001 ss.21 & 22)

Examples of items treated as expenditure on plant and machinery include:

- electrical, cold water, gas and sewerage systems provided mainly to meet the particular requirements of the trade or to serve particular items of plant and machinery;
- manufacturing or processing equipment, storage equipment including cold rooms;
- space or water heating systems and powered systems of ventilation, air cooling or purification;
- cookers, washing machines etc;
- refrigeration or cooling equipment;
- partitions which are moveable and which are intended to be moved in the course of the business;
- decorative assets which are provided for the enjoyment of the public in a hotel, restaurant or similar trades.

(CAA 2001 s.23)

Allowances may be claimed on expenditure on the alteration of land or buildings for the purpose of installing qualifying plant or machinery. In order to qualify, the main purpose of the alterations must be the installation of the machinery, and the acquisition of the plant must have given rise to the expenditure *(CAA 2001 s.25)*. This will generally include professional fees allocated to the installation of plant and machinery where separate fee notes, or carefully itemised fee notes, are issued, but not where such fees are allocated on a percentage basis.

Expenditure on the following items is deemed to be plant and machinery and the exclusions relating to building, land and structures in *CAA 2001 ss.21-23* do not apply:

1. thermal insulation of buildings *(CAA 2001 s.28)*;
2. safety at sports grounds *(CAA 2001 ss.30-32)*;
3. personal security *(CAA 2001 s.33)*;
4. provision or replacement of an integral feature of a building or structure. The following qualify as integral features, provided that their principal purpose is not to insulate or enclose the interior of a building or provide a permanent interior wall, floor or ceiling:
   a) an electrical system (including a lighting system);

b) a cold water system;
c) a space or water heating system, powered system of ventilation, air cooling or air purification and any floor or ceiling comprised in such a system;
d) a lift, an escalator or a moving walkway;
e) external solar shading.

(CAA 2001 s. 33A)

An integral feature is treated as having been replaced if a person incurs expenditure amounting to more than 50% of the cost of replacement, either immediately or over a 12-month period starting with the initial expenditure *(CAA 2001 s.33B)*;

5. software and rights to software, to the extent that expenditure is not treated as revenue *(CAA 2001 s.71)*.

3.2.2. Case law

The statutory definition essentially formalised the definition of plant and machinery which had developed over the years through case law.

In order to qualify as plant, an asset must be kept for permanent use in the business. In practice, any asset which has an expected life of two years or more will qualify. Plant and machinery specifically excludes assets held as stock in trade.

Plant and machinery must be used for carrying on the business and must not be part of the setting in which the trade is carried on. This means that the asset must perform a function in the context of the particular trade. Normal lighting is therefore part of the building, whereas specialised lighting such as lighting in display windows and spotlights for diamond cutting have a specific function in the trade, and qualify for capital allowances. Doors in a warehouse which simply grant normal access do not qualify for capital allowances, whereas electrically operated roller doors, which specifically allow for vehicles such as fork-lift trucks to move about the warehouse easily, do qualify. It has also been held in the case of *IRC v Scottish and Newcastle Breweries Ltd (1982) (55 TC 252)* that part of the trade of hotelier and innkeeper consisted of providing 'atmosphere' or 'ambience', and that wall decor such as pictures, murals, tapestries and other items which contribute to the creation of an appropriate atmosphere perform a function in this context, rather than merely being a part of the setting. More recently there have been contrasting decisions in two cases with similar facts. In *IRC v Anchor International Ltd (Court of Session (2005) 97)* an artificial five-a-side football pitch was held to be plant and its foundations were expenditure on the alteration of land for its installation. In *Lingfield Park 1991 Ltd v Shove (HMIT) CA (2005) 89* an all-weather racing track was held to be a part of the premises. The respective decisions were based on analyses of the particular trades. In the former case, the provision of artificial five-a-side pitches was the sole activity by which the company generated profits, whilst, in the latter case the company also had a grass racing track and the trade was held to be the provision of facilities to watch horse racing. The all-weather track merely allowed those activities to be carried on more often and in worse weather.

In order to qualify as plant, an item must have a separate identity from the premises. In *J.D.Wetherspoon Plc v Revenue & Customs Commissioners (2012) (UKUT 42)* it was held that wood panelling which had been installed in a pub, having been moved from another pub, was held to be a part of the premises, because, unlike works of art etc., it did not have a separate identity, even though the taxpayer argued that it had been installed to provide a more inviting atmosphere than painted walls. Similarly, incidental expenditure must have a sufficient connection with the plant installed in order to qualify. In the above case the taxpayer argued that kitchen wall tiles which provided wipe-clean surfaces in order to comply with health and safety regulations should be building alterations incidental to the installation of plant because it would not be possible to use the cookers if the safety provisions were not satisfied, but the tribunal found against the taxpayer on the grounds that the tiles 'did not have a sufficient nexus with the installation of equipment such as cookers to be incidental thereto.' The tribunal gave examples of other types of expenditure which would be classified as plant, such as expenditure on strengthening the kitchen floor to take the weight of commercial cookers, fridges and dishwashers. Partitions and doors to toilets and cubicles were, however, held to be relevant alterations because they had a sufficient nexus with the toilets themselves, since the toilets could not be used without the doors and partitions.

3.3. Assets Deemed to be Plant and Machinery

3.3.1. Thermal insulation of industrial buildings

Expenditure on the heat insulation of an industrial building occupied for the purpose of a trade, or which has been let in the course of an ordinary property business or an overseas property business, e.g. double-glazing, roof-lining or cavity wall insulation, qualifies for capital allowances. Where expenditure is incurred by a lessor who lets the property other than in the course of a trade, relief is given primarily against the property rental income or any balancing charge in respect of industrial buildings or structures *(CAA 2001 s.28)*.

3.3.2. Assets acquired for personal security

Allowances are available on expenditure on assets to counteract a security threat to a trader arising wholly or mainly from his trade *(CAA 2001 s.33(1)&(2))*. Examples of assets falling within this section are alarm systems, floodlighting and bullet-resistant windows. The sole object of the expenditure must be to counteract the threat and to improve personal physical security, and the fact that it may also have another use or also improves the security of other family members is irrelevant *(CAA 2001 s.33(3)&(4))*. Where the asset is only partly used to improve personal physical security the above test is not necessarily failed, but only the relevant portion of the expenditure qualifies for allowances *(CAA 2001 s.33(5))*. Cars, ships, aircraft and dwellings are specifically excluded, although the asset may become attached to land or a dwelling *(CAA 2001 s.33(6))*.

3.3.3. Computer software

Expenditure on computer software qualifies as plant and machinery where it is expected to have an economic useful life of two years or more *(CAA 2001 s.71(2))*. This is irrespective of whether it is supplied electronically or in a tangible form *(CAA 2001 s.71(1))* or whether the purchaser acquires the software itself or merely a licence to use it. Software with an expected economic useful life of less than two years is treated as revenue expenditure. Apportionment may be necessary where hardware and software are purchased together as a single package. The question as to whether expenditure is capital or revenue will apply where software is acquired outright (including the salaries of in-house computer professionals) and will depend on the function of the software. Software is not defined by statute and therefore has its normal meaning and covers both programs and data. The exclusions relating to buildings, structures and land in CAA 2001 ss.21-23 do not apply to expenditure on software falling within CAA 2001 s.71.

There is a disposal where rights to computer software are granted to another person in consideration of a capital sum of money. The disposal value to be brought in is:

Consideration does not consist entirely of money	Market value of right at date of disposal.
Grant made for no consideration or at undervalue	Market value of right unless there is a charge on the buyer under *ITEPA 2003*.
Any other case	Net consideration received plus any insurance monies or compensation.

These rules are subject to the overriding rule that the disposal value cannot exceed the amount of the original expenditure.

3.4. Definition of Expenditure

3.4.1. General principle

Allowances are calculated by reference to capital expenditure incurred on the provision of plant and machinery. The cost of an item will therefore exclude the VAT if a trader is registered and can recover the VAT, but will include VAT if the trader is not registered or if the VAT cannot be reclaimed even by registered traders, such as the irrecoverable portion of VAT on motor cars.

3.4.2. Grants, subsidies and contributions

Capital allowances are claimed on expenditure net of any grant or subsidy from the Crown or other government, public or local authority *(CAA 2001 s.532)* with the exception of a grant under Northern Ireland legislation corresponding to part II of the Industrial Development Act 1982 *(CAA 2001 s.534(1))*. It does not matter whether the grant or subsidy is mandatory or discretionary.

A person making a contribution towards expenditure incurred by another person may claim allowances on the amount of the contribution provided:

- it is made for the purpose of his trade, profession or vocation *(CAA 2001 s.538)*;
- the two parties are not connected; and
- the person to whom the contribution is made would have been entitled to claim allowances on the expenditure if they had incurred it themself, or would have been able to claim allowances, but for the fact that it is a public body *(CAA 2001 s.537(2)(b)&(c))*.

Where a grant or contribution is subsequently repaid, capital allowances may be claimed on the amount repaid (*ESC B49*). If the contributor has claimed capital allowances on the contribution, a trader can only claim additional allowances if the repayment gives rise to a balancing adjustment in the hands of the contributor.

The following contributions are not deducted from the expenditure on assets:

- insurance or compensation proceeds;
- contributions made by a person (other than a public body) who cannot claim capital allowances on the contribution.

3.4.3. Loan interest

Allowances cannot be claimed on interest charged on loans to purchase an asset, even if the interest is properly charged to capital under accepted accounting practice *(Ben-Odeco Ltd v Powlson (1978) (52 TC 459))*.

3.4.4. Exchange rate fluctuations

Additional costs due to exchange rate fluctuations will be allowable. In *Van Arkadie v Sterling Coated Metals (1983) (56 TC 479)* the sterling price for an item of machinery was payable in instalments. Sterling Coated Metals subsequently entered into a finance agreement with a Swiss bank whereby it paid its instalments to the bank. Due to the depreciation of sterling against the Swiss franc, the eventual cost to the company was greater than the original sterling cost. The additional cost was held to qualify for allowances, although the additional cost would not have qualified if the agreement with the bank had been made before the purchase of the machinery.

3.4.5. Assets originally acquired for non-qualifying purposes

If a person brings an item of plant and machinery into use for a qualifying activity which was originally acquired for another purpose, allowances may be claimed on the lower of:

1. the market value of the asset on the date it is brought into use for qualifying activities *(CAA 2001 s.13(3))*; and
2. the amount of the expenditure originally incurred less any amount required to be left out by CAA 2001 ss.218 & 224 *(CAA 2001 s.13(4))*.

3.4.6. Assets acquired at undervalue

If an asset is acquired as a gift or at undervalue, allowances are claimed on the market value of the asset at the date of acquisition *(CAA 2001 s.14(3))*.

3.5. Date of Expenditure

For the purpose of claiming capital allowances, the basic rule is that expenditure is incurred on the date when the obligation to pay becomes unconditional *(CAA 2001 s.5(1))*. The date will not necessarily be the date a contract is signed or an invoice is issued, but will depend on the terms of the contract.

The basic rule is modified in the following circumstances:

- where payment is due to be made more than four months after the date on which the obligation becomes unconditional, the date of acquisition will be the date the payment is due *(CAA 2001 s.5(5))*;
- where an asset is being constructed under a long-term contract, and progress payments are made when certain milestones specified in the contract are reached, the obligation to pay becomes unconditional once it has been certified that a milestone stage of completion has been reached. The work may, however, be certified some time after it has been completed. Therefore:
    1. if the work is certified before the end of the same accounting period in which the work was completed, the normal rules apply;

2. if the work is certified no later than one month after the end of the accounting period in which the work was completed, the date of expenditure for capital allowances purposes is the last day of the accounting period;
3. if the work is certified more than one month after the end of the accounting period in which the work was completed, the date of expenditure for capital allowances purposes is the date on which the work is certified.

(CAA 2001 s.5(4))

- expenditure incurred before the commencement of trading is treated as having taken place on the first day of trading *(CAA 2001 s.12)*;
- where computer equipment or land and buildings are acquired under the capital goods scheme, the date of expenditure is the last day of the VAT period in which the acquisition was made *(CAA 2001 s.548)*;
- expenditure on assets acquired under an HP agreement is deemed to have been made on the date the asset is brought into use *(CAA 2001 s.67(1)-(3))*.

Where a date is inserted into an agreement wholly or mainly to accelerate capital allowances, the expenditure is treated as having been incurred on the date that payment is due *(CAA 2001 s.5(6))*.

3.6. Disposal of Assets

When an asset is sold, the disposal value which is brought into account is the lower of the original cost of the asset and the net sale proceeds plus any insurance monies receivable, insofar as they are received as a result of an event affecting the sale value, or compensation receivable insofar as it consists of a capital sum *(CAA 2001 ss.61 & 62)*. Where an asset is not pooled, a disposal will give rise to a balancing allowance or balancing charge equal to the difference between the disposal value and the tax written down value of the asset at the date of disposal. Where an asset which has been pooled is sold, the disposal value is deducted from the pool balance. Any expenditure on the asset which has not yet been written off will remain in the pool and allowances will be claimed on this expenditure in subsequent years. Where an asset is demolished or destroyed, the sale proceeds will be the net scrap proceeds, i.e. after deducting costs of demolition and adding any insurance monies receivable *(CAA 2001 s.26)*. Where an asset is donated to a 'designated educational establishment' *(ITTOIA 2005 s.108(2))* or to a charity or body listed under ITTOIA 2005 s.108(4)4, the disposal value is nil.

If the asset is sold to a connected party, so that the sale proceeds may not reflect the market value of the asset, HM Revenue & Customs may substitute the market value for the actual proceeds. This market value will also become the purchaser's deemed acquisition cost *(CAA 2001 ss.567 & 568)*. An election may be made under CAA 2001 ss.569 & 570 for the transfer to be made at the 'alternative amount', i.e. the tax written down value of the assets at the date of transfer. No balancing allowance or charge will therefore arise, and the transferee will continue to claim allowances on the same basis as the transferor. The time limit for making the election is two years from the date of the sale *(CAA 2001 s.193(3))*.

Where assets qualifying for capital allowances are sold along with other assets which do not qualify, there must be a 'just apportionment' of the sale proceeds between the various items *(CAA 2001 s.562(1), ITTOIA 2005 s.193 (3))*, even where assets are sold under separate contracts or a separate price is agreed for certain assets. Any apportionment agreed in a contract may therefore be revised for tax purposes and any dispute between the parties must be resolved by a tribunal.

Where there has been a transfer at undervalue, the actual transfer price will also be used in the transferor's computation, unless the transferee does not claim allowances on the expenditure, or the expenditure is not used for the purpose of calculating employee benefits, in which case the market value at the date of transfer is used *(CAA 2001 s.62)*.

3.7. Allowances

3.7.1. Writing down allowance (WDA)

A WDA of 18% may be claimed on expenditure not previously written off *(CAA 2001 s.56(1)&(3))*. This allowance is available unless the asset is treated as special rate expenditure (see section **3.8.1**) *(CAA 2001 s.56(2)(a))*.

For accounting periods of any other duration, a WDA is available *pro rata*, e.g. a WDA of 9% is available for the six-month accounting period ending 31 December 2018 *(CAA 2001 s.56(2))*. Allowances are also available on expenditure by tenants on fixtures which under general law become the property of the landlord (see section **3.12.1**).

CAA 2001 s.56A allows small balances of unrelieved expenditure of up to £1,000 in either the main pool or the special rate pool to be claimed in full in an accounting period. The limit is increased or reduced *pro rata* for accounting periods of lengths other than 12 months and where a qualifying activity has only been carried on for part of the period *(CAA 2001 s.56A(4))*.

A taxpayer may elect for the WDA to be reduced to a specified amount and it may be disclaimed entirely *(CAA 2001 s.56(5))*. If a WDA is claimed in the year the expenditure is incurred the full WDA due for the period may be claimed, regardless of the date on which the expenditure is incurred.

3.7.2. Annual investment allowance (AIA)

An AIA is available where an individual, partnership or company incurs qualifying expenditure. The maximum allowance was raised to £1,000,000, originally for expenditure from 1 January 2019 to 31 December 2020, but this has now been extended to 31 December 2021. It will currently revert to £200,000 for expenditure from 1 January 2022 onwards. The limit is increased or reduced *pro rata* for accounting periods of more or less than 12 months *(CAA 2001 s.51A(1)-(6))*. Where an accounting period straddles the date of the change, the two AIA limits must both be time-apportioned. However, if all expenditure has been incurred after the date of the change, the limit will simply be £200,000 as reduced by time-apportionment, i.e. £50,000 for a 3-month period.

A person is not compelled to claim the full allowance available and may claim only a part, or none at all *(CAA 2001 s.51A(7)*. The allowance will be reduced appropriately if the plant and machinery is provided partly for a non-qualifying purpose *(CAA 2001 s.51A(11)(b))*. The following expenditure is excluded from the definition of qualifying expenditure:

1. the expenditure is incurred in the period in which the qualifying activity is permanently discontinued;
2. expenditure on plant and machinery incurred in connection with a change in trade or business carried on by a person other than the person incurring the expenditure and the main benefit, or one of the main benefits expected to arise from this change is the obtaining of an AIA. The aim of this exclusion is to prevent a business which has exhausted its entitlement to AIA circumventing the limit by transferring an asset to another business which has not exhausted its entitlement;
3. notional expenditure (as defined by CAA 2001 s.13) on an asset brought into use for a qualifying purpose during an accounting period, but which was previously owned by the same person and was used for another purpose;
4. the asset was acquired as a gift.

(CAA 2001 s.38B)

There are a number of other exclusions relating to companies and groups of companies (see section **14.2.1**).

The AIA is restricted where two or more qualifying activities are carried on by a person or persons other than a company, are controlled by the same person or persons and these activities are related to one another *(CAA 2001 s.51H(1))*. Where all the qualifying activities are carried on by a single person, that person is entitled to a single AIA in respect of expenditure relating to all their qualifying activities *(CAA 2001 s.51H(3))*. Where the qualifying activities are

carried on by more than one person, these are entitled to a single AIA in respect of expenditure relating to all their qualifying activities *(CAA 2001 s.51H(4))*. The person or persons may allocate the allowance to the relevant qualifying activities as they see fit *(CAA 2001 s.51H(5))*. A qualifying activity is controlled by the person or persons carrying on the activity at the end of the chargeable period *(CAA 2001 s.51I(1)-(2))* or, in the case of a business carried on by a partnership, by the persons controlling the partnership *(CAA 2001 s.51I(3))*. If two or more partnerships are controlled (as defined by CAA 2001 s.574(3)) by the same person or persons, the qualifying activities controlled by the partnerships are treated as being controlled by the same person *(CAA 2001 s.51I(5))*. Qualifying activities are related to one another if the activities are either carried on from the same premises *(CAA 2001 s.51J(3))* or if more than 50% of the turnover for each business is derived from activities sharing the same first-level NACE classification[2] *(CAA 2001s.51G(6),(7);51J(4),(5))*.
Where an asset is used only partly for a qualifying purpose or where a partial depreciation subsidy is claimed, the amount of the expenditure qualifying for an AIA is reduced to a just and reasonable amounts *(CAA 2001 ss.205 & 210 as amended by FA 2008 Sch. 24 paras 6 & 7)*.

An AIA is not available where an asset is acquired for a connected person, as defined by CAA 2001 ss.575 & 575A *(CAA 2001 s.217)*. An AIA will also not be available where an arrangement is entered into, the main purpose, or one of the main purposes, of which is to obtain an AIA to which the person would not otherwise be entitled *(CAA 2001 s.218A)*.

If expenditure qualifying for an AIA gives rise to an additional VAT liability, that VAT liability will also qualify for an AIA *(CAA 2001 s.236(3A)-(3C))*.

3.7.3. Assets elligle for 100% ECA

An ECA of 100% is available for expenditure on certain categories of assets, the most important of these being:

1. energy-saving plant and machinery *(CAA 2001 s.45A)*;
2. cars with low CO_2 emissions *(CAA 2001 s.45D)*;
3. zero emission goods vehicles *(CAA 2001 s.45DA)*;
4. plant or machinery for gas-refuelling stations *(CAA 2001 s.45E)*;
5. electric vehicle charging points *(CAA 2001 s.45EA)*
6. environmentally beneficial plant or machinery *(CAA 2001 s.45H)*.

Other than low-emissions cars, these allowances need only be claimed if the total expenditure on all plant and machinery exceeds the level of the AIA, which at its current level is highly unlikely for small businesses.

---

[2]See:http://ec.europa.eu/eurostat/documents/3859598/5902521/KS-RA-07-015-EN.PDF.

Energy-saving plant and machinery

Equipment for the purpose of efficient energy use includes the following categories:

- combined heat and power systems;
- boilers;
- motors;
- variable speed drives for liquid and gas movements;
- lighting;
- pipe insulation;
- refrigeration;
- thermal screens;
- uninterruptible power supplies.

(CAA 2001 s.45A)

The assets must be unused and no FYA allowance may be claimed where another payment or incentive under the Energy Act 2008 s.41 (or an act having similar force in Northern Ireland), s.100 or Energy Act 2011 s.113 has been received *(CAA 2001 s.45AA)*. Relief on expenditure will cease to be available after 5 April 2020 (31 March 2020 for companies).Cars with low CO_2 emissions

Cars with low CO_2 emissions

An ECA may be claimed on the purchase of unused cars which are either electrically-propelled or which do not emit CO_2 *(CAA 2001 s.45D(1)-(4))*. The definition of a car includes a taxi, but excludes a motorcycle *(CAA 2001 s.45D(8))*. In the case of a bi-fuel car, the CO_2 emissions figure is taken as the lowest figure specified by the certificate *(CAA 2001 s.45D(6))*.

Expenditure on zero-emission goods vehicles

An ECA may be claimed on unused zero-emission goods vehicles *(CAA 2001 s.45DA(1)&(2))*.

Expenditure on plant or machinery for gas refuelling stations

An ECA may be claimed on unused plant and machinery purchased for use in connection with refuelling vehicles with natural gas, biogas or hydrogen fuel *(CAA 2001 s. 45E(1)&(2))*.

Expenditure on electric vehicle charging points

An ECA may be claimed on unused plant and machinery for an electric vehicle charging point incurred between 23 November 2016 and 31 March 2019 for companies and 5 April 2019 for individuals (*CAA 2001 s.45EA)*.

Expenditure on environmentally beneficial plant and machinery

An ECA may be claimed on the acquisition of plant and machinery, other than a long-life asset, which has been certified as being environmentally beneficial.

Where components of plant and machinery, but not the whole asset, have been certified as being environmentally beneficial an ECA may be claimed on the part of the acquisition cost apportioned to such components *(CAA 2001 ss.45H-45J)*. The Water Technology Criteria List includes the following types of expenditure which will qualify:

- efficient taps;
- efficient toilets;
- flow controllers;
- leakage detection;
- meters;
- rainwater harvesting equipment;
- efficient showers;
- efficient washing machines;
- efficient industrial cleaning equipment.

Expenditure incurred before the relevant Treasury Order was issued will qualify provided that it fulfils all the conditions, but relief can only be claimed when the order was issued.

3.8. Calculation of Capital Allowances

3.8.1. Categories of plant and machinery

The following classes of assets must each be treated separately in calculating the allowances due to a taxpayer *(CAA 2001 s.54)*:

- general pool expenditure (this includes any expenditure not included elsewhere) *(CAA 2001 s.54(6))*. Cars which either have a low emissions rating or are electrically propelled are included in the general pool, but no AIA or ECA may be claimed *(CAA 2001 s.104AA(1))*. A car has a low emissions rating either if it was first registered on the basis of a qualifying emissions certificate or if it has an emissions rating of 110g/km or less *(CAA2001 s.104AA(3)&(4))*. Cars which do not satisfy the above criteria are treated as special rate expenditure (see section 0)*(CAA 2001 ss.104A-104E)*;
- special rate pool expenditure;
- short-life assets *(CAA 2001 s.86)*;
- assets with an element of private use *(CAA 2001 s.206)*;
- assets in respect of which a partial depreciation subsidy has been received (see section 0) *(CAA 2001 s.211)*;
- contributions to expenditure on plant and machinery acquired by a third party *(CAA 2001 s.538)*;
- assets which it is intended to lease out in certain circumstances *(CAA 2001 s.107)*.

Cars are defined as mechanically propelled road vehicles, other than motor cycles, vehicles primarily suited to carrying goods or which are otherwise not commonly used as private vehicles and are unsuitable for use as such *(CAA2001 s.268A).*

General pool expenditure

All expenditure on items included in the general pool in the course of an accounting period is added together and added to the balance of the expenditure not written off in previous years, known as the Tax Written Down Value (TWDV). The identity of the individual assets is therefore lost and ceases to be relevant, except in the rare situation where a particular item is later sold for more than its original cost (see below).

Layout of computation

Tax WDV b/f		X	Balance of expenditure not written off in previous periods
Additions not qualifying for ECA or AIA		X	Cars, or assets where ECAs have been disclaimed acquired before relevant date
Additions qualifying for AIA	X		Assets acquired after relevant date
AIA	(X)		Lower of qualifying expenditure and AIA limit
		X	
Disposals		(X)	Lower of original cost and sale proceeds
		X	
WDA		(X)	
		X	
Additions qualifying for ECA	X		Assets acquired before relevant date
ECA	(X)		
		X	
Tax WDV c/f		X	

Example

Mr Bean has been trading for many years making up his accounts to 31 March each year. The TWDV of the pool at 1 April 2021 is £160,000 and his pool expenditure in the year ended 31 March 2022 is as follows:

15 April 2021	Purchases lathe for £25,000;
30 June 2021	Purchases shelving for storeroom for £7,000;
1 September 2021	Purchases three grinders for £42,000;
30 September 2021	Sells grinder for £2,500, which had originally cost £8,000;
18 October 2021	Purchases car with emissions rating of 100g/km for £20,000;
15 December 2021	Purchases cash registers for £6,000;
28 February 2022	Sells polisher for £4,000, which had originally cost £7,500;
10 March 2022	Purchases two polishers for £40,000.

Expenditure qualifying for AIA

	£
Lathe	25,000
Shelving	7,000
Grinders	42,000
Cash registers	6,000
Polishers	40,000
Total	£120,000

Expenditure not qualifying for AIA

Motor car	£20,000
Sale proceeds	
Grinder	2,500
Polisher	4,000
	£6,500

The pool computation will therefore be:

	£	£	£
Tax WDV 1 April 2021		160,000	
Additions not qualifying for AIA		20,000	
Additions qualifying for AIA	120,000		
AIA	(120,000)		120,000
		NIL	
Disposals		(6,500)	
		173,500	
WDA @ 18%		(31,230)	31,230
Tax WDV 31 March 2022		£142,270	
Total Allowances			£151,230

Special rate expenditure

The special rate pool includes the following types of expenditure incurred wholly and exclusively for the purposes of a qualifying activity and which is not required to be allocated to a single-asset pool *(CAA 2001 s.104A):*

1. thermal insulation under CAA 2001 s.28;
2. integral features under CAA 2001 s.33A;
3. long-life assets;
4. cars which are not electrically propelled and which have an emissions rating of over 110g/km.

(CAA 2001 s.104A)

If only part of the expenditure on plant and machinery is special rate expenditure, the expenditure is apportioned on a just and reasonable basis and each part is treated as if it were expenditure on separate items of plant and machinery *(CAA 2001 s.104B).*

The allowance is given at 6% on the reducing balance basis, adjusted *pro rata* for long or short chargeable periods *(CAA 2001 s.104D).* Where there is a disposal of a special rate asset at less than the notional written down value of the asset in the pool and the disposal is part of, or occurs as a result of, a scheme that has the obtaining of a tax advantage as its main purpose, or one of its main purposes, the disposal will be deemed to have taken place at the notional written down value of the asset *(CAA 2001 s.104E)*. An example of a situation where this might apply is where there is a sale and lease-back arrangement in order to accelerate allowances.

FA 2008 Sch. 26 para. 15 is an anti-avoidance provision to prevent allowances being claimed on sales between connected persons (as defined by CAA 2001 ss.575 & 575A) of integral features acquired before 1 April 2008 (for companies) or 6 April 2008 (for unincorporated businesses) and which did not qualify for allowances when they were acquired.

Assets with private use

Where there is an element of private use of an asset by the proprietor, the asset is not pooled and the WDA is calculated is as follows:

- each year the TWDV of the asset is reduced by the full WDA;
- only the business proportion of the WDA may be claimed in the computation;
- on the disposal of the asset, only the business proportion of any balancing allowance may be claimed, and only the business proportion of any balancing charge is deducted.

(CAA 2001 s.207)

If the proportion of business use changes, the calculation of allowances must be changed accordingly *(CAA 2001 s.208)*.

The changes to capital allowances in FA 2009 Sch. 11 have not changed this method of calculating allowances, except that the WDA available will be determined by the car's emissions rating.

Example

Jane Thomas draws up accounts to 31 March. In September 2019 she purchased a motor car for £13,000 with an emissions rating of 100g/km. The business use has been agreed as 70%. In August 2021 the car is sold for £6,000.

Allowances Claimed

	£		
Addition	13,000		
WDA y/e 31.3.20	(2,340)	x 70%	£1,638
TWDV 31.3.20	10,660		
WDA y/e 31.3.21	(1,919)	x 70%	£1,343
TWDV 31.3.21	8,741		
Disposal	(6,000)		
Balancing allowance y/e 31.3.22	£2,741	x 70%	£1,919

This does not apply where an asset is used privately by an employee. The employer claims the full WDA, and the employee is taxed on the asset as a benefit in kind.

Partial depreciation subsidies

Where a partial depreciation subsidy, which is not taken into account in computing the profits of the recipient, is received in respect of an asset, the asset is not pooled and the allowances and charges are reduced in a 'just and reasonable' manner, i.e. if the subsidy is to cover half the depreciation, the allowances and charges are reduced by a half.

3.9. Short-life Assets

If a claim is made to treat an asset as a short-life asset, it is removed from the general pool and WDAs are claimed in the normal manner *(CAA 2001 ss.83 & 84)*. Provided that the assets are sold or cease to be used in the business within the relevant period a balancing allowance may be claimed on disposal. If at the end of this period the assets are still in use, the balance of the expenditure not written off is added to the general pool *(CAA 2001 s.86(2)-(4))*. The relevant period is eight years from the end of the accounting period in which they were acquired for assets acquired on or after that date *(FA 2011 s.12)*, The election is irrevocable, so if the sale proceeds were to exceed the TWDV at the date of sale, a balancing charge would arise. The election must be made within two years from the end of the accounting period in which the expenditure is incurred, and must specify the asset and the date that the expenditure was incurred *(CAA 2001 s.85)*. A single election may be made in respect of all short-life assets acquired in a particular accounting period.

Where an asset in respect of which an election is made is transferred to a connected person within the first four years of ownership, the transferee may continue to claim the same allowances that the transferor could have claimed *(CAA 2001 s.89)*.

The following types of assets cannot be the subject of a short-life assets election:

- motor cars (except for cars hired out to individuals receiving disability allowances);
- assets with an element of private use;
- long-life assets;
- assets acquired by way of gift;
- assets in respect of which a subsidy is received.

(CAA 2001 s.84)

HM Revenue & Customs accept that it may not be practicable to identify individual assets in cases where large numbers of identical assets are held

(SP1/86). In such cases, an election which gives information about the assets by reference to batches and aggregates their value in one amount will be accepted provided that HMRC are satisfied that none of the assets are specifically excluded, and enough information is given to make it clear which assets are covered by the election. SP1/86 gives two examples which cover two different situations.

Where assets are held in very large numbers and separate identification is impossible, the total assets acquired in an accounting period are aggregated and the actual (not economic) useful life of these assets is agreed with HMRC. A balancing allowance may be claimed in the last year of the agreed life.

Disposal proceeds are matched with the remaining pool expenditure of the assets concerned, and where the pool contains assets which relate to more than one period, the proceeds are matched on a FIFO basis, i.e. related to the earliest period for which assets are still in the pool.

Example

Stephen has an accounting date of 5th April. It has been agreed that a particular class of assets in Stephen's business has an actual useful life of three years and that assets acquired in year one are therefore disposed of in year four. It is assumed that no AIA is claimed on the expenditure.

Year ended 31 March	**2019**	**2020**	**2021**	**2022**	**Allowances**
	£	**£**	**£**	**£**	**£**
Cost of tools	1,000	1,200	800	1,000	
WDA y/e 5.4.2019 @ 18%	(180)				£180
	820				
WDA y/e 5.4.2020 @ 18%	(148)	(216)			£364
	672	984			
WDA y/e 5.4.2021 @ 18%	(121)	(177)	(144)		£442
	551	807	656		
Disposal y/e 5.4.2021	(NIL)				
	551				
Balancing allowance	(551)				551
	(£NIL)				
WDA y/e 5.4.2022 @ 18%		(145)	(118)	(180)	443
Tax WDV y/e 5.4.2022		£662	£538	£820	
Allowances y/e 5.4.2022					£994

Where separate identification is possible but impractical in the circumstances of the case, an alternative method may be used.

Example

A taxpayer uses a large number of small items, such as scientific and technical instruments. The accounting records enable him to identify for each kind the number and cost of acquisition, and the number and sale proceeds of disposals, and the number on hand at the end of the short-life asset period related to those acquisitions.

Technical Instruments	Number	Cost	Disposal Proceeds
Acquisition – y/e 5.4. 2020	100	£10,000	
Sold – y/e 5.4. 2021	20		£500
Sold – y/e 5.4.2022	40		£400
On hand – y/e 5.4.2022	40		
Allowances	**£**	**£**	
Additions – y/e 5.4.2020		10,000	
WDA – y/e 5.4.2020 @ 18%		(1,800)	£1,800
		8,200	
WDA – 5.4.2021 @ 18%		(1,476)	£1,476
		6,724	
y/e 5.4.2022 – disposal Expenditure £6,724 x 20/100	1,345	(1,345)	
Proceeds	(500)		
Balancing allowance	£845		845
		5,379	
WDA – y/e 5.4.2022 @ 18%		(968)	968
		4,411	
Total allowances			£1,813

This example assumes that all the items cost the same. This computation may still be used where different items have a similar, but not identical, cost.

HM Revenue & Customs accept that given the wide variety of assets which might be covered by this election, other forms of computation may also be acceptable.

3.10. Cessations and Successions

3.10.1. Cessations

In the final period of trading no WDAs are available. The sale proceeds of assets sold, or market value if assets such as cars are taken over by the proprietor, are entered in the computation as disposal proceeds, and balancing allowances or balancing charges are calculated as appropriate *(CAA 2001 s.62)*.

3.10.2. Successions

If a person takes over the trade of another and the change is treated as a cessation, assets of the old trade which are used in the new trade which have not actually been sold to the successor, are treated as having been sold at their market value at the date of the succession (*CAA 2001 ss.265 & 268* for plant and machinery and *ss.557 & 559* for other types of assets eligible for capital allowances). If the trade passes from one connected person to another, they may jointly elect within two years from the date of cessation that the purchaser take over the assets at their TWDV. In this case the vendor may claim ECAs and WDAs in the final period of trading, and no balancing allowances or balancing charges will arise *(CAA 2001 s.266)*.

3.11. Hire Purchase and Leasing

Where an asset is purchased on hire purchase, the amount payable under the hire purchase agreement is split between the capital cost of the asset and finance charges. For the purpose of claiming capital allowances, capital instalments paid before the asset is brought into use are treated as having been made on the date of payment. All other capital instalments are treated as having been paid on the date that the asset is brought into use, even though legal title does not pass until the final payment has been made *(CAA 2001 s.67)*. Finance charges are an allowable expense when they are incurred. Where a hire purchase agreement is terminated before all payments have been made, the amount of the outstanding payments which are no longer to be made is brought into the computation as a disposal value *(CAA 2001 ss.67 & 68)*. These provisions override the general provision that allowances may only be claimed on amounts payable more than four months after the contract becomes unconditional at the time they are required to be paid. Where a chattel is purchased under a hire purchase agreement and subsequently becomes a fixture, so that another person becomes entitled to claim allowances on it, the original owner is treated as having made a disposal. If a fixture is purchased on hire purchase, allowances cannot be claimed on amounts payable more than four months after the contract becomes unconditional until they are actually required to be paid.

No capital allowances are available in respect of assets which are leased. In principle, the whole of the leasing charge is strictly treated as a revenue payment, but HM Revenue & Customs' practice is to allow the finance charge as an allowable expense in the period in which it is incurred, and to accept that the depreciation charged on the asset in the accounts equates to the capital repayment element of the leasing charge, provided that this has been computed using accepted accounting principles *(SP 3/91)*. There is a restriction on the leasing charges which may be deducted in respect of some cars (see section **2.28**).

Capital allowances on leased assets may normally be claimed by the lessor, although there are a number of anti-avoidance provisions. Allowances may only be claimed on expenditure as it is actually incurred *(CAA 2001 s.229(3))*.

3.12. Fixtures

3.12.1. Definition

A fixture is an asset which is installed or otherwise fixed in or to a building or land and which has as a result become, in property law, a part of the building. In the case of leased property, property law distinguishes between landlords' fixtures and tenants' fixtures, a tenant's fixture being one which may be removed by the tenant when the lease expires. This distinction is not relevant for the purpose of claiming capital allowances. Two situations must be distinguished:

1. a taxpayer incurs expenditure on a fixture which is installed in a building or on land on which they are carrying on a qualifying activity, but does not own;
2. a taxpayer incurs expenditure on a fixture which is leased under an equipment lease.

3.12.2. Fixture installed in building in which qualifying activity is carried on

Allowances may be claimed by the person who has incurred the expenditure, provided that they has an interest in the land on which the fixture is situated at the time the plant and machinery becomes a fixture *(CAA 2001 s.176(1))*. The interest in the land includes any interest, including a licence (interpreted by HM Revenue & Customs to mean an exclusive licence) to occupy or an agreement to acquire an interest in the land *(CAA 2001 s.175(1))*. Where more than one person has an interest in the same land, allowances will be given to the person with the most subordinate interest *(CAA 2001 s.176(3))*.

3.12.3. Transfer of allowances to lessee

Where a new lease is granted and the lessee pays a sum in respect of an item of plant and machinery which is a fixture, the lessor and lessee may make a joint election within two years of the date on which the lease is to take effect to transfer the allowances to the lessee *(CAA 2001 s.183(1))*, provided that the following conditions are satisfied:

1. the lessor would be entitled to allowances on the fixture, or would have been entitled to allowances if they had been within the charge to tax; and
2. the lessee and lessor are not connected *(CAA 2001 s.183(1))*.

The lessee is also entitled to allowances where a capital sum is paid for the fixture if the lessor would not be entitled to allowances, provided that the fixture has not been used for the purposes of the trade by the lessor or a person connected with him *(CAA 2001 s.184(1))*. This does not apply where immediately after the grant of the lease a person has a prior right in relation to the fixture *(CAA 2001 s.184(2))*.

Where an interest in land is acquired and part of the purchase price may be apportioned to fixtures, allowances may be claimed on that part *(CAA 2001 s.81(1))*. Where a part of the sum paid to acquire the interest in the land is to discharge the obligations of an equipment lessee or a client under an energy services agreement in respect of a fixture on that land, allowances may be claimed on that part *(CAA 2001 s.182(1)&182A(1))*.

3.12.4. Equipment leases

Where a fixture is leased, the lessor may claim allowances provided that the lessor and lessee are not connected and a joint election is made by 31 January in the second tax year after the end of the tax year in which the chargeable period in which the expense was incurred ends *(CAA 2001 s.177)* and either:

- the fixture is to be used by the lessee for a qualifying activity, and the lessee would have been entitled to allowances if they had incurred the expenditure *(CAA 2001 s.178)*; or
  - i) the equipment lease is treated as an operating lease under generally accepted accounting principles; and
  - ii) the fixture is fixed to land, that is not a building, in which the lessee has an interest when the equipment is installed; and
  - iii) the fixture is not for use in a dwelling house; and
  - iv) the fixture can be removed in a useable state by the lessor at the end of the lease, and the lessor has a right to do this *(CAA 2001 s.179)*; or
- the fixture consists of a boiler, heat exchanger, radiator or heating control that is installed in a building as part of a space or water heating system under the Affordable Warmth Scheme *(CAA 2001 s.180)*.

Where an energy services provider incurs expenditure on installing a fixture as part of an energy services agreement in a building in which the energy services provider has no interest, but the client does have an interest, the energy services provider may claim allowances provided that:

1. the energy services provider and the client are not connected;
2. the fixture is not provided for leasing or for use in a dwelling house;
3. the operation of the fixture is carried out wholly or substantially by the energy services provider or a person connected with him; and
4. a joint election is made by the energy services provider and the client.

(CAA 2001 s.180A)

3.13. Disposal of Fixtures

3.13.1. Sale of qualifying interest

Where a person entitled to allowances by virtue of:

1. having incurred expenditure on a fixture installed in a building in which they are carrying on a qualifying activity *(CAA 2001 s.176)*; or
2. giving consideration for fixtures as part of the purchase price for land *(CAA 2001 s.181)*; or
3. discharging the obligations of equipment lessees or energy service providers *(CAA 2001 ss.182, 182A)*; or
4. the transfer of allowances from a lessor *(CAA 2001 ss.183, 184)*,

and that person ceases to have a qualifying interest in the land or building in which the fixture is installed, that person is treated as having sold the fixture *(CAA 2001 s.188)*. The disposal value is the part of the sale price apportioned to the fixture, or which would have been apportioned to the fixture if the purchaser were entitled to allowances unless either:

1. the sale is at less than market value and the purchaser cannot claim allowances on the expenditure *(CAA 2001 s.196(2)*; or
2. the qualifying interest continues in existence after the disposal, or would do so apart from the fact that it has been merged with another interest *(CAA 2001 s.196(1))*.

In these situations the disposal value is the part of the disposal proceeds which would have been apportioned to the fixture if the qualifying interest had been sold at market value.

3.13.2. Expiry of qualifying interest

If the disposal of a fixture is due to the expiry of the qualifying interest, i.e. ownership of a fixture passes to the lessor on the termination of a lease, the disposal value is the amount of any capital received as compensation or which is otherwise attributable to the fixture *(CAA 2001 s.196(1))*.

3.13.3. Discontinuance of qualifying activity

If the qualifying activity is discontinued and the fixture is demolished or otherwise lost, the disposal value is the net proceeds for any remains of the fixture, i.e. after deducting any demolition costs, plus any insurance or compensation monies received *(CAA 2001 s.196(1))*.

3.13.4. Use of fixture for purpose other than qualifying activity

If a fixture begins to be used for a purpose other than a qualifying activity, the disposal value is the part of the sale proceeds which would have been apportioned to the fixture if the qualifying interest had been sold at its market value on the date the qualifying activity ceased *(CAA 2001 s.196(1))*.

3.13.5. Transfer of allowances to lessee

Where a lessor transfers the right to allowances on a fixture on the grant of a lease to a lessee who is entitled to claim allowances *(CAA 2001 s.183)*, there is a disposal, the disposal value being the capital sum paid by the lessee in respect of the fixture *(CAA 2001 s.196(1))*.

3.13.6. Severance of fixture

Where an asset is severed from the land or building to which it was previously attached, and the person who was entitled to claim allowances no longer owns the fixture, there is a disposal at the market value of the fixture at the date of severance *(CAA 2001 s.196(1))*.

3.13.7. Fixture which is subject of an equipment lease or is owned by energy services provider

Where a fixture is a subject of an equipment lease or is owned by an energy services provider, and the rights of the equipment lessor or the energy services provider are assigned or discharged, the disposal value is the capital sum received in consideration of the assignment or discharge of the rights *(CAA 2001 s.196(1))*.

3.13.8. Merger of interest

There is no disposal where the qualifying interest is merged with another qualifying interest held by the same person, the lease or licence expires and a new lease or licence is granted, or the lessee remains in occupation on the expiry of the lease with the consent of the lessor *(CAA 2001 s.189(2)-(5))*.

3.13.9. Apportionment of sale proceeds

It is possible for the purchaser and vendor to make a joint election which determines the apportionment of the sale proceeds on the disposal of a qualifying interest *(CAA 2001 ss.198 & 199)*. This amount cannot exceed the actual total sale price or the amount on which the former owner originally claimed allowances. HM Revenue & Customs have indicated that they will accept an election covering groups of assets and, in particular groups of assets or all assets in a single building, providing that this does not distort the tax computation. However, they will not accept a single election covering fixtures in different properties which are being sold together.

3.13.10. Allowances claimed by subsequent owner

The expenditure on which the owner of a fixture may claim allowances is restricted to the original cost. Therefore, if a previous owner has claimed plant and machinery allowances or scientific research allowances on the fixture, the expenditure on which allowances may be claimed is restricted to the disposal value of the previous owner *(CAA 2001 s.185)*. For purchases on or after 6 April 2012 a subsequent owner may only claim allowances on expenditure if, where the previous owner was entitled to claim capital allowances:

1. the previous owner has either allocated the expenditure to a pool in a chargeable period beginning on or before the date of the transfer or has claimed a ECA on any part of this expenditure; and
2. the previous owner has brought the disposal value into account; and
3. within two years of the date of sale, an apportionment of the sale price has been made or the current owner has obtained written statements from the previous owner to support the disposal value brought into account; and

4. a joint election under CAA 2001 s.198 or s.199, or an application to the First-tier Tribunal to fix the disposal value of the fixtures, is made within two years of the date of disposal.

(CAA 2001 s.187A(3)-(9))

Where the purchaser acquires the fixtures from a non-taxpayer, who had previously acquired the property from someone who had claimed capital allowances, the two-year limit above will not apply, but the current owner must provide a written statement to support the disposal value brought into account on the earlier disposal *(CAA 2001 s.187A(8))*. If the vendor has claimed capital allowances, but a joint election is not possible (for example if the vendor ceased his business some time ago, bringing the disposal value into account in the year of cessation, but later decides to sell his former business premises), the vendor must confirm the disposal value of the fixtures in a written statement within two years of the dates of sale *(CAA 2001 s.187A(10))*. There are no exceptions to this requirement and no appeal to the First-tier tribunal is possible.

3.13.11. Fixtures – anti-avoidance provision

Where a fixture is sold for less than its notional tax written value, i.e. the tax written down value at the date of sale assuming that all ECAs and WDAs have been claimed, and the disposal is a part of a transaction, or series of transactions, the main purpose, or one of the main purposes, of which is to obtain a tax advantage, the deemed disposal value will be the notional tax written down value *(CAA 2001 s.197(1)&(2))*. The allowances claimed by the purchaser will, however, be calculated on the actual consideration given.

3.14. Anti-avoidance

Anti-avoidance provisions restrict the allowances available on the sale of property or plant and machinery where there has been no change of control or the transaction has been structured to enable one party to claim allowances. These provisions apply where:

- the parties are connected or (for assets other than plant and machinery) one party has control over the other or the two parties are under common control; or
- in the case of plant and machinery, the asset continues to be used in a trade carried on by the seller, or a person connected with the seller; or
- where it appears that the sole or main aim of the transaction was to enable one of the parties to obtain allowances or to accelerate the rate at which allowances may be claimed *(CAA 2001 s.215)*.

The provisions may apply to the sale of an asset, a hire purchase contract or the assignment of the benefit of a hire purchase-type contract *(CAA 2001 s.213)*.

Where these provisions apply, for plant and machinery, the amount on which the buyer claims allowances will be restricted to the proceeds which have been brought into the vendor's computation, or where there are no sale proceeds, the lower of market value and the original expenditure *(CAA 2001 s.218(3))*. For other assets the amount on which the buyer may claim allowances is restricted to the market value of the assets, or, where an election has been made under CAA 2001 ss.567-569, the tax written down value. These provisions do not apply in the case of a sale and leaseback transaction in respect of plant and machinery where the buyer and seller make an irrevocable election under CAA 2001 s.227(1). The election must be made within two years of the sale *(CAA 2001 s.227(4))*. The election may be made where:

- the buyer and seller are not connected;
- the transaction is not part of an avoidance scheme;
- the seller has incurred capital expenditure on the equipment;
- the seller did not acquire the equipment from a connected person, under a sale and leaseback arrangement or as part of a tax avoidance scheme;
- the equipment was new (i.e. unused) at or after the time it was acquired by the seller;
- the equipment is sold within four months of being first brought into use;
- the seller has not claimed any capital allowances on the expenditure.

(CAA 2001 s.227)

The effect of such an election is that the expenditure on which the buyer may claim allowances is restricted to the expenditure incurred by the vendor, or a person connected to the vendor, if lower *(CAA 2001 s.228(2))*.

Chapter 4. Other Allowances

4.1. Business Premises Renovation Allowance

4.1.1. Qualifying expenditure

The relief is given on expenditure on:

- the conversion of a qualifying building into qualifying business premises;
- the renovation of a qualifying building which is, or will be, qualifying business premises;
- repairs to a qualifying building, or to a building of which a qualifying building forms part, to the extent that these are incidental to the conversion or renovation and provided the expenditure may not be deducted from the profits of a trade, profession or vocation.

Expenditure must be incurred on:

1. building works;
2. architectural or design work;
3. surveying or engineering services;
4. planning applications; or
5. statutory fees or statutory permissions.

Relief is available on expenditure not falling within one of the above categories if it does not exceed 5% of the total qualifying expenditure incurred on items falling within heading 1 to 3 above.
(CAA 2001 s.360B(2A)-(2C))

Qualifying expenditure does not include expenditure on:

- acquiring rights to the land; and
- extending the building, apart from providing access to or from qualifying premises;
- the development of land adjoining a qualifying building;
- the provision of plant and machinery, other than plant and machinery qualifying as a fixture under CAA 2001 s.173(1).

(CAA 2001 s.360B(3))

Fixtures falling within CAA 2001 s.360B(3) are:

1. integral features within meaning of CAA 2001 s.33A;
2. automatic control systems for opening and closing doors, windows and vents;
3. window cleaning installations;
4. protective installations such as lightning protection, sprinkler and other equipment for containing or fighting fires, fire alarm systems and fire escapes;
5. fitted cupboards and blinds;

6. building management systems;
7. cabling in connection with telephone, audio-visual data installations and computer networking facilities, which are incidental to the occupation of the building;
8. sanitary appliances and bathroom fittings which are hand-driers, counters, partitions, mirrors or shower facilities;
9. kitchen and catering facilities for producing and storing food and drink for the occupants of the building;
10. signs;
11. public address systems;
12. intruder alarm systems.

(CAA 2001 s.360B(3A))

Expenditure is excluded if, and to the extent that, it exceeds the normal market value for the works or services *(CAA 2001 s.360B(3B))* or if the building was used at any time during the 12 months ending on the date that the expenditure is incurred *(CAA 2001 s.360B(3D))*.

Relief is not available if, and to the extent that, works, services or other matters are not completed or provided within 36 months of the expenditure being incurred *(CAA 2001 s.360BA(1)&(2))*. Notice of the failure to complete within the 36 months must be give to HM Revenue & Customs within three months of the date on which the person claiming the relief first became aware that the original return had become incorrect due to the operation of this section and must specify how the original return should be amended *(CAA 2001 s.360BA(4)-(5))*. If the works, services or other matters are completed or provided after the end of the 36 months, relief may be claimed in the period in which the works are completed or the services are provided *(CAA 2001 s.360BA(6))*.

4.1.2. Qualifying building

A qualifying building is defined as a building:

- situated in an area designated as disadvantaged on the date the conversion or renovation began;
- which has been unused for at least one year before that date;
- which, before falling into disuse, had not been used as a dwelling, or part of a dwelling, or, in the case of a part of a building, had not been last occupied and used in common with any other part of the building other than a part which had been disused for at least a year or which had been used as a dwelling.

(CAA 2001 s.360C(1))

Qualifying business premises mean premises in a qualifying building which are to be used, or available and suitable for use, for the purpose of a trade, profession or vocation or as offices. Where the premises are to be used as offices, there is no requirement that they be used for the purpose of a trade, profession or vocation. The premises must not be used, or be available for use, as a dwelling *(CAA 2001 s.360D(1))*. Premises will remain qualifying business premises during a period when they are temporarily unsuitable for use for qualifying purposes, provided that they were qualifying business premises immediately before the start of that period *(CAA 2001 s.360D(3))*.

4.1.3. Relevant interest

The relevant interest is the interest held by the person incurring the expenditure at the time it was incurred *(CAA 2001 s.360E(1))*. Where the person holds more than one interest and one of these interests is reversionary on all the others, the reversionary interest is the relevant interest *(CAA 2001 s.360E(3))*. A relevant interest is not affected if a lease is granted out of it *(CAA 2001 s.360E(4))*. If the relevant interest is a leasehold interest and this interest is merged with the freehold interest through the purchase of the reversionary interest, the merged interest becomes the relevant interest *(CAA 2001 s.360E (5))*.

If a person incurs qualifying expenditure, but only acquires an interest in the flats on completion of conversion, they are treated as having held that interest at the date the expenditure was incurred *(CAA 2001 s.360F)*.

4.1.4. Initial allowance

An initial allowance of 100% of the qualifying expenditure may be claimed in the period the expenditure is incurred. This allowance may be reduced to a specified amount *(CAA 2001 s.360G)*. An initial allowance given on the basis that the premises are to be qualifying business premises is withdrawn if the premises are not, in fact, qualifying business premises when they are first used or if the person to whom the allowance is made sells the relevant interest before the premises are first used *(CAA 2001 s.360H)*. Where a person incurs an additional VAT liability in respect of qualifying expenditure, an initial allowance may be claimed on the additional liability in the period it is incurred, whether this is before or after the date on which the premises are first used for, or are suitable for use for business purposes *(CAA 2001 ss.360U & W)*.

4.1.5. Writing down allowance

If an initial allowance of 100% is not claimed, a WDA of 25% on cost (adjusted *pro rata* for periods of more or less than 12 months) may be claimed, provided that a long lease (over 50 years) has not been granted on the qualifying building in consideration of a capital sum at the end of the chargeable period

(CAA 2001 s.360I & J). Where a person incurs an additional VAT liability in respect of qualifying expenditure and does not claim an initial allowance of 100%, the remainder is added to the residue of expenditure and writing down allowances may be claimed *(CAA 2001 s.360V)*. Where a VAT rebate is received, the rebate will reduce the residue of qualifying expenditure *(CAA 2001 s.360Y)*.

4.1.6. Grants and payments towards expenditure

No initial or writing down allowances are given to the extent that expenditure is taken into account for the purpose of a relevant grant or relevant payment towards the expenditure or any other expenditure incurred by any person in respect of the same building and on the same single investment project (as defined by *Commission Regulation (EU) No. 800/2008 (General Block Exemption Regulation)* as the expenditure *(CAA 2001 s.360L(1))*. A relevant grant or payment is defined as a State aid or any other grant or subsidy which the Treasury may specify in regulations *(CAA 2001 s.360L(6))*. Any allowance which has already been given will be withdrawn to the extent a relevant grant or payment is given towards expenditure, or, within the period of three years beginning when that expenditure was incurred, a relevant grant or relevant payment is made towards any other expenditure which is incurred by any person in respect of the same building, and on the same single investment project, as that expenditure *(CAA 2001 s.360L(2))*. Notice of the receipt of a grant must be give to HM Revenue & Customs within three months of the date on which the person claiming the relief first became aware that the original return had become incorrect due to the operation of this section and must specify how the original return should be amended *(CAA 2001 s.360L(4)-(5))*.

4.1.7. Balancing adjustments

A balancing adjustment is calculated if, within a period of five years commencing on the date the building is first used *(CAA 2001 s.360M(4))*:

- the relevant interest is sold;
- a long lease is granted on the qualifying building in consideration of a capital sum;
- where the relevant interest is a leasehold, the leasehold ends other than through the person acquiring the reversionary interest;
- the person holding the relevant interest dies;
- the building is demolished or destroyed or otherwise ceases to be a qualifying building.

(CAA 2001 s.360N)

The proceeds taken into account are:

Balancing Event	Proceeds
Sale of relevant interest	Net proceeds of sale
Grant of long lease	Capital sum received in consideration, or the commercial premium receivable if this is greater than the sum received
Expiry of a lease where the lessee and person entitled to a superior interest are connected	Market value of relevant interest at date of expiry of lease
Death of person holding relevant interest	Market value of relevant interest at date of death
Demolition or destruction of building	Net proceeds for remains of flat plus any insurance or compensation monies received, so far as they are capital in nature
Building ceases to be qualifying business premises	Market value of relevant interest at date of event

(CAA 2001 s.360O)

A balancing charge cannot exceed the amount of allowances given on the qualifying expenditure *(CAA 2001 s.360P(5))*.

Where a building is demolished and the person holding the relevant interest incurs the cost of demolition, these costs are added to the residue of expenditure when calculating any balancing adjustment (*CAA 2001 s.360S)*.

If a VAT rebate is received in respect of qualifying expenditure, a balancing charge will arise to the extent that the rebate exceeds the residue of qualifying expenditure *(CAA 2001 s.360X)*.

Where part of a sum receivable on the sale of a relevant interest is attributable to assets qualifying for allowances, an apportionment must be made on a 'just and reasonable basis' *(CAA 2001 s.360Z2)*.

4.1.8. Termination of lease

- Where on the termination of the lease the lessee remains in possession with the consent of the lessor, the lease is deemed to continue until the lessee vacates the property *(CAA 2001 s.360Z3(2))*.
- Where a new lease is granted under an option contained in the old lease the lease is deemed to continue *(CAA 2001 s.360Z3(3))*.
- Where the lessor makes a payment to the lessee in respect of the building which is the subject of the lease, the payment is treated as consideration for the surrender of the lease *(CAA 2001 s.360Z3(4))*.
- Where a lease is granted to a new lessee, who makes a payment to the old lessee, the lease is treated as having been assigned to the new lessee in consideration for the payment *(CAA 2001 s.360Z3(5))*.

4.2. Patents

'Patent rights' are defined as 'the right to do or authorise the doing of anything which would, but for that right, be an infringement of a patent' *(CAA 2001 s.464(2))*. These include expenditure on licences in respect of a patent, and on obtaining the right to obtain a future patent right where no patent right on an invention has yet been granted *(CAA 2001 ss.465 & 466)*. Expenditure on patent rights qualifies for WDAs where they are used for trading purposes or where income arising from these rights is taxable. All such rights are pooled and a WDA of 25% may be claimed on the reducing balance basis (reduced *pro rata* for accounting periods of less than one year) *(CAA 2001 ss.470-472)*. Where rights are disposed of, the sale proceeds are deducted from the pool balance *(CAA 2001 s.476(2),(3))*. Where the disposal proceeds exceed the original cost, as with plant and machinery, the amount deducted from the pool is restricted to the original cost *(CAA 2001 s.477)*.

Where patent rights are purchased from a connected person, the amount on which a purchaser may claim allowances is restricted to the disposal value which the vendor has brought into account. This also applies where the parties are not connected, but it appears that the sole or main purpose of the sale is the obtaining of an allowance *(CAA 2001 s.481)*. On the subsequent disposal by the purchaser, any balancing adjustment is calculated by reference to the greater of the expenditure by the purchaser and the expenditure by the vendor *(CAA 2001 s.477(2)&(3))*. Where any sum received by the vendor is taxable as income, the amount upon which a purchaser may claim allowances is restricted to that sum *(CAA 2001 s.481(5))*. In any other cases the allowable expenditure is the smallest of:

- open market value;
- capital expenditure of the vendor;
- capital expenditure of any person connected with the vendor.

(CAA 2001 s.481(6)).

Expenses incurred in connection with the grant or maintenance or obtaining an extension of a patent are deductible against profits of the trade *(ITTOIA 2005 s.600)*. A non-trader may also obtain allowances by offsetting them against income from patents received during the year *(CAA 2001 s.479)*. Expenses incurred by an inventor in devising an invention are deductible in the year in which the expenditure is incurred *(ITTOIA 2005 s.600)*.

4.3. Know-how

Know-how is defined as information and techniques of a technical nature (rather than commercial knowledge such as marketing and customer lists) which is likely to assist in the manufacturing or processing of goods and materials, the working of mineral deposits or the carrying out of agricultural, forestry or fishing operations. Payments to acquire know-how exclusively for the purpose of a trade will normally be a revenue payment and are therefore deductible, but where such expenditure is treated as capital, it is pooled in the same way as expenditure on patent rights, but in a separate pool, and allowances are claimed at 25% on the reducing balance basis (reduced *pro rata* for accounting periods of less than 12 months) *(CAA 2001 ss.456-458).* Disposal proceeds are deducted from the pool balance in full and are not restricted to original cost, with any excess over original cost being taxed as a receipt of the trade. Receipts from imparting or disclosing know-how accumulated in the course of carrying on a trade will, however, generally be treated as being revenue, whether or not the receipts are in the form of a lump sum or are of a recurring nature *(British Dyestuffs Corporation (Blackley) Ltd v IRC (1924) (12 TC 586), Jeffrey v Rolls Royce Ltd (1962) (40 TC 443)).* A receipt will be treated as being capital where it relates to either:

- a disposal of one element of a comprehensive arrangement under which a trader effectively gives up an established business in a particular territory *(Evans Medical Supplies Ltd v Moriarty (1957) (37 TC 5400));* or
- a covenant against competition (a 'keep- out' covenant) and that covenant is ancillary to the grant of a licence under a patent which is a fixed capital asset of the grantor *(Murray v ICI (1967) (44 TC 175))*

A disposal made as part of the disposal of all or part of a business is treated as a sale of goodwill, unless an election is made within two years that this should not apply *(CAA 2001 s.531(2)&(3)).* Where an election is made the buyer may claim allowances on the expenditure, and the seller will be taxed on the receipt.

Expenditure incurred before the commencement of trade is treated as having been incurred on the commencement of trade *(CAA 2001 s.454(3)).*

4.4. Structures and Buildings Allowances

4.4.1. Introduction

There was no general allowance for construction expenditure on buildings and structures since Industrial Buildings Allowances (IBAs) were abolished in 2011. However FA 2019 s.29 re-introduced a similar allowance for expenditure on buildings or structures for non-residential use incurred on or after 29 October 2018, although expenditure incurred in relation to a contract for works entered into before that date is treated as having been incurred before that date *(CAA2001 s.270AB).* This has therefore updated and broadened the scope of the allowance, since its predecessor had previously been rooted in the era of the smokestack industries.

4.4.2. Rate of allowance and relevant interest

The allowance was originally given at 2% p.a. on a straight line basis, but this was increased to 3% with effect from 6 April 2020 for individuals and 1 April 2020 for companies *(CAA2001 s.270AA(5))*. For the accounting straddling the date of the change the allowance is calculated as a weighted average of the two rates, i.e. for the year ended 30 June 2020 the rate would be 2.23% (2% x 280/366 + 3% x 86/366) *(CAA2001 s.270GD)*.

The allowance is adjusted pro rata for chargeable periods of either more or less than one year or if the person did not hold the relevant interest for the whole of the chargeable period or the building or structure is demolish during a chargeable period *(CAA2001 s.270EA)*.

The allowance is given to the person holding the relevant interest in the building. A person who incurs expenditure on a building or structure and is entitled to to an interest in it on completion is treated as having that interest at the time the expenditure is incurred *(CAA2001 s.270DA)*. A relevant interest will be either a freehold interest or a leasehold interest with an effective duration of 35 years or more, provided the market value of the reversionary interest in the building or structure is less than one third of the lease premium given as consideration for the lease and that, on expiry of the lease, the lessor will acquire the relevant interest from the lessee *(CAA2001 s.270DD(1),(2))*.

The allowance may be claimed from the later of the date on which the expenditure is incurred and the building is first brought into use and is available for a period of 33 ⅓ years from that date *(CAA2001 s.270AA(2))*.

Where a building falls into temporary disuse the allowance may still be claimed, provided that, immediately prior falling into disuse, it was being ued for non-residential purposes. However, the allowance ceases to be available if the building or structure is demolished*(CAA2001 s.270AA(3),(4))*.

4.4.3. Qualifying activities and use

The following are qualifying activities, provided that the activities are chargeable to tax:

1. a trade;
2. an ordinary UK or overseas property business;
3. a profession or vocation,
4. a mining or quarrying concern;
5. management of investments of a company with investment business (as defined by CTA2009 pt 16).
   (CAA270CA)

Trades carried on through a permanent establishment outside the UK in respect of which an election under CTA2009 s.18A to exempt the profits are treated separately from any other activities of the company and are not qualifying activities *(CAA2001 s270CC).*

A building is in qualifying use if it is in non-residential use, but any non-qualifying use will be disregarded if the extent of that use is insignificant *(CAA2001 s.270CE).* Residential use includes use as a:

1. dwelling house
2. residential accommodation for pupils, students, members of the armed services or persons requiring care due to age, disability or current or past dependence on alcohol or drugs;
3. prison or similar establishment.
   (CAA2001 s.270CF)

Where a property is put to two or more qualifying use, or to multiple uses, some of which are non-qualifying, expenditure may be apportioned between the various activities on a just and reasonable basis *(CAA2001 s.270EB).*

4.4.4. Qualifying expenditure

The following expenditure is excluded from qualifying expenditure:

1. costs on acquisition of land or rights over land;
2. incidental costs of acquisition of land or rights over land, e.g. professional fees or stamp duty and other taxes;
3. expenditure on land reclamation or remediation;
4. expenditure qualifying as plant and machinery.
   (CAA2001 s.2001BG,BI)

Qualifying expenditure will, however, include expenditure on the preparation of land, e.g. levelling or tunnelling *(CAA2001 s.270BK).*

Expenditure incurred for the purposes of a qualifying activity on or after 29 October 2018, but before the date on which the person starts to carry on that activity, is treated as having been incurred on the date the qualifying activity commences *(CAA2001 s.270BN).*

Where expenditure must be apportioned between qualifying expenditure and other expenditure, the apportionment must be done on a just and reasonable basis *(CAA2001 s.270BL).*

Expenditure on the renovation or conversion of a building or structure, including repairs which are incidental to the renovation or conversion, are treated as expenditure on the construction of the building or structure for the first time to the extent that they are not an allowable deduction in calculating taxable profits *(CAA2001 s.2001 s.270BJ).*

Where an interest in a building or structure is sold and the sum paid by the purchaser is the qualifying expenditure, any excess of the sum paid over the market value of the interest at date of the sale is treated as excluded expenditure *(CAA2001 s.270BH).*

Expenditure is not qualifying expenditure if the building or structure is sold before it is brought into non-residential use *(CAA2001 s.270BB).* Where expenditure is incurred after the building or structure is brought into use, it may be treated as having been incurred either on the latest date on which expenditure is incurred or on the first day of the following chargeable period *(CAA2001 s.270BB).*

Where a building or structure is sold unused, the purchaser is treated as having incurred the qualifying expenditure. Where the person actually incurring the expenditure is a developer, the amount of the qualifying expenditure is the sum paid by the purchaser. Where the person incurring the the expenditure is not a developer, the qualifying expenditure is the lower of the actual qualifying expenditure incurred by the vendor and the capital sum paid by the purchaser *(CAA2001 s.270BC,BD).*

Where a developer sells a building or structure after it has been brought into use, the purchaser will acquire the qualifying interest and the qualifying expenditure is the amount of qualifying expenditure actually incurred by the developer *(CAA2001 s.270BE).*

Chapter 5. Basis Periods

5.1. Current Year Basis (CYB)

Continuing businesses, i.e. businesses that have been trading for some time, are assessed on a CYB, and so the profits assessed in a tax year are the adjusted profits of the accounting period ending in the tax year *(ITTOIA 2005 s.198 (1))*. There are special rules for the opening and closing years.

Example

Peter has been in business for many years, drawing up accounts annually to 30 September. His adjusted profits for the years ended 30 September 2020 and 2021 have been £20,000 and £30,000 respectively. The assessments for the tax years 2020/21 and 2021/22 will therefore be:

Tax Year	Basis Period	Profits
2020/21	Y/e 30.9.20	£20,000
2021/22	Y/e 30.9.21	£30,000

5.2. Opening Year Rules

There are special rules in the opening year, which are designed to ensure that a business is first assessed to tax in the tax year that it commences. The basis periods for the first three tax years are as follows:

1st year

- From date of commencement to following 5 April *(ITTOIA 2005 s.199)*.

2nd year

- If there is an accounting date falling in the second tax year and this date is at least 12 months after the date of commencement, the basis is the 12 month period ending on that accounting date *(ITTOIA 2005 s.200(3))*;
- if there is an accounting date falling in the second tax year but this date is less than 12 months after the date of commencement, the basis is the first 12 months of trading *(ITTOIA 2005 s.200(2))*;
- if there is no accounting date falling in the second tax year, i.e. the trader starts with a long accounting period, the basis period is the tax year itself *(ITTOIA 2005 s.200(4))*.

3rd year

- The basis period will be the 12 months ending on the accounting date falling in the third tax year.

A consequence of the opening year rules is that some of the profits of the early periods will be normally be taxed twice (this can only be avoided if a trader draws up accounts to 5 April). These are known as overlap profits. Where an accounting period straddles two or more tax years, the profits are time-apportioned.

Example

1. Rooney started trading on 1 July 2020 and makes up accounts to 31 December. The agreed adjusted profits are as follows:

6m/e 31.12.20	£8,000
y/e 31.12.21	£20,000

Rooney's assessments will be:

Tax Year	Basis Period			Assessment
2020/21	1.7.20 – 5.4.21	6m/e 31.12.20		8,000
		1.1.21 – 5.4.21	£20,000 x 95/365	5,205
				£13,205
2021/22	Y/e 31.12.21			£20,000

The overlap profits will be £5,205, i.e. the profits of the period from 1 January 2021 to 5 April 2021.

2. Crouch started trading on 1 July 2020 and makes up accounts to 30 April. His agreed adjusted profits are as follows:

10m/e 30.4.21	£12,000
y/e 30.4.22	£15,000

Tax Year	Basis Period			Assessment
2020/21	1.7.20 – 5.4.21		£12,000 x 279/304	£11,013
2021/22	1.7.20– 30.6.21	10m/e 30.4.21		12,000
		1.5.21– 30.6.21	£15,000 x 61/365	2,507
				£14,507
2022/23	Y/e 30.4.22			£15,000

The overlap profits will be those arising in the period from 1 July 2020 to 5 April 2021 (taxed in 2020/21 and 2021/22) and the period from 1 May 2021 to 30 June 2021 (taxed in 2021/22 and 2022/23), and total £13,520.

3. Owen started trading on 1 January 2020 and made up his first accounts to 30 April 2022. The agreed adjusted profit for the period is £24,000.

Tax Year	Basis Period		Assessment
2020/21	1.1.21 – 5.4.21	£24,000 x 95/486	£4,691
2021/22	6.4.21 – 5.4.22	£24,000 x 365/486	£18,024
2022/23	1.5.21 – 30.4.22	£24,000 x 365/486	£18,024

The overlap profits will be £16,739, i.e. the profits of the period from 1 May 2021 to 5 April 2022. These can also be calculated by taking the aggregate assessments of the three tax years less the adjusted profits of the accounting period.

Where a trader receives a business start-up allowance which is not a lump sum payment in a period which falls within two basis periods, the payment is included in the profits of the first basis period and excluded from the profits of the second basis period *(ITTOIA 2005 s.207(1)&(2))*. The payments included in this section are those made in England and Wales by the Skills Funding

Agency under the *Learning and Skills Act 2000*. The equivalent payments in Scotland are those made by a local enterprise company under the *Enterprise and New Towns (Scotland) Act 1990 s.2(4)(c)* and in Northern Ireland payments by, or on behalf of, the Department for Employment and Learning under *Employment and Training Act (Northern Ireland) 1950 s.1(1A)(d)*.

5.3. Closing Year Rules

The final tax year of assessment will be the tax year in which the business ceases, and the basis period will start immediately after the end of the basis period for the penultimate year and run to the date of cessation *(ITTOIA 2005 s.202(1))*. In many cases this will result in a basis period of longer than 12 months. The overlap profits are then deducted to arrive at the final assessment *(ITTOIA 2005 s.205)*.

Example

Giggs ceases trading on 31 March 2021, having previously made up accounts to 30 June. The overlap profits arising on commencement were £10,000. His results for the last three periods have been:

y/e 30.6.20	£30,000
y/e 30.6.21	£50,000
9m/e 31.3.22	£25,000

Tax Year	**Basis Period**		**Assessment**
2020/21	Y/e 30.6.20		£30,000
2021/22	1.7.20 – 31.3.22	Y/e 30.6.21	50,000
		9m/e 31.3.22	25,000
			75,000
	Less: Overlap Profits		(10,000)
			£65,000

5.4. Tax Planning on Commencement

The opening and closing year rules ensure that, whichever accounting date is chosen, the aggregate assessments will equal the aggregate adjusted accounting profits over the total life of a business. The choice of accounting date will, therefore, only change the tax years in which the various profits are taxed. The actual tax liabilities arising are unlikely to be the same due to changes in rates and allowances, but the effect of this cannot be predicted at the time of commencement. A cash flow advantage can be gained by choosing an accounting date which gives rise to low assessments in the opening years. The only disadvantage is that there is likely to be a high assessment in the final year of trading and the trader must be prepared for this. It is often possible to achieve this, since profits of a business will often show a rising trend over the first few years and the level of taxable profits in the first period of trading can often be reduced by the use of, for example, pre-trading expenditure. By judicious choice of accounting date it can be ensured there are low taxable profits in accounting periods which are taxed twice.

A date early in the tax year will give the maximum delay between earning the profits and paying the tax and, where profits are rising, will mean that the tax will be paid on profits which are lower than the profits being earned at the date the tax is paid. The converse will, however, be true where profits are falling. A date early in the tax year will also allow the level of taxable profits to be known earlier so that a better estimate of payments on account can be made.

An accounting date late in the tax year will be advantageous where it is expected to make losses in the opening years since it will maximise the ability to carry back the losses against other income. It will also reduce the amount of overlap profit and avoid a large tax liability in the year of cessation.

5.5. Tax Planning on Cessation

Whilst in many cases it may not be possible to plan the date of cessation, a certain amount of planning is possible to minimise the tax liability in the final years. In the example in section **5.3** above, Giggs is paying higher rate tax on much of the 2020/21 assessment. If they were to delay his retirement until 30 April 2021, the year of cessation would be 2021/22. The basis period for 2020/21 would be the year ended 30 June 2020, giving an assessment of £50,000. The profits of the 10 months ended 30 April 2021 less the overlap profits would be assessable in 2021/22, and would, therefore, probably be taxable at the basic rate (depending on the amount of other income in that year).

5.6. Change of Accounting Date

If a trader wishes to change his accounting date, the following conditions must be met:

1. the change must be notified to HM Revenue & Customs by 31 January following the tax year in which the change is made *(ITTOIA 2005 s.217(2))*;
2. the first accounts to the new accounting date must not be for a period longer than 18 months, otherwise two sets of accounts must be prepared *(ITTOIA 2005 s.217(3))*; and
3. there must not have been a change of date in the previous five tax years, unless it can be shown that the change is for commercial, not tax, reasons *(ITTOIA 2005 ss.217(4),s.218(3))*.

Where the above conditions are not met, HMRC will ignore the change and the basis period will be the 12 months running to the old date. A taxpayer has the option of making a fresh attempt to change the accounting date the next year, in which case the previous failure will be ignored for the purpose of condition three, or they can revert to the old date.

The change can result either in a period of less than 12 months or a period of more than 12 months and there are different rules for each case.

Where a trader draws up his accounts to a mean accounting date, e.g. the nearest Saturday to 31 December, HMRC will not treat this as a change provided that the accounting date does not vary by more than four days from the mean accounting date.

5.7. Period Less than 12 Months

Where the accounting period is less than 12 months, the basis period will be the 12 months ending on the new accounting date, and any profits assessed twice will become additional overlap profits *(ITTOIA 2005 s.216(2))*.

Example

Beckham has been trading for a number of years making up accounts to 31 December. In 2021 he decided to change his accounting date to 30 September. His results for the relevant periods were:

y/e	31.12.20	£35,000
9m/e	30.9.21	£20,000

The basis period for 2021/22 will be 1 October 2020 to 30 September 2021, giving an assessment of:

		£
1.10.20 – 31.12.20	92/365 x £35,000	8,822
9m/e 30.9.21		20,000
		£28,822

5.8. Period More Than 12 Months

Where the accounting period is of more than 12 months, the basis period will run from the old accounting date to the new accounting date *(ITTOIA 2005 s.216(3))*. This will give a basis period of more than 12 months' duration. Therefore, a proportion of the overlap profits arising on commencement may be deducted. These overlap profits will not be available on cessation.

The overlap profits deductible are:

$$\frac{\text{No. of days in basis period - 365}}{\text{No. of days in overlap period}} \times \text{Overlap profits}$$

(ITTOIA 2005 s. 220(3))

Example

Scholes has been trading for a number of years, making up accounts to 30 June. In 2021 he decides to change his accounting date to 30 September and the profits for the 15 months ended on 30 September 2021 were £60,000. The overlap period on commencement was 279 days and overlap profits were £15,000.

The basis period for 2021/22 will be the 15-month (457 day) accounting period, giving an assessment of:

	£
15m/e 30.9.21	60,000
Less: Overlap profits £15,000 x $\frac{457-365}{279}$	(4,946)
	£55,054

5.9. Two Accounting Dates in Tax Year

If, as a result of a short accounting period, there are two accounting periods ending in the same tax year, the basis period will cover both accounting periods. This will create a basis period of more than 12 months and a portion of overlap profits will be deductible.

5.10. No Accounting Date in Tax Year

If a long accounting period results in there being no accounting date in a year of assessment, the profits assessed will be those of the 12 month period ending one year before the new accounting date. This will, therefore, result in a basis period of less than 12 months, and additional overlap profits will arise.

5.11. Transitional Overlap Relief

Up to 1995/96, businesses which had commenced before 6 April 1994 were assessed on the preceding year basis, i.e. the assessment was the adjusted profits of the accounting period which ended in the preceding tax year. For a business with an accounting date of 31 December, the basis period for 1995/96 would, therefore, have been y/e 31 December 1994. To bring about the change to the CYB (current year basis) the assessment for 1996/97 was the average of the profits which would have been assessed on a preceding year basis and the profits which would have been assessed on the current year basis. However, due to the workings of the complicated opening year rules under the previous regime, this averaging process did not give full relief for profits assessed more than once on commencement. Therefore, the profits arising from 6 April 1997 to the next accounting date following 6 April 1997 are treated as transitional overlap profits and may be deducted from the assessment in the year of cessation *(FA 1994 Sch. 20 para. 3)*.

Example

Butt has an accounting date of 30 June and his adjusted profit for the year ended 30 June 1997 was £30,000. The transitional overlap relief runs from 6 April to 30 June 1997 and is £30,000 x 86/365, i.e. £7,068.

5.12. Overlap Profits and Trading Allowance

Where full relief under ITTOIA 2005 s.783AF has been claimed for either of the tax years to which overlap profits relate, these are reduced to £NIL *(ITTOIA 2005 s.204A(2)(a))*.

Where partial relief is claimed and the deductible amount for either of the tax years to which the overlap profits relate is greater than or equal to the amount of the overlap profits, these are reduced to £NIL *(ITTOIA 2005 s.204A(2)(b))*.

Where partial relief is claimed for both tax years to which the overlap profits relate, but the deductible amount for both tax years is less than the amount of the overlap profits, these are reduced by whichever of the deductible amounts for the two years is higher *(ITTOIA 2005 s.204A(7),(8))*.

Where partial relief is claimed for one of the tax years to which the overlap profits relate and the deductible amount for this tax year is less than the amount of the overlap profits, these are reduced by the deductible amount *(ITTOIA 2005 s.204A(4)-(6))*.

5.13. Changes in Size and Nature of Operations

Where there is a sudden increase or decrease in the size of a business's operations or there is a significant change in its nature, this may be treated as a cessation of one business and the commencement of another. A gradual increase, decrease or change will not be so treated. Where an identifiable part of a trade ceases, it will be a question of fact whether this is to be treated as a cessation of the whole business or not, as there cannot be a cessation simply of the part which is closed. A change in location may be a cessation and recommencement, for example if a shopkeeper sells one shop and opens a new shop in a completely different locality, or may be a continuation, for a mail-order business for example. A key question would be whether the business had the same customer base before and after the change. Similarly, where a trader carries on more than one trade, it will be a question of fact whether an increase or decrease will be the commencement or cessation of a new trade or not, and HM Revenue & Customs will resist arguments that a trade which has been treated as a single trade is in fact several trades, so that a cessation of one trade can be treated as a cessation of that trade. Activities will be considered to be separate trades if they are so fundamentally different that they cannot constitute a single trade and are not interconnected, interlaced or interdependent *(Scales v George Thompson & Co Ltd (1927) (13 TC 83))*. Where a new business is acquired which is fundamentally different from the old trade, there may either be a commencement of the new trade alongside a continuation of the existing trade or the cessation of the previous trade and a commencement of a new trade, depending on the degree to which the stock, staff and customers etc. of the two businesses are common and the degree of central co-ordination and control.

In the case of inactivity, whether there has been a cessation will be determined by the period of inactivity and the intentions of the parties.

A trade is considered to cease where it ceases in circumstances which turn out to be permanent, even if it was originally hoped to continue trading (*Marriott v Lane (1996) (69 TC 157)*).

The following have been held to be the cessation of a trade, and the commencement of a new trade where appropriate:

- brewer ceasing to brew beer, but continuing to distribute it (*Gordon & Blair Ltd v IRC (1962) (40 TC 358)*);
- ceasing trade as Lloyds underwriter but continuing trade as ship-owner (*Scales v George Thompson & Co Ltd (1927) (13 TC 83)*); and
- trader sold confectionery manufactured by themself and purchased from third parties. These trades ceased and shops and factories were closed. He commenced purchasing and reselling sugar and cellophane (*Seaman v Tucketts (1963) (41 TC 422)*).

The following have been held to be the commencement of a new trade:

- land dealers funded unsuccessful film production (*Laver & Anor v Wilkinson (1944) (26 TC 105)*); and
- hire-purchase trader sold trade to company, but retained right to receive instalments on outstanding contracts (*Parker v Batty (1941) (23 TC 739)*).

The following have been held to be the continuation of a trade:

- two mills used for baking bread and flour milling were closed. One re-opened a year later to supply bakeries (*Bolands Ltd v Davis (1925) (4 ATC 526)*); and
- taxpayer continued to fulfil orders from existing stock and from goods purchased under existing contracts, even though he had announced his intention to retire (*J & R O'Kane & Co v IRC (1922) (12 TC 303)*).

In the case of professions, it is less likely that there will be deemed to be a cessation before a person dies or retires since a professional's activities all derive from the exercise of his natural personal skills. However, a deemed cessation and recommencement is not precluded if the nature of the activities changes. In the case of *Seldon v Croom-Johnson (1932) (16 TC 740)* it was held that a barrister had not commenced a new profession when he became a King's Counsel. In *Davies v Braithwaite (1931) (18 TC 198)* the various engagements of an actress were considered to be a single profession, rather than a number of employments, but in *Elliot v Guastavino (1924) (8 TC 632)* the freelance activities of a correspondent (taxed as trading income) were held to be a separate profession from his employment with a bank (taxed as employment income).

5.14. Death of Trader

Where a trader dies and the trade is continued by his executors, this is not treated as a cessation and recommencement *(Newbarns Syndicate v Hay (1939) (22 TC 461))*. Trading losses incurred by the deceased trader may, however, not be carried forward, since continuity of ownership is required.

5.15. Mergers and Demergers

A merger of two or more businesses may, depending on the facts, be treated as a cessation of both, or all, businesses or the continuation of one business and the cessation of the other(s), and HM Revenue & Customs will often require to see the merger agreement to establish the facts. HMRC will, however, often treat mergers of firms of accountants, solicitors etc. as a continuation of all the businesses.

In the case of demergers it will again be a question of fact whether the previous trade is being continued by one of the parties or not. The purchase of a business by a person already trading will be a continuation if the purchaser has simply acquired assets, whereas where a business is acquired as a going concern it is less clear and will depend on the facts of the case.

5.16. Date of Commencement and Cessation

A trade will be treated as commencing when a trader is ready to supply goods, and preparatory activities, such as finding premises, acquiring machinery or hiring staff will not be so treated. Any expenditure incurred before the date trading commences is treated as a separate trading loss incurred on the date of commencement (see section **2.32**). Retail shops commence trading on the date that they open their doors to customers. Where a high-technology business raises finance etc. to exploit intellectual property, it is the view of HM Revenue & Customs that trading does not commence until the business has decided the manner in which it will realise the value of the intellectual property, e.g. manufacture and sale of a product or granting licences to produce it. Costs incurred up to that point will be preparatory expenses and will not be trading losses, but may be pre-trading losses.

The date of cessation is again decided on the facts of each case and will be determined by the same factors as those which determine that the trade has ceased.

5.17. Successions

The following criteria determine whether a person has taken over and continued a trade or whether there has been a cessation and recommencement*)*:

- whether the person carries on a similar trade after the transfer. In *Maidment v Kibby (1993) (BTC 291)* the acquisition of a second fish and chip shop was held to be the expansion of an existing business;
- length of inactivity between cessation of business by predecessor, the transfer of the business and the resumption by successor. In general, the longer the period of inactivity, the greater the likelihood that the transfer will be treated as a cessation and recommencement. This may depend on the reason for the inactivity since in *Wild v Madame Tussaud's (1926) Ltd (1932) (17 TC 127)* a four-year gap due to a fire in the waxworks was not held to prevent a succession by the company buying the business;
- intention of the transferee. If the transferee does not intend to run the business for a significant period of time after acquiring it, the transfer will not be treated as a succession;
- if the successor takes over the goodwill this will be an important, but not a conclusive, indicator that there is a succession *(Kenmir Ltd v Frizzell (1968) (1 All ER 414))*;
- similarly, if the successor takes over staff this will be an important, but not conclusive, indicator that there is a succession;
- taking over stock and work in progress may be an indicator, but in general it is less important than the taking-over of staff and goodwill;
- if the successor takes over the business premises this will be an important, but not conclusive, indicator;
- where the transferor has been forced to sell due to losses there is less likely to be a cessation.

In the case of a profession there cannot be a succession where the profession relies on the personal qualities of the individual, e.g. a musician, but in the case of a general practitioner there may be a continuation where there is a change of ownership.

A personal representative succeeds to the business of the deceased.

5.18. Trader Becoming, or Ceasing to be, UK Resident

Where a person carrying on a trade wholly or partly outside the UK becomes or ceases to be resident in the UK, there is a deemed cessation and recommencement of a trade etc. There is, however, specific provision for losses incurred before the cessation to be carried forward to be offset against profits arising after the recommencement *(ITTOIA 2005 s.17(1)-(4))*. Where a person carrying on a trade etc. wholly in the UK becomes or ceases to be resident there is no deemed cessation and recommencement.

Chapter 6. Trading Losses

Note: For the treatment of trading losses by companies see section **14.14**

6.1. Introduction

There are three main ways in which a trading loss may be relieved:

- carry forward against future trading profits *(ITA 2007 ss.83&84)*;
- offset against general income *(ITA 2007 ss.64&65; FA 2009 Sch. 6)*; or
- offset against capital gains *(TCGA 1992 ss.261B-261D)*.

There are, in addition, special reliefs available for a loss incurred either in the early periods of trading *(ITA 2007 ss.72-74)* or the final period of trading *(ITA 2007 ss.89-92)*.

There are no special rules concerning adjustments to profits, basis periods and capital allowances for the period concerned *(ITA 2007 ss.61(2)&62(2))*. It is worth remembering that one situation in which it may be worthwhile disclaiming all or some of the capital allowances available is in loss-making periods. An assessment can never be negative; if the adjusted figure for the basis period is a loss the assessment for the tax year concerned is nil and the question of how the loss can be relieved is an entirely separate issue.

It is never possible to claim relief for a loss more than once *(IRC v Scott Adamson (1932) (16 TC 670))*. Therefore, if relief has been claimed for a loss under one section, relief cannot be claimed again under another section, nor may relief be claimed for a loss which has been offset against profits in calculating the assessable profits of a tax year ('relief by aggregation'). A loss relief claim will be accepted on the basis of estimated figures, but a final loss figure must be notified as soon as possible.

6.2. Offset Against Future Trading Income

The loss is carried forward and offset against the first available trading income arising in subsequent periods from the same trade *(ITA 2007 s.84)*. Subject to this proviso, the loss may be carried forward indefinitely (although there is clearly a limit to the length of time that a trader can commercially afford to sustain losses). If a trader is carrying on more than one trade, the profits and losses of each trade must be computed separately, since a loss carried forward arising from one trade may not be offset against profits arising from the other trade. Two or more activities carried on by the same person are considered to be one trade, unless:

- they are so dissimilar that they cannot reasonably constitute one trade; or
- they are not interconnected, interlaced or interdependent *(Scales v George Thompson & Co Ltd (1927) (13 TC 83))*.

There is no discretion in the amount of loss offset; in any period this will be the lower of the total loss still unrelieved and the trading profits of the tax year.

This loss relief must be claimed and the time limit is 31 January in the sixth tax year following the tax year of the loss, i.e. for 2021/22 this will be 31 January 2028 *(TMA 1970 s.43)*.

Example

Phil has been trading for many years and his recent adjusted results have been as follows:

y/e 30.9.18	£(30,000)
y/e 30.9.19	£6,000
y/e 30.9.20	£8,000
y/e 30.9.21	£20,000

The assessments will be:

	2018/19	**2019/20**	**2020/21**	**2021/22**
	£	**£**	**£**	**£**
Trading income	NIL	6,000	8,000	20,000
Loss: s.84	____	(6,000)	(8,000)	(16,000)
	£NIL	£NIL	£NIL	£4,000

Loss Memorandum

	£
Loss 2018/19	30,000
s.84 2019/20	(6,000)
	24,000
s.84 2020/21	(8,000)
	16,000
s.84 2021/22	(16,000)
	£NIL

6.3. Transfer of Business to a Company

Where a business is transferred to a company, unrelieved losses of the unincorporated business at the date of transfer may be offset against income received by the taxpayer from the company in future years, i.e. remuneration or dividends, provided that:

- the business was transferred wholly or mainly for shares;
- the taxpayer has a beneficial interest in the shares for the whole of the tax year in question;
- the company carries on the business throughout the tax year in question.

(ITA 2007 s.86)

6.4. Offset Against Total Income and Carry-back

A trading loss may be offset against the taxpayer's general income for the year (defined as the total income from all sources less charges on income) *(ITA 2007 s.64(1))* of:

- the tax year of the loss *(ITA 2007 s.64(2)(a))*; or
- the preceding tax year *(ITA 2007 s.64(2)(b)*; or
- both the tax year of the loss and the preceding tax year *(ITA 2007 s.64(2)(c))*.

A trading loss incurred in 2021/22 may therefore be offset against the general income (i.e. total income after deducting charges, but before deducting the personal allowance) of 2020/21 and/or 2021/22.

In order to make a claim under ITA 2007 s.64, it must be shown that in the period in question the business had been carried on on a commercial basis and with a view to and in reasonable expectation of the realisation of profits throughout the basis period *(ITA 2007 s.66)*. Relief for a loss incurred in the trade of farming or market gardening may generally only be claimed under ITA 2007 s.64 if there has been a profit in at least one of the five preceding years *(ITA 2007 s.67)*.

If a taxpayer makes a loss from one or more trade in a non-active capacity (otherwise than as a partner in a partnership), the total loss which may be carried back and offset against general income and capital gains is restricted to £25,000, unless the loss is being offset against profits of the same trade *(ITA 2007 s.74A)*. Losses which arise directly or indirectly from an arrangement, the main purpose, or one of the main purposes, of which, is obtaining a tax advantage, may not be carried back or offset against capital gains *(ITA 2007 s.74ZA)*.

A claim under ITA 2007 s.64 is not compulsory, but as with ITA 2007 s.83, it is not possible to make a partial offset; the loss offset will be the lower of any unrelieved loss and the general income of the tax year. Where the loss is greater than the general income of either the current or the preceding tax year, but less than the combined general income, the taxpayer may choose whether to make the maximum offset against the total income of the year of the loss, and only offset the balance against the general income of the preceding tax year or vice versa. Therefore, if a taxpayer incurs a trading loss of £30,000 in 2021/22 and has a general income of £20,000 in both 2020/21 and 2021/22, they may either offset £20,000 of the loss in 2020/21 and the remaining £10,000 in 2021/22, or £20,000 in 2021/22 and the remaining £10,000 in 2020/21.

The time limit for making an ITA 2007 s.64 loss relief claim is 31 January in the second tax year following the year of the loss, i.e. 31 January 2024 for losses incurred in 2021/22 *(ITA 2007 s.64(5))*.

Example

Brenda has been trading for many years and her recent adjusted results have been as follows:

y/e 31.12 19	£14,000
y/e 31.12.20	£(20,000)
y/e 31.12.21	£17,000

She also received rental income of £2,000 p.a.

	2019/20	**2020/21**	**2021/22**
	£	**£**	**£**
Trading income	14,000	NIL	17,000
Loss relief s.84			(4,000)
	14,000	NIL	13,000
Property income	2,000	2,000	2,000
	16,000	2,000	15,000
Loss relief: s.64	(16,000)		
	£NIL	£2,000	£14,000

Loss Memorandum

	£
Loss 2020/21	20,000
2019/20 s.64	(16,000)
	4,000
2021/22 s.84	(4,000)
	£NIL

An ITA 2007 s.64 claim against the general income of 2020/21 would be theoretically possible, but would not achieve any tax saving and would simply waste more of the personal allowance.

It is an inevitable consequence of making losses and obtaining loss relief that some personal allowances will be wasted, but these can often be minimised by disclaiming capital allowances. This will reduce the amount of the loss and also increase the trading income against which the losses may be offset.

6.5. Temporary Extension of Carry-back Period

Where a taxpayer incurs a trading loss in either 2020/21 or 2021/22 and either;

1. Makes a s.64 loss relief claim in respect of the loss; or
2. Is unable to make a s.64 loss relief claim in respect of the loss, due to there being no income against which the loss can be offset in either of the relevant years;

the remaining loss, up to a maximum of £2,000,000, may be carried back a further two tax years, but may only be offset against the trading profits of those years. The loss is offset against the trading profits of the later year before the earlier year.

(FA 2021 Sch. 2 paras. 1&2)

Example

If Brenda (see section 6.4) had trading profits of £12,000 in y/e 31.12.2017 and £3,000 in y/e 31.12.2018 and also had property income of £2,000 in both of those years, she could make the following loss relief claims as an alternative to carrying the remaining £4,000 forward under s.83.

	2017/18	2018/19	2019/20	2020/21
			£	£
Trading income	12,000	3,000	14,000	NIL
Loss relief FA 2021 Sch. 2	(1,000)	(3,000)		
	11,000	NIL	14,000	NIL
Property income	2,000	2,000	2,000	2,000
	13,000	2,000	16,000	2,000
Loss relief: s.64			(16,000)	
	£13,000	£2,000	£NIL	£2,000

Loss Memorandum

	£
Loss 2020/21	20,000
2019/20 s.64	(16,000)
	4,000
2018/19 FA 2021 Sch. 2	(3,000)
	1,000
2017/18 FA 2021 Sch. 2	(1,000)
	£NIL

A claim must be made by 31 January in the second tax year following the tax year of the loss.

6.6. Offset Against Capital Gains

If, but only if, a claim under ITA 2007 s.64 is made to offset a loss against the general income of the tax year and some of the loss remains unrelieved, a further claim may be made under TCGA 1992 ss.261B-261D to offset the loss against the net capital gains of the tax year. This relief is covered in more detail in section **13.5.1**.

6.7. Losses in the Early Years of Trading

Under the basis period rules for the early years of trading, a period can form part of the basis period for two tax years and thus be taxed twice. If a loss is incurred in such a period, relief cannot be obtained twice. For the purpose of claiming loss relief, the loss is incurred in the basis period for the earlier tax year, and must be excluded from the loss of the later tax year *(ITTOIA 2005 s.206)*.

Example

Anne started trading on 1 October 2020 and draws up accounts to 30 June.

The results for the first two periods of trading were:

9m/e 30.6.21 Loss £12,000

y/e 30.6.22 Profit £9,000

The loss available for relief will be:

Tax Year	Basis Period		
2020/21	1.10.20 – 5.4.21	£12,000 x 187/273	£8,220
2021/22	1.10.20 – 30.9.21	9m/e 30.6.21	12,000
		Less: Relief given in 2020/21	(8,220)
		Profit of 1.7.21 – 30.9.201	
		£9,000 x 92/365	(2,269)
			£1,511

There is a special relief (*ITA 2007 ss.72-74*) available for losses incurred in the first four tax years. These can be carried back against the net income (i.e. total income after deducting charges, but before deducting the personal allowance) of the three years preceding the year of the loss. The following points are relevant to the relief:

- the loss is offset against the general income of the earliest year first;
- the loss relief claim applies to all three of the preceding years, provided that the loss is large enough; and
- an earlier claim takes precedence over a later claim.

The taxpayer must show that the business was being carried on on a commercial basis throughout the basis period. A claim under these sections must be made by 31 January in the second tax year following the year of the loss *(ITA 2007 s.72(3))*.

Example

Peter started trading on 1 July 2020. He incurred a loss in the year ended 30 June 2019 of £40,000. He has no other source of income and does not anticipate making a profit in the year ended 30 June 2021. His employment income before starting the business was:

2017/18	£20,000
2018/19	£15,000
2019/20	£30,000

If Peter were to make a claim under ITA 2007 s.72 the apportionment of the loss would be:

2020/21	279/365 x £40,000	£30,575
2021/22	£40,000 - £30,575	£9,425

This may be relieved as follows:

	2017/18	**2018/19**	**2019/20**
	£	**£**	**£**
Employment income	20,000	15,000	30,000
Loss relief: s.72 (2020/21)	(20,000)	(10,575)	
Loss relief: s.72 (2021/22)		(4,425)	(5,000)
	£NIL	£NIL	£25,000

It would also be possible for Peter to claim under ITA 2007 s.64 for the loss in 2020/21 and offset the loss against the employment income in 2020/21, carrying the remaining £575 forward. If a claim under ITA 2007 s.73 were then made in 2021/22, the whole of the loss would be offset against the income of 2020/21. This would mean that the personal allowances were wasted only in 2020/21.

6.8. Terminal Loss Relief

A special loss relief is available for losses incurred in the last 12 months of trading *(ITA 2007 ss.89-92)*. Since the final period of trading will often be of less than 12 months duration, part of a loss incurred in the penultimate period of trading may also be included. Any loss for which relief has been obtained under ITA 2007 s.64 must be excluded from a terminal loss claim and terminal loss relief is to be used with other reliefs in such a way as to minimise the claimant's total tax liability.

The terminal loss will be offset against the trading income of the three tax years preceding the tax year of cessation *(ITA 2007 s.89(2)-(3))*. In contrast to the relief for losses in early years, the loss is offset against the latest year first.

The terminal loss must be calculated in two parts, one relating to the tax year in which the cessation takes place and the other relating to the previous tax year. Apportionments are made on a time basis. Where the final 12 months of a business covers part of the penultimate accounting period of a business, profits of that period must be aggregated with the loss of the final period, but if the result is a net profit it is disregarded in the terminal loss calculation.

Example

Sarah has traded for many years, but ceased trading on 30 September 2021. The loss for the nine months ended 30 September 2021 was £30,000. She made a profit of £45,000 in the year ended 31 December 2020 and has overlap relief of £5,000 available.

Sarah's terminal loss is:

	£	£
Loss 2021/22 (6.4.21 – 30.9.21)		
£30,000 x 178/273	19,560	
Overlap relief	5,000	
		24,560
Loss 2020/21 (1.1.21 – 5.4.21)		
£30,000 x 95/273	10,440	
Profit 1.10.20 – 31.12.20 (£45,000 x 92/365)	(11,342)	
Net profit	£902	
		NIL
Terminal loss		£24,560

A claim must be made by 31 January in the sixth tax year following the year of cessation *(TMA 1970 s.43)*.

6.9. Tax planning and loss relief

There are two objectives when planning how to obtain relief for a loss:

- obtain tax relief at the highest possible rate and thus maximise the tax saving;
- obtain relief as soon as possible.

These two aims are often incompatible, since in order to obtain relief at the highest rate it may be necessary to carry the loss forward under ITA 2007 s.83. In this case, each situation must be considered on its own facts, and the taxpayer must weigh up the benefits of obtaining immediate relief against the prospect of future relief at a higher rate. This will, however, be based on projected profits and, particularly if they are some time in the future, may well be speculative.

6.10. Restriction of Loss Relief

Loss relief will be restricted where activities are not being undertaken on a commercial basis or are not undertaken with a view to profit *(ITA 2007 s.66).* In order to satisfy the first test it is not sufficient simply to be conducting a trade *(Wannell v Rothwell (1996) (68 TC 719))* and an important factor will be whether there might be other non-commercial reasons for undertaking an activity, such as an interest in the activity as a hobby. The second test is satisfied if the taxpayer has a realistic expectation of profits, even if these may not occur until some time in the future.

6.11. Late Claims

There is no specific authority for HM Revenue & Customs accepting late claims, but they are prepared to do so in the following circumstances:

1. where illness of the taxpayer or a close relative, or an agent prevented a claim being made within the time limit, and it was not reasonable to expect alternative arrangements to have been made. HMRC would expect alternative arrangements to be made once it became clear that the illness would last more than three months, and the claim should be made within three months of arrangements being made or of recovery;
2. where information must be obtained from a third party and reasonable and persistent efforts have been made to obtain the information in time;
3. where an informal notification was made by the taxpayer or his agent, but they were not invited to make a formal claim. The taxpayer or agent must have reasonably believed that a valid claim had been made;
4. where the taxpayer was unaware of the income against which the loss could be offset at the date the time limit expired;
5. where the existence of a profit or loss was dependent on negotiations with HMRC which had not been completed at the date the time limit expired.

A claim in headings 2 to 5 must be made within a reasonable period of becoming aware of the need to make or the possibility of making a claim, which is normally considered to be three months, or such shorter time as may be specified in a letter from HMRC, for example in the case of heading 3.

Chapter 7. Property Income

Note: Where provisions apply equally to companies and unincorporated businesses only the ITTOIA 2005 reference is cited for brevity.

7.1. Introduction

Property income covers all income from furnished and unfurnished property situated in the UK. It is not treated as trading income, even if it is being run in an organised fashion as a trade (income from property situated overseas is taxed using the same rules, but is treated as foreign income). This includes caravans and houseboats which are not moved *(ITTOIA 2005 s.266(4))*. Where a proprietor of a caravan site carries on activities associated with the site which constitutes trading, rent from the letting of pitches for caravans may be treated as a receipt of the trade *(ITTOIA 2005 s.20)*. Receipts for the use of furniture are treated as property income unless the taxpayer is carrying on a trade of furnished lettings *(ITTOIA 2005 s.308)*. Receipts from the grant of sporting rights, e.g. shooting permits or fishing licences are generally treated as property income. The property income rules were revised in the 1990s to bring them broadly into line with the trading income rules, so that income from property is taxed in much the same way as income from any other type of business.

Property income includes casual receipts from letting, even if a business is not being run on an organised basis. Chargeable gains incurred in the course of letting are not treated as property income *(ITA 2007 s.989)*.

The following are excluded from property income:

1. receipt of yearly interest;
2. profits from occupation of woodlands managed on a commercial basis;
3. profits from farming and market gardening *(ITTOIA 2005 ss.9&10)*, mines, quarries and other concerns *(ITTOIA 2005 s.12)*;
4. rent from letting tied premises *(ITTOIA 2005 s.19)*. These rents are treated as trading income;
5. rent from the letting of surplus business accommodation;
6. rent from UK electric-line wayleaves, if a trade is being carried on on all or some of the land to which the wayleave relates. The rent is treated as a trading profit *(ITTOIA 2005 s.22)*.

The term 'rent' includes any payment in respect of a licence to occupy or otherwise use land, 'rent charges', 'ground annuals' or 'feu duties' and any other payments arising from the land and, in certain circumstances, royalty payments *(Tollemache Settled Estates Trustees v Coughtrie (1961) (AC 880))*.

7.2. Basis of Assessment

Tax is charged on the total profit arising on the letting of qualifying properties during the tax year itself *(ITTOIA 2005 s.270(1))*. The income from all properties let by a taxpayer is pooled. Therefore, a loss arising on one property may be offset against the profit arising on other properties. HMRC encourage the adoption of a fiscal year[3] in order to prevent the need to time-apportion rents etc. Where a partnership receives property income, the basis of assessment is the same as for trading income.

The profits of a property business must be calculated using GAAP where:

- it is carried on by a company, LLP, corporate firm or the trustees of a trust; or
- it has cash basis receipts for the tax year exceeding £150,000; or
- it is carried on by an individual, but a share of the profits is brought into account by another individual whose profits are calculated using GAAP; or
- an allowance under CAA 2001 Part 3A (business renovation allowances is made at any time in calculating the profits of the business; or
- an election has been under this section by 31 January in the second tax year following the endo f the tax year to which it relates.

  (ITTOIA 2005 s.271A)

Where none of these conditions apply, the cash basis may be used *(ITTOIA 2005 s.271C)*.

See table in **7.6** for provisions which do not apply where the cash basis is in force.

See **2.10.4** for the treatment of adjustment income arising from leaving the cash basis.

7.3. Dilapidations

Shortly before the expiry of a lease the property will normally be inspected by the landlord, and a list of repairs which the tenant is required to carry out will be drawn up. If the tenant does not, in fact, carry out these repairs they may pay the landlord a sum in compensation. HM Revenue & Customs will treat this as a capital receipt for breach of the terms of the lease, if the landlord disposes of the property or occupies it themself on the expiry of the lease. Where the payment can be seen as compensation for lost profits, e.g. the

---

[3] For the self-employed and others who pay personal tax the **fiscal year** starts on 6 April and ends on 5 April of the next calendar **year**.

property could only be let at a lower rent, HMRC will treat the payment as property income.

7.4. Lease Premiums

7.4.1. Premium taxable as property income

Where a lease of 50 years or less is granted during the year, a portion of any premium received by the landlord or any person connected with him is taxable as property income. A premium is defined as any similar sum paid either to the immediate or superior landlord, or to any person connected with either the immediate or superior landlord *(ITTOIA 2005 s.364(1))*. The portion is given by the formula:

$$\text{Premium} \quad \times \quad \frac{51 - n}{50}$$

Where n is the number of years for which the lease has been granted *(ITTOIA 2005 s.277(4))*.

Example

Keegan granted a 30 year lease to Owen on 1 September 2021 and received a premium of £12,000. Owen has an accounting date of 31 December. The proportion of the premium which is taxable in 2021/22 is:

$$£12{,}000 \quad \times \quad \frac{51\text{-}30}{50} = £5{,}040$$

Where the lease is granted to a trader, the lessee can obtain a deduction from his trading income for the portion of the lease premium which is taxable in the hands of the lessor, but this deduction must be spread over the term of the lease. In the above example, Owen can therefore obtain a deduction of £168 for each of the 30 years. In the year the lease is granted the relief is given *pro rata,* calculated to the nearest month, i.e. in the year ended 31 December 2021 Owen will claim £168 x 4/12 = £56.

7.4.2. Duration of lease

For this purpose a lease will be treated as expiring on the earliest date when the lease is likely to expire *(ITTOIA 2005 ss.303 & 304)*. If either the lessor or lessee has an option to terminate the lease which it is likely that they will exercise, i.e. unless the lease has been granted on an arm's length basis and the premium payable was substantially greater than would have been payable on the grant of a seven-year lease, a 20 year lease with an option on either side to terminate after seven years will be treated as a seven-year lease. Conversely, if the tenant can give, and is likely to give, notice to extend the term of the lease, or the tenant, or a person connected with him, may become entitled to a further lease, the duration of the extended lease or the combined leases will be taken.

7.4.3. Amount of premium

The following anti-avoidance provisions apply in calculating the amount of any premium to be taken into consideration:

- where any benefit other than the right to vacant possession or to receive a reasonable, commercial rent in respect of this right is granted in order to obtain a tax advantage, or payments are made which would not be made if the parties had been acting at arm's length and no other benefits had been conferred, it will be assumed for the purpose of calculating the premium that the payments had not been made or the benefits had not been conferred *(ITTOIA 2005 s.304(3)-(6))*;
- a deemed premium will arise where the landlord stipulates that work is to be carried out on the property at the tenant's expense. The amount of the deemed premium is the difference between the value of the property before and after the work is carried out (not necessarily the cost incurred by the tenant) *(ITTOIA 2005 s.278(1)-(3))*. This does not apply to work carried out of a revenue nature which would have been deductible if the work had been carried out by the landlord *(ITTOIA 2005 s.278(4)&(5))*;
- a lump sum paid in lieu of rent payable for a period is treated as a premium. The premium is treated as relating to the period of the rent covered by the payment, e.g. if a sum is paid in order to reduce the rent payable for the following ten years, the payment is treated as a premium in respect of a ten-year lease *(ITTOIA 2005 ss.279 (1) & 280(1)-(4))*;
- an amount payable by the tenant to the landlord on the surrender of a lease is treated as a premium, paid in consideration of the lease from the commencement of the lease to its surrender *(ITTOIA 2005 ss.279(1) & 280(1)-(4))*;
- payments to vary or waive terms of the lease are treated as a premium arising in the period in which the contract is entered into, and relating to a period for which the variation or waiver has effect *(ITTOIA 2005 s.281(1)-(4)&(6))*.

Where a premium is payable by instalments, the tax charge on it may, at the option of HM Revenue & Customs, be paid by instalments over a period not exceeding eight years, and ending no later than the date of the payment of the last instalment. HMRC will only permit this if the landlord can show that they would otherwise suffer hardship *(ITTOIA 2005 s.299)*.

7.4.4. Premiums on grant of sub-lease

Where a premium is payable on the grant of a sub-lease, part of that premium may be taxable *(ITTOIA 2005 ss.287-290)*. The portion taxable is given by the formula in section **7.4.1** less a portion of the premium payable by the person granting the sub-lease to the superior landlord. This deduction is:

Premium taxable under Property Income on superior landlord	x	Duration of sub-lease / Duration of head lease

(ITTOIA 2005 s.288(4)&(6))

Example

Keane granted a 30-year lease to Scholes in 2008, Scholes paying a premium of £50,000. In 2021 Scholes granted a 10-year lease to Giggs in consideration of a premium of £10,000. The amount of the premium chargeable on Giggs is:

	£
Premium chargeable £10,000 x (51 – 10)/50	8,200
Less: £21,000* x 10/30	(7,000)
	£1,200

*Premium chargeable on grant of head lease

£50,000 x (51-30)/50 = £21,000

If the deduction in respect of the premium on the head lease exceeds the taxable amount of the premium on the sub-lease chargeable, the excess can be offset against income received from the sub-lessee over the term of the sub-lease.

7.4.5. Reverse premiums

Reverse premiums are sums paid by landlords to tenants in order to induce them to take out a lease. Reverse premiums are treated as revenue receipts in the hands of the tenant *(ITTOIA 2005 ss.101 & 102)*. This applies where a sum is payable as an inducement in connection with a transaction being entered into by the person, or a person connected with him within ITA 2007 ss.993 & 994 or CTA 2010 s.1122, under which the recipient or connected person becomes entitled to an estate or interest in, or a right over, land. The payment must be made by the grantor of the estate or a person connected with him or his nominee *(ITTOIA 2005 s.99(4))*.

The reverse premium is taxable as trading income if it is received in connection with a trade, profession or vocation carried on by the recipient; otherwise it is treated as property income *(ITTOIA 2005 s.101)*. Where the two parties are connected and the transaction is clearly not at arm's length, the premium is brought into account in the 'first relevant period of account', i.e. the period of account in which the transaction takes place, or the first period of account if the transaction takes place before the commencement of trading *(ITTOIA 2005 s.102)*.

These provisions do not apply to the extent that the payment is treated as a contribution to reduce the recipient's expenditure qualifying for capital allowances *(ITTOIA 2005 s.100(1))*, if the transaction concerns the recipient's main residence *(ITTOIA 2005 s.100(2))* or it is a sale and leaseback arrangement within ITA 2007 pt 12A ch. 1 *(ITTOIA 2005 s.100(3),(4))*.

HM Revenue & Customs have issued guidance stating which payments are within ITTOIA 2005 ss.99-103. Payments within these sections include:

- contributions towards specified costs of the tenant, e.g. fitting out, start of tenancy or relocation. These should be payments contributing to expenditure which is normally the responsibility of the tenant. Where a landlord is merely reimbursing the tenant for expenditure on fittings and chattels or completing the building there is no benefit under ITTOIA 2005 ss.99-103;
- sums paid to third parties to meet obligations of the lease, such as rent to a landlord under an old lease;
- the effective payment of cash by another means, e.g. the writing off of debts.

Payments not within ITTOIA 2005 ss.99-103 include:

- the grant of a rent-free period of occupation;
- replacement by agreement of an existing lease, which has become onerous due to changes in the market, by a lease at a lower rent;
- replacement by agreement of a lease containing a condition, which the tenant finds onerous, by a lease not containing that condition.

7.4.6. Assignment of leases granted at undervalue

Where a lease is granted for 50 years or less and the lessor could have demanded a premium, but did not, or could have charged a greater premium than the premium actually demanded and the lease is later assigned for a consideration greater than that for which it was granted, an additional amount will be charged on the assignor. The charge will be based on the 'additional amount', defined as the lower of the difference between the premium (if any) which was actually charged; and

1. the premium which could have been charged ('the amount forgone'); or
2. the consideration for the assignment of the lease.

(ITTOIA 2005 ss.282 & 283).

The same proportion of the additional amount is taxed as would have been taxable if it had been paid on the grant of the original lease *(ITTOIA 2005 s.282(4))*.

Example

Peter granted a 30-year lease to Mary on 1 October 2009, charging a premium of £20,000 instead of a premium of £30,000, which could have been demanded. On 1 October 2021 the lease was assigned to David for £40,000.

Premium taxable as income.

$$£20,000 \times \frac{(51-30)}{50} = £8,400$$

Amount assessable on Mary

Amount forgone £30,000 - £20,000 = £10,000

Excess consideration on assignment £40,000 - £20,000 = £20,000

The amount assessable on Mary will be based on the amount forgone of £10,000.

$$£10,000 \times \frac{(51-30)}{50} = £4,200$$

Note that the proportion of the additional amount chargeable is based on the duration of the original lease, not the remaining period at 1 October 2021.

If the lease had been assigned for £25,000, the charge on Mary would have been based on the £5,000 excess over the premium originally charged giving an amount of £2,100.

Where such a lease is assigned a second or further time, a charge arises where the consideration for the assignment exceeds the consideration on the immediately preceding assignment *(ITTOIA 2005 s.283(5))*. The assessment is based on the amount of the lower of that excess and the 'amount forgone' on the grant of lease, reduced by amounts already charged on a previous assignment.

Example

If, where in the above example the lease had been assigned for £25,000, David were later to assign the lease to Fiona for £55,000, a charge would be made on David based on the lower of:

1. the excess consideration of £30,000 (£55,000 - £25,000); and
2. the amount forgone of £10,000.

This would give:

	£
$£10,000 \times \frac{(51-30)}{50} =$	4,200
Less charge on Mary	(2,100)
	£2,100

7.5. Sale with Right of Conveyance

Where land, or an interest in land, is sold under terms which require that it will, or may be, reconveyed to the seller, or a person connected with him, at a price which is less than the sale price, an amount may be assessed on the seller *(ITTOIA 2005 s.284)*.

Where land, or an interest in land, is sold under terms which require that it will, or may be, reconveyed to the seller, or a person connected with him, at a price which is less than the sale price, some or all of the difference between the original sale price and the reconveyance price is assessed on the seller. The amount of the difference which is to be assessed is given by the formula:

$$\text{Excess} \times \frac{51-n}{50}$$

where n is the number of complete years between the date of sale and the earliest date on which the reconveyance could take place *(ITTOIA 2005 s.284(1)-(4))*.

If the reconveyance price is variable, depending on the date of the reconveyance, the amount is calculated on the lowest possible reconveyance price under the terms of the agreement, and a repayment will be made if the reconveyance price is actually greater than this amount *(ITTOIA 2005 s.286(3))*.

Example

Jane sold a property to Harry on 1 January 2022 for £250,000 , on the condition that it could be reconveyed to Jane at any time up from 31 March 2026 for £125,000.

The amount assessable is:

	£
Sale price	250,000
Lowest possible reconveyance price	(125,000)
Excess	£125,000
Assessed on seller £125,000 x ((51 – 4)/50)	£115,000

If a sale permits a lease to be granted to the seller, or a person connected with him, the lease is treated as a reconveyance at a price equal to the sum of any premium payable on the grant of the lease and the value at the date of sale, to receive a conveyance of the reversion immediately after the lease starts to run, unless the lease is granted and starts to run within a month of the sale *(ITTOIA 2005 s.285(2))*.

7.6. Expenditure Deductible

Expenditure incurred wholly and exclusively in the course of letting may be deducted from the rent receivable, if it is a proper debit item under normal accounting principles *(IRC v Land Securities Investment Trust Ltd (1969) (45 TC 495))* and is not prohibited by statute. Examples include:

- repairs and maintenance; the distinction between repairs and improvements applies to property income in the same way as to trading income. By concession where improvements obviate the need for repairs an amount of expenditure equal to the estimated cost of the repairs is deductible. This concession does not apply where the repairs are so extensive as to amount effectively to the reconstruction of the property, or where there is a change of use which would have made the repairs unnecessary. Where an improvement is very small or is purely due to the use of modern materials, the whole of the expenditure is treated as a repair. See *Law Shipping Co Ltd v IRC (1923) (12 TC 621)* for initial repairs (section 2.17);

- wages of porters and maintenance staff;
- cost of collecting rent;
- legal and accountancy fees;
- insurance;
- ground rent;
- service charges not recoverable from tenant;
- installation of energy-saving items in a dwelling house, or in a building containing the dwelling house, if no allowance is available under CAA 2001 and a deduction is not prohibited by the wholly and exclusively rule, but would otherwise be prohibited by ITTOIA 2005 s.33;
- loft insulation or any other expenditure of an energy-saving nature as may be specified in regulations *(ITTOIA 2005 s.312)*. The deduction is not available if:
  1. the item is installed in a dwelling house that is in the course of construction; or
  2. the taxpayer does not have an interest, or is in the course of acquiring an interest or further interest; or
  3. the dwelling house forms part of a business of furnished holiday lettings; or
  4. the person derives rent-a-room receipts from the dwelling house; or
  5. the expenditure is not for the benefit of the dwelling house.

  (ITTOIA 2005 s.313)

  From 2020/21 relief for interest on a loan to purchase property has been restricted to the basic rate, with the relief being given as a reduction of the tax liability, rather than as a deduction from property income .

The provisions relating to the following deductions from trading income apply to property income *(ITTOIA 2005 s.272)*:

Reference	**ITTOIA**	**Chapter**
Capital expenditure	*ss.33*	*2.10*
Expenses not wholly and exclusively for trade and unconnected losses	s.34	2.12
Bad and doubtful debts	*s.35*	*2.22*
Unpaid remuneration	*ss.36 & 37*	*2.24*
Employee benefit remuneration	ss.38-44	2.24
Business entertainment and gifts	ss.45-47	2.25 & 2.26
Car or motor cycle hire	*ss.48-50*	*2.28*
Patent royalties	*s.51*	*2.48*
Exclusion of double relief for interest	s.52	2.31
Social security contributions	s.53	2.24
Penalties, interest and VAT surcharges	s.54	2.30
Crime-related payments	s.55	2.30

Expenditure on integral features	s.55A	
Pre-trading expenses	s.57	2.32
Incidental costs of obtaining finance	ss.58 & 59	2.29
Payments for restrictive undertakings	s.69	2.16.5
Seconded employees	ss.70 & 71	2.16.5
Payroll deduction scheme; contributions to agents' expenses	s.72	2.16.5
Counselling and retraining expenses	ss.73-75	2.40
Redundancy payments etc	ss.76-80	2.35
Personal security expenses	s.81	2.16.5
Contributions to local enterprise organisations	ss.82-86	2.16.5
Contribution to flood and coastal erosion risk management projects	s.86A & 86B	
Scientific research	ss.87 & 88	2.16.5
Expenses connected with patents, designs and trade marks	ss.89 & 90	2.29
Payments to ECGD	s.91	2.16.5
Expenditure on vehicles	ss.94D-94G	2.16.4

The items in italics do not apply where an election to use the cash basis is in force.

The following provisions relating to trading income are not applicable to property income *(ITTOIA 2005 s.272(2))*:

- treatment of premiums taxed as rent *(ITTOIA 2005 s.60-65)*;
- farming and market gardening, relief for fluctuating profits *(ITTOIA 2005 ss.221-224)*.
- tied premises, receipts and expenses treated as those of trade *(ITTOIA 2005 s.19)*.

Relief for the following is specifically prohibited:

- interest on tax *(TMA 1970 s.90)*;
- expenditure not wholly and exclusively for the purpose of the business;
- domestic and private expenditure *(ITTOIA 2005 s.34)*;
- losses not arising out of the business *(ITTOIA 2005 s.34)*;
- expenditure on integral features under CAA 2001 s.33A(3)*(CTA 2009 s.60)*;
- debts, other than bad debts or debts released as part of a voluntary arrangement *(ITTOIA 2005 s.35)*;
- sums recoverable under insurance or indemnity contract *(ITTOIA 2005 s.106)*;
- rent exceeding a notional commercial rent under sale and leaseback arrangements *(ITA 2007 pt 12A ch.1)*;
- interest under a scheme or arrangements solely or primarily made to reduce a tax liability *(ITA 2007 s.809ZG)*;
- VAT penalties *(ITTOIA 2005 ss.54 & 869)*.

7.7. Sea Walls

An allowance of 1/21st of expenditure on sea walls, embankments and river defences may be claimed each year *(ITTOIA 2005 s.315)*.

7.8. Mutual Business

The rules relating to mutual trading do not apply to property income, and the computational rules therefore apply as if there were no mutual relationship *(ITTOIA 2005 s.321)*. HM Revenue & Customs have stated that residential service charges received by occupier-controlled flat management companies are not taxable, since under correct accountancy principles the landlord is not beneficially entitled to the receipts. Such sums are to be treated as capital in the landlord's capacity as trustee, and interest arising in a designated bank account will be subject to tax at the trust rate *(Landlord and Tenant Act 1987 s.42)*. Rents receivable by these companies are taxable.

7.9. Relief for Capital Expenditure

Capital allowances are available on plant and machinery used in the running of a letting business, and the computation uses an accounting date of 5 April. Capital allowances are not normally available on plant and machinery used in a dwelling, and therefore they are not available on the cost of furniture in a furnished property *(CAA 2001 s.35)*. From 2016/17 the wear and tear allowance has been abolished and relief for capital expenditure on items for domestic use is now given on a renewals basis, i.e. the initial cost of an item is not deductible, but the cost of any subsequent replacement is deductible in full in the year the expenditure is incurred, unless the business consists of the commercial letting of furnished holdiday accommodation, in which case capital allowances may be claimed (see **7.11.**), or if rent-a-room relief applies (see **7.12.**) *(ITTOIA 2005 s.311A)*. If the replacement item is the same, or substantially the same, as the item being replaced, the full cost is deductible. Otherwise the deduction is restricted to an amount which would have been incurred to purchase an item which is the same, or is substantially the same *(ITTOIA 2005 s.311A(9))*. If the taxpayer incurs capital expenditure in connection with the disposal of the old item, that expenditure is added to the cost of the replacement item *(ITTOIA 2005 s.311A(10))*. Where any proceeds are received on the disposal of the old item or the expenditure on the replacement item is reduced because the old item has been taken in part exchange, the cost of the replacement item must be restricted by the amount of the proceeds or part exchange value *(ITTOIA 2005 s.311A(11),(12))*. This allowance is not available for fixtures, such as boilers and heating systems.

See chapter 2.10.2 and 2.10.3 for provisions relating to capital receipts and capital expenditure where an election to use the cash basis has been made, with the additional provision that no deduction is available on capital expenditure incurred on, or in connection with, the provision, alteration or disposal of an asset for use in ordinary residential property. Where expenditure has been incurred partly for use in ordinary residential property and partly for other purposes, an apportionment may be made *(ITTOIA 2005 ss.307B & 307E)*. Where a business enters the cash basis, profits having previously been calculated according to GAAP, relief for any unrelieved capital expenditure may claimed in the first period in which the cash basis is used *(ITTOIA 2005 s.334B)*.

Example

Atkinson rents out three properties; properties 1 and 2 are unfurnished and property 3 is furnished:

Property 1 was let for the first time on 1 July 2021 at an annual rental of £4,000.

Property 2 was let at an annual rental of £2,500 p.a. until 30 September 2021, when the lease was terminated. The tenant had left the country and the rent outstanding for the last quarter was never recovered. The property was re-let from 1 December 2021 at an annual rent of £3,000.

Property 3 was let throughout the year at a rent of £4,800.

Atkinson made the following payments in respect of the properties during the year.

Property	**1**	**2**	**3**
Council Tax	£350	£300	£600
Electricity and Gas	£250	£200	£500
Insurance	£200	£200	£300
Redecoration	£300	£1,200	£350
Water Rates	£150	£100	£250
Interest on Mortgage	£500	£400	£1,250
Replacement furniture			£800
Gardener's Wages	£250		£520
Advertising	£100	£50	

Property		1	1	2	2	3	3
		£	£	£	£	£	£
Rent	£4,000 x 279/365		3,057				4,800
	£2,500 x 178/365				1,219		
	£3,000 x 126/365				1,035		
					2,254		
Council Tax		350		300		600	
Electricity and Gas		250		200		500	
Insurance		200		200		300	
Redecoration		300		1,200		350	
Water Rates		150		100		250	
Replacement of furniture						800	
Bad Debt				625			
Gardener's Wages		250				520	
Advertising		100		50			
			(1,600)		(2,675)		(3,320)
			£1,457		£(421)		£1,480

The loss on property 2 will be offset against the profit on properties 1 and 3, giving a total assessment of £2,516. In addition, Atkinson will be able to claim a reduction from their tax liability of £430, i.e. 20% of the total interest payable of £2,150.

7.10. Losses

As stated above, the profits and losses from each property are pooled, so that the property income assessment will be the net profit from all the properties. If there is a net loss, this will be carried forward and offset against the property income of future years *(ITA 2007 ss.118-124)*. The following points should be noted:

- the loss must be offset against the earliest property income;
- the maximum loss offset must be made, i.e. the amount offset must be the entire loss or the total property income, if lower *(ITA 2007 s.119)*;
- where a loss of more than one tax year is carried forward, the loss of the earlier tax year is offset before the loss of the later tax year;
- to the extent that a loss is wholly or partly attributable to the claiming of capital allowances, or the property business has been carried on in relation to land which consists of or includes an 'agricultural estate' to which 'allowable agricultural expenses' deducted in claiming the loss, are attributable, a claim may be made to offset some or all of the loss against general income *(ITA 2007 s.123)*. A claim must be made by 31 January in the second tax year after the tax year of the loss *(ITA 2007 s.124(1))*. No relief is given against general income for property losses arising directly or

indirectly from arrangements, the main purpose, or one of the main purposes, of which, is obtaining a tax advantage, to the extent that the loss is attributable to an annual investment allowance (AIA) *(ITA 2007 s.127A(1),(2))*. In determining whether a loss is attributable to an AIA, the loss is treated as being attributable to capital allowances before anything else and to an AIA before any other capital allowances *(ITA 2007 s.127A(3))*.

Where the conditions in *ITA 2007 s.123* are satisfied, the amount of the claim is the lowest of:

a. the relievable income of the year for which the claim is made;
b. the net capital allowances;
c. the amount of the allowable agricultural expenses for the year of the loss;
d. the sum of the net loss and the allowable agricultural expenses *(ITA 2007 s.122)*.

Relievable income is the income of a year after offsetting losses carried forward under ITA 2007 s.119, or under ITA 2007 s.121(2)&(3) where a claim has been made under that section. Where relief is claimed for the same loss for two years, the total relief may not exceed the smallest of the amounts in ITA 2007 s.122(2). 'Allowable agricultural expenses' are defined as any expenses attributable to the estate which are deductible as maintenance, repairs, insurance or management of an agricultural estate, but excluding any interest payable on a loan *(ITA 2007 s.123(5))*.

7.11. Furnished Holiday Lettings

Income from furnished holiday lettings is treated as property income, but is classified as earned income rather than unearned income. This has a number of advantages:

- the same loss reliefs are available as for trading losses (see **Chapter 1**);
- capital allowances are available on furniture, rather than the renewals or wear and tear basis;
- Capital gains tax reliefs which are available to traders may be claimed (see section **13.31– 13.35.**).

All the furnished holiday lettings of the taxpayer are treated as a single business *(ITA 2007 s.127(3) & ITTOIA 2005 s.323)* and must be calculated separately from the liability from other property income.

To qualify as furnished holiday lettings these conditions must be fulfilled:

- the properties must be let on a commercial basis with a view to realising profits *(ITTOIA 2005 s.323(2))*. In *Brown v Richardson (HMIT) (1997) (SpC 129)* the taxpayers acquired a property in 1992 and occupied it for three weeks in July and August (the most expensive letting times) and at other times during the year on an *ad hoc* basis. It was held by the Special

Commissioners that, although the letting was commercial in that a commercial rent was charged, the property was let 'with a view to generating revenue to offset costs, rather than with a view to the realisation of profits', and the losses from the letting of property did not therefore arise from furnished holiday letting. HM Revenue & Customs have stated that a property's status as furnished holiday lettings may be prejudiced if it is purchased as a second or retirement home, or with a view to realising a capital profit, or if the size of the mortgage to purchase the property is so large as to put the prospect of earning profits and the credibility of the acquisition as a commercial undertaking in doubt. HMRC may require a business plan in such cases. Where losses are expected in the early years, HMRC will expect a profit to be earned in 'a reasonable time thereafter'. This is regarded as an indefinite, but fairly short period;

- the property must be available for letting for at least 210 days during the year *(ITTOIA 2005 s.325(2))*;
- the property must be actually let for at least 105 days *(ITTOIA 2005 s.325(3))*. Where a landlord rents out more than one property, all the properties will qualify as furnished holiday lettings if the average number of days for which they are let is greater than 105. Additionally, a landlord may omit certain properties from this calculation, if this would bring the average below 105 days *(ITTOIA 2005 s.326)*;
- if a property qualifies as furnished holiday lettings in a tax year, a taxpayer may make an election that the property be treated as furnished holiday lettings in either the following or the following two tax years, provided that the property only fails to qualify in those tax years because it was let for less than 105 days and there was a genuine intention to satisfy this condition *(ITTOIA 2005 s.326A(1))*. An election must be made by 31 January in the second tax year following the year to which it relates, but if an election is not made for the first of the two years, no election may be made for the second year *(ITTOIA 2005 s.326A(4),(5))*;
- a property must not be in 'long-term occupation', i.e. let to the same occupant for a continuous period of more than 31 days, for more than 155 days in a year. This does not include situations where a property is in the same occupation for more than 31 days continuously for reasons which are not normal, e.g. illness *(ITTOIA 2005 s.325(4)-(6))*.

The year referred to above is the tax year or accounting period in question unless the property was first let or ceased to be let as furnished holiday lettings during the tax year or accounting period. In this case the period is the 12 months commencing on the date it was first let, or the 12 months ending on the date it ceased to be let *(ITTOIA 2005 s.324)*.

Where a taxpayer rents out a number of properties, only some of which qualify as furnished holiday lettings, two profit & loss accounts must be drawn up, so that the profit from furnished holiday lettings can be distinguished from other property income.

Example

Stephen has let out four properties during 2021/22. None of these were let to the same occupants for more than 31 consecutive days.

Property	No. of days available for letting	No. of days let
1	225	128
2	187	112
3	240	98
4	255	84

Property 2 cannot qualify as furnished holiday lettings, since it was available for letting for less than 210 days. Stephen cannot claim all of properties 1, 3 and 4 as furnished holiday lettings, since the average number of days for which the three properties were let was less than 105. He may, however, claim either in respect of properties 1 and 3 or properties 1 and 4, since the average number of days for which they were let exceeds 105.

7.12. Rent a Room Scheme

Where an individual lets a furnished room or rooms in a property in the UK which is his main residence at some time during (but not necessarily throughout) the basis period, the rental income will be exempt provided that the gross rent does not exceed £7,500 *(ITTOIA 2005 ss.795-802)*. The exemption may also apply to the provision of services such as laundry or meals. The room must not be a self-contained living unit. This exemption does not apply if the income is part of a wider business carried on either in the same property or different properties, e.g. bed and breakfast *(ITTOIA 2005 ss.785 (1) & 786(1))*. Where another person also receives rent from the letting of rooms in the same property, this limit is halved. Where the rents do not exceed the limit, it is sufficient simply to state that fact on the tax return.

Where the gross rent exceeds the limit, the taxpayer may either be taxed on the rent-a-room receipts plus any balancing charges less expenses in the normal way, or they may elect to be assessed on the excess of the gross rent plus balancing charges over less £7,500 (or £3,750 if the limit is halved) without any deduction for expenses. An election must be made by 31 January in the second tax year after the tax year to which it relates.

This relief only applies where accommodation is let for furnished residential use and it is not available where a room is used as an office or for the purpose of trading. Relief is, however, available where a student, to whom a room is let, is provided with study facilities.

Chapter 8. Employment and Self-employment

8.1. Introduction

The question of whether a worker is performing work for another person, in the capacity of an employee or as a self-employed contractor, is of fundamental importance for tax purposes.

If a worker is treated as being self-employed:

- their business profits are taxed as trading income;
- they are liable to pay class 2 and class 4 national insurance contributions (NIC).

If a worker is treated as being an employee:

- payments to the worker by the person for whom the work is performed are treated as employment income;
- the worker is liable to pay primary class 1 NIC;
- the employer is liable to pay secondary class 1 and 1A NIC.

In the past it has been common for a worker to avoid being treated as an employee by providing services through an intermediary, typically through a personal service company (PSC), i.e. a company which merely exists as a vehicle for the worker to provide his services, and in which they are the main shareholder and director. An associated person such as a spouse may also be a shareholder in order to comply with company law requirements. The company is liable to corporation tax on its profits, at a rate of 19%, and the worker is remunerated by the company. The salary is a deductible expense for the company, but the salary payments are structured in a tax efficient manner in order to minimise the worker's tax liability. There is also the possibility of remuneration by payment of dividends. PSCs are still legal and they can still enable workers to reduce personal financial risk through limited liability.

Legislation now contained in ITEPA 2003 ss.49-61 was introduced in FA 2000 (preceded by the notorious Budget Press Release IR35 by which name the legislation is commonly referred to) and has removed the tax advantages of such an arrangement in many circumstances. The effect of the legislation is to look through the company, and whether an individual is to be treated as an employee or to be self-employed is determined by the normal tests relating to employment and self-employment.

8.2. Benefits of Self-employment

As regards security and benefits it is more beneficial to be an employee than to be self-employed, but for tax purposes there are a number of advantages of being self-employed. These include:

- it is easier to deduct work-related expenses and capital allowances from trading income than from employment income;
- tax is deducted at source from employment income under the PAYE system, whereas there can be a considerable delay between earning trading income and paying the related tax;
- the self-employed may make more generous pension contributions than employees.

8.3. Definition of Employment and Self-employment

There is no single definition of 'employment' or 'self-employment' for the purpose of income tax. For the purpose of NIC, an employed earner is defined as 'a perso n who is gainfully employed in Great Britain either under a contract of service, or in an office (including elective office) with general earnings' *(SSCBA 1992 s.2(1)(a))*. A contract of service must be a legally binding contract with an agreement for valuable consideration to pass from one party to another and may be written, oral, or implied. SSCBA 1992 s.2(1)(b) defines a 'self-employed earner' by default as 'a person who is gainfully employed in Great Britain otherwise than in employed earner's employment (whether or not he is also employed in such employment)'.

There are two fundamental questions in determining a person's status for the purpose of income tax and NIC:

- whether they are employed or not;
- if they are not an employee, whether they are to be treated as self-employed.

8.4. Tests for Employment

8.4.1. General principles

Many employees are keen to become self-employed for tax purposes, but being accepted as self-employed by HM Revenue & Customs involves more than simply putting the appropriate documentation and business structure in place. The status depends on the nature of the relationship between the person doing the work and the person for whom the work is performed.

Although the tests determining whether an individual is an employee for taxation purposes interact with the employment law rules determining whether they are a worker, the two sets of rules are different and an employee for employment law purposes need not be an employee for taxation purposes.

A number of tests have been developed over the years by the courts to determine a taxpayer's status, but these are not applied mechanically and each case is considered on its individual facts. A quote from the leading case of *Hall v Lorimer (1994) (66 TC 349)* makes this clear.

> 'In order to decide whether a person carries on business on his own account, it is necessary to consider many different aspects of that person's work activity. This is not a mechanical exercise of running through a checklist to see whether they are present in, or absent from, a given situation.... It is a matter of evaluation of the overall effect, which is not necessarily the same as the sum total of all the individual details. Not all details are of equal weight or importance in any given situation. The details may also vary in importance from one situation to another.'

Broadly speaking, self-employment has been defined as a 'contract for services', whereas employment has been defined as a 'contract of service', with connotations of the master/servant relationship. A number of tests are applied to the contract between the worker and the person for whom the work is performed, which may be written, oral or implied.

A single contract may contain services which are separable between employment income and trading income *(McManus & Another v Griffiths (HMIT) (1997) (BTC 412))*. In this case the taxpayer was contracted by a club as a stewardess and to provide catering. She was responsible for buying food and hiring staff relating to the provision of catering, and the club had no knowledge of the profit from the catering. The catering profits were held to be trading income, whereas the profits from activities as a stewardess were held to be employment income.

In determining the status of a taxpayer it is necessary to look at the terms of any contract, whether written, oral or implied, and also at standard practices which may exist in certain industries. Under general law, where there is a written contract, the subsequent conduct of the parties is not normally admissible evidence in interpreting the contract *(Hooper v British Railways Board (1998) (IRLR 517))*. A contract should be distinguished from a framework document, which sets out the terms and conditions of engagements which may be offered in the future and may be intended to apply to all workers in general.

8.4.2. Mutuality of obligations

An employer is obliged to offer work to an employee, or at least pay an employee even if it is unable to offer work, and an employee is obliged to carry out that work, unless there is a good reason for not doing so. A business is, however, not obliged to offer work to a self-employed contractor and the contractor is not obliged to accept work offered. If there are no mutual obligations it is unlikely that a worker will be considered to be an employee, although, while this may be persuasive, it will not in itself be conclusive. In *Mailway (Southern) Ltd v Willsher (1978) (IRLR 322)* a casual labourer was not held to be an employee, since he turned up only when he wanted to work and this was held to be volunteering for work.

The question of mutuality of obligations will cause most problems when there is a series of engagements with the same engager. If it can be demonstrated that there is an ongoing mutual obligation, the contractor will be treated as an employee for the entire period. Otherwise each engagement will be considered separately.

8.4.3. Control

An employer is able not only to specify what work is carried out, but also the exact way in which it is to be carried out. A self-employed person will be contracted to perform specific tasks, but will use his professional skill and expertise to determine exactly what work needs to be carried out and how it should be performed. Control need not be present in all areas and the critical factor is the right of control, rather than the amount of control actually exercised since many highly qualified employees, such as surgeons, have a very high degree of autonomy. This test is also likely to encompass control over where the work is carried out. In *Ansell Computer Services Limited v Richardson (HMIT) (2004) (SpC 3061/03)* the ability to take time off, without seeking permission from the client, was given as an example of lack of control by the client which meant that the contractor was not caught by the provisions of ITEPA 2003 ss.49-61. An employee will generally, but not always, have to carry out his duties at the employer's premises or another place nominated by the employer, even if that is not strictly necessary for the performance of those duties. The self-employed can, in principle, choose where to carry out their work, although sometimes the nature of the task e.g. plumbing, will dictate this. Where a taxpayer is engaged by the hour or day they may be required to complete timesheets. This merely certifies that the taxpayer has worked for a certain period of time and has completed the work to a satisfactory standard and does not indicate by itself that the taxpayer is an employee.

8.4.4. Right to use a substitute or obtain assistance

A self-employed contractor has the right to obtain assistance or sub-contract part of an engagement, e.g. a builder may sub-contract work to an electrician. In the case of *Express and Echo Publications Ltd v Tanton (1999) (IRLR 367)* (an unfair dismissal case rather than a tax case), the fact that the worker had the right to use his own nominated substitute to carry out the work, and actually did so, was the sole factor which determined that they were self-employed rather than an employee. It is not necessary for the right of substitution to have been exercised, but it must be demonstrated that the right is a genuine one. The engager may have a certain degree of veto over the appointment of a substitute, but where there is an unrestricted right of veto, or a substitute must be chosen from a list approved by the engager, the right is unlikely to be considered genuine. Where a contractor has been engaged specifically on the basis of his personal reputation and expertise, no right of substitution is likely to exist.

The details of any contract and other documentation must therefore be considered carefully to determine the degree to which, and the terms on which, substitution is permitted whether the obligation to pay the substitute and the responsibility for the work carried out lies with the taxpayer or the client. The case of *Tilbury Consulting Ltd v Gittins (2003) (SpC 390)* has emphasised that giving the contractor a real right to provide a substitute is possibly the most effective way to avoid being treated as an employee of a client under ITEPA 2003 ss.49-61. However, *Autoclenz v Belcher (2011) (UKSC 4)* has held that HM Revenue & Customs have the power to take a more purposive view of any clause in a contract granting the right of substitution than in normal commercial contracts. This is because of the unequal bargaining power of the two parties and the fact that the contract is nearly always written by the engager and HMRC may therefore rule that the clause is a sham.

8.4.5. Provision of equipment

An employee will normally expect his employer to supply the essential equipment to perform the task, whereas a self-employed contractor is normally expected to provide his own equipment. Once again this test does not always apply; the *Hall v Lorimer* case (*Hall v Lorimer [1993] EWCA Civ 25*) involved a sound engineer who was held to be self-employed and who was hiring out his personal skill, although the other party provided the equipment. Conversely, orchestral musicians may be employees, even though they are obliged to purchase their own musical instruments. Where a taxpayer is only expected to supply minor pieces of equipment e.g. small tools, this will not be a significant factor in determining his status.

8.4.6. Financial risk

An individual who is in business on his own account will be taking a far greater degree of financial risk than an employee, and there is a far greater opportunity to profit from good work and sound business management. For example a self-employed person must rectify faulty work in his own time and at his own expense, and will bear the costs of an overrun where a fixed price has been quoted for a contract.

In *Addison and others v The London Philharmonic Orchestra Society Limited (1981) (ICR 261),* session musicians were held to be self-employed even though they did not have their own business structure or risk their own capital. This was because they were held to be freelance musicians with individual reputations, even though they were playing for an orchestra.

8.4.7. Part and parcel of organisation

An employee will normally be more closely integrated into a business than a self-employed contractor. For example, a contractor will not be required to wear a client's uniform and is unlikely to be responsible for managing a client's staff. Where such factors are present, the individual is likely to be treated as an employee. HM Revenue & Customs argued in *Ansell Computer Services Limited v Richardson (HMIT) (SpC 3061/03)* that a lack of sick or holiday pay and lack of membership of the company social club were mere consequences of the contractor not being treated as an employee by the client and were thus not relevant in determining status, but it was held that negotiating away these benefits in order to retain flexibility was part of the process that was considered by the contractor and the client in determining the nature of their relationship, and therefore indicated that they were not an employee.

8.4.8. Employee benefits and right of dismissal

A contractor will not enjoy employee benefits, such as paid holiday, and will not be entitled to a fixed period of notice. If these features are present, the worker is likely to be considered an employee. This does not apply where an entitlement to paid leave exists solely due to rights under the Working Time Regulations.

8.4.9. Method of payment

Employees will normally receive a regular salary, whereas self-employed contractors will generally charge an agreed amount for an assignment. This is not, however, conclusive, since many employees are paid commission or by the piece *(Airfix Footwear v Cope (1978) (IRLR 396))* and many self-employed individuals may charge by the day or hour. HM Revenue & Customs consider that in this latter case an engager is likely to exercise a greater degree of supervision in order to ensure value for money, and that this may be indicative of employment.

8.4.10. Intention of the parties

While the purpose of the above tests is to ensure that the legal form of the contract and the intention of the parties is not decisive in determining the status of a worker *(Ferguson v John Dawson & Partners (Contractors) Ltd (1976) (1 WLR 1213))*, it will be relevant where the above factors are evenly balanced, i.e. where a client and contractor enter into a self-employed arrangement, the contractor will be treated as being self-employed unless the other factors clearly point to him being an employee.

8.4.11. Zero-hours contracts

Where an employer engages a worker on a zero-hours contract there are no guaranteed hours and the employer will only pay the worker for the hours worked. However, many of the other characteristics of employment will generally be present and it is therefore necessary to scrutinise any such contract carefully before concluding that a worker under such a contract can be treated as self-employed.

8.4.12. The Gig Economy

A similar approach is now being taken in determining whether a person operating in the 'gig' economy is a worker or self-employed. In *Dewhurst v Citysprint UK Ltd (ET/2202512/2016),* Ms Dewhurst signed a standard contract which expressly stated that she agreed that she was self-employed, but, in ruling that she was a worker, the employment tribunal took into account that there was a two-day recruitment process, training was given on how she should perform her role, uniform and other equipment, she has expected to perform the work personally and was paid weekly without submitting an invoice.

Similarly, in *Aslam and Farrar and others v Uber BV and others (ET2202550/2015),* the decision that the drivers were workers was based *inter alia,* that Uber interviewed and recruited drivers, controlled key information, such as the passenger's surname and contact details, and required drivers to accept trips, a requirement which was enforced by logging off drivers who breached it. Whilst these are employment law, rather than tax cases, the tests applied are consistent with those used in determining an individual's status for tax purposes.

8.5. Workers Supplied by Agencies

Where a worker personally provides services to a client and there is a contract between the client, or a person connected with the client, and a person other than the worker or client, or person connected with the client, and as a consequence of this contract services are provided or the client or connected person pays for the services, the worker is to be treated as an employee of the agency and remuneration received is treated as earnings from that employment. These provisions do not apply if the payments are taxable under any other provisions or if the worker is not subject to, or to the right of, supervision, direction or control by any person (*ITEPA 2003 s.44*). In the DSS case of *Staples v Secretary of State for Social Services (1985) (unreported)* it was held that the agency rules did not apply to the engagement of a relief head chef, since the level of autonomy enjoyed by the chef showed that they were not subject to the direction of the management. The agency is therefore liable to deduct PAYE on amounts received from the client. This does not apply where the agency simply introduces the worker to the client and leaves them to draw up a contract between themselves *(Brady v Mrs M A Hart trading as*

Jaclyn Model Agency (1985) (58 TC 518)). In these circumstances the agency passes on any amounts received after deducting commission.

The following types of service are excluded from the above provisions:

- service as actor, musician, singer or other entertainer or fashion, photographic or artist's model. This heading only covers cases where the worker is performing services in the relevant capacity, not where they are, for example, doing promotional work;
- services provided wholly in the home of the worker or at other premises which are neither controlled nor managed by the client nor prescribed by the nature of the services *(ITEPA 2003 s.47(2)).*

A worker engaged in a profession, the income from which is taxable as trading income, falls within these provisions if they undertake work through an agency, if they are subject to the right of control or direction. This will be the case even if in practice they have complete autonomy, unless the exemption set out in ESC A37 applies (see section **9.14**).

8.6. Non-executive Directors

Non-executive directors are not employees of a company. However, they are considered as office-holders, and therefore PAYE and NIC must be deducted from payments to them, if they are remunerated as individuals.

8.7. Self-employment or a Number of Separate Employments

Where a professional person performs services under a number of separate contracts, the question arises whether each contract might be seen as a separate employment, or whether all the contracts are carried out in the course of a single profession. The answer will depend on the facts of the individual case, but some important cases can be compared. In *Davies v Braithwaite (1931) (18 TC 198)* an actress was held to be self-employed in relation to all her activities, but in *Fall v Hitchen (1973) (49 TC 433)* a professional ballet dancer at Sadler's Wells was held to be an employee. In the former case Miss Braithwaite worked for a number of people, whereas in the latter case Mr Hitchen did not do so, although his contract allowed for this with the permission of Sadler's Wells. Furthermore, his contract was for a minimum of 22 weeks, or until notice was given by either side, and during this time they were to work full-time for a regular salary.

HM Revenue & Customs have, since 1990, insisted on all stage managers, actors and performers engaged on standard Equity contracts being treated as employees, unless they had been treated as self-employed for three years before that date. Under ITEPA 2003 s.352, actors and musicians etc. may, however, deduct up to 17.5% of their fees, inclusive of VAT, paid to a licensed employment agency or *bona fide* co-operative society which acts as their agent.

In 1993, as a result of the Special Commissioners' decision in *McCowen and West v IRC (1993)*, HMRC agreed that actors and musicians on standard Equity contracts may, under certain circumstances, be self-employed.

8.8. Provision of Services Through an Intermediary – Income Tax

8.8.1. Legislative framework

The legislation may potentially apply whenever services are provided for another person through an intermediary *(ITEPA 2003 s.49)*. This will most typically be a Personal Service Company (PSC), but may also be a partnership or a third party individual. The rules only apply where a client is acting in the course of business. Therefore, if personal gardening or DIY services are provided through an intermediary to the chief executive of a company, these are not affected by these provisions.

The rules will apply in the case of a company, which is not an associated company of the client, where:

- the worker or an associate (spouse or unmarried partner, brother, sister or direct ancestor or descendant) controls more than 5% of the ordinary share capital of the company or is entitled to more than 5% of any dividend; or
- the worker receives, or could receive, payments or benefits from the company, which, while not salary, might reasonably be taken to be a reward for services provided to the client *(ITEPA 2003 s.51(4); Social Security Contributions (Intermediaries) Regulations 2000 (SI 2000/727) reg.5(4))*. This may apply, for example, where a composite PSC has been set up comprising more than 20 contractors, at least some of which will hold less than 5% of the share capital. It is then necessary to look at whether a worker receives remuneration directly from the intermediary and whether this represents remuneration for services provided to the client.

In the case of a partnership the rules apply where:

- the worker or a member of their family (including an unmarried partner) is entitled to at least 60% of the profits;
- all or most of the partnership income is derived from services provided to a single client; or
- the profit-sharing arrangements are designed to reward the worker on the basis of the services provided to the client *(ITEPA 2003 s.52(2); Social Security Contributions (Intermediaries) Regulations 2000 (SI 2000/727) reg.5(6))*.

A third party individual may be an intermediary where the payment or benefit is received or receivable by the worker directly from the intermediary, and can reasonably be taken to represent remuneration for services provided by the worker to the client *(ITEPA 2003 s.53; Social Security Contributions (Intermediaries) Regulations 2000 (SI 2000/727) reg.5(8))*.

The legislation will only apply where the relationship between the contractor and the client is such that, had it not been for the interposition of the intermediary, the contractor would have been classified as an employee using the tests in section **8.4** ('the relevant engagements') or the contractor is an office-holder who holds that office under the client and the services relate to that office *(ITEPA 2003 s.49(1))*. If the contractor is genuinely providing services on a self-employed basis they will be unaffected by the legislation. It may well be the case that the legislation will apply to some of the engagements during the period, but not to others and in this case an apportionment of income and expenses will be made.

HM Revenue & Customs have clarified that the rules will not apply to a taxpayer if his only relationship with the intermediary is in a non-executive capacity. The legislation also does not affect the clients for whom services are performed.

If the worker is resident in the UK for tax purposes, the deemed payment will be taxable in the UK, regardless of where the duties are carried out. Where profits from the relevant engagements exceed the salary drawn by the contractor during the period, the intermediary is deemed to make a payment of employment income on the last day of the tax year.

8.8.2. Calculation of deemed payment

Where the profits from relevant engagements exceed the salary paid, the calculation of the deemed payment is set out in ITEPA 2003 s.54(1). Under the *Welfare Reform and Pensions Act 1999 s.75* and *Social Security Contributions (Intermediaries) Regulations 2000 (SI 2000/727)* payments received by an intermediary which are taxable as employment income are to be treated as earnings of employment, whether as a payment of salary, a benefit or as a deemed payment at the end of the tax year for the purpose of NIC *(Social Security Contributions (Intermediaries) Regulations 2000 (SI 2000/727) (Regs. 2, 4, 8(1) & 8(2))*, and the provisions of ITEPA 2003 s.54 are replicated in the *Social Security Contributions (Intermediaries) Regulations 2000 (SI 2000/727) reg.7(1)* for the purpose of determining the element of the deemed payment represented by secondary class 1 contributions. The method of calculation is as follows:

1. All payments received by the company or partnership from relevant engagements are aggregated.
2. A deduction of 5% of the aggregate payments in step 1 is given to allow for expenses of running the company or partnership. If the intermediary is a partnership, any sums in excess of the sum of 5% of the payments received

by the partnership and sums which would be deductible in step 4 are omitted in calculating the amount of the deemed payment *(ITTOIA 2005 s.164).*

3. Any payments or benefits received directly from the client which have not already been taxed are added.
4. Any expenses incurred by the company or partnership which would have been deductible had they been incurred personally by the worker (see section **9.16**). This includes pension contributions to a registered pension scheme and the business proportion of any revenue expenses incurred by the intermediary in providing a benefit to the worker, such as a car. The following points should be noted:
   - Where a car is provided, either the actual expenditure on the provision of the car or the statutory mileage allowances which would be available to employees using their own car for business travel may be deducted *(ITEPA 2003 s.54(3))*. If the intermediary is a partnership of which the contractor is a member and the contractor has provided a car to the partnership, the car is treated as having been provided by the intermediary and the contractor is entitled to the same allowance that they could have claimed if they had been employed by the client *(ITEPA 2003 s.54(5))*.
   - All engagements are treated as a single employment with the intermediary. Therefore, the expenses incurred by the worker in travelling between home and clients may be deducted, unless they expect to spend more than 40% of his time working for a particular client for a period of more than two years.
   - If at this point, or any later point, the sub-total at the end of the step is nil or a negative figure, there is no deemed employment payment.
5. Any capital allowances on expenditure incurred by the intermediary, which could be claimed by the worker if they had incurred the expenditure directly, may be deducted. Where a car is provided to a worker and the statutory mileage allowances are claimed in step 4, no capital allowances may be claimed.
6. Any earnings or benefits in kind already received by the worker from the company or partnership which are taxable as employment income, or which constitute either remuneration from the contractor's employment or benefits subject to class 1A NIC and on which PAYE and NIC have been operated are deducted, i.e. salary or bonus. Statutory mileage allowances which are exempt from tax may also be deducted *(ITEPA 2003 s.54(7))*.

7. Secondary class 1 and/or 1A NIC on the above earnings are deducted. The NIC must be calculated using annualised limits (see section **11.1**) regardless of whether the contractor is a director or not.
8. The balance represents the deemed payment made to the contractor. The payment is normally deemed to have been made at the end of the tax year, but if the contractor ceases to be employed by the intermediary or a company ceases to trade at an earlier date the payment is treated as having been made on the date the contractor left or the trade ceased. This payment must be analysed between the gross deemed salary and secondary NIC. The portion relating to the employer's NIC is given by:

$$\frac{\text{Rate of employer's NIC}}{100 + \text{Rate of employer's NIC}}$$

Example

David provides services through a limited company. The income in 2021/22 from contracts falling within ITEPA 2003 ss.49-61 was £60,000. The company has also provided David with a car which gives rise to a benefit-in-kind charge of £3,000 and has paid pension contributions of £5,000 on David's behalf into a registered pension fund. David has paid himself a salary of £20,000 during the year.

The deemed payment on 5 April 2022 will be:

	£	£
Income		60,000
Less:		
5% deduction	3,000	
Benefit-in-kind already taxed	3,000	
Pension contributions	5,000	
Salary	20,000	
Secondary Class 1 NIC (£20,000 - £9,568) x 13.8%	1,440	
Employer's Class 1A NIC £3,000 x 13.8%	414	
		(32,854)
		£27,146
Deemed payment 100/(100 + 13.8) x £27,146		£23,854
Secondary Class 1 NIC on deemed payment		£3,292

8.8.3. Deemed payment – treatment by intermediary

The deemed payment and the related secondary NIC is a deductible expense in calculating the taxable profits of the intermediary, but where the intermediary is a partnership, the deemed payment may not create or increase a loss and no expense may be deducted by the partnership other than those taken into account in calculating the deemed payment.

8.8.4. Provision of services through an intermediary – national insurance

The provisions of ITEPA 2003 ss.49-61 are replicated in *Social Security Contributions (Intermediaries) Regulations 2000 (SI 2000/727)*, but these will only apply where a contractor meets the condition of being in the employment of the client as an 'employed earner' within SSCBA 1992 s.2(1)(a). Where the services are provided outside the UK, the contractor is liable to pay the social security contributions of the country in which the services are performed, unless the services are provided in a country within the EEA and either:

- the contractor is seconded overseas by a UK employer for a period of not more than 12 months, and they are not being sent to replace another person who has completed his posting, in which case UK NIC continues to be payable. An application must be made by the employer on form E101 and the 12 months period may be extended by a further 12 months if the employer applies for an extension on form E102; or
- a contractor is employed to work in two or more member states, in which case UK NIC is payable.

Where services are provided through an intermediary in a country outside the EEA, social security contributions are payable in that country unless there is a reciprocal agreement between that country and the UK. The terms of each agreement must therefore be looked at individually to determine any liability.

8.8.5. Payment of tax on deemed payment

The income tax and primary and secondary NIC on the deemed payment must be accounted for by the intermediary under the PAYE system. In the case of a partnership being the intermediary the deemed payment is treated as being received by the contractor in a personal capacity, rather than as partnership income *(Social Security Contributions (Intermediaries) Regulations 2000 (SI 2000/727) reg. 8(4)).*

8.8.6. Multiple intermediaries

Where there is more than one intermediary, amounts received from each intermediary are taken into account to avoid double counting. All intermediaries are jointly and severally liable to pay NIC on the contractor's attributable earnings, unless a particular intermediary has not received payments or benefits under the arrangements or other arrangements.

Where income tax cannot be recovered from any of the intermediaries income tax and primary NIC may be collected from the worker *(Income Tax (Employment) Regulations 2003 SI 1993 No. 744 reg. 72; Social Security (Contributions) Regulations 2001 (SI 2001/1004) reg. 86).*

A contractor's earnings from all intermediaries are aggregated and treated as a single payment.

8.9. Managed Service Companies

HM Revenue & Customs have found the PSC legislation difficult to administer, since it requires them to rule whether each contract falls within its scope. The Finance Act 2007 introduced legislation aimed at counteracting the use of managed service companies (MSC), namely composite companies which provide services to coordinate and administer the activities of workers, who would otherwise have formed their own PSCs. These individuals will be employees and shareholders of the MSC and may be remunerated through a tax-efficient mixture of salary and dividends. The legislation looks at the activities of the MSC and is therefore simpler to administer.

A company is a MSC if:

1. its business consists wholly or mainly of providing, directly or indirectly, the services of an individual to other companies;
2. payments are made, directly or indirectly, to the individual (or associates of the individual) and the amount of these payments is equal to, or greater than, the consideration for the provision of the services;
3. the way in which the payments are made would result in the individual (or associates) receiving an amount (net of tax and national insurance) which is greater than the amount (net of tax and national insurance) that they would have received in respect of the services, if the payment had been treated as employment income of the individual; and
4. a person who carries on a business of promoting or facilitating the use of companies to provide the services of individuals (the MSC provider) is involved with the MSC.

(ITEPA 2003 s.61B(1))

An MSC provider is involved with the MSC if they (or an associate):

1. benefits financially on an ongoing basis from the provision of the services of individuals;
2. influences or controls the provision of those services and the way in which payments to individuals (or their associates) are made; and
3. influences or controls the company's finances or gives or promotes an undertaking to make good a tax loss.

(ITEPA 2003 s.61B(2))

A person is not treated as controlling the company's finances merely by providing legal or accountancy services in a professional capacity or carrying on a business consisting of placing individuals with persons who wish to obtain their services (e.g. employment agencies) *(ITEPA 2003 s.61B(3)&(4))*.

Where an MSC provides the services of an individual and that individual receives a payment or benefit which can reasonably be taken as being in respect of these services and the payment or benefit is not treated as earnings from an employment with the MSC, the MSC is treated as making a deemed employment payment to the individual at the same time as the payment or benefit is made *(ITEPA 2003 s.61D).*

The amount of any non-cash benefit is taken as its cash equivalent, except in the case of the provision of living accommodation, where it is the greater of the cash equivalent and the amount determined in accordance with ITEPA 2003 s.398(2) *(ITEPA 2003 s.61F(4))*. The time of the payment or benefit is determined in the same manner as payments or benefits received by reason of an individual's employment (see section 9.4) *(ITEPA 2003 s.61F(5)).*

The deemed employment payment is the amount of any payment or benefit received falling within ITEPA 2003 s.61D less any expenses met by the individual which would have been deductible from taxable earnings from the employment, if they had been employed by the client to provide the services and had met the expenses out of these earnings. Where the MSC is a partnership of which the individual is a member the expenses may include expenses incurred by the individual on behalf of the partnership. This includes mileage allowance relief where the individual uses a car provided by the MSC, or, where the MSC is a partnership of which the individual is a member, the car has been provided by the individual for use in the partnership.

If the above amount is nil, or a negative figure, there is no deemed payment. If the amount is a positive figure, this amount is the total of the deemed payment and the secondary NIC on that payment. To find the amount of the deemed payment this figure must be multiplied by 100/113.8 and to find the amount of the NIC the figure must be multiplied by 13.8/113.8 *(ITEPA 2003 s.61E).*

Any deemed employment payment is made under PAYE, except that no deduction is to be made for expenses or mileage allowance relief *(ITEPA 2003 s.61G(1)-(3)).*

The payment is not taxable if:

1. the individual is resident or domiciled outside the UK;
2. the client is resident outside the UK; and
3. the services are provided outside the UK.

(ITEPA 2003 s.61G(4)&(5))

Where the MSC is a partnership of which the individual is a member, the payment is treated as being received by the individual in a personal capacity and not as a member of the partnership *(ITEPA 2003 s.61G(6)).*

Where the individual is resident in the UK and the services are provided in the UK the MSC is treated as having a place of business in the UK, irrespective of whether it, in fact, does so *(ITEPA 2003 s.61G(7)).*

Where an MSC is a body corporate and the MSC makes a distribution, either in the same year as a deemed employment payment or a subsequent year, a claim may be made by 31 January in the sixth tax year following the tax year in which the distribution is made for the deemed employment payment to be set against the distribution. Where there is more than one distribution the deemed employment payment will be set, as far as possible, against:

1. distributions of the same tax year before distributions of other years;
2. distributions received by the individual before those received by other persons; and
3. distributions of earlier years before distributions of later year.

(ITEPA 2003 s.61H)

PAYE regulations may make provision for the recovery of any amount which should have been deducted from a deemed employment payment by an MSC from the following persons:

1. a director, or office-holder, or an associate of the MSC;
2. an MSC provider;
3. a person who has directly or indirectly encouraged or been actively involved in the provision of the services of an individual by the MSC. A person does not fall within these provisions merely by providing legal or accountancy services in a professional capacity or carrying on a business consisting of placing individuals with persons who wish to obtain their services (e.g. employment agencies);
4. a director or office-holder, or an associate, of a person (other than an individual) falling within 2 or 3 above.

(ITEPA 2003 s.688A)

The deemed employment payments, and the associated NIC, are an allowable deduction in the computation of the profits of the MSC in the period of account in which the payments are made. The payments may, however, only reduce the taxable profits to nil and may not create a loss *(ITTOIA 2005 s. 164A(4); FA 2007 Sch. 3 para.10(4))*.

8.10. National Insurance – Deemed Employment

Certain categories of persons are deemed to be employees and therefore liable to pay class 1 contributions. These are:

Employment	Person liable to pay secondary contributions
Office and telephone kiosk cleaners	Agent supplying cleaner, or if there is no agent, person with whom cleaner contracted to do work.
Person employed by his or her spouse	The spouse
Lecturer, teacher or instructor	Person providing the education

Church of England minister other than under a contract of service	Church Commissioners for England
Employment by the liquidator of a company in voluntary liquidation	Liquidator for the time being
Other ministers of religion not under a contract of service and whose remuneration consists wholly or mainly of income other than salary or stipend	Person responsible for fund out of which minister is paid.
Employment in chambers as a barristers' clerk	Head of chambers
Employment within the agency rules	Where partner's services are supplied by partnership, the partnership or third party through whom services are provided. If third party or partnership is resident outside the UK and not liable to pay secondary class 1 NIC, the person to whom the services are provided.

(Social Security (Categorisation of Earners) Regs 1978 (SI 1978/1689) reg.5 & Sch.3)

8.11. National Insurance – Deemed Self-employment

The only categories of persons who are deemed to be self-employed are contained in *Social Security (Categorisation of Earners) Regs 1978 (SI 1978/1689) Sch. 1 pt. II*. These are persons employed through an agency as examiners, moderators or invigilators or in a similar capacity, whose contracts are to be completed in less than 12 months, where the examination leads to the award of any certificate, diploma, degree or professional qualification.

8.12. National Insurance – Persons Deemed not to be Employed

The following are deemed not to be employment for the purpose of NIC *(Social Security (Categorisation of Earners) Regs 1978 (SI 1978/1689 Sch. 1 pt. III):*

- employment by close member of family (other than spouse) in a private dwelling house other than for the purposes of the family member's business;
- employment by spouse other than for the purpose of spouse's employment;
- employment as self-employed earner where the earner is 'not ordinarily employed in such employment or employments'
- employment for purposes of election or referendum authorised by Act of Parliament as a returning officer or deputy or as a Chief Counting Officer or counting officer or person employed by them;

- employment by visiting military forces, either as member or civilian employee, except for civilians ordinarily resident in the UK;
- employment as member of duly designated international headquarters or defence organisation, other than a serving member of HM Forces or civilians ordinarily resident in the UK who are not members of the organisation's retirement scheme.

Chapter 9. Employment Income

9.1. Income Tax – Introduction, Charging Legislation and General Definitions

Most unincorporated businesses are small and may have no employees, or may employ only part-time administrative assistance, which may be a family member. Some unincorporated businesses, particularly partnerships, are, however, substantial and will have a number of employees. Even if a business is small, it is still important to ensure that employments are remunerated in a tax-efficient manner by making the best use of exemptions and that no unexpected liabilities arise due to the failure to make the correct deductions from amounts paid to employees.

'Employment income' is classified as either 'general earnings' or 'specific employment income' *(ITEPA 2003 s.7)*. 'Specific employment income' covers benefits from registered non-approved pension schemes *(ITEPA 2003 Part 6)* and income relating to securities *(ITEPA 2003 Part 7)* and excludes any income which is exempt under Part 4, but the great majority of earnings are classified as 'general earnings', including the following:

- wages and salaries;
- bonuses (whether in cash or in kind);
- lump sum payments in substitution for benefits in kind (*Bird (HMIT) v Allen; Bird (HMIT) v Martland (1982) (56 TC 89))*;
- benefits in kind (see **Chapter 10**);
- tips and gratuities;
- round-sum allowances, subject to deduction for certain expenses (see section **9.16** & **9.17**).

The distinction between 'general earnings' and 'specific employment income' is important because there are special rules for taxing the 'general earnings' of a taxpayer who is either not resident, or not domiciled in the UK. However, these provisions do not apply to 'specific employment income'.

9.2. National Insurance Contributions – Charging Legislation and General Definitions

The main charging act for NIC is the *Social Security Contributions and Benefits Act 1992 (SSCBA 1992)*. This is supplemented by a number of regulations enacted by way of statutory instrument, the most important being the *Social Security (Contributions) Regulations 2001 (SI 2001/1004)(*Abbreviated here to *SSCR 2001)*. NICs are levied on earnings, and earnings from employment are subject to primary class 1 contributions (payable by the employee), secondary class 1 contributions (payable by the employer) and class 1A contributions (payable by the employer). There are also class 1B contributions, payable by the employer on benefits included in a PAYE settlement agreement. For the purpose of class 1 NIC 'earnings' include any remuneration or profit derived from an employment *(SSCBA 1992 s.3(1)(a))*.

9.3. Income Tax and National Insurance – a Comparison

9.3.1. General

The rules for income tax and NIC are often drafted in a rather different manner, but cash payments are generally either liable to both income tax and class 1 NIC or neither. Earnings are liable to income tax and class 1 NIC if they arise by reason of a person's employment and need not be received from the employer. Where a payment is received in the form of a right or opportunity to acquire 'employment-related' securities or a securities option the term 'employment' includes either a former or prospective employment and the right or opportunity is deemed to arise by reason of a person's employment unless it is made available by an individual in the normal course of domestic, family or personal relationships *(ITEPA 2003 s.471)*. Payments received from third parties may therefore, in certain circumstances, be liable to income tax and NIC.

The position for income tax and class 1 NIC can be summarised as follows:

9.3.2. Cash payments

Payments in cash arising from employment are liable to both income tax and primary and secondary class 1 NIC unless the payment represents the reimbursement of a business expense or is covered by a specific exemption. An exception is tips and gratuities received direct from customers; these are liable to income tax, but not class 1 NIC. Where the payment is covered by an exemption, the exemption for income tax contained in ITEPA 2003 is mirrored by a similar exemption for class 1 NIC in *SSCR 2001*.

9.3.3. Expenses

The treatment of expenses for the purpose of income tax differs from the treatment for class 1 NIC. For income tax, expenses are deductible from income if they are wholly, exclusively and necessarily incurred in the performance of the duties or if a deduction is specifically permitted by statute. Where the employer reimburses an employee for a deductible expense, the expense is exempt from tax, provided that:

1. the amount reimbursed does not exceed the amount of the expense;
2. the reimbursement is calculated in accordance with HM Revenue & Customs regulations;

3. the employer, or other person making the reimbursement, operates a system to check that the expense being reimbursed and would be deductible against employment income;
4. the employer, or other person making the reimbursement, does not know or suspect, nor could be reasonably expected to know or suspect, that the expense has not actually been incurred or would not be deductible against employment income.

(ITEPA 2003 s.289A)

This exemption is a special case exemption under ITEPA 2003 s.228A. Therefore it still applies where it is provided under a salary sacrifice arrangement.

An employer may apply for approval to pay or reimburse expense at a flat rate. The approval notice must specify:

1. the type of expense(s) to which the application relates;
2. the rate of payment or reimbursement;
3. the date from which approval takes effect and ceases to have effect. The approval period will be for a maximum of five years.

(ITEPA 2003 s.289B)

Otherwise the payment is taxable and the employee may make a claim to deduct the expense. For class 1 NIC, no deduction is allowed for expenses, business or otherwise, but the reimbursement of expenses which are either business expenses under general principles or where a specific deduction is available are not treated as earnings. The reimbursement of non-business expenses is treated as earnings.

9.3.4. Capital allowances, pension contributions and other deductions

For income tax, capital allowances are available to employees on expenditure which is wholly, exclusively and necessarily incurred on plant and machinery used in their employment. Relief is also given for pension contributions, either to occupational pension schemes or personal pension schemes within certain limits and also for charitable donations made through the payroll. For class 1 NIC, no deduction is permitted for these items. Therefore, it may be more beneficial to pay pensions through a salary sacrifice.

9.3.5. Benefits in kind

Most employees are subject to income tax on a range of benefits in kind received by reason of their employment. In general, the value of benefits is the cost to the employer of providing them. There are a number of exceptions to the general rule. These are cash vouchers, non-cash vouchers and credit tokens, to the extent that they do not qualify for an exemption, and accommodation which is not job-related. Class 1 NIC is only payable on loans to employees written off and gifts to employees of cash vouchers, non-cash vouchers and certain assets listed in *SSCR 2001 Sch. 3 pts III & IV*. Other benefits in kind are only subject to a secondary class 1A contribution.

No liability to income tax arise in respect of a benefit where an amount equal to the benefit would be allowed as a deduction *(ITEPA 2003 s.289A)*. This exemption is a special case exemption under ITEPA 2003 s.228A. Therefore it still applies where it is provided under a salary sacrifice arrangement.

9.4. Time of Receipt

Earnings are taxed in full in the year in which they are received *(ITEPA 2003 s.15(2))*. Earnings taxed under ITEPA 2003 s.26 are taxed in full in the tax year in which they are remitted to the UK. This applies regardless of the tax year to which the earnings relate or whether the office or employment exists in the year of receipt or remittance *(ITEPA 2003 s.15(3))*. Tax on earnings received after the date of death of an employee is payable by the estate of the deceased. There are, however, anti-avoidance rules to prevent manipulation of this rule for tax purposes. The basic rule is that the date of receipt for tax purposes is the earlier of the date of actual receipt and the date on which the earnings are available to the employee *(ITEPA 2003 s.18(1))*. If an employee can choose to receive a bonus on any date from 15 March 2021 onwards it will be taxed in 2020/21, even if the employee chooses not to collect it until the end of April. There are more stringent rules for directors and the date of receipt is the earliest of:

1. the date of receipt determined under the general rule above; and
2. the date that the earnings are credited in the company's accounts, (whether or not there is any restriction on the right to draw the sums); and
3. a) if the amount of the earnings is determined before the end of the accounting period to which they relate, the end of the accounting period; and

   b) if the amount of the earnings is determined after the end of the accounting period to which they relate, the date on which the amount is determined.

Benefits in kind are, in principle, taxed at the time at which they are provided. There are more precise rules relating to certain benefits:

- non-cash vouchers – taxed in the later of the year of the person providing the voucher incurred the expenses and the year in which the employee receives the voucher *(ITEPA 2003 s.82(3))*;
- credit token – taxed in year in which employee uses it *(ITEPA 2003 s.94(1))*;

- cash voucher – taxed in year in which employee receives voucher *(ITEPA 2003 s.73(3))*; and
- termination payment or payment in respect of change of duties – taxed in year of date of change unless payment commutes annual or other periodical payments when it is taxed in the year of commutation *(ITEPA 2003 s.403(2))*.

9.5. Cash Payments to Employees

The HM Revenue & Customs booklet *Employer's further guide to PAYE and NICs, Chapter 5,* gives a comprehensive list of payments which are subject to income tax and class 1 NIC. Some of these are discussed below.

9.6. Payments Arising by Reason of Employment

9.6.1. Inducements ('Golden Hellos')

A leading case in this area is *Shilton v Wilmshurst (1990) (BTC 66),* which involved Peter Shilton, the former England goalkeeper. He was paid a sum of money by Southampton Football Club to induce him to move from his then employer, Nottingham Forest. This payment was held to be taxable since Southampton only paid the money because Shilton was Nottingham Forest's goalkeeper and it thus arose from his employment, even though it was not paid by his current employer. Payments of this nature have often been referred to as 'golden hellos'.

9.6.2. Employment income provided through third parties

ITEPA 2003 ss.554A-554Z21 deem that where a person (A) is a current, former or prospective employee of another person (B), a reward for that employment is paid to a relevant third party and that third party takes a relevant step, the amount so paid may be treated as employment income of A. A relevant person may refer to A, B or any other person acting as a trustee, or, if B is a limited liability partnership or a company which is a member of group, to a company which is a subsidiary of the partnership or to another group company *(ITEPA 2003 s.554A(7)-(9))*.

A relevant step may include the situations where a sum of money or an asset is held by any person and there are arrangements, including informal arrangements whereby the money, asset, or a sum derived directly or indirectly from the asset, may be transferred to A *(ITEPA 2003 s.554B, C)* or where an asset is made available to A *(ITEPA 2003 s.554D)*. There are a number of exclusions, some of the most important of which are where a transfer is a normal commercial transaction *(ITEPA 2003 s.554F)*, part of an employment benefit package *(ITEPA 2003 s.554G)* or is earmarked as part of an employee benefit scheme *(ITEPA 2003 s.554J)*.

9.6.3. Tips and gratuities

Tips and gratuities received, for example, by restaurant staff, are liable to income tax on the basis that they arise by reason of a person's employment, even if the restaurant does not operate a tronc system (where tips received by all staff are pooled) and tips are paid directly to the staff by the customers. Tips are not, however, subject to class 1 NIC where either:

1. the tips are not made directly or indirectly by the secondary contributor, i.e. the employer, and they do not represent sums previously paid to the secondary contributor; or
2. the secondary contributor does not allocate the tips directly or indirectly to the employee.

(Social Security (Contributions) Regs 2001 (SI 2001/1004) Sch. 3 pt. X para. 5).

Tips are spontaneous payments by customers and include service charges added to a bill, where it is made clear that payment of this charge is purely voluntary. NIC is always payable on a compulsory service charge.

NIC will therefore be payable on tips paid by debit or credit card, since they are paid to the employer and the employer is allocating the tips to the staff. For the same reasons, NIC is also payable where cash tips are collected by the employer in order, for example, to ensure that they are shared amongst staff other than waiting staff. If the employer is under a contractual agreement to pay a certain amount to staff, e.g. there is a guaranteed minimum payment to each member of staff, NIC is payable on the amount of the minimum payment, but not on any excess, provided that all other conditions are satisfied.

Where tips are paid through a tronc the liability for paying any NIC due lies with the employer, not the tronc-master. The employer must notify HM Revenue & Customs of the name of the tronc-master. No NIC is payable on tips paid through a tronc if the above conditions are satisfied. Therefore, if the tronc-master operates independently of the employer, no NIC is payable, but NIC must be paid if the employer interferes directly or indirectly in the allocation of the tips. It is acceptable for the employer to appoint a tronc-master and to recommend a points system for allocating tips, provided that the staff agree to accept this system. If the employer allocates some of the tips, but the balance is allocated by the tronc-master, NIC is payable on the amounts allocated by the employer. The employer may also be considered to allocate the tips if the tronc-master is a director or proprietor, or an associate or relative, and it is advisable to avoid such a situation arising. HMRC accept that the employer's payroll may be used to deduct PAYE, but maintain that the tronc-master must keep records to ensure that tips are properly allocated. If an employee has a contractual right to participate in the tronc, all tips paid by the tronc are subject to NIC. If an employee has a contractual right to receive a minimum sum from the tronc, NIC is payable on the minimum amount, but not on any excess, provided that all other conditions are satisfied. However, a contractual right to participate in the tronc does not constitute a contractual right to payment, if no minimum amount is specified, and the NIC exemption will apply.

9.6.4. Payments to sales representatives

Sales representatives may also receive bonuses and payments in kind (such as a holiday) from the manufacturers of the products which they sell, rather than their employers. Such payments are taxable and subject to class 1 NIC if they represent rewards for past services or are made in anticipation of specific future services. Corporate entertaining by the manufacturers in order to foster good relations and generate future sales will, however, not normally give rise to taxable earnings in the hands of the sales representative.

9.6.5. Other payments arising by reason of employment

The following types of payments to employees are liable to tax and class 1 NIC on the grounds that they arise from the employment:

- payments to encourage an employee not to leave ('Golden handcuffs');
- payments in anticipation of future services to employer *(Cameron v Prendergast (1940) (23 TC 122));*
- compensation for restriction of employee's freedoms, e.g. to join a trade union *(Hamblett v Godfrey (HMIT) (1987) (59 TC 694));*
- payments to employees on the variation of their duties or terms of employment or a change in their earnings *(ITEPA 2003 s.401(1));*
- capital payments received from a trust fund set up by employer for benefit of employees *(Brumby v Milner (1976) (51 TC 583);*
- reward for future services *(Riley v Coglan (1967) (44 TC 481)).* The payment was made to a football player on signing a contract binding him to a club for 12 years or the rest of his career;
- study loan subsequently waived *(Clayton v Gothorp (1971) (47 TC 168));*
- compensation for giving up future commission payments *(McGregor v Randall (1984) (58 TC 110));*
- gifts and presents in cash from the employer;
- Christmas presents in cash from persons other than the employer are taxable earnings if it is a widespread custom for such presents to be given and the expectation that presents will be received attaches to the employment. This was the case in *Wright v Boyce (1958) (38 TC 160)* where it was customary for a huntsman, whoever he was, to receive cash presents from members of the hunt at Christmas.

The following payments have been held not to be taxable as earnings:

- allowance paid to teacher to attend extra-curricular activities *(Donnelly v Williamson (1982) (54 TC 636));*
- lump sum payments in compensation for loss of rights under a redundancy scheme *(Mairs (HMIT) v Haughey (1993) (BTC 339))*. The payment was held to take on the character of the payment it replaced and the payment was held not to be taxable since the redundancy payment would not have been taxable;
- *ex gratia* payment to former employee *(Wilcock (HMIT) v Eve (1994) (BTC 490))*. The payment was made in compensation for loss of rights under an option scheme and was held not to be 'intimately connected' with the employment;
- loss of job status *(Pritchard v Arundale (1972) (47 TC 680))*. A senior partner in a firm of chartered accountants was given 4,000 shares by a controlling shareholder to induce him to enter into a seven-year contract to work for the company. The value of the shares was held not to be taxable because the employment was not the direct cause of the transfer, but was simply a 'necessary preliminary circumstance' and because it was not the employer who transferred the shares. This case would be likely to be decided differently today because of part 7 of ITEPA 2003.

9.7. Payments on Termination of Employment or Variation of Employment Terms

Payments made to an employee on the termination of employment may either be:

- fully taxable;
- exempt;
- exempt up to a limit of £30,000 with the excess being taxable as earnings. These exclude 'relevant termination awards', i.e. redundancy payments or approved contractual payments up to the amount which would have been due if a redundancy payment had been payable. Any amounts which represents post-employment notice pay are also excluded from the £30,000 exemption *(ITEPA 2003 ss.402A-C)*.

Payments made on the variation of the terms of employment may either be fully taxable or exempt up to a limit of £30,000.

9.7.1. Payments in lieu of notice (PILONs) and 'gardening leave'

There is a distinction between PILONs and gardening leave in that in the latter case, proper notice of the termination of employment is given, but the employee is told not to attend work during the period of notice, whereas in the former case, proper notice is not given but payment is made instead. A payment therefore represents the payment of the normal salary for the period and is liable to tax and class 1 NIC in full *(ITEPA 2003 s.62).*

A PILON is fully taxable under ITEPA 2003 s.62 and is liable to class 1 NIC if:

- the right to a PILON is contained in an employee's contract. The right need not be contained in the main contract but may also be contained in another document such as a side document, a staff handbook or the letter of appointment. The payment will be fully taxable even where the contract gives the employer a choice between giving notice and making a PILON *(EMI Group Electronics v Caldicott (1999) (BTC 294));*
- it is customary to make such a payment, even if nothing exists in writing. In *SCA Packaging Ltd v HMRC (2007) (EWHC 270 (Ch))* it was held that the policy must have been communicated to the employees, or followed without exception for a substantial period, so that employees are able to read this custom into the contract. If an individual assessment is made in each case as to whether to make a PILON, the payment will not be considered to be customary and the payment will be treated as a payment for breach of contract under ITEPA 2003 s.401;
- the employer and employee agree before termination is in prospect that the employment may be terminated without giving proper notice on payment of a PILON;
- a compromise agreement is reached between the employer and the employee and the employee has a contractual right to a PILON. The PILON will be treated as a payment for breach of contract if the paymentof the PILON by the employer is discretionary;
- the PILON represents post-employment notice pay (see section **9.7.6**).

In other situations the payment is treated as a payment for breach of contract under ITEPA 2003 s.401 and the first £30,000 of any payment is exempt. This may also include cases of unfair dismissal or situations where an employee is forced to resign in circumstances which constitute constructive dismissal *(ICAEW Technical Release 851 November 1991).*

For the purpose of class 1 NIC, contractual and customary PILONs paid are treated as earnings, but not in other cases, such as negotiated settlements.

9.7.2. Payments on death or disability

Where a payment is made on an employee's accidental death it will not be taxable. Where the death occurs as a result of natural causes the payment will be treated as a relevant benefit under a pension scheme (see below).

HM Revenue & Customs' approach in relation to termination payments as a result of illness or disability is in this respect more generous, provided that the payment is made solely to meet this situation. These will be exempt regardless of whether the disability occurs suddenly, e.g. a heart attack or an accident or gradually due to a chronic condition, e.g. multiple sclerosis, but the disability must not be due to the normal process of ageing *(SP 10/81)*. In order to qualify, the illness or disability must be the motive for the payment. Where an employer makes a commercial decision to dismiss an employee due to a decline in his performance the total exemption will not apply, even if the illness or disability is the cause of the decline.

9.7.3. Compensation for loss of office or variation of terms of employment

In situations where a payment is not a PILON and is not made on death or disability, it is fully taxable where:

- the employee is contractually entitled to the payment or it relates to services previously performed, such as a terminal bonus *(Henry v Foster (1932) (16 TC 605))*. In *Allum v Marsh (2005) (STC (SCD) 191)* a statement that *ex gratia* payments to two former directors were 'in appreciation of their services to the company over many years' was sufficient for the Special Commissioners (now replaced by the tribunals) to decide that the payments were taxable under ordinary principles;
- there is a reasonable expectation that it will be made, even if the right is not contained in any contract. This is interpreted broadly and includes situations where:
  i) there is any formal or informal understanding with the employee;
  ii) a payment is made by a manager under delegated authority; or
  iii) it is common practice to make such a payment.

  In *Allum v Marsh (2005) (STC (SCD) 191)* it was held that the fact that a decision to make a payment was made at a board meeting did not constitute a prior arrangement;
- an *ex gratia* payment is made to a spouse or dependant, regardless of whether it was paid from an registered pension scheme *(ITEPA 2003 s.401(1))*;
- it is made in return for certain restrictive undertakings concerning the former employee's future conduct, such as not divulging the employer's secrets or not establishing a business in competition *(ITEPA 2003 ss.225 & 226)*. This does not include undertakings given by an employee on reaching a financial settlement on the termination of employment that they will not commence, or will discontinue, legal proceedings against their employer in a court or industrial tribunal *(SP 3/96)*. Where SP 3/96 applies the payment must be considered under other sections to determine whether and to what extent it is taxable. If the compromise agreement includes a repayment

clause whereby the former employee must repay some or all of the sum paid if they commence litigation, HMRC has indicated that no charge will arise under ITEPA 2003 ss.225 & 226 on the amount repayable except in exceptional cases where, for example, the amount exceeds a reasonable sum for the settlement of the claim;

- a payment is made in circumstances such that the employee is unlikely to work again. In this case the termination payment will be taxable as a relevant benefit under an unapproved pension scheme. The payment will be taxed under either ITEPA 2003 s.15(1) or ss.393 & 394. There is no tax charge if the payment is made from a registered pension scheme and it is possible to obtain approval to treat an *ex gratia* payment as having been made from a registered scheme where:
  i) the employee is not already a member of a registered pension scheme or a scheme which is being considered for registration, unless the payment is made on retirement and the scheme only provides for death in service benefits; and
  ii) the payment also satisfies the normal requirements for registration of the pension scheme (see section **12.3**).
- the payment represents post-employment notice pay.

A payment as part of a redundancy package 'in recognition of any entitlements under the consultation process' was held not to be earnings under ITEPA 2003 s.15(1) and was therefore not taxable under ITEPA 2003 s.401(1), but was held to be a compensation for breach of contract where the employer had failed to honour its statutory obligation to consult trade union representatives about any redundancy proposal *(Mimtec Ltd v IRC (2001) (SpC 277)).*

Where a termination payment is not fully taxable and is not paid on death or disability, the first £30,000 of an *ex gratia* payment is exempt, but the excess is taxable *(ITEPA 2003 s.406).*

For the purpose of class 1 NIC any redundancy payments are not treated as earnings *(SSCR 2001 Sch. 3 pt. X para. 6).*

9.7.4. Calculation of Termination Payment

The £30,000 exemption may be made up of cash and any benefits which would be taxable as earnings, or which would be so chargeable but for any exemption, e.g. being allowed to keep the company car *(ITEPA 2003 s.404, George v Ward (HMIT) (1995) (SpC 30))*. The value of a non-cash payment is the 'cash equivalent', defined as the higher of the amounts which would be chargeable in accordance with ITEPA 2003 s.15(1) if the benefit were earnings of the employment or under ITEPA 2003 s.415(3)-(7) in relation to benefits received under non-approved pension schemes. Where a non-cash payment is a beneficial loan, relief may be obtained for notional interest payable on a beneficial loan that is a qualifying loan under ITEPA 2003 ss.174 & 175. Where a payment is made on the variation of the terms of employment a non-cash payment will be taxed as a benefit under ITEPA 2003 s.201 rather than as a payment within ITEPA 2003 s.401.

Any benefit which would be exempt if provided during the course of employment is also exempt if provided on termination of employment *(ITEPA 2003 s.402(2),(3))*, e.g. retraining courses.

Payments received in different tax years or in respect of different employments with the same or associated employers must be aggregated *(ITEPA 2003 s.404)*. Employers are treated as being associated if one employer is under the control of the other or both are under common control *(ITEPA 2003 s.404(2))*.

Statutory redundancy payments are not taxable, but these payments reduce the £30,000 exemption, so that if a statutory redundancy payment of £5,000 is received, only the first £25,000 of any *ex gratia* payment may be exempt *(ITEPA 2003 s.309(2),(3))*. This exemption is an excluded exemption under ITEPA 2003 s.228A. Therefore it still applies where it is provided under a salary sacrifice arrangement.

Payments for service abroad are exempt if the earnings from the employment were tax-free. If only part of the payment relates to such service the exception applies to that part *(ITEPA 2003 ss.413 & 414)*.

Cash payments are taxable in the year payment is made or the recipient becomes entitled to require payment *(ITEPA 2003 s.403(3)(a))* and non-cash payments are taxable when they are used or enjoyed *(ITEPA 2003 s.403(3)(b))*.

Where amounts could be charged both under ITEPA 2003 s.401 and as a payment to a non-approved retirement benefits scheme under ITEPA 2003 s.386, they will be charged under ITEPA 2003 s.386 in precedence to ITEPA 2003 s.401.

9.7.5. Legal Costs Associated with Termination of Employment

Where an employee obtains compensation for loss of employment through legal action and also succeeds in recovering some or all of his legal costs, the legal costs recovered are taxable under ITEPA 2003 s.401(1) and there is no deduction for costs incurred by an employee in pursuing the claim for wrongful dismissal. ITEPA 2003 s.413A, however, exempts recovered legal costs in the following circumstances where the case is resolved without recourse to the courts:

- the costs are paid directly to the former employee's solicitor; and
- the costs are in full or partial discharge of the solicitor's costs incurred solely in connection with the termination or loss of employment; and

- the payment of costs is made under a specific term in the settlement agreement providing for such a payment.

HM Revenue & Customs have stated that where a case goes to court, legal fees paid to the former employee under a court order will also be exempt in addition to those paid in the above circumstances.

The concession only applies to legal costs and not to other costs, e.g. accountants' fees, and does not apply to legal fees above the amount which the former employer may pay in the circumstances mentioned. Exceptionally, where it is necessary for a solicitor to consult other professionals for the specific claim, the cost to the solicitor will represent a disbursement and will qualify as a legal cost.

It is not necessary for the solicitor's bill to relate solely to the termination of employment, but fees attributable to this must be identified.

9.7.6. Post-employment notice pay (PENP)

The concept of PENP has been introduced by Finance (no. 2) Act 2017 as ITTOIA 2005 s.402D to exclude any amounts which would have been subject to PAYE and national insurance, if employment had not been terminated. A non-contractual PILON which was previously covered by the £30,000 exemption will now be fully taxable to the extent that it represents PENP.

PENP is calculated as follows:

$$\text{Basic pay for last pay period ending before trigger date (BP)} \times \frac{\text{Number of days in post-employment notice period}}{\text{Number of days in BP}}$$

Where the last pay period was a month and the notice period is given by contractual terms expressed as a whole number of months, the fraction is calculated by reference to the number of months.

Where there is no pay period ending before the trigger date, e.g. the employee leaves very shortly after joining, BP is calculated from the start of the employment.

Basic pay excludes overtime, bonuses allowances and benefits in kind and any amounts in connection with the termination of the employment.
(ITEPA 2003 s.402D)

The trigger date is the day that notice is given, or if no notice is given, the last day of employment. Where notice is given it does not matter whether the notice is more or less than the minimum notice period required to be given by law and the contractual terms of employment. If the employment ends before the notice expires and the minimum notice period commences immediately before notice is given. Where no notice is given the minimum notice period takes effect immediately before the employment ends, or, where the employment is terminated by agreement, immediately before the agreement is entered into.

The post-employment notice period commences on the last day of employment and ends on the earliest lawful termination date, or, in the case of a limited-term contract, the occurrence of the event limiting the term of employment.
(ITEPA 2003 s.402D)

9.8. Damages and Compensation Paid to Employee

A payment of damages or compensation to an employee by an employer is taxable and subject to class 1 NIC where it is made under a contractual liability, for example where an employee is injured at work. Where there is no contractual liability and a payment genuinely represents compensation either for injury or for breach of contract there is no liability. An example of compensation for breach of contract would be the reimbursement of bank interest and charges suffered by an employee due to the late payment of salary.

Where an employer makes payments to an employee whilst the employee pursues a claim for damages against a third party following an accident the payments are liable to income tax and class 1 NIC unless the employee is obliged to repay the employer, regardless of whether the claim is successful.

An Employment Tribunal award made either as a protective award or an order for re-instatement or re-engagement or continuation of employment is liable to tax and class 1 NIC.

9.9. Sick Pay and Sickness and Other Benefits

Amounts paid to, or for the benefit of, an employee or his family for any period during which they are absent from work due to sickness or disability and which are paid under any arrangement entered into by the employer are taxable as employment income *(ITEPA 2003 s.221)* unless part of the sum paid is attributable to contributions by the employer and part to sums contributed by the employee, in which case only the portion attributable to contributions made by the employer is taxable *(ITEPA 2003 s.221(4); SSCR 2001 Sch. 3 pt. X para. 7)*.

ITTOIA 2005 ss.735-743 exempts certain payments under insurance policies for financial protection in the event of accident, sickness, disability, infirmity or unemployment. Where an employer has taken out a group policy for the costs of sick pay, payments under that policy are exempt to the extent that they relate to contributions made by the employee *(ITTOIA 2005 s.743)*. This is extended to cases where an employee retires due to illness or disability and benefits continue to be paid under a separate policy derived from the employer's policy *(ITTOIA 2005 s.741)*.

Reasonable lump sums paid as compensation for a specific injury suffered are not earnings within ITEPA 2003 s.62 and are not treated as employment income by ITEPA 2003 s.403. Sums which are calculated on a weekly, monthly, or similar basis and paid for periods of absence from work, or for periods after the employee returns to work when they are unable to earn as much as they did before the injury, will usually be taxable as earnings in the same way as sick pay (or ordinary pay when paid after the employee returns to work).

Statutory Sick Pay, Statutory Maternity or Paternity Pay and Statutory Adoption Pay are all liable to income tax and class 1 NIC.

9.10. Commission, Cashbacks and Discounts

SP 4/97 sets out HM Revenue & Customs' detailed practice concerning the taxation of receipts such as commission, cashbacks and discounts on the sale of financial services products such as insurance policies, personal pension schemes or life annuity contracts.

- An employee is taxable on the full amount of commission which is due from his employment, regardless of whether the commission is passed on by him to the customer, the commission is paid by the employer or a third party (para. 25) or whether they consent to the commission being passed on to the customer or a third party or being invested for the benefit of themself or a third party (para. 26).
- Where a purchaser pays a discounted price, there is no liability provided that the purchaser is not a member of the employee's family or household and neither the employee nor their family and household receive any money or benefits as a consequence. Where the above exemption does not apply the provision of the goods or services may constitute a taxable benefit on the employee, although this will not be the case where the discounted price paid covers the cost to the provider. The cost of the goods or service to the provider will be a question of fact, but no benefit will arise on the sale of an insurance policy provided that the discount is no greater the total of the commission which the insurer would otherwise have paid to the third party on the sale of the policy and the anticipated profit on the policy (para. 27).
- No benefit will arise where commission is available to an employee on the same basis as it is available to the general public since it is not considered to arise from the employment (para. 28).
- Commission is taxable if it arises from the purchase by the employee of his own goods and services even if the employee can request or permit all or some of it to be applied for the benefit of another person (para. 29).

- Where an employee receives a right with a monetary value from his employment, e.g. where an additional amount is invested in an employee's investment and that investment can be disposed of, that monetary value is taxable (para. 30).
- Where a liability arises it will be calculated in the same manner as the liability on discounts detailed in para. 27.
- Where an employee receives a cashback from his employer or a third party there will be no liability provided that it is received on the same basis as it is available to members of the general public or if the contract with the employer is dissociated from the contract of employment and the employee gives fair value for the cashback under that contract or by entering into another contract with the employer or a third party. Where the above does not apply, a benefit may arise under ITEPA 2003 s.201 (para. 32).
- Where commission is assessable, a deduction may be claimed for any portion which is passed on to, or is applied for the benefit of, another party if the employee is obliged to expend the sum wholly, exclusively and necessarily in the performance of his duties. This may well arise where the transaction occurs between independent parties at arm's length in the normal course of the employer's business (para. 33).
- Where commission or a cashback is assessable, PAYE must be applied. Where the commission is in the form of tradeable assets PAYE must be operated under ITEPA 2003 s.696 (para. 34).

Where employees have the right to purchase goods from the employer at a discount, no liability arises under ITEPA 2003 s.62 since the right cannot be converted into money and no benefit arises, provided that the amount paid by the employee is at least equal to the cost to the employer.

9.11. Tax-free Lump Sum Payments

Lump sum payments under ITEPA 2003 s.386(1) from registered retirement benefit schemes, relevant statutory retirement benefit schemes, retirement benefit schemes established by foreign governments for their employees, payments under a personal pension scheme or under 'retirement benefit schemes' where payments made by the employer were taxable on the employee are tax-free. The lump sums do not have to be paid on retirement, but may be made at any time before or after the employee has retired. Pension scheme members are able to take lump sums up to a maximum of 25% of the value of the pension fund, or lifetime allowance if this is less. Lump sums must be taken before the age of 75, or before an earlier crystallisation date, and before the member's lifetime allowance has been used up. It will be possible to take more than one lump sum, provided that the lifetime allowance has not been used up. Excessive lump sum payments will be taxable at 55%, but may be repaid.

9.12. Payment of Expenses to Third Parties on Behalf of Employee

Where an employer makes a payment of expenses to a third party on a behalf of an employee (e.g. private telephone calls, mortgage payments or insurance premiums) the tax treatment depends on whether the contract for the provision of the goods or service and hence the obligation to pay, is between the employer and the third party or between the employee and the third party. Where the contract is between the employee and the third party the employer is simply reimbursing the employee for a private expense incurred by them and the payment is therefore taxable as earnings under ITEPA 2003 s.62 and is subject to class 1 NIC. Where the contract is between the employer and the third party the payment is treated as a benefit in kind under ITEPA 2003 pt. 10. This has two consequences:

1. the payment is not liable to income tax in the hands of a lower paid employee;
2. class 1 NIC is not payable, but a secondary class 1A contribution is payable by the employer.

Where an employee makes a purchase on behalf of their employer, it is assumed that they are not acting as an agent for the employer unless they make it clear in advance of making the purchase that they are acting in that capacity. Where they are not held to be acting as an agent of the employer, the contract is between the employee and the vendor, therefore any amount reimbursed to the employee (net of any VAT charged on the purchase) is liable to income tax and class 1 NIC as earnings, subject to a deduction under ITEPA 2003 s.336. Where the employee is held to be acting as an agent, the contract is between the employer and the vendor and there is no income tax and class 1 liability, but the bill is settled. Where, in these circumstances, the employee is given the use of the asset purchased, a benefit arises which is subject to an income tax and class 1A liability (see section **10.15**).

Similar principles apply where an employer pays a fixed penalty motoring fine on behalf of an employee:

- if the penalty is fixed to a car registered solely in the employer's name, and the employer pays the penalty (or reimburses the employee for payment), there are no tax consequences for the employee;
- if the penalty notice is fixed to a car registered in the employee's name, the fixed penalty notice does not impose a personal liability on the employee. So if the employer pays the penalty direct to the relevant authority, it does

not discharge a personal debt of the employee. In that case, the payment represents a benefit under ITEPA 2003 s.203, but if the employer reimburses the employee for payment of the fixed penalty, the employer's payment is taxable as earnings within ITEPA 2003 s.62, or as an expenses payment within ITEPA 2003 s.70;

- if the penalty notice is handed to the employee, but the employer pays the penalty direct to the relevant authority, the payment represents a benefit under ITEPA 2003 s.203, regardless of whether the car is registered in the name of the employee or employer. If the employer reimburses the employee for payment of the fixed penalty, the employer's payment is taxable as earnings within ITEPA 2003 s.62, or as an expenses payment within ITEPA 2003 s.70.

9.13. Payments for Clothing

Allowances paid to uniformed staff in lieu of a uniform are not taxable, but payments to employees to purchase personal clothing or uniform which can be worn outside work are liable to tax and class 1 NIC. Payments for non-durable items such as hosiery are excluded.

9.14. Directorships Held by Partners

Where partners hold directorships director's fees are taxed as trading income provided that:

- the directorship is a normal incident of the profession and the particular practice;
- the fees are only a small part of the profits; and
- under the partnership agreement the fees are pooled for division amongst the partners.

(ITTOIA 2005 s.16B)

The payments are also exempt from class 1 NIC, but may be liable for class 2 and class 4 NIC *(SSCR 2001 reg. 27(1) & (2))*.

9.15. Payment of Employee's Tax by Employer

Where an employer pays an employee's income tax liability, the gross salary is the total of the salary paid to the employee plus the associated tax *(Hartland v Diggines (1926) (10 TC 247))*. Any payment must be grossed up by 100/80, i.e. the rate of income tax is treated as being 20% *(Companies Act 1985 s.311)*.

9.16. Income Tax – Deduction of Expenses

In order for expenses to be deductible against employment income for income tax they must be wholly, exclusively and necessarily incurred in the performance of the employee's duties. This is a notoriously restrictive provision which has, however, been upheld on a number of occasions and contrasts with the rule for deducting expenses from trading income, where expenses merely need to be wholly and exclusively incurred in the course of the business.

The words 'wholly and exclusively' preclude a deduction where expenditure has a dual purpose unless the expenditure can be apportioned between a part of the expenditure which satisfies the definition and part which does not, in which the part satisfying the definition is deductible.

In *Hillyer v Leeke (1976) (51 TC 90)* a deduction for the cost of two suits was denied because the suits were worn to provide "cover and comfort" as well as to comply with a dress code (this case can be compared with *Mallalieu v Drummond (1983) (2 AC 386, BTC 380)* where a deduction from trading income was denied for the same reasons).

The definition of whether an expense is necessary is not determined by whether the employer considers it to be so, but whether the duties could be performed without incurring the expense. Examples of expenses which have been held not to be deductible are:

1. expense of a bank manager joining a club, which was a requirement of the employment, since on an objective basis the job could have been performed without incurring the expense *(Brown v Bullock (1961) (40 TC 1))*;
2. costs of clothing, since it is possible to perform duties as an accountant, for example, without wearing a suit (*Hillyer v Leeke (1976) (51 TC 90))* (see above). The cost of uniform and protective clothing is deductible. Examples include corporate clothing with non-detachable logos (not including shoes, socks or underwear) and games kit worn by PE teachers. See EIM32450ff for a more exhaustive list. In many cases a deduction is available on a set scale for the laundering and upkeep of such clothing (see EIM67210 and EIM66790) and a deduction of £60 (reduced *pro rata* where the employer bears a part of the cost) is available where no agreement has been reached.
3. the cost of an employee of HM Revenue & Customs using his own car to travel from home to various tax offices and premises of employers in excess of the amount reimbursed by HMRC was held not to be deductible. The taxpayer was not required to use his own car and could have travelled by public transport. However, the judge, Pennycuick J, did concede the principle that the choice of the mode of transport could be influenced by factors such as speed and convenience *(Marsden v IRC (1965) (42 TC 326))*. Whilst this case illustrates the general principle, the introduction of the fixed profit car scheme (FPCS) means that this decision is no longer applicable.

An example of a case in which expenditure has been held to be necessarily incurred is *Elwood v Utitz (1965) (42 TC 482)* in which the subscription to a

London club which gave the taxpayer the right to accommodation and facilities when he visited London was held to be deductible. The taxpayer successfully argued that he was simply obtaining suitable accommodation at the least possible cost, even though HMRC argued that he obtained personal benefit from membership of the club. This can be distinguished from *Brown v Bullock* above in that it was accepted that it was necessary for the taxpayer to travel to London from Northern Ireland on business, and therefore to incur accommodation costs, whereas the taxpayer in *Brown v Bullock* could have performed the duties of the office without being a member of the club. Joining the club was, therefore, a means to obtain the necessary accommodation more cheaply.

The phrase 'in the performance of the duties' has similarly been interpreted in a very restrictive manner. Cases where deductions have been denied include:

1. normal commuting costs since the costs are not incurred in the performance of duties, but in order to put oneself in position to perform duties (see section **9.18**);
2. cost of meals incurred whilst attending late meetings (not incurred in the performance of duties);
3. costs of attending evening classes, purchasing textbooks and examination fees since they are not necessary to perform current job, but are incurred in order to obtain a better job *(Blackwell v Mills (1969) (26 TC 468))*;
4. expenditure on employing a child-minder *(Halstead v Condon (1970) (46 TC 289))*;
5. costs incurred by journalists in Scotland in purchasing newspapers in order to keep themselves up to date *(Fitzpatrick v IRC (No. 2) (1994) (BTC 66))*. The journalists were putting themselves in a position to perform their duties. Two recent cases have reaffirmed this point. In *Perrin v HMRC (2008) (SpC 671)* the taxpayer claimed unsuccessfully that payments in respect of course fees and the cost of reference materials in order to qualify as a Chartered Accountant were incurred wholly, exclusively and necessarily in the course of his duties. In *Emms v HMRC (2008) (SpC 668)* the taxpayer, a rugby player, similarly claimed unsuccessfully that the cost of diet supplements was incurred wholly, exclusively and necessarily in the course of his duties. In both cases it was held that the taxpayer incurred the expenses in order to put himself in a position to perform his duties;
6. in *Consultant Psychiatrist v R & C Commissioners (2006) (SpC 557)* a qualified doctor employed by an NHS trust paid for her CPD personally because the trust was short of funds. Although the CPD was necessary to continue to be qualified for her post, relief was denied because she was not carrying

out her duties whilst undertaking the training, and therefore the expenditure was not incurred in the performance of her duties.

The costs involved in preparatory work may sometimes be deductible.

9.17. Reimbursement of Expenses

9.17.1. Income tax

Where an employer reimburses an employee for deductible expenses, the payment is taxable as employment income, but the employee may claim a corresponding deduction under ITEPA 2003 s.336. Where an employer reimburses an employee for specific expenses incurred, the deduction will be equal to the payment made, but this will not be the case if an employer pays an employee a round sum expense allowance.

The expense and reimbursement may both be disregarded where the employer, or a third party, has a system in place to check that the employee has actually incurred the expense, that it is deductible, and that neither the employer nor the third party has any reason to suspect that the employee has not incurred the expense or that it is not, in fact, deductible, both This exemption does not apply where the reimbursement of expenses forms part of a salary sacrifice arrangement *(ITEPA 2003 s.289A).*

9.17.2. Expenses – Class 1 NIC

Expenses incurred are not an allowable deduction from earnings for the purpose of calculating class 1 NIC. Therefore, there is no relief where the employee must bear them personally. Where business expenses are reimbursed by the employer they are disregarded in the calculation of earnings and no class 1 or 1A liability arises *(SSCR 2001 Sch. 3 pt. VIII, para. 9).*

9.18. Qualifying Travel Expenses

9.18.1. Case law

As stated in section **9.16** above the costs of normal commuting are not deductible on the grounds that an employee is merely putting themself in a position to perform their duties, but the situation is not always clear-cut and a deduction is available under ITEPA 2003 s.337 where travel is undertaken in the performance of duties and the reimbursement of such expenses is disregarded in the calculation of earnings under *SSCR 2001 Sch. 3 pt. VIII, para. 3.*

In *Elderkin (HMIT) v Hindmarsh (1988) (BTC 129)* the taxpayer worked away from home for up to two months at a time, during which time his company paid him a subsistence allowance. The taxpayer failed in an attempt to claim a deduction for subsistence expenses, but he did not try to claim a deduction for his travel expenses between his home and his temporary place of employment. The court agreed that the subsistence expenses had been incurred necessarily, but the failure to claim travel expenses effectively conceded that the temporary workplace was his place of employment; therefore the expenses were not incurred in the course of his duties.

In *Miners v Atkinson (Inspector of Taxes) [1997] (STC 58)* it was held that the director of a one-man company could not deduct the cost of travelling from his home to his clients from his salary, since the company was run from home purely for convenience and the expenses were therefore not necessarily incurred.

Where an employee is a home-worker the expenses of travelling to the employer's office periodically and the costs of maintaining a part of the house as an office are not deductible *(Kirkwood (HMIT) v Evans (2002)* (74 TC 481) (but see section **9.20** below for relief for additional household expenses incurred by home-workers).

In *HMRC v Dr Piu Bannerjee (2010) (EWCA civ 843)* it was held that Dr Bannerjee, a specialist registrar, should be allowed a deduction for training costs, since she was employed on a training contract and the courses were an intrinsic part of her employment.

9.18.2. Statutory relief for travel to temporary place of employment

Relief is given under ITEPA 2003 ss.338 & 339 if an employee is required to work at a temporary place of employment. The full costs of travelling from home to the temporary place of employment may be deducted, not just the excess over the normal commuting costs. The reimbursement of such expenses is disregarded in the calculation of class 1 NIC earnings *(SSCR 2001 Sch. 3 pt. VIII para. 3).*

Example

Peter lives in Pontypridd and works in Cardiff, a distance of 12 miles. He is required to work in Merthyr Tydfil for a period, a distance again of 12 miles. Despite the fact that the costs of travel to Merthyr Tydfil are no greater than the normal commuting costs, they will be deductible in full.

The conditions for claiming the relief are:

- a temporary place of employment is one where the employee either spends less than 40% of their time or where they will be working for a continuous period of up to 24 months, unless this period comprises all or almost all of the period during which the person is likely to hold the employment *(ITEPA 2003 s.339(5));*
- if the period during which the person is to be working at a place of employment is not fixed, it will not be a temporary place of employment if

it is reasonable to assume that they will be working there for more than 24 months *(ITEPA 2003 s.339(5));*

- if the secondment is initially for a period not exceeding 24 months, but is then extended so as to exceed that period, the costs will cease to be deductible from the time the employee is made aware of the change;
- the costs will be deductible even if the employee visits the office on the way to or from the temporary place of employment, provided that the duties performed there are merely incidental, e.g. making a telephone call or picking up a file;
- conversely the costs of travel will not be deductible if the duties performed at the temporary place of employment are merely incidental, nor if the journey to the temporary place of work is essentially the same as the normal journey to work *(ITEPA 2003 s.338(2), (4));*
- a place of work is treated as a permanent place of employment if either:
  1. it is the base from which employment duties are performed; or
  2. it is the place at which the tasks to be carried out in performing the employment duties are allocated *(ITEPA 2003 s.339(4)).*

9.18.3. Travel expenses – agency workers

The permanent workplace of an agency worker will normally be the premises of the agency. Therefore, no relief is available on the cost of travelling between home and the agency's premises. A deduction may, however, be allowed where the worker is engaged by a client and subsequently sent on a period of detached duty at a temporary workplace. Where a worker travels between the workplaces of different clients the expenses of travelling from one to the other are allowable under ITEPA 2003 ss.337-339, provided that:

- the clients were all obtained through the same agency; and
- the worker starts and finishes the day at his own home.

9.18.4. Travel expenses of workers providing services through intermediaries

Where a worker provides services for a client through an intermediary other than a managed service company, each engagement is to be regarded as a separate employment and no relief is therefore available for travel between engagements *(ITEPA 2003 s. 339A).* Where the intermediary is a managed service company ITEPA 2003 s. 339A applies to deny relief for travel expenses where the worker is subject to the control (or to the right of control) by any person, but not where they are not so subject *(ITEPA 2003 s. 339A(3)).*

9.18.5. Other deductible travel expenses

Where a spouse accompanies a person on a business trip abroad because they are unable to make the trip alone due to health reasons and the employer pays the spouse's travel expenses, no benefit arises on the employee *(ESC A4(d))*. Travel expenses include cost of hotel accommodation and the employee need not be UK resident. It should be noted that this relief is concessionary and there is no corresponding exemption for the purpose of class 1 NIC.

9.18.6. Overnight allowances – lorry drivers

By agreement with the Road Haulage Association lorry drivers have been able to claim an overnight tax-free allowance without needing to produce documentary evidence. This allowance has for a number of years remained at £34.90, reduced to £26.20 where they driver has a sleeper cab. From 6 April 2017 it has only been possible to make this payment free of tax where the employer has entered into a 'bespoke agreement' with HM Revenue & Customs, which requires drivers to retain receipts for expenditure and the employer to implement a system for auditing them.

9.19. Entertainment

HM Revenue & Customs will not generally assess an employee on amounts paid by the employer on entertainment or paid to the employee in order to reimburse them for specific entertainment expenses. However, HMRC may, on occasions, raise an assessment if, for example, they consider that the entertainment has little connection with the trade. If the employer gives a general expense allowance, entertaining expenses paid out of this are not deductible.

Where the entertainment is provided by third parties no benefit arises provided that the entertainment is neither in recognition of past services nor in anticipation of specific future services *(ITEPA 2003 s.265)*.

9.20. Expenses Incurred by Homeworkers

ITEPA 2003 s.316A provides that no liability arises on reasonable payments by employers to employees in respect of additional household expenses as a result of homeworking arrangements. There is no limit to the amount of the payments, provided that it can be shown that they are reasonable. HM Revenue & Customs have indicated that they will not require supporting documentation for payments of up to £6 per week per employee. However, evidence will be required for larger payments. An employer may agree bespoke scale rates with HMRC or reimburse actual expenses incurred.

The relief is only available if the employer makes a payment to the employee, rather than the employee claiming a deduction for the unreimbursed expenses.

HMRC will accept that employees who work at home are entitled to a deduction under ITEPA 2003 s.336 for additional household expenses only if all the conditions below are satisfied:

1. the duties that the employee performs at home are substantive duties of the employment, i.e. they represent duties that are all or part of the central duties of the employment;
2. the duties cannot be performed without the use of appropriate facilities;
3. no such facilities are available at the employer's premises, or the job requires the employee to live so far from the employer's premises that it is not practical to travel there on a daily basis;
4. at no time before or after the contract is drawn up is the employee able to choose between working at the employer's premises or elsewhere. If an employee takes up a new post and would normally be required to relocate, or has the option of relocating, but negotiates to work from home, no deduction is available. If the requirement to work at home is inserted in the contract after negotiation with the employee, no deduction is available.

These conditions preclude employees, such as academics, claiming the payment if they are allowed to work from home, if they wish, although they will be able to do so if their university is closed and they are required to work from home due to Covid-19.

Where relief is available, the expenses must satisfy the normal test and HMRC consider that relief may only be claimed for the following:
1. additional costs of gas and electricity consumed while a room is being used for work;
2. the *metered* cost of water used in the performance of the duties;
3. the unit cost of business telephone calls, including dial-up internet access.

No relief is available for the following expenses:
1. council tax;
2. rent;
3. water rates;
4. mortgage repayments and endowment premiums;
5. household insurance premiums.

No relief is available for the costs of travel between home and the employer's premises, since the deduction for the costs of travel between places of work does not apply where one of those places is the employee's home *(Miners v Atkinson (Inspector of Taxes) [1997] (STC 58)* and *Kirkwood (HMIT) v Evans (2002) (74 TC 481))*.

9.21. Other Deductible Expenses

Other expenses which are deductible include:
1. contributions to registered pension schemes up to certain limits (see section **12.6**);

2. cost of board and lodging where employee is working away from home, provided that the employee's earnings are taxable and the employee is resident in the UK. Any amount reimbursed is disregarded in the calculation of earnings for the purpose of class 1 NIC *(ITEPA 2003 s.376; SSCR 2001 Sch. 3 pt. VIII, para. 4D)*. Where an employee is away from home partly for the purpose of work and partly for other purposes (e.g. taking a holiday after completing an assignment) the proportion of the cost which relates to work is allowable (see section **9.22.30**);
3. Where an employee is engaged in qualifying travel the following subsistence payments may be made:
   a) five or more hours of qualifying travel £5;
   b) ten or more hours of qualifying travel £10;
   c) fifteen or more hours of qualifying travel £25.

   In the case of payments falling within a) or b) an extra £10 may be paid if the travel is ongoing at 8pm *(SI 2015/1948)*.
4. ITEPA 2003 s.304 exempts allowances paid by the European Commission to detached national experts (private sector employees or civil servants seconded to the European Commission to advise and assist officials). This is a concessionary relief, and therefore there is no corresponding exemption for class 1 NIC;
5. subscriptions to approved professional bodies, where membership of that body is relevant to employment or is a condition of the employment *(ITEPA 2003 ss. 343 & 344; SSCR 2001 Sch. 3 pt. VIII, para. 11)*. The section contains a list of approved bodies. Where a subscription is paid voluntarily, e.g. by a retired person who wishes to remain eligible to practise, the payment may not be deducted against any occupational pensions since there is no employment and there are no duties *(Singh v Williams (HMIT) (2000) (SpC 250))*;
6. cost of insurance against liabilities incurred by an employee as a result of acts or omissions in the course of their duties, e.g. damages for negligence and associated legal costs *(ITEPA 2003 s.346; (SSCR 2001 Sch. 3 pt. VIII, para. 10)*. No deduction is available if the payment is made as part of arrangements, the main object, or one of the objects of which is the avoidance of tax *(ITEPA 2003 s.346(2A)*;
7. payment of costs incurred in connection with the employee giving evidence to any investigation or proceeding about matters related to the employment, or in which acts of the employee or any other matters related to the employment are likely to be considered *(ITEPA 2003 s.346BA & 346BB)*;

8. capital allowances may be claimed on plant which is acquired wholly, exclusively and necessarily for the purpose of the employment. Capital allowances may only be claimed in rare instances, for example musicians in an orchestra are usually employees, but are required to provide their own instruments *(CAA 2001 s.15(1)(e))*;
9. cost of providing tools and protective clothing. In many cases a fixed allowance has been agreed with trade unions and this amount may be claimed without an employee needing to prove the actual level of expenditure. If an employee's actual level of expenditure is greater than the fixed allowance, the actual expenditure may be claimed *(ITEPA 2003 s.367)*;
10. class 1 employee NIC contributions are not a deductible expense, but, where an employee themself pays another person in a capacity as an employer, and the payment represents a deductible expense, the associated employer class 1 or class 1A NIC contributions will also be deductible *(ITEPA 2003 s.360A)*.

9.22. Payments and Benefits Exempt from Income Tax and Class 1 National Insurance Contributions

9.22.1. Job-related accommodation

See section **10.14**.

9.22.2. Loans to employees

See section **10.22**.

9.22.3. Suggestion schemes

Awards under suggestion schemes are exempt from tax and class 1 or 1A NIC if:

- there is a formal scheme, open to all employees on equal terms;
- the suggestion does not fall within the employee's normal duties. This test looks at whether, in the light of the employee's experience, they could have been expected to come up with the suggestion as part of his normal duties. Where meetings are held for the purpose of putting forward suggestions, these will always be regarded as being part of the employees' duties;
- if the decision to make the award is taken before the suggestion is implemented, the award must not exceed £25. Any award exceeding £25 must only be made after the suggestion has been implemented and must reflect the financial significance of the suggestion to the organisation. The award must not exceed 50% of the expected financial benefit in the first year or 10% of the expected financial benefits over a period not exceeding 5 years;

- an award over £5,000 will always be taxable. Therefore, an award of £5,000 which falls within the above provisions will be preferable to one of, say £5,200;
- if more than one employee makes the same suggestion, awards over £25 must be shared between them on a reasonable basis;
- an 'encouragement' award of £25 or less will be exempt. This is an award made in order to acknowledge that a suggestion has intrinsic merit, even though it will not be implemented;
- income or gains arising from the exploitation or disposal of rights in an invention are always taxable.

A non-cash voucher provided in connection with a suggestion scheme is not liable to Class 1 NIC.
(ITEPA 2003 ss.321 & 322; SSCR 2001 Sch. 3 pt. V para. 6(c))

9.22.4. Long service awards

Long service awards are exempt from tax and class 1 or 1A NIC provided:

- they are not in the form of cash;
- the period of service has been at least 20 years;
- no similar award has been made to the employee in the previous 10 years;
- the cost of the award does not exceed £20 per year of service.

A non-cash voucher provided in connection with a long service award is not liable to Class 1 NIC.
(ITEPA 2003 s.323; SSCR 2001 Sch. 3 pt. V para. 6(d))

9.22.5. Gifts to employees and payments made to employees in a personal capacity

Reasonable gifts to employees on occasions such as marriage are exempt. In determining whether such payments are taxable, important factors will be the regularity of the payments and whether the employee has an expectation that they will receive it. The regularity of payments relates only to a particular employee, not to general business policy, i.e. where payments have been made to employees in the past, but such a payment has not been made regularly to the particular employee and the employee does not expect the payment, it will not be taxable *(IRC v Morris (1967) (44 TC 685)).*

Following the decision in *Ball v Johnson (1971) (47 TC 155)* examination awards paid by employers to employees for passing a recognised examination are not taxable as earnings within ITEPA 2003 s.62, but only where the employee is lower paid (earnings of £8,500 or less), and so the exemption is now of limited benefit. In addition, all the following conditions must be satisfied:

1. the award is made at the discretion of the employer (that is, the employer is under no legal obligation to make the award);

2. it is not part of the employee's duties to sit and pass the examination (for example, dismissal does not automatically follow failure);
3. the award takes the form of a lump sum paid once and for all;
4. the award is reasonable in amount and there is no evidence to suggest that it represents disguised remuneration.

For employees who are not in lower paid employment, the award is treated as earnings by *ITEPA 2003 s.203*.

There is a strong presumption that cash gifts are a reward for services, e.g. tips and gratuities, but where a payment can be shown to have been made as a mark of esteem or appreciation it is not taxable. For example, in *Moore v Griffiths (1972) (48 TC 338)*, a one-off bonus unexpectedly received by Bobby Moore and the entire 1966 World Cup winning English football team was held not to be taxable.

Receipts by sportsmen from testimonial matches will not generally be taxable, provided that the sportsman has no contractual right to the benefit. As testimonial matches become more frequent HM Revenue & Customs may well in future successfully argue that the degree of expectation is such that they constitute a receipt from the employment and are therefore taxable.

9.22.6. Entertainment

See section **9.19** above.

No liability arises on the use of a credit token used to procure hospitality or entertainment satisfying the above conditions *(ITEPA 2003 s.267(2)(f))*.

No class 1 NIC liability arises on the above items under general principles.

9.22.7. Small gifts from third parties

No tax or class 1 or 1A NIC arises on gifts provided to employees by third parties provided:

- the gift is not provided by the employer or a person connected with him;
- neither the employer nor any person connected with him has directly or indirectly procured the gift;
- the gift is not in recognition of specific past services nor in anticipation of future services;
- the gift must not be in the form of cash or securities;
- where the gifts are in the form of vouchers or tokens they must only be exchangeable for goods;
- the total cost to the donor of gifts to a particular employee must not exceed £250 in a tax year. If this limit is exceeded, the full amount is taxable.

(ITEPA 2003 ss.270 & 324; SSCR 2001 Sch. 3 pt. V para. 6(a)&(e))

9.22.8. Staff entertainment

Functions such as staff Christmas parties are exempt provided that:

- they are open to all employees;
- the cost does not exceed £150 per head (including VAT and any transport and accommodation costs incurred by the employer).

(ITEPA 2003 s.264; SSCR 2001 Sch. 3 pt. V para. 5B(c)).

Functions may be treated as entertaining, even if entertaining is not the purpose of the event, such as a lunch to discuss budgets where only staff are present.

Where the £150 limit is exceeded the full amount is taxable. Where two or more functions are held during the year and the total cost exceeds £150 per head the exemption will apply to the function(s) which make best use of the exemption, i.e. if two functions costing £120 and £100 per head respectively are held during the year, the function costing £120 will be exempt and the function costing £100 will be taxable.

Where staff attend a business conference or event, particularly where it is held overseas, HMRC will require details of the itinerary and the time spent at the conference or event as a proportion of the total time spent on the trip to establish whether it should be taxable either as entertaining or as an incentive. If more than 50% of the time is spent on business, HMRC will generally consider the primary objective to be business and ignore any element of entertaining, such as a drinks reception. However, if the main purpose is to provide entertainment, it will be treated as a benefit in kind. Events held outside of normal working hours are more likely to be treated as entertaining and the more exotic the location, the more critically HMRC will examine the event and it is important to be able to justify why the event was held where it was. For example, employees of a fashion house attending the London or Milan fashion week could be justified as business, but running such an event in an exotic, distant location would be more likely to be treated as entertaining.

The costs of a conference may be treated as work-related training if it can be shown than employees' attendance was wholly, exclusively and necessarily in the performance of their duties (see section **9.16**. for general guidance on this).

A gala dinner during the business section of an event may be treated as subsistence if all employees attend it, since it would be necessary to incur some level of subsistence costs, even if the meal is more lavish than would normally be provided.

There are only limited circumstances where an event can be considered to be work-related if spouses, or civil partners, are allowed to accompany employees.

9.22.9. Crèche and childcare facilities

The cost of providing a place in a crèche **run by the employer** is not taxable and is not liable to class 1A NIC and any amount provided by the employer towards the cost of private crèche facilities will not be taxable or liable to class 1 NIC *(ITEPA 2003 ss.318, 318A, 318B & 318C)* provided that the following conditions are met:

1. the employee must have parental responsibility for the child or the child must reside with him or the child must be the child or stepchild of the employee and must be maintained at his expense;
2. the relief continues until the end of the week following 1 September following the child's 15th birthday (16th birthday if the child is receiving free in-patient care in hospital or is disabled) *(ITEPA 2003 s.318B(1))*;
3. the childcare must not be provided on premises which are used wholly or mainly as a dwelling;
4. the care is provided on premises which are made available by the employer alone or through a partnership arrangement whereby care is provided under arrangements made by persons including the employer on premises belonging to one of those persons and the employer is at least partly responsible for financing and managing the provision of the care. The level of financial commitment must extend beyond buying childcare places on an *ad hoc* basis and must take the form, for example, of a commitment to fund a set proportion of the overall costs of care provision. The employer does not have to manage the care provision on a day-to-day basis, but must be closely involved in matters such as the appointment and performance monitoring of carers, the extent of care provided, the conditions under which it is provided and the allocation of places;
5. the scheme must be open to all employees or all employees at a particular location and the employee must be employed by the employer providing the care. In the case of partnership arrangements, the scheme must be open to any employee working at the same location as the scheme employer and need not necessarily be an employee of the scheme employer. If the scheme is provided under salary sacrifice or flexible remuneration arrangements, this condition is not prevented from being met solely by virtue of the scheme not being open to low-paid employees *(ITEPA 2003 ss.270A(5A)&*,318A(5A)).

Other forms of employer-supported childcare and childcare vouchers are exempt up to a maximum limit. This limit is £55 per qualifying week (£243 per month) plus the 'voucher administration costs', i.e. the difference between the cost to the employer of providing the vouchers provided that:

1. the employee joined the scheme before 6 April 2011; and

2. the employee has not ceased to be employed by the employer during the period beginning on 6 April 2011 and ending with the week in question; and
3. during that period there has not been a continuous period of 52 weeks throughout which vouchers were not, or care was not, being provided for the employee under the scheme.

This scheme has been closed to new entrants from 4 October 2018. An employee is deemed to have joined the scheme as soon as the employer has agreed that vouchers or care will be provided by the employer under the scheme for the employee and there is a child for whom the employee has childcare responsibility falling within ITEPA2003 s.270A(3)(a) or (b) or s.318A(3)(a) or (b). An employee must have submitted an application to join the scheme before this date and this application must have been accepted by the employer, but it is not necessary for them to have already received any vouchers or directly contracted childcare under the scheme on order to be eligible under the old rules. However, it is also necessary that the child was born before that date *(FA 2011 Sch. 8 para. 8).*

Where an employee does not fulfil the above conditions the limit is:
1. £22 per qualifying week (£95 p.m.) for employees whose relevant income exceeds the higher rate threshold;
2. £28 per qualifying week (£121 p.m.) for employees whose relevant income exceeds the basic rate threshold;
3. £55 per qualifying week (£238 p.m.) in other cases;

plus the 'voucher administration costs', i.e. the difference between the cost to the employer of providing the vouchers and their face value. An employer must make an estimate of an employee's relevant income *(ITEPA 2003 ss.270A (5C),(6A),(6ZA)& 318(5C),(6A)).*

Relevant income is defined as salary, wages and fees and any other earnings to which the employee is contractually entitled, such as guaranteed overtime payments or London weighting allowance, plus any amounts treated as earnings under ITEPA 2003 Pt. 3, Chapters 2-12 (benefits in kind), less excluded amounts, which are amounts, such as pension contributions, donations and removal expenses, which an employee is entitled to deduct from their earnings. Discretionary overtime payments or performance-related payments are excluded. Where an employee becomes employed by the employer during the tax year this must be adjusted *pro rata (ITEPA 2003 ss.270B&318AA).* Employers are required to make a basic earnings assessment for employees who fall within the new rules. This must be carried out when an employee first joins the scheme and thereafter at the start of each tax year, and remains valid for the whole of the tax year, even if the employee's earnings change during the tax year.

The term 'qualifying week' is defined as one of the successive periods of seven days, starting on the first day of the tax year, with the additional day (or two days in the case of a leap year) counting as a separate 53rd week *(ITEPA 2003 ss.270A & 318A(7))*.

'Care' covers any form of supervised activity provided on either a regular or irregular basis excluding any activity primarily provided for educational purposes *(ITEPA 2003 s.318B(1))*.

The exemptions for employer-provided care and for other care are excluded exemptions under ITEPA 2003 s.228A. Therefore they still apply where they are provided under a salary sacrifice arrangement.

9.22.10. Sports and recreational facilities

Sports and recreational facilities made available to employees and non-cash vouchers provided for this purpose are not liable to tax or class 1 NIC, unless they are provided on domestic premises (e.g. an exercise bicycle for use at home) or consist of an interest in any mechanically propelled vehicle or of overnight accommodation *(ITEPA 2003 ss.261 & 262; SSCR 2001 Sch. 3 Pt. V para. 5B(b))*.

9.22.11. Free or subsidised meals

Free or subsidised meals provided in a staff canteen are exempt from income tax and class 1A NIC, provided that they are available to all employees and are reasonable in scale *(ITEPA 2003 s.317; SSCR 2001 Sch. 3 pt. V para. 5B(e))*. A separate dining facility for senior staff will therefore not qualify. Where hotel or restaurant staff take meals in the dining room whilst meals are being served to the public, the exemption will only apply where the meals are taken in a section of the room designated for the use of employees *(ITEPA 2003 s.317(4))*. The provision of meals must not be under salary sacrifice or flexible remuneration arrangements *(ITEPA 2003 s.317(4A))*. Employers who do not have a canteen may designate a restaurant as a staff canteen. This will not give rise to a benefit for lower paid employees since the facility cannot be converted into cash, but for other employees it will be an assessable benefit.

This exemption is a special case exemption under ITEPA 2003 s.228A. Therefore it still applies where it is provided under a salary sacrifice arrangement.

9.22.12. Removal costs

The first £8,000 of eligible removal expenses and benefits paid by the employer is exempt from income tax and class 1 or 1A NIC, provided the conditions set out below are satisfied *(ITEPA 2003 ss.271-287)*. Payments in excess of £8,000 are taxable, but are not subject to PAYE *(ITEPA 2003 s.287(1))*. This exemption covers:

- estate agent's, auctioneer's and legal fees, penalties for loan redemption, public utility disconnection charge, cost of maintenance, insurance, security and residence whilst the property is unoccupied, incurred in connection with the disposal of the employee's former residence *(ITEPA 2003 s.279)*;
- transport costs for moving domestic belongings of the employee and members of his family to the new residence, including insurance cover, packing and unpacking, temporary storage, detaching, attaching and adapting of domestic fittings *(ITEPA 2003 s.280)*;
- costs of acquisition of new residence including legal expenses and procurement fees incurred in obtaining a loan, cost of mortgage protection, surveyor's and inspector's fees, registry fees and SDLT and connection charges to public utilities *(ITEPA 2003 s.277)*. The cost of property in some parts of the UK means that the payment of the SDLT can use up a significant proportion of the £8,500 limit;
- abortive costs connected with the acquisition of a new residence where the sale did not proceed due to circumstances beyond the employee's control or because they decided reasonably not to proceed *(ITEPA 2003 s.278)*;
- cost of travel and subsistence expenses including the cost of temporary accommodation, costs of employee and family making temporary visits to the new area, costs of travel between the former residence and the temporary accommodation, travel by employee and family between former residence and new residence, subsistence of a child under 19 (a 'relevant' child) in either the old or new area to ensure continuity of education, travel by relevant child between such accommodation and new residence *(ITEPA 2003 ss.281-283)*;
- interest on a bridging loan raised to cover time between purchase of new residence and disposal of former residence. If the amount of the bridging loan exceeds the value of the former residence or part of the loan is not used to purchase the new residence, no relief is available on the excess or the part of the loan not so used *(ITEPA 2003 s.284)*;
- cost of obtaining duplicate domestic goods where the similar goods used in the former residence are not suitable for the new residence *(ITEPA 2003 s.285)*.

In order to qualify for the relief:

- the move must be due to the taking up of employment or a change in an employee's duties or place of work;

- the move must be made wholly or mainly in order to permit the employee to live within a reasonable travelling distance of his place of work; and
- the former residence must not be within a reasonable travelling distance of the employee's new place of work *(ITEPA 2003 s.273).*

(ITEPA 2003 ss.271-287 SSCR 2001 Sch. 3 Pt. VIII para. 2)

9.22.13. Fixed profit car scheme (FPCS)

Where an employer reimburses an employee for using his own car for business purposes, the payment is strictly taxable and the employee must claim a deduction for the cost of motoring by showing that it was incurred wholly, exclusively and necessarily in the course of his duties.

The FPCS allows reimbursement to be made tax-free up to a maximum amount per mile. The rate for all cars and vans is 45p per mile up to 10,000 miles and 25p per mile thereafter. Any payment in excess of this amount will be taxable and liable to class 1 NIC *(ITEPA 2003 ss.229 & 230; SSCR 2001 reg. 22A).*

If an employee is not reimbursed for motoring expenses they can use the amounts set by the FPCS as a basis for his expenses claim *(ITEPA 2003 s.232).*

9.22.14. Passenger payments

No tax or class 1 NIC liability arises on payments made by passengers to a driver of up to 5p per mile where the passengers are also employees of the same employer and the journey represents business travel for both the driver and the passenger(s) if:

- the employee receives a mileage allowance for the use of the car or van; and
- the car or van is taxable as a benefit in kind on the employee where the car or van is provided by the employer by reason of his employment.

(ITEPA 2003 ss.233 & 234; SSCR 2001 Sch. 3 Pt. VIII para. 7C)

9.22.15. Bicycles and motorcycles

Employers can pay employees a tax-free amount for using a bicycle (20p) or motorcycle (24p) for business travel. If the employer pays less than this amount, the employee can claim any difference as a deduction *(ITEPA 2003 ss. 229 & 230; SSCR 2001 Sch. 3 Pt. VIII para. 7B)*).

The provision of a cycle or cycle safety equipment is not liable to tax or class 1 NIC provided that the facility is available to all employees, the cycle is used mainly for qualifying journeys and there is no transfer of ownership of the cycle or the equipment *(ITEPA 2003 ss.244(3) & 249).* The condition relating to the use of the cyle mainly for qualifying journeys is deemed to have been met for the period from 16 March 2020 to 5 April 2022 *(FA 2021 s.25).* If the cycle or equipment is subsequently transferred to the employee, the general rule does not apply and the tax charge is the market value of the asset at the date of transfer less any amounts made good by the employee *(ITEPA 2003 s.206).*

Where a non-cash voucher gives an employee the entitlement to use a cycle or safety equipment and the above conditions are satisfied, no benefit arises *(ITEPA 2003 s.266(2), (5)); (SSCR 2001 Sch. 3 Pt. V para. 5A(c)).*

This exemption is an excluded exemption under ITEPA 2003 s.228A. Therefore it still applies where it is provided under a salary sacrifice arrangement.

9.22.16. Car parking facilities

No benefit arises where an employer provides free parking space for cars, cycles or motorcycles at, or near, the place of employment or reimburses an employee for the cost of using such a car park *(ITEPA 2003 ss.266(1) & 267)* or provides a non-cash voucher or credit token *(ITEPA 2003 ss.266(1) & 267; SSCR 2001 Sch. 3 pt. VIII para. 8*).

9.22.17. Provision of vehicle-battery charging

No liability arises in respect of the provision at, or near, an employee's workplace of facilities for charging a battery used by the employee, provided that it is made generally available to all employees at a workplace. This exemption includes the provision of electricity, but not of workplace parking *(ITEPA 2003 s.237A).*

9.22.18. Works bus services

No tax liability arises in respect of the provision of a works bus service; i.e. 'a service provided by means of a bus or minibus for conveying employees of one or more employers on qualifying journeys' *(ITEPA 2003 s.242).*

A qualifying journey is a journey between an employee's home and place of work or between places of work, provided that the employee's attendance is necessary for the performance of the duties *(ITEPA 2003 ss.242(3) & 249).*

The bus or minibus must have been designed to have a minimum seating capacity of nine (to prevent overcrowding by unscrupulous employers), must be available to all employees of the employer(s) and must be mainly used for qualifying journeys *(ITEPA 2003 s.242(1))*. It may only be used by employees and their children or step-children under the age of 18 *(ITEPA 2003 s.242(1))*. If an employee is given a non-cash voucher to be used on a service which meets the above conditions there is no liability to tax or class 1 NIC *(ITEPA 2003 s.242(4), (6); SSCR 2001 Sch. 3 Pt. V para. 5A(a)*).

9.22.19. Subsidies provided to public bus services

Subsidies provided to public bus services do not give rise to a tax liability so long as the service is used for 'qualifying journeys' and is generally available to all employees *(ITEPA 2003 s. 243).*

There is a further condition that employees pay the same fare as the general public *(ITEPA 2003 s.243(1)& (4))*, although this does not apply to employer-subsidised local bus services (as defined by the *Transport Act 1985 s.2) (ITEPA 2003 s.243(3))*. This exemption covers qualifying journeys, defined as above *(ITEPA 2003 ss.243(5) & 249)*.

A non-cash voucher provided to employees in respect of a subsidised bus service does not give rise to a class 1 NIC liability *(SSCR 2001 Sch. 3 Pt. V para. 5A(b))*.

9.22.20. Transport and accommodation provided due to industrial action

No income tax or class 1 or 1A NIC liability arises on reasonable expenditure on behalf of or payments to employees in respect of transport and overnight accommodation provided due to industrial action which disrupts public transport services *(ITEPA 2003 s.245; SSCR 2001 Sch. 3 Pt. V para. 5B(a))*.

9.22.21. Taxis provided for employees required to work late

No income tax or class 1 or 1A NIC liability arises on the payment by an employer of taxi fares for employees required to work later than 9pm *(ITEPA 2003 s.248; SSCR 2001 Sch. 3 Pt. V para. 5(c))*.

This relief is limited to the following circumstances:

- the employee must be *required* to work late, they must not be doing so by choice;
- this must not be a regular requirement of the job;
- relief is given for a maximum of 60 such journeys during a tax year. However, if there are more than 60 such journeys, the exemption will still apply to the first 60, provided that the other conditions are satisfied;
- public transport must have ceased or must not be a reasonable option;
- the transport must be a taxi or hired car used solely to take the employee home.

In determining whether working late is a regular requirement of the job, the decisive factor is whether there is a pattern in the late working, rather than the number of occasions. For example, an employee who is required to work late once a month to complete a specific monthly task, such as preparation of the payroll, or who is required to work late each year for a month following the year-end will not qualify for this exemption. The requirement to work late is determined by reference to the employee's actual normal work pattern, rather than the contractual hours of work. If an employee normally works until 9.30pm, even though they are only contracted to work until 8.30pm, the exemption is not available. Public transport will not be considered a reasonable alternative if the journey home takes more than an extra hour to complete or if there is a significantly higher risk to personal safety from using public transport after 9pm. Travelling home when tired with a heavy briefcase to an unmanned station and having to cope with less frequent services do not qualify for the exemption.

9.22.22. Breakdown of car sharing arrangements

No income tax or class 1 or 1A NIC liability arises on the payment of transport costs incurred where car sharing arrangements unavoidably break down *(ITEPA 2003 s.248 (3); SSCR 2001 Sch. 3 Pt. V para. 5(b))*.

9.22.23. Transport – disabled employees

No income tax or class 1 or 1A NIC liability arises on the provision of alternative means of transport and financial assistance with the costs of journeys between home and work for employees who are severely and permanently disabled and who are incapable of using public transport *(ITEPA 2003 ss.246 & 247; SSCR 2001 Sch. 3 Pt. V para. 5(a))*.

Where a car is provided for the use of such an employee no car or fuel benefit arises if the car has been adapted for his use, or is a car with automatic transmission where the employee can only drive such a car. The terms on which it is made available must prohibit use other than for business travel and ordinary commuting and the car must actually only be used on those terms.

9.22.24. Scholarships and apprenticeships

An employer may pay up to £15,480 to or on behalf of an employee without giving rise to a taxable benefit where the employee is allowed to enrol on a full-time course at a university, technical college or similar institution lasting at least a year and where the employee is required to attend for a minimum of 20 weeks per year. The institution must offer more than one course of practical or academic instruction and the course must be open to members of the public generally. The payments may cover lodging, travelling and subsistence, but exclude tuition fees *(SP4/86)*. These payments are also exempt from class 1 NIC *(SSCR 2001 Sch. 3 Pt. III para. 12)*.

Where the £15,480 limit is exceeded, the full amount is taxable, and not just the excess.

9.22.25. Work-related training

No liability to tax or class 1 NIC arises where an employer pays any costs of work-related training or any related costs. Work-related training is any training which is likely to improve the employee's performance of his job or of a charitable or voluntary activity associated with his work. Related costs means incidental costs such as examination fees *(ITEPA 2003 ss.250-254; SSCR 2001 Sch. 3 Pt. VII para. 2)*. The re-imbursement of the costs incurred by an employee on training commenced or completed before taking up employment will not normally be covered by this exemption. However, the exemption may apply in certain cases where there is a strong link between the employment and the pre-commencement training. For example, the exemption may apply where an employee has accepted an offer of employment to commence in the reasonably near future and then undertakes training related to the future employment.

9.22.26. Contributions to individual learning account (ILA) training

No liability to tax or class 1 NIC arises in respect of contributions made by an employer to a third party towards training of an employee which qualifies under the Learning and Skills Act 2000 ss.108 & 109 (Education and Training Act 2000 (Scotland) s.1 in Scotland) or the provision of a benefit incidental to such training or the payment or reimbursement of expenses connected with such training *(ITEPA 2003 ss.255 & 256; SSCR 2001 Sch. 3 Pt. VII para. 3).*

The person providing the training must be qualified under the Learning and Skills Act 2000 ss.105 & 106 (Education and Training Act 2000 (Scotland) s.2 in Scotland) *(ITEPA 2003 s.255(2)).*

Travel expenses will be exempt if the employee would have been able to claim a deduction for the travel expenses if they had not been paid by the employer, and the employee is undertaking the training as one of the duties of his employment *(ITEPA 2003 s.257).* Subsistence payments made by the employer will, likewise, only be deductible if the employee is undertaking the training as one of the duties of his employment *(ITEPA 2003 s.257).*

No relief is available if the employee is undertaking the training for entertainment or recreational purposes or if an employer or former employer is paying for the training as a reward for past services *(ITEPA 2003 s.258).*

The cost of providing assets or materials which will be used in the course of the training and the duties of the employee's employment, e.g. stationery, books or CDs is exempt. The assets must not be used for any other purposes to any significant extent *(ITEPA 2003 s.259).*

The training must be generally available to all staff *(ITEPA 2003 s.260).*

9.22.27. Retraining courses

ITEPA 2003 s.311 gives relief for the costs of attending a 'qualifying course' for the purpose of retraining. These cover:

- course and examination fees;
- essential books;
- daily travel expenses which would have been deductible under ITEPA 2003 ss.337 & 338 if the course had been relevant to the previous employment and the employee had still been employed.

The employee must begin the course while still employed or within one year of ceasing employment, having been employed for two years before the beginning of the course or before employment ceases, if earlier, and the employee must cease employment no later than two years after the end of the course. The course will not qualify where the employee resumes employment with the employer within two years of ceasing to be employed. The exemption is available to both full-time and part-time employees and there is no requirement that the course be full-time or substantially full-time.

No class 1 NIC liability arises on the payment since it does not arise from the employment and is thus not treated as earnings under general principles.

This exemption is an excluded exemption under ITEPA 2003 s.228A. Therefore it still applies where it is provided under a salary sacrifice arrangement.

9.22.28. Air miles and car fuel coupons

No taxable benefit arises in respect of air miles and car fuel coupons obtained through business travel, even if these are used for private purposes.

9.22.29. Payment of expenses for employees temporarily absent from normal place of employment

In addition to the costs of travel to and from the temporary place of employment, the cost of accommodation and subsistence is not taxable if paid by the employer. If the employee must bear these costs themself, they may obtain a deduction for the cost in the following circumstances *(ITEPA 2003 ss.240, 241 & 268(1)-(5); SSCR 2001 Sch. 3 pt. X para. 4)*:

- the period for which an employee is working at the temporary place of employment is not expected to last, and does not actually last, more than 12 months; and
- the employee returns to his normal place of employment at the end of this period;
- where the employee is initially not expected to be working at the temporary place of employment for more than 12 months, but that period is subsequently extended, the payments are tax-free up to the date when the change in circumstances becomes known;
- the payment of personal incidental expenses incurred by an employee, such as telephone calls, whilst staying away from home on business is exempt up to a maximum of £5 per day when staying in the UK and £10 when staying outside the UK *(ITEPA 2003 s.241(3))*. It does not matter how the employer deals with or reimburses these expenses;
- where expenses are reimbursed for a number of days, HMRC will, in principle, apply the exemption on the basis of the average expenses reimbursed per day. If, therefore, over a three-day period when an

employee is abroad, expenses of £12, £11 and £6 are reimbursed the exemption will apply to all amounts;

- this rule need not be applied to a period in its entirety. If the amounts were £8, £9 and £15 the period could be broken into two periods, one consisting of the first two nights and the other consisting of the third night. In this case the amounts reimbursed for the first two nights will be exempt;
- the exemption also applies where non-cash vouchers or credit tokens are used to obtain such goods or services and the cost is not otherwise deductible *(ITEPA 2003 s.268(1)-(5));*
- the limit applies to the aggregate of all expenses, whether they are paid in cash or by vouchers or credit *(ITEPA 2003 s.241(1), (2));*
- this exemption also applies if an employee is away from home on a training course.

9.22.30. Expenses incurred whilst employed abroad

Taxpayers who are resident in the UK, but the duties of whose employment are performed wholly outside the UK, may deduct the following costs from their earnings, or claim a deduction equal to the employment income benefit charge where these are paid or reimbursed by the employer. Where the employee is not domiciled in the UK, the deduction is only available where the employer is a foreign employer:

1. travel from any place in the UK at the start of the employment and the return journey to any place in the UK when it terminates *(ITEPA 2003 s.341);*
2. travel between employments whilst abroad *(ITEPA 2003 s.342);*
3. travel costs of return journeys between the place of work and the UK whilst employed abroad, provided that the duties can only be performed outside the UK *(ITEPA 2003 s.370);*
4. board and lodging incurred for the purpose of performing the duties of the overseas employment *(ITEPA 2003 s.376 (1)-(3)).*

Where the costs are reimbursed by the employer they are not treated as earnings for the purpose of class 1 NIC and there is no class 1A NIC liability *SSCR 2001 Sch. 3 pt. VII paras. 4, 4A, 4B & 4D*).

Where expenses are only partly incurred for the above purpose, an apportionment must be made.

Where an employee has more than one employment and the duties of one or both employments are performed wholly or partly outside the UK, the expenses of travelling to or from the UK, or between places outside the UK, are deductible where they are travelling in order to perform the duties of one employment, having previously performed the duties of another employment

(ITEPA 2003 s.342(1)-(7)). Where the travel is only partly attributable to performing duties of the employment, only the portion of the expenses so attributable is deductible *(ITEPA 2003 s.342(8)).*

There is also a deduction equal to the benefit charge which would otherwise arise where the employer pays or reimburses the cost of up to two visits per year by his spouse and children (including step-children, adopted children and illegitimate children) who are under 18 at the time of the outward journey where the employee is absent from UK for more than 60 days *(ITEPA 2003 s.371(3)-(7); SSCR 2001 Sch. 3 pt. VII para. 4C*). There is no class 1 or 1A liability on payments to employees under this heading. This deduction is not available where the employee bears the cost themself.

9.22.31. Travel and other costs of non-domiciled individuals working in the UK

Similar deductions and exemptions for class 1 and 1A NIC are available to taxpayers who are not domiciled in the UK, but who receive earnings in respect of duties performed in the UK for more than 60 days *(ITEPA 2003 ss.373 & 374; SSCR 2001 Sch. 3 pt. VII para. 5*).

The occasional day's absence will be ignored and the conditions will be treated as having been met if a taxpayer is present in the UK for at least two-thirds of the working days in the 60 day period and is present in the UK both at the start at the end of the period. This will also apply for NIC for the purpose of Social Security (Contributions) Regulations 2001.

The amount of a deduction given is the lower of the cost actually incurred and the cost which would have been incurred if the journey had commenced from the normal place of work.

Relief is also given where the duties of an employment are performed partly within the UK and partly outside the UK. Relief is given for travel from any place in the UK to the overseas place of employment and from the place of employment to any place in the UK, provided that the duties are only capable of being performed outside the UK.

Relief is also available where an employee has more than one employment and it is necessary to perform the duties of one or more of these employments outside the UK.

9.22.32. Mobile telephones

Mobile telephones provided for an employee's use are exempt for tax under ITEPA 2003 s.319 and from class 1 NIC under general principles. This benefit is restricted to one telephone per employee.

9.22.33. Workplace counselling

Workplace counselling is exempt, provided that the service is available to all employees *(ITEPA 2003 ss.210 & 266(4)); Income Tax (Benefits in Kind) (Exemption for Welfare Counselling) Regulations 2000 (SI2000/2080)).* This exemption is available to both full-time and part-time employees. The exemption covers any counselling services other than:

1. medical treatment;
2. financial advice (other than debt counselling);
3. tax or legal advice;
4. advice on recreation and leisure.

It is not necessary for the services to be provided by the employer.

There is also a specific relief for counselling given to employees on the cessation of employment *(ITEPA 2003 s.310).* This exemption covers the cost to the employer of providing such services or the payment or reimbursement of an employee for such costs or of the employee's travel costs.

In order to qualify the services must consist of the following *(ITEPA 2003 s.310(2)-(7)):*

1. enabling an employee to adjust to the cessation of employment and/or finding other gainful employment or self-employment;
2. improving skills and providing or making available office equipment or similar facilities.

The employee must have been employed by the current employer for at least two years ending at the earlier of the date of the commencement of the services and the cessation of employment.

The services must be performed in the UK. Where the services are only partly performed in the UK, a reasonable apportionment will be made.

The services may be available either to current or past employees and may be available to all current and past employees or only to current and past employees of a particular class.

The exemption under ITEPA 2003 s.310 is an excluded exemption under ITEPA 2003 s.228A. Therefore it still applies where it is provided under a salary sacrifice arrangement.

9.22.34. Pension advice

No liability arises on the the provision of pensions advice to an employee or a former or prospectiveemployee, or the reimbursement of costs incurred by the employee or former or prospective employee. However, where the advice is provided directly the exemption is limited to £500 *(ITEPA 2003 s.308C).* This exemption applies where either:

1. the advice is available to all employees generally, or all employees at a particular location; or
2. the advice is available to all employees generally, or all employees at a particular location, who have reached a minimum qualifying age, which must be within five years of the employee's relevant pension ago, or who meet the ill-health condition.

9.22.35. Medical check-ups and payment of medical expenses

The provision of one medical check-up and one screening per employee per year, whether carried out by the employer's own staff or an outside firm, does not give rise to a benefit in kind, and there is no class 1 or 1A NIC liability. The health screenings must be available to all employees and the check-ups must either be available to all employees, or to all employees identified as requiring a check-up by health screenings *(ITEPA 2003 s.320B, Income Tax (Exemption of Minor Benefits) Regulations 2002 (SI 2002/205 reg. 7)).*

A taxable benefit will arise where the employer reimburses an employee for medical treatment or diagnosis.

There is also an exemption from class 1 NIC for payments of or contributions to the cost of overseas medical treatment where the need for treatment arises whilst an employee is working outside the UK (*SSCR 2001 Sch.3 pt. VIII para. 14).*

9.22.36. Eye tests and special corrective appliances

No benefit arises where an employer provides free eye tests and any special corrective appliances found to be necessary as a result of the test where the test and appliances are required under the Health and Safety at Work etc. Act 1974, provided that tests and appliances are generally made available to all employees covered by this act *(ITEPA 2003 s.320A).*

9.22.37. Recommended medical treatment

There is no liability on:

1. the provision by an employer of recommended medical treatment;
2. or the payment or reimbursement of the cost of such treatment; or
3. the provision of non-cash vouchers for the purpose of obtaining such treatment;

up to a maximum value of £500, provided that the treatment is not under salary sacrifice arrangements or flexible remuneration arrangements. Recommended medical treatment is defined as any procedure for diagnosing or treating any physical or mental illness, infirmity of defect which is provided as occupational health services under the Employment and Training Act 1973 s.2 in order to assist an employee to return to work after a period of absence due to injury or ill health *(ITEPA 2003 s.320C).*

This exemption is a special case exemption under ITEPA 2003 s.228A. Therefore it still applies where it is provided under a salary sacrifice arrangement.

9.22.38. Health and employment insurance payments

There is no liability where an employer makes payments to an employee which are attributable, on a just and reasonable basis, to premiums paid by the employee under an insurance policy taken out by another person wholly or partly for the benefit of the employee or his spouse, provided that such a payment would be exempt under ITTOIA 2005 s.735, if it were an annual payment *(ITEPA 2003 s.325A)*. In order to be deductible the policy must insure against a health or employment risk, i.e. the employee becoming unable to continue employment due to physical or mental illness, disability, infirmity or defect or a deterioration in a condition resulting from such illness etc. *(ITTOIA 2005 s.736)*.

9.22.39. Coronavirus tests

No liability to income tax will arise in respect of a coronavirus test provided to an employee by their employer or the reimbursement of the cost of a test incurred by the employee . This exemption applies for the 2020/21 and 2021/22 tax years *(FA 2021 s.26)*.

9.22.40. Security assets

Amounts expended by the employer or reimbursed to the employee in relation to the provision of assets and services which are provided in order to counter a specific threat to the personal physical security of the employee arising as a result of the job are exempt *(ITEPA 2003 s.377)*. Examples of such assets and services are floodlighting, alarms, bullet-resistant windows and bodyguards.

9.22.41. Accommodation, supplies or services used in the performance of duties

No benefit arises where an employer provides an employee with accommodation or supplies or services which are used by the employee in the performance of his duties *(ITEPA 2003 s.316)*, provided that the private use by the employee or his family is not significant *(ITEPA 2003 s.316(2))*. This will include private use of an internet connection provided by the employer where no breakdown between business and private calls is possible and private use does not affect the cost of the package.

Where the accommodation is being simultaneously used for the performance of the employees' duties and for private purposes the asset is considered for the purpose of this exemption as being used for private purposes *(ITEPA 2003 s.316(3))*. The word 'significant' is not defined.

Where the benefit is provided other than on premises owned by the employer, the exemption will only apply if:

1. the benefit is provided for the sole purpose of enabling the employee to perform their duties;
2. private use is not significant;
3. it is not an excluded benefit. These are high value assets such as motor vehicles, boats and aircraft or a benefit involving an extension, conversion or alteration to living accommodation or a building or other structure on land adjacent to and enjoyed by the accommodation.

(ITEPA 2003 ss.210 & 266(4))

9.22.42. Employee liabilities and indemnity relief

ITEPA 2003 s.346 gives relief to employees for:

1. the cost of discharging a qualifying liability of the employee;
2. costs arising out of or connected with a claim that the employee is subject to a qualifying liability;
3. so much of any premium paid under a qualifying contract of insurance as relates to covering the employee.

Relief is also available from class 1 NIC under *SSCR 2001 Sch.3 pt. VIII, para. 10.*

An insurance contract must not be 'connected' with any other contract, i.e. where two associated contracts are taken out, only one of which relates to liability insurance and the premiums of that policy are artificially weighted to inflate the amount qualifying for relief, no relief will be available. Where a job contract stipulates that an employee must take out a work indemnity policy, such a connection will not, however, preclude relief for the premiums under ITEPA 2003 s.346.

Relief is denied where it would be 'unlawful' for any employer to enter into a contract of insurance in respect of particular liabilities or costs, e.g. insurance against fines, penalties and costs arising out of criminal or other offences. The costs of insuring against the costs of defending a criminal case are deductible. This exclusion only relates to contracts which are illegal under English law, rather than contracts which are outside a company's articles of association *(ITEPA 2003 s.346(2))*. Relief will also be denied if the payment is made as part of arrangements, the main object, or one of the objects of which is the avoidance of tax *(ITEPA 2009 s.346(2A))*.

Relief is available both where payments are made by an employee and where they are made by the employer or another person on behalf of the employee.

Payments to or on behalf of an employee other than under an insurance policy are earnings of the employment in respect of which the liability claim arises.

9.22.43. Apprenticeship bursaries for care leavers
Apprenticeship bursary payments made out of the public revenue to a person who is, or was, looked after by a local authority are not liable to income tax *(ITEPA 2003 s.254A)*.

9.22.44. Payment of expenses to voluntary office-holders
Payments of expenses to the holder of voluntary office in respect of reasonable expenses incurred in connection with that office are not liable to income tax. This applies both to advance payments and the reimbursement of expenses and regardless of whether the payment is made by the person with whom the office is held *(ITEPA 2003 s.299B)*.

9.22.45. Contributions to retirement benefit schemes
See **Chapter 12**.

Chapter 10. Benefits in Kind

10.1. Valuation of Benefits in Kind

Under ITEPA 2003 s.203 the benefit assessable on employees is the 'cash equivalent' of the benefit, which is defined as the cost to the employer of providing the benefit less any amounts contributed by the employee by 6 July following the end of the tax year. This general rule is, however, overridden by statute in the case of certain high value benefits such as cars and accommodation. ITEPA 2003 ss.70-72 states that payments to employees in respect of expenses are to be treated as earnings even where they are not held to be so treated by another section, but a corresponding deduction may be claimed where the expense is incurred wholly, exclusively and necessarily in the course of the employee's duties (see section **9.16**). The value of benefits is added to an employee's cash salary when calculating the amount of tax due.

10.2. Benefits – Definition of Cost

The cost to the employer is defined as the additional or marginal cost to the employer *(ITEPA 2003 s.204)*. This was established in the landmark case of *Pepper v Hart (1995) (BTC 591)*, which concerned the provision of education at reduced fees to the children of teachers at a public school. It was held that provided the fees charged covered the additional costs of books and catering etc, no benefit arose. The same principle applies to free rail or bus travel for employees. Provided that no fare-paying passengers are displaced no benefit arises. Where goods are sold to employees at a discount no benefit arises provided that the price paid by the employee covers the wholesale price paid by the employer. If professional services are provided to employees which do not require additional staff or partners and the costs to the employer are negligible, no benefit arises.

Where there is mixed business and private use of an asset, some fixed costs may be disregarded (e.g. the road fund licence for a fitter's van) where private use is incidental to business use, but full tax will be charged on assets provided solely for non-business purposes.

Where a benefit is only provided for a part of a tax year, the charge is reduced *pro rata*.

If an employee sacrifices salary in order to obtain the benefit, the money's worth of the benefit is the amount of salary given up *(Heaton v Bell (1970) (46 TC 211))*, subject to any specific exemptions.

10.3. Exemption for Trivial Benefits

No taxable benefit arises where:

1. the benefit is not cash or a cash voucher;
2. the cost of the benefit to the employer does not exceed £50. Where the benefit is provided to more than one employee and it is not practicable to apportion the cost between the employees, the cost of providing the benefit must be divided by the number of employees to which it is provided;
3. the benefit must not be provided under any relevant salary sacrifice arrangement or other contractual obligation;
4. the benefit is not provided in recognition of particular services performed in the course of employment or in anticipation of such services;
5. where the employee is a close company and the benefit is provided to a director of the company or a member of his family or household who is not an employee of the company, the total benefits provided to the employee and members of his family not employed by the company must not exceed £300 in a tax year.

(ITEPA 2003 ss. 323A, 323B)

These exemptions are special case exemptions under ITEPA 2003 s.228A. Therefore they still apply where it is provided under a salary sacrifice arrangement.

10.4. Ministers of Religion

Ministers of religion earning less than £8,500 p.a. (pro-rated where they are employed for part of the year) are exempt from the following provisions of ITEPA 2003:

1. expenses payments *(ITEPA 2003 ss.70-72)*;
2. cars vans and related benefits *(ITEPA 2003 ss.114-172)*;
3. loans *(ITEPA 2003 ss.173-191)*
4. use of and transfer of assets *(ITEPA 2003 ss.204-206)*;
5. scholarships *(ITEPA 2003 ss.211-216-72)*.

(ITEPA 2003 s.290C(2))

Where a car or van is provided during the year and an alternative to the car is also offered which would be treated as earnings under ITEPA 2003 Pt 3 ch. 1 and that amount exceeds the amount which would have been chargeable in respect of the car or van, but for the exemption under ITEPA 290C(2), the excess is treated as earnings. ITEPA 2003 s.290C(2) is to be disregarded for the purpose of this calculation *(ITEPA 2003 s.290F)*.

The calculation of earnings includes the salary or stipend, benefits not exempted under ITEPA 2003 s.290C(2), any other amounts treated as earnings and any extra amounts to be added in connection with a car *(ITEPA 2003 s.290E(1))*. Where a minister of religion has two or more related employments, i.e. they are with the same employer or with bodies or partnerships controlled by the same individual, partnership or body, the earnings must be aggregated. Where one or more of these employments is not as a minister of religion, ITEPA 290C will not apply to any of the employments *(ITEPA 2003 s.290G).*

10.5. Carers

No liability to income tax arises in respect of the provision of board and lodging to an individual by reason of their employment as a home care worker, provided that it is at the home of the recipient and is on a reasonable scale. The employment must consist wholly or mainly of the provision of personal care to the recipient because of either the recipient's:

1. old age;
2. mental or physical disability;
3. past or present dependence on alcohol or drugs;
4. past or present illness; or
5. past or present mental disorder.

(ITEPA 2003 s. 306A)

10.6. Benefits in Kind and National Insurance Contributions

The only benefits which are liable to class 1 NIC are loans written off, and the following assets specified in *SSCR 2001 Sch. 3 pts II, III and IV:*

1. cash vouchers;
2. non-cash vouchers unless covered by a specific exemption (*SSCR 2001 Sch. 3 pt. II para. 2(b));*
3. readily convertible assets (*SSCR 2001 Sch. 3 pt. III);*
4. the following assets listed in *SSCR 2001 Sch. 3 pt. IV:*
   (a) securities;
   (b) options to acquire assets, currency, precious metals or other options;
   (c) alcoholic liquor on which duty has not been paid;
   (d) gemstones;
   (e) certificates etc. conferring rights in respect of assets;
   (f) vouchers which are capable of being exchanged for any other asset falling within this paragraph.

Where benefits are not liable to class 1 NIC, secondary class 1A contributions are payable. Therefore, no liability arises to the employee, only to the employer.

10.7. Payment of Expenses by Employer

There is a difference between the situations where an employer provides a benefit directly to an employee, e.g. where the employee has the use of a telephone provided by the employer and the situation where an employer reimburses an employee for expenses which the employee has incurred, e.g. private telephone calls. The determining factor is that in the first case the contract is between the employer and the third party, whereas in the second case the contract is between the employee and the third party.

In the first situation no benefit arises on a lower paid employee since the benefit cannot be converted into cash, whereas in the second situation the employer is meeting the liability of an employee and a benefit arises, subject to a deduction under ITEPA 2003 s.336.

For other employees, a benefit will arise in both situations unless a deduction is available under ITEPA 2003 s.336. No class 1 NIC is payable where the benefit is provided directly, but class 1A NIC will be payable by the employer. So, it is advisable for any contract for the provision of services to an employee or a mortgage etc. to be made directly between the employer and the supplier.

10.8. Salary Sacrifice Arrangements

Where a benefit is provided under a salary sacrifice arrangement the amount of the benefit is generally the greater of the cash equivalent using the usual rules and the amount of salary foregone, although this is amended in certain instances.

Specific exemptions for benef its do not apply where they are provided under a salary sacrifice arrangement, unless they are either a 'special case exemption' or an 'excluded exemption' *(ITEPA 2003 s.228A(3))*. These exemptions are noted in the relevant sections of the book.

10.9. Gift of Assets to Employees

10.9.1. General rule

Where a new asset other than a cash voucher, non-cash voucher or a credit token is given to an employee, the benefit will be the cost to the employer of providing it, less any amount reimbursed *(ITEPA 2003 s.203(3))*.

Where an asset is first made available for private use and then subsequently given to the employee, the taxable benefit will be the higher of:

1. market value of asset at date of gift less the amount paid by employee; or
2. cost of asset less amounts already assessed on the employee (see section **10.15**) and the amount paid by the employee *(ITEPA 2003 s.206)*.

Example

William was given the use of a new suit with an original cost of £400 by his employer on 5 July 2020. He bought the suit on 6 April 2021 for £50, at which date it had a market value of £120.

The benefit arising in 2020/21 will be £400 x 20% x 9/12 = £60

The benefit arising in 2021/22 will be the higher of:

1.

Second-hand value	120
Amount paid	(50)
	£70

and

2.

Cost	400
Assessed 2020/21	(60)
Amount paid	(50)
	£290

Where the asset is used partly for business purposes and partly for private purposes, the benefit charge will be reduced by an appropriate amount.

Under general principles, a class 1A NIC liability arises on the gift of assets to employees. However, a class 1 liability arises where the asset is a 'readily convertible asset' or comes within *SSCR 2001 Sch. 3 pt. IV.*

10.9.2. Readily convertible assets

'Readily convertible assets' are valued at the best estimate of the amount which will be chargeable to income tax as employment income. Therefore, for an employee who is not lower-paid, the value will be the cost to the employer of providing the asset. This is reduced by the amount of any consideration given *(SSCR 2001 Sch. 2 para. 5).*

Where one asset may be exchanged for another and the value of the interest in the second asset is greater than the value of the interest in the first asset, earnings will be the value of the second asset. Where the amount of consideration which might be given is variable, the lowest possible value of the consideration is taken.

A readily convertible asset is defined as:

1. an asset capable of being sold or otherwise realised on:
   i) a recognised investment exchange; or
   ii) the London Bullion market; or
   iii) the New York Stock Exchange; or
   iv) a market for the time being specified in PAYE regulations *(ITEPA 2003 s.702(1)(a));*
2. an asset consisting in:
   i) the rights of an assignee, or any other rights, in respect of a money debt (in sterling or another currency) that is or may become due to the employer or any other person; or

ii) property that is subject to a warehousing regime within VATA 1994 ss.18-18F or corresponding arrangements in another state which is a contracting party to the Agreement on the European Economic Area; or

iii) anything that is likely (without anything being done by the employee) to give rise to, or to become, a right enabling a person to obtain an amount or total amount of money which is likely to be similar to the expense incurred in the provision of the asset *(ITEPA 2003 s.702(1)(b))*;

3. an asset for which trading arrangements are in existence, or are likely to come into existence in accordance with:

   i) any arrangements of another description existing when the asset is provided; or

   ii) any understanding existing at the time;

   (ITEPA 2003 s.702(1)(c))

   by which the employee or a member of his household may receive an amount of money similar to the expense incurred;

4. an amount is received which enhances the value of an asset of the employee, or member of their family or household, and the asset in its enhanced state would be a readily convertible asset *(ITEPA 2003 s.697)*.

10.9.3. Beneficial interest in assets listed in Social Security (Contributions) Regulations 2001 Sch. 3 Pt. IV

Class 1 NIC is payable on any asset listed in the *SSCR 2001 Sch. 3 Pt. IV*. The liability is calculated on the amount which the asset might fetch in the open market. Where the asset is not quoted on a recognised stock exchange, the open market value is taken as the value which would be agreed in an arm's length transaction between a willing seller and a willing buyer in possession of the full facts *(SSCR 2001 Sch. 2 Pt. V para. 2(1))*.

In the cases of alcoholic liquor upon which duty has not been paid and gemstones, a value is estimated on the basis of the cost of the asset in question. A value is estimated in a similar manner for an asset which cannot be exchanged for a readily convertible asset or a non-cash voucher which is not capable of being so exchanged *(SSCR 2001 Sch. 3 Pt. IV)*.

The value of a conditional interest in shares is the difference between the market value of the interest immediately after it ceases to be conditional, or the disposal of the interest if earlier, and the amount of the consideration given for the interest plus any other amounts previously included as earnings *(SSCR 2001 Sch. 2 para. 7)*.

10.9.4. Gift to employees of computers and bicycles

The gift to an employee of either computer equipment or a bicycle, where the asset has previously been loaned and has enjoyed an exemption under ITEPA

2003 s.244 or s.320 is deemed to take place at the market value of the asset at the time the gift is made *(ITEPA 2003 s.206 (6)(b)&(c))*.

10.10. Cash Vouchers, Non-cash Vouchers and Credit Tokens

10.10.1. General principles

Subject to the exemptions below, cash vouchers given to any employees are liable to income tax and class 1 NIC. The liability is calculated on the amount of cash for which the voucher can be exchanged, unless the voucher is issued under a salary sacrifice arrangement, in which case the liability is calculated on the greater of the cash equivalent and the amount of salary foregone. No benefit arises if the benefit of the voucher would be exempt from income tax but for ITEPA 2003 s.228A *(ITEPA 2003 s.81)*.

Cash vouchers are treated as salary and PAYE must be operated. National savings certificates on which the interest is exempt and other vouchers where any sum of money obtainable would not be taxable are not treated as cash vouchers.

Subject to the exemptions below, non-cash vouchers given to employees are liable to income tax and Class 1 NIC. The liability is calculated on the cost to the person providing them less any amounts paid by the employee, unless the voucher is issued under a salary sacrifice arrangement, in which case the liability is calculated on the greater of the cost of provision and the amount of salary foregone reduced by any amount made good by 6 July following the end of the tax year *(ITEPA 2003 s.87; SSCR 2001 Sch. 2 Pt. V para. 14(2),(3))*. The tax year in which the benefit arises is the later of the tax year in which the employer incurs the cost of provision and the tax year in which the employee receives the voucher, unless it is a cheque voucher, when the benefit arises in the tax year in which the voucher is handed over in exchange for money or services *(ITEPA 2003 s.87(6))*.

Where a voucher is provided for two or more earners, the cost must be apportioned in accordance with the benefit to which each earner is entitled, if this is known at the time of the payment. Otherwise the cost will be apportioned equally *(SSCR 2001 Sch. 2 para. 15)*.

Subject to the exemptions below, credit tokens, i.e. credit card, debit card or other documents giving right to credit, given to any employee are liable to income tax. The liability is calculated on the cost to the person providing them less any amounts paid by the employee *(ITEPA 2003 s.94(2))*, unless the credit token is issued under salary sacrifice arrangements, in which case it is calculated on the greater of the cost of provision and the amount foregone reduced by any amount of the cost of provision made good by 6 July following the tax year *(ITEPA 2003 s.94A)*. However, no class 1 NIC liability arises, since the token cannot be exchanged for cash.

The benefit arises on the later of the date on which the employer incurs the expenditure and the date on which the employee receives the token or voucher *(ITEPA 2003 s.88)*.

10.10.2. Vouchers and credit tokens exempt from income tax class 1 NIC

Cash vouchers, non-cash vouchers and credit tokens are exempt from income tax and class 1 NIC if:

1. they are provided in the normal course of the employer's domestic, family or personal relationships *(ITEPA 2003 ss.73(2), 82(2), 90(2))*; or
2. they are of a kind made available to the general public and the terms on which they are made available to the employee are no more favourable than those on which they are made available to the general public *(ITEPA 2003 ss.78, 85, 93)*.

Cash vouchers will also be exempt from income tax and class 1 NIC if they were issued under a scheme which was approved by HM Revenue & Customs at the time they were issued *(ITEPA 2003 s.79)* or if the voucher enables the employee to obtain a sum which would not have been employment income if it had been received directly *(ITEPA 2003 s.80)*.

Non-cash vouchers and credit tokens for the following purposes will also be exempt from income tax and class 1 NIC:

1. transport under pre-26 March 1982 transport arrangements *(ITEPA 2003 s.86; SSCR 2001 Sch. 3 pt. V, para. 2)*;
2. car parking places near to place of employment *(ITEPA 2003 ss.266(1)(a),267(2)(a); SSCR 2001 Sch. 3 pt. V para. 3)*;
3. transport between work and home for disabled employees *(ITEPA 2003 ss.266(1)(b),267(2)(c); SSCR 2001 Sch. 3 pt. V para. 5 (a))*;
4. provision of cars for disabled employees *(ITEPA 2003 ss.266(1)(c),267(2)(d); SSCR 2001 Sch. 3 pt. V para. 5(b))*;
5. transport home for late-night working and transport provided due to the failure of car-sharing arrangements *(ITEPA 2003 ss.266(1)(d),267(2)(e); SSCR 2001 Sch. 3 pt. V para. 5(c))*.
6. third party entertainment *(ITEPA 2003 s s.266(1)(e),267(2)(f))*;
7. works transport services *(ITEPA 2003 s.266(2)(a); SSCR 2001 Sch. 3 pt. V para. 5A(a))*;
8. supporting public bus services *(ITEPA 2003 s.266(2)(b); SSCR 2001 Sch. 3 pt. V para. 5A(b))*;

9. cycles and cyclist's safety equipment *(ITEPA 2003 s.266(2)(c); SSCR 2001 Sch. 3 pt. V para. 5A(c));*
10. mobile telephones under ITEPA 2003 s.319 (exemption restricted to one phone per employee for phones available from 6 April 2006) *(ITEPA 2003s s.266(2)(d),267(2)(g); SSCR 2001 Sch. 3 pt. V para. 5A(d));*
11. travelling and subsistence during public transport strikes *(ITEPA 2003 ss.266(3)(a),267(2)(b); SSCR 2001 Sch. 3 pt. V para. 5B(a));*
12. recreational benefits *(ITEPA 2003 s.266(3)(b); SSCR 2001 Sch. 3 pt. V para. 5B(b));*
13. annual parties and functions *(ITEPA 2003 s.266(3)(ac); SSCR 2001 Sch. 3 pt. V para. 5B(c));*
14. armed forces' travel leave facilities *(ITEPA 2003 s.266(3)(d); SSCR 2001 Sch. 3 pt. V para. 5B(d));*
15. subsidised meals *(ITEPA 2003 s.266(3)(e); SSCR 2001 Sch. 3 pt. V para. 5B(e));*
16. provision of eye tests and corrective appliances for employees covered by ITEPA 2003 s.320A *(ITEPA 2003s s.266(3)(f),267(2)(h); SSCR 2001 Sch. 3 pt. V para. 5B(e)*);
17. provision for health screening or medical check-ups covered by ITEPA 2003 s.320B *(ITEPA 2003 s.266(3)(g), 267(2)(i) SSCR 2001 Sch. 3 pt. V para. 9) (see* section 9.22.37*);*
18. meal vouchers up to a maximum of 15p per day *(ITEPA 2003 s.89; SSCR 2001 Sch. 3 pt. V para. 6A*);
19. minor benefits exempted under regulations *(ITEPA 2003 s.210).*

The following non-cash vouchers and credit tokens are exempt from income tax and class 1 NIC if, and to the extent that, the conditions contained in the relevant sections are satisfied:

1. small gifts of vouchers *(ITEPA 2003 s.270; SSCR 2001 Sch. 3 pt. V para. 6(a));*
2. offshore oil and gas workers: mainland transfers *(ITEPA 2003 s.305; SSCR 2001 Sch. 3 pt. V para. 6(b));*
3. suggestion rewards *(ITEPA 2003 s.321; SSCR 2001 Sch. 3 pt. V para. 6(c));*
4. long service awards *(ITEPA 2003 s.322; SSCR 2001 Sch. 3 pt. V para. 6(d));*
5. small gifts from third parties *(ITEPA 2003 s.324; SSCR 2001 Sch. 3 pt. V para. 6(e));*
6. vouchers for childcare *(ITEPA 2003 s.270A; SSCR 2001 Sch. 3 pt. V para. 7));*
7. vouchers for incidental overnight expenses *(ITEPA 2003 s.268; SSCR 2001 Sch. 3 pt. X para. 4);*
8. vouchers or credit tokens for use in connection with a car or van in respect of which a taxable benefit arises or an exempt heavy goods vehicle *(ITEPA 2003 s.269).*

Where a voucher or token is taxable, or would be taxable there is no charge on an employee in respect of goods, cash or services obtained as a result of the use of the voucher or token *(ITEPA 2003 s.95).*

10.11. Payment Made to a Registered Pensions Scheme for the Benefit of Two or More People

If a payment is made under a registered pensions scheme with a view to providing benefits for more than one person, the amount to be treated as earnings will depend on whether the separate benefits to be provided for each of these people is known at the time the payment is made. If this is known the payment is apportioned on the basis of benefits secured by the payment. If not the payment is apportioned equally among all persons who might benefit *(SSCR 2001 Sch.2 para. 13).*

10.12. Waiver of Loan

The waiver of a loan is treated as earnings under ITEPA 2003 s.62 and is subject to income tax and class 1 NIC under general principles, unless the waiver is due to death *(ITEPA 2003 s.190).* Where a loan is made to a relative of an employee, no charge arises on the waiver of the loan provided that the employee has not received any benefit from the loan.

The loan waiver is also not assessable if it is taxable under any other provisions *(ITTOIA 2005 s.415).* These provisions take precedence over any charge under ITEPA 2003 s.403 in relation to golden handshakes.

10.13. Job-related Accommodation

10.13.1. Scope of benefit charge

Accommodation provided for employees by reason of their employment (not necessarily by the employer) is assessable on all employees unless it is:

1. job-related *(ITEPA 2003 s.99)*; or
2. provided in the normal course of personal and domestic arrangements, i.e. no benefit arises where a child is employed part-time in the parents' business *(ITEPA 2003 s.97(2))*;
3. the accommodation is provided by a local authority on terms which are no more favourable than those offered on other accommodation *(ITEPA 2003 s.98).*

It is immaterial whether the terms on which the accommodation is provided constitute a fair bargain *(ITEPA 2003 s. 97(1A)).*

Accommodation is job-related if it is:

1. necessarily provided in order for the employee to perform their duties, e.g. caretaker. In order to qualify it is necessary to demonstrate that 'for the performance of his duties the employee must live in that house and no

other'. It is not sufficient for the employer to require that the employee occupy a property under the terms of a contract of employment;

2. provided in order that the employee can perform duties better and it is usual for such accommodation to be provided, e.g. clergy. The test of whether the accommodation is required so that the employee can carry out their duties better is an objective one and is not simply a matter of the employer's opinion. For example, this will include situations where the employee is required to be on call outside their normal hours, and is in fact frequently called out and the accommodation is provided so that they have quick access to his place of employment. In order to establish whether the practice is customary, consideration must be given to how long the practice has existed and the extent to which it has achieved general acceptance by employers;
3. provided due to a threat to an individual's security arising from their work, e.g. workers at animal research laboratories.

Where the accommodation is job-related the payment by the employer of council tax and water or sewerage charges is exempt from income tax and class 1 and 1A NIC *(ITEPA 2003 s.314; SSCR 2001 Sch.3 pt. VIII para. 10)*. If the accommodation is not job-related these payments are subject to a class 1 NIC liability, whereas the accommodation itself is subject to a class 1A liability.

No benefit arises in respect of accommodation outside the UK provided by a company for a director or other officer of the company or a member of their family or household, if:

1. the company is, or is a subsidiary of a company which is, wholly owned by the director or officer or by the director or officer and other individuals and no interest in the company is partnership property;
2. the company's only or main asset is the property and its only activities are those incidental to its ownership of the property;
3. the company has either owned the interest in the property at all times since the 'relevant time'. The relevant time is defined as the time when the company first acquired the interest in the property or, if the director or officer did not acquire their interest in the company from a connected person and the company owned an interest at the time the director or officer first acquired an interest in the company, at all times since the director or officer acquired their interest.

(ITEPA 2003 s.100A)

This section is intended to give relief where a taxpayer has set up or acquired a company abroad to own a property. It does not apply where:

1. the company's interest in the property was acquired directly or indirectly from a connected company at an undervalue or derives from a interest so acquired; or
2. at any time since the relevant time expenditure on the property has been incurred directly or indirectly by a connected company; or
3. at any time since the relevant time any borrowing of the company directly or indirectly from a connected company has been outstanding, unless the borrowing is at a commercial rate or has given rise to a taxable benefit; or
4. the main purpose, or one of the main purposes, of the providing the living accommodation is the avoidance of tax or national insurance contributions.

(ITEPA 2003 s.100B)

10.13.2. Calculation of benefit

Where accommodation is not job-related, the basic benefit if the employer owns the property is its rental value less any amount reimbursed by the employee by 6 July following the end of the tax year *(ITEPA 2003 ss.105 & 106(1))*. It does not matter whether the contribution is voluntary or made under the terms of employment *(ITEPA 2003 s.105(2))*. Where a property costs more than £75,000 there is an additional benefit (see section **10.14.3** below).

The rental value is now defined by ITEPA 2003 s.110 as the rent which a landlord might reasonably be expected to obtain from letting the property if the tenant undertook to pay all the taxes and charges usually paid by a tenant and the landlord undertook to pay all the expenses, such as insurance and repairs, which are necessary to maintain the property in a state to command the rent *(ITEPA 2003 s.110(1))*.

Notwithstanding this section, HM Revenue & Customs continue to follow the previous practice (as set out in the *Employment Income Manual*) of using the annual value of a property derived from the rateable value of domestic property, which was used to calculate domestic rates before they were abolished in order to ensure continuity of treatment and prevent the need for annual revaluations. Where a property in the UK has been built, or substantially altered, since that time, HMRC will continue their practice of determining a figure for the rental value. In Scotland, the rateable value of properties was adjusted in 1985 to bring them up to a more realistic level. This was not done in the rest of the UK, and so ESC A56 provides that the rateable value in 1978 is to be used for properties in Scotland. The rental value as defined by ITEPA 2003 s.110 will therefore, in practice, only be used for properties situated outside the UK and for such properties any value used for the purpose of local property taxes will not be used.

Where an employer rents the property the basic benefit will be the higher of the rental value and the rent paid by the employer *(ITEPA 2003 s.105(4),(4A))*. Where the employer has at any time paid a lease premium in respect of lease of 10 years or less (or where there is an option to terminate the lease within 10 years of its inception) which is entered into, or is extended, on or after 22 April 2009, the benefit will be the total of the rent paid during the period and a portion of the lease calculated using the following formula:

$$\frac{\text{No. of days in period (in days)}}{\text{Term of lease (in days)}} \times \text{Amount of lease premium}$$

(ITEPA 2003 s.105A(2))

The period referred to in the numerator is the tax year, or part thereof (if the property is only occupied by the employee for part of the tax year).

Where there is an option to terminate the lease by the employer, the lessee (if not the employer) or the lessor, where the lessor is involved in providing the accommodation, the term of the lease is determined on the assumption that the option will be exercised at the earliest possible time *(ITEPA 2003 s.105B(4),(5))*.

Where a lease was extended on or after 22 April 2009, the term of the lease is taken as the period of the extension and any premium payable on the unextended lease is ignored *(FA 2009 s.71(5))*.

The value of the property used in calculating the benefit is not reduced by any loan made by the employee to the employer for the purpose of acquiring the property (it would therefore be advisable in this situation for the employee to become a part owner).

On a strict reading of the legislation it would appear that it is necessary for the payment to be made by the employee, rather than a member of their household. Although HM Revenue & Customs are unlikely to raise this point, it may be prudent to ensure that payment is made by the employee.

10.13.3. Additional accommodation benefit

There is an additional benefit chargeable if the cost of the property exceeds £75,000 *(ITEPA 2003 s.106)*.

The cost is defined as the original purchase price of the property plus the cost of any improvements before the start of the current tax year *(ITEPA 2003 s.104)*. Carrying out improvements in April or May instead of March will therefore delay their inclusion in the calculation by one year. The cost will include any amounts incurred by the person providing the property, the employer or any person connected with either of these.

The formula for calculating the additional benefit is:

(Cost of property - £75,000) x Official rate of interest at start of tax year *(ITEPA 2003 s.106(2))*

The amount of the benefit is reduced by any amount contributed by the employee.

By concession (*ESC A91*) the additional charge does not apply where the charge under ITEPA 2003 s.105 is calculated on the open market rental value.

Example

On 1 July 1998, Howard was provided with a house by his employer. The accommodation is not job-related. The rental value of the house is £1,500 and cost the employer £65,000 in 1996. In 1997, an extension was installed at a total cost of £15,000, in September 1998 a conservatory was added at a cost of £10,000 and in May 2021 there was a further capital improvement costing at a cost of £3,500. The market value of the house at 1 July 1998 was £100,000 and Howard pays £100 per month to his employer in respect of the accommodation.

The official rate of interest at 6 April 2021 was 3%.

	£	£
Rental Value		1,500
Purchase price of property	65,000	
Kitchen and Bathroom (1997)	15,000	
Conservatory (1998)	10,000	
Cost of property	90,000	
	(75,000)	
	£15,000	
Additional benefit £15,000 x 3%		450
		1,950
Less: Contribution 12 x £100		(1,200)
Total benefit		£750

Note: The cost of the improvement in 2021/22 will be included in the cost of the property from the 2022/23 tax year onwards.

10.13.4. Properties acquired more than six years before first occupied by current occupant

The formula for calculating the cost of the property is modified where:

1. the property was acquired by the employer more than six years before it was first occupied by the current employee; and
2. the cost of the property using the basic rule exceeds £75,000.

In this case, the cost used is the market value of the property at the time it was first occupied by the employee, plus subsequent improvements (excluding those made in the tax year) *(ITEPA 2003 s.107)*.

This modified rule is designed to cover properties which were acquired many years ago and whose market value is now many times the purchase price.

It is important to note that if the total of the original cost plus improvements (i.e. using the basic rule) does not exceed £75,000, this modified rule cannot apply, however high the market value. It is therefore worth noting that if a property was acquired in the 1970s for £70,000, was first occupied by the current employee in the mid 1990s and an improvement costing £10,000 is made in June 2019, the modified rule will apply for the first time in 2020/21. If the market value at the time the property was first occupied by the employee was £300,000 this will lead to a very substantial increase in the accommodation benefit.

Example

Assuming that the property in the previous example had been acquired in 1989 the calculation would be:

	£	£
Rental Value		1,500
Market Value July 1998	100,000	
Conservatory (1998)	10,000	
Cost of property	110,000	
	(75,000)	
	£35,000	
Additional benefit £35,000 x 3%		1,050
		2,650
Less: Contribution 12 x £100		(1,200)
Total benefit		£1,450

10.13.5. Salary sacrifice option

If the employee has the choice between the provision of accommodation and additional salary, the amount of the benefit will be the higher of the figure obtained using the normal rules and the salary sacrificed *(ITEPA 2003 s.103A)*. Where the cost of providing the accommodation does not exceed £75,000, the benefit is reduced by any amounts made good by 6 July following the tax year *(ITEPA 2003 s.103A(7),(8))*.

Where the amount of the salary sacrifice is less than the amount calculated under ITEPA 2003 ss.103-107, the salary sacrifice will be taxed under the general charging provisions and only the excess will be charged under ITEPA 2003 ss.103-107.

No benefit arises where the provision of accommodation would be exempt, but for ITEPA 2003 s.228A.

10.13.6. Living accommodation provided to more than one employee in same period

Where the same accommodation is provided to more than one employee in the same period, e.g. a married couple who are both employees, the total benefit assessed on all relevant employees will not exceed the charge which would have arisen had the accommodation been provided to a single employee *(ITEPA 2003 s.108).*

10.13.7. Accommodation used partly for business purposes

Where an employee uses part of the accommodation as an office, a deduction may be claimed in respect of the portion of the benefit charge which relates to the part of the property used for business purposes *(ITEPA 2003 s.364).* If there are two separate parts to a property, one domestic and one business, a benefit charge only arises on the portion of the annual value and the cost of the property which is attributable to the domestic part.

10.14. Assets Available for Private Use

Where an employer loans an asset to an employee, or a member of his family or household, there will be an annual taxable benefit of 20% of the 'annual value' of the asset, unless the terms on which it is made available prohibit private use and no private use is made of the asset during the tax year. This is defined as the annual rental value in the case of land *(ITEPA 2003 s.205(3)(a))* and the market value of the asset when first provided in the case of other assets *(ITEPA 2003 s.205(3)(b)).* In both cases any further costs in providing the asset must be added *(ITEPA 2003 s.205(4)* and any amount reimbursed by the employee must be deducted *(ITEPA 2003 s.203(2)).*

Where the employer rents the asset, the taxable benefit will be the higher of the 20% charge and the rent paid by the employer *(ITEPA 2003 s.205(2)(b)).*

A deduction may be made *pro rata* where, for more than 12 hours during a day the asset:

(i) is not in a condition fit for use;
(ii) is undergoing repair or maintenance;
(iii) cannot be lawfully used;
(iv) is in the possession of someone other than the employee, member of his family or household or his employer;
(v) is used by someone other than the employee, member of his family or household; or
(vi) is used by the employee solely in the performance of his duties of employment.
(ITEPA 2003 s.205A(2))

Where an asset is shared between more than one employee at the same time, the amount of the benefit charged to each employee is first determined in the usual manner and then reduced in a just and reasonable manner *(ITEPA 2003 s.205B).*

In practice, HM Revenue & Customs will ignore incidental costs of acquisition. A benefit will arise, for example, if an employee sells an asset to the employer for more than its market value or transaction costs incurred by an employee are reimbursed.

In many cases the market value of the asset will be the same as the cost to the employer, but this will not be the case where the asset is second-hand or the asset consists of, for example, a uniform bearing the employer's name and logo. In these cases the market value is likely to be considerably less than the original cost.

This benefit will continue to be charged as long as the employee has the use of the asset. Therefore, if this period exceeds five years, the employee will be taxed on more than the original cost of the asset.

No benefit arises if the asset is provided solely for work purposes, or if private use of the asset is 'not significant' *(ITEPA 2003 s.316(2))*. In interpreting this phrase HMRC do not solely look at the proportion of use which is private, but also at the motive of the employer in giving the employee use of the asset. The mixed-use problem is likely to arise in the case of computers provided to employees, and if the sole motive for providing the computer is to enable them to perform work duties at home, e.g. downloading work rosters, any private use will be considered to be not significant, even if the amount of time for which the computer is being used privately is as great as, or even greater than, the amount of time for which it is being used for work purposes. In order to ensure that the 'not significant' test is met, employers should ensure:

1. that the policy about private use is clearly stated to the employees; and
2. the circumstances in which private use is permitted, which may include asking employees signing an agreement acknowledging company policy and the disciplinary consequences of misuse; and
3. any decision not to recover costs of private use from employees must be a commercial one based on the impracticality of doing so, rather than be motivated by a desire to reward employees.

If there is a separately identifiable cost relating to the asset which is incurred by the *employee* and reimbursed by the employer, e.g. broadband, this will be taxed as a benefit. If there is mixed use of this additional facility and there is no practical way to identify the business proportion, e.g. the broadband package provides unlimited access and there are no separate billing arrangements, the benefit is exempt provided that the private use is not significant and does not affect the cost of the package.

If an employee purchases a fractional share of the asset the decision in *Vasili v Christensen (2004) (STC 935)* means that they are likely to be taxable on the full cost of the asset, with no deduction for the proportion of the asset which they own.

10.15. Expenses Connected with Living Accommodation

A taxable benefit arises where an employer provides accommodation, and also pays ancillary expenses, such as utility bills, wages of a housekeeper or provides furniture (assessed at 20% of the cost to the employer) *(ITEPA 2003 s.315).*

This benefit is assessable regardless of whether the accommodation itself is job-related, but if the accommodation is job-related the amount of the benefit is restricted to 10% of the employee's net earnings. These are an employee's total earnings (excluding any benefit under this heading) less allowable deductions.

The payment by the employer of an employee's council tax is exempt if the accommodation is job-related *(ITEPA 2003 s.314).*

Example

Clarke occupies a house provided by his employer. The following ancillary services were paid by the employer in 2021/22:

Electricity	£500
Gas	£350
Wages of gardener	£1,000
Furniture	£3,000

Clarke made no payment in respect of the property. Their salary was £16,000 and they made a payment of £1,000 p.a. to a registered pension scheme.

If the accommodation is not job-related the assessable benefit will be:

Electricity	500
Gas	350
Wages of gardener	1,000
Furniture £3,000 x 20%	600
	£2,450

If the accommodation is job-related the benefit is restricted to 10% x (£16,000 - £1,000) = £1,500.

10.16. Cars

10.16.1. Scope of benefit

A benefit will arise where a car is made available for private use by an employee or member of his family by reason of his employment. The benefit is reduced by the amount of any contribution made by the employee, provided that the contribution is made by 6 July following the end of the tax year *(ITEPA 2003 s.114).* It is immaterial whether the terms on which the car is made available constitute a fair bargain *(ITEPA 2003 s. 114(1A))*. A car is not treated as being made available to an individual by reason of his employment where:

1. it is made available in the normal course of the employer's domestic, family or personal relationships; or
2. the employer carries on a vehicle hire business, the vehicle made available is of the same kind as those made available to the public, the vehicle is hired to the employee in the normal course of business, so that the employee is acting as an ordinary member of the public.
   (ITEPA 2003 s.117)

Two points should therefore be noted:

1. in order to avoid a charge the employee should not be allowed to use the car for private purposes and must not actually do so. It would be advisable to include the prohibition on private use in the employee's contract of employment and/or to take out business-only insurance or ensure that it is kept overnight at the employer's premises. If these precautions are taken, the car may qualify as a pool car. It should be remembered that travel between home and work will count as private use;
2. where a car is not supplied by the employer, e.g. a car supplied by a third party to a local sports personality, there will be a benefit.

10.16.2. Cost of car

The amount of the benefit is based on the cost of the car. This is defined as the list price when new, i.e. before any fleet discounts etc. obtained by the employer and including any customs duty, VAT and delivery charge, plus the list price of additional extras, whether installed at the time of purchase or later *(ITEPA 2003 ss.122, 123 & 126-131)*. This includes the cost of a number plate, although the additional cost of providing a personalised number plate does not give rise to an additional benefit.

Where there is no list price, a notional price will be used, i.e. a price which might reasonably be expected to equate to a list price *(ITEPA 2003 s.124))*.

This, however, excludes:

1. mobile phones made available for use with the car;
2. optional extras costing less than £100 *(ITEPA 2003 s.126(3))*;
3. features to enable a car to be driven by a person holding a disabled person's badge either where they are fitted at the time when the car is first provided or when the employee first becomes disabled *(ITEPA 2003 s.125(2)(c))*. This includes not only features designed specifically for the disabled, but also features such as power steering which facilitate driving for the disabled *(ITEPA 2003 s.172)*; and

4. security features, such as armour or bullet-resistant glass installed in order to counter a threat to the employee's personal physical security which arises wholly or mainly because of the nature of the employee's employment *(ITEPA 2003 s. 125A).*

The cost of converting a car to run on road fuel gases is not included in the cost of the car *(ITEPA 2003 s.125(2)(b)).* If a car is manufactured to run on such gases, the cost of the car may be reduced by an amount which reasonably represents the cost of manufacture attributable to enabling the car to do so *(ITEPA 2003 s.146).*

If an employee is required to drive a car with automatic transmission by reason of disability and the cost of such a car is greater than that of an equivalent manual car, the benefit charge is calculated on the cost of the equivalent manual car *(ITEPA 2003 s.124(A)).*

A capital contribution to the cost of the car by the employee may be deducted from the cost up to a maximum of £5,000 *(ITEPA 2003 s.132).*

10.16.3. Cost of classic cars

The benefit is calculated by reference to the market value (including accessories) on the last day of the tax year (or on the last day on which the car was provided to the employee) if the car is:

1. over 15 years old at the end of the tax year; and
2. has a market value of over £15,000; and
3. the open market value is greater than cost.

(ITEPA 2003 s.147)

10.16.4. Calculation of benefit

The benefit is calculated as a percentage of the cost of the car. The percentage is graduated according to the car's emission of carbon dioxide and other pollutants. The percentages applicable are given in the table on page **231**.

Where no information on CO_2 emissions is available and the car has an internal combustion engine, the percentage will depend on the engine capacity.

Engine Capacity	
Up to 1,400cc	24%
1,401 – 2,000cc	35%
2,001 and above	37%

(ITEPA 2003 s.140(2))

Where a car does not have an internal combustion engine, the percentage is 0% if the car cannot emit CO_2 under any circumstances (such as an electically-powered car); otherwise the percentage is 37% *(ITEPA 2003 s.140).*

A voucher in respect of private use of a car, where this use is subject to a class 1A liability, is exempt from class 1 NIC.

Where a disabled person is obliged to drive an automatic car due to their disability, the percentage will be based on the closest available model with manual transmission *(ITEPA 2003 s.138).*

The benefit charge covers all the normal running expenses paid by the employer, such as the road fund licence, insurance, MOT and repairs and maintenance, even where these are provided under a salary sacrifice arrangement. The benefit charge does not cover:

1. the cost of a chauffeur *(ITEPA 2003 s.239(5))*. This could prove very expensive for an employee who is disqualified and who is required to drive as part of his job;
2. fuel provided for private motoring *(ITEPA 2003 s.149).*

Example

Emma's employer made a petrol car available to her in 2021/22 which cost £18,500 in 2018. At the time of purchase a CD player costing £350 was fitted and in 2020 a mobile telephone was fitted at a cost of £140. Emma paid £150 p.m. for the use of the car. The car's emissions rating is 130g/km.

The assessable benefit will be:

	£
Purchase price	18,500
CD player	350
	£18,850

The percentage applicable will be 31%.

The benefit will therefore be

	£
£18,850 x 31%	5,844
Contribution £150 x 12	(1,800)
	£4,044

10.16.5. More than one car made available

Where more than one car is made available to the employee at different times during the year, the benefit must be calculated separately for each car. The benefit charge for each car will be reduced *pro rata.*

10.16.6. Car unavailable for part of year

The benefit will be reduced *pro rata* where:

1. a car is first made available or ceases to be available during the year;
2. a car is unavailable for a continuous period during the year of at least 30 days *(ITEPA 2003 s.143).* The 30-day period may span more than one tax year. Where a car is unavailable for a period of less than 30 continuous days and a replacement car is provided during that period, no benefit

arises on the replacement car where it is of similar quality and the provision of the replacement is not part of a scheme to give an employee a better car *(ITEPA 2003 s.145).*

The withdrawal of a car must be made in writing and it may be advantageous to do this where an employee will not be in position to use the car, e.g. illness or working abroad. A car is not treated as being unavailable simply due to the employee not being in a position to drive, either through illness, absence abroad or disqualification.

10.16.7. Use of car by family members and shared use

An employee will not be taxed on a car made available for private use to a member of their family or household if the person to whom the car is made available is chargeable on the benefit in their own right, i.e. the family member is also an employee *(ITEPA 2003 s.169).*

Where two or more employees have the use of a single car the total benefit charged will not exceed the benefit which would have been charged if it had been made available to a single employee. The benefit will be apportioned on a reasonable basis *(ITEPA 2003 s.148(2)).*

10.16.8. Salary Sacrifice Arrangements

Where a salary sacrifice is made in order to obtain the car and the emissions' rating does not exceed 75g/km, the benefit will be the higher of the benefit charge calculated using the normal rules and the salary sacrificed in cases *(ITEPA 2003 s.119).* Where the emissions' rating exceeds 75g/km and the benefit charge on the employee is the relevant amount, where this is greater than the modified cash benefit.

The relevant amount is defined as:

i) the salary foregone in respect of the car or any other benefit connected with the car provided to the employer or member of their household other than the provision of fuel or a driver; less
ii) any allowable capital contribution (see section **10.17.2)** multiplied by the appropriate percentage and pro-rated if the car was unavailable for part of the year (see section **10.17.6**); and less
iii) any payments made by the employee for the private use of the car.

The modified cash benefit is the benefit charge calculated using the normal rules, except that any capital contribution towards the cost of the car is ignored. There are special rules for determining the modified cash benefit in the case of classic cars.

(ITEPA 2003 ss.120A, 121A, 121B).

Example

Peter had the use of a petrol-driven car costing £30,000 with an emissions' rating of 140g/km throughout 2021/22 except for a period of 42 days when it was off the road for repairs following an accident. At the time of purchase accessories costing £1,000 were fitted and Peter made a capital contribution of £3,000 towards the cost of the car and paid £2,000 for the use of the car in 2021/22. He forewent salary of £15,000 in 2021/22 for the use of the car.

Relevant amount

	£
Salary foregone	15,000
Less: Capital contribution x 33%	(990)
Payment for use of car	(2,000)
Relevant amount	£12,010

Modified cash benefit

	£
Cost of car	30,000
Accessories	1,000
	£31,000
Modified cash benefit £31,000 x 33% x 323/365	£9,053

Since the relevant amount exceedsthe modified cash benefit, the benefit charge on Peter is £12,010.

10.16.9. Summary of car benefit percentages

Cars registered before 6 April 2020

Emissions' rating (g/km)	Petrol/RDE2 Diesel	Non RDE2 Diesel[4]
0	1	
1-50	14	
51-54	15	
55-59	16	
60-64	17	
65-69	18	
70-74	19	
75-79	20	24
80-84	21	25
85-89	22	26
90-94	23	27
95-99	24	28
100-104	25	29
105-109	26	30
110-114	27	31
115-119	28	32
120-124	29	33
125-129	30	34
130-134	31	35
135-139	32	36
140-144	33	37
145-149	34	37
150-154	35	37
155-159	36	37
160 and over	37	37

[4] The supplement does not apply where a car registered on or after 1 September 2017 meets the Real Driving Emissions Step 2 standard.

Cars registered on or after 6 April 2020

Emissions' rating (g/km)	Petrol/RDE2 Diesel	Non RDE2 Diesel[5]
0	1	
1-50	13	
51-54	14	
55-59	15	
60-64	16	
65-69	17	
70-74	18	
75-79	19	23
80-84	20	24
85-89	21	25
90-94	22	26
95-99	23	27
100-104	24	28
105-109	25	29
110-114	26	30
115-119	27	31
120-124	28	32
125-129	29	33
130-134	30	34
135-139	31	35
140-144	32	36
145-149	33	37
150-154	34	37
155-159	35	37
160-164	36	37
165 and over	37	37

(ITEPA 2003 ss.140 and 141)

Electric Cars

Range (miles)	Registered before 6 April 2020	Registered from 6 April 2020
130 or over	2	1
70-129	5	4
40-69	8	7
30-39	12	11
Under 30	14	13

[5] The supplement does not apply where a car registered on or after 1 September 2017 meets the Real Driving Emissions Step 2 standard.

10.17. Fuel for Private Use

An additional benefit will arise if the employer provides fuel for private use *(ITEPA 2003 s.149).* No benefit will arise if:

1. the employer only provides fuel for business motoring; or
2. the employee is required to, and does, reimburse the employer for all fuel provided for private use by 6 July following the end of the tax year. There is no reduction for partial reimbursement.

(ITEPA 2003 s.151)

If a benefit arises, the amount of fuel provided for private use is irrelevant; the benefit is calculated as a notional figure (£24,600 in 2021/22) multiplied by the percentage used for calculating the car benefit *(ITEPA 2003 s.150).* The fuel charge is reduced *pro rata* where a car is unavailable for at least 30 days *(ITEPA 2003 s.152(1)).* The charge will also be proportionately reduced where, for a part of the year, either fuel is not made available, it is only made available for business use or the the employee is required to, and does, reimburse the cost of fuel for private use by 6 July following the end of the tax *(ITEPA 2003 s.152(2)).* The reduction under ITEPA 2003 s.152(2) does not apply if there is a time later in the tax year where none of these exclusion apply *(ITEPA 2003 s.152(3).* HM Revenue & Customs publish a table of minimum rates, which they will accept as being full reimbursement. These are liable to change frequently in line with changes in fuel prices and the up-to-date rates are to be found at:

www.hmrc.gov.uk/cars/advisory_fuel_current.htm.

Where fuel is provided under a salary sacrifice arrangement, the benefit charge is the greater of the charge calculated using the normal rules and the amount of salary foregone *(ITEPA 2003 s.149A).* No fuel benefit arises where the fuel would be exempt, but for ITEPA 2003 s.228A.

It is important to remember that, unlike contributions towards the provision of the car itself, there is no reduction in the benefit for any partial contribution towards the cost of fuel. Therefore, it would be more tax-efficient to treat any contribution made by the employee as being for the provision of the car rather than fuel.

If reimbursement for fuel provided for private use has not been made by the end of the tax year, later settlement will be acceptable where there is no unreasonable delay. If there is an unintentional administrative error by the employer and it is found that not all the cost of fuel for private use has been reimbursed, a subsequent settlement of the outstanding amount is acceptable provided it is made within 30 days of the discovery of the error.

References in this section to fuel do not include any energy supplied to a car which cannot, under any circumstance, emit CO_2 *(ITEPA 2003 s.149(4))*.

10.18. Pool Cars and Vans

No benefit arises on an employee in respect of a pool car or van *(ITEPA 2003 ss.167 & 168)*. A pool vehicle must satisfy the following conditions:

1. the car must be used by more than one employee and not used predominantly by one employee;
2. the car must normally be kept overnight at the premises of the employer;
3. any private use by an employee must be merely incidental to the business use.

Where a vehicle fails to qualify as a pool vehicle, the benefit charge is apportioned between all employees using the vehicle.

SP2/96 gives guidance on incidental private use. Its interpretation requires consideration of whether the private use is independent of the business use or follows on from the business use. Examples of the latter would be where an employee takes a pool car home due to an early start the next morning or uses the car to go to a restaurant whilst away on business. Incidental private use will always be a small proportion, although the reason for private use is also relevant.

There is also no fixed definition of what constitutes use predominantly by one employee or incidental private use. In the latter case the private mileage must clearly be small in relation to the business mileage, but even where this is the case a proportion of private use will not always be allowed. An example may be where an employee uses a pool car for their annual holiday. It would be advisable to have strict rules on the use of such cars to ensure that no benefit inadvertently arises.

Where a car and driver are provided to take an employee between work and home in order for the employee to work on confidential papers in the car, HM Revenue & Customs at one time accepted that all such journeys constituted incidental private use, regardless of their frequency. HMRC will now look at all the circumstances, e.g. whether the papers are needed for a meeting at the employee's home or are to be delivered to a client.

Where a person employed as a chauffeur takes a pool car to their home overnight this will not in itself disqualify the car from being treated as a pool car.

10.19. Vans and Heavier Commercial Vehicles

10.19.1. Scope of benefit

A benefit arises where a van or other commercial vehicle is made available for private use by an employee or his family *(ITEPA 2003 s.154).* ITEPA 2003 s.114(3) ensures that no double charge arises by excluding any charge under any other sections.

A van is considered to be available for private use unless the terms under which it is made available prohibit private use *(ITEPA 2003 s.118(1)).* A van is considered to be made available by reason of employment unless the employer is an individual and the van is made available as part of normal family or domestic arrangements *(ITEPA 2003 s.118(2)).*

ITEPA 2003 s.155 provides that there is no benefit if the van may only be used, and is in fact only used, for business purposes and for the purpose of commuting between home and work or if the van cannot, under any circumstances, emit CO_2.

A van is a vehicle up to 3.5 tonnes in weight which is designed for carrying goods *(ITEPA 2003 s.115).* Vehicles designed for carrying goods over this weight are classified as heavier commercial vehicles.

10.19.2. Vans and heavier commercial vehicles – calculation of benefit

If a van is provided wholly or mainly for business use and normal commuting, so that and private use is insignificant, there is no benefit *(ITEPA 2003 s.155(4)).* Otherwise, if a van is provided for private use by one employee only, the benefit charge is £3,500 if the van is capable of emitting CO_2 *(ITEPA 2003 s.155(1B)(b)),* reduced by any amounts which the employee is required to and does actually pay for the use of the van *(ITEPA 2003 s.159).* If the vehicle cannot produce CO_2 emissions under any circumstances there is no benefit charge from 2021/22 onwards *(ITEPA 2003 s.155(1B)(a)).*

Where a van is only available for a part of the year or is unavailable for a period of at least 30 days the charge is reduced *pro rata (ITEPA 2003 s.158).*

Where a van is available for private use by more than one employee on a shared basis, the benefit is shared equally amongst all users on a just and reasonable basis *(ITEPA 2003 s.158).*

Where a van is made available under a salary sacrifice arrangement, the benefit is the amount of salary foregone for the van or any other benefit connected with the van provided to the employee or member of their household, other than fueld or a driver, less any amounts paid for the use of the van by 6 July following the tax year, where the amount of salary foregone is greater than the benefit calculated using the normal rules, but ignoring any reduction for unavailability or shared use *(ITEPA 2003 s.154A).* No benefit arises where the van would have been exempt, but for ITEPA 2003 s.228A.

Where a van is temporarily replaced (i.e. for a period of less than 30 days) the replacement van is ignored and the benefit is calculated on the original van for the entire period *(ITEPA 2003 s.159).*

There is an additional benefit of £669 if fuel is provided for private use unless the employee is required to, and actually does, reimburse the employer for all fuel for private use *(ITEPA 2003 ss.160-162).* There is no relief for partial reimbursement. The fuel benefit is reduced if the van is not available for any part of the tax year *(ITEPA 2003 s.163(1)).* The charge will also be proportionately reduced where, for a part of the year, either fuel is not made available, it is only made available for business use or the the employee is required to, and does, reimburse the cost of fuel for private use by 6 July following the end of the tax *(ITEPA 2003 s.163(3)).* The reduction under ITEPA 2003 s.152(2) does not apply if there is a time later in the tax year where none of these exclusion apply *(ITEPA 2003 s.163(4).* There is no benefit if the vehicle cannot produce CO_2 emissions under any circumstances.

Where a van is available to more than one employee the fuel benefit is shared in a similar manner to the benefit charge for the van itself *(ITEPA 2003 s.164).*

Where the fuel is provided under a salary sacrifice arrangement, the benefit is the greater of the amount foregone and the benefit calculated using the usual rules *(ITEPA 2003 s.160A).* No benefit arises where the provision of fuel would be exempt, but for ITEPA 2003 s.228A.

Pool vans (defined in the same way as pool cars) are exempt *(ITEPA 2003 s.168).*

Where a van is made available to a member of the family or household of an employee, who is themselves an employee of the same employer, ITEPA 2003 s.169A provides that there can be no double charge on both the employee and the member of the family or household provided that the van is made available to the member of the family or household on the same terms as vans made available to other employees in similar employment and it is normal commercial practice to provide a van to such employees.

No benefit arises in respect of a heavier commercial vehicle, except in the unlikely event that it is provided wholly or mainly for private use *(ITEPA 2003 s.238).* Non-cash vouchers or credit tokens provided to be used for obtaining the use of such a vehicle are exempt *(ITEPA 2003 s.269(1)).*

10.20. Emergency Vehicles

No benefit arises where an emergency vehicle is available mainly for business travel provided that the terms on which the vehicle is provided prohibit private use other than when the employee is on call or engaged in on-call commuting and no private use is actually made of the vehicle except in those circumstances *(ITEPA 2003 s.248A(1)&(2))*.

An emergency vehicle is defined as a vehicle with a flashing light attached to it for use in emergencies or a vehicle which would have such a light attached to it except for the fact that it would present a security risk to the user by making it apparent that they were a member of the emergency services *(ITEPA 2003 s.248A(3))*.

On-call commuting is defined as using the vehicle for travel between two places which comprises, or substantially comprises, ordinary commuting where it is necessary to do so in order that the person is available to respond to emergencies as part of his normal duties *(ITEPA 2003 s.248A(8))*.

10.21. Beneficial Loans

10.21.1. Calculation of benefit

A benefit may arise where an employer makes a loan to an employee which is either interest-free or at a low rate of interest *(ITEPA 2003 s.174)*. This also covers loans made to the employee's relatives (defined as his spouse, siblings, lineal ancestors and descendants and their spouses) unless no benefit arises to the employee *(ITEPA 2003 s.174(1)(b), 174(5)(b))*. It is immaterial whether the terms on which the loan is made constitute a fair bargain *(ITEPA 2003 s. 173(1A))*.

A benefit does not, however, arise where such a loan is made to any other member of the employee's household *(ITEPA 2003 s.174(5)(a))*, but any loan made by an employer will be treated as having been made by reason of his employment unless covered by the above exemption *(ITEPA 2003 s.174(1), (2))*.

Where a loan is made jointly to two or more employees the benefit is apportioned between them in a 'fair and reasonable manner' *(ITEPA 2003 ss.183(4) & 185)*, although no guidance is given as to how this is applied in practice.

There are two possible ways of calculating the amount of the benefit:

1. the balances outstanding at the start of the tax year (or the date the loan is first made) and the end of the tax year (or date that the loan is repaid in full) are averaged and interest is charged on this amount using the official rate(s) of interest in force during the tax year *(ITEPA 2003 s.182); or*

2. interest is charged at the official rate of interest on the amount outstanding on a daily basis *(ITEPA 2003 s.183).*

Interest paid by the employee is deducted from these amounts *(ITEPA 2003 s.175(3)(b)).*

HM Revenue & Customs will normally use the first method, but either the employee or HM Revenue & Customs may insist on using the second method. HMRC will, however, only do this if the amounts outstanding during the year were considerably higher than at the start or end of the year and a large amount of tax is likely to be at stake. An election to use the exact method must be made by the first anniversary of the filing date of the return to which the loan relates *(ITEPA 2003 s.183(2)).*

Example

Paul has a loan from his employer. The balance at 6 April 2021 was £11,000 and on 5 July 2021 he repaid £2,400 of the loan. The official rate was 3% until 5 September 2021, when it rose to 4%. Paul paid interest of £150 during the year.

Using the averaging method the benefit would be:

$\frac{£11{,}000 + £8{,}600}{2}$ x 3% x 153/365	123
$\frac{£11{,}000 + £8{,}600}{2}$ x 4% x 212/365	227
	350
Less: Interest paid	(150)
Benefit	£200

Using the second method the benefit would be:

£11,000 x 3% x 91/365	82
£8,600 x 3% x 62/365	43
£8,600 x 4% x 212/365	199
	324
Less: Interest paid	(150)
Benefit	£174

It would therefore benefit Paul to elect for the second method to be used.

Where a loan is provided under a salary sacrifice arrangement where the amount foregone is less than the amount of interest which would be payable on the loan at the official rate of interest (i.e. any interest actually paid is ignored), the benefit is the amount of salary foregone less any interest actually paid *(ITEPA 2003 s.175A).* No benefit arises where the loan would be exempt, but for ITEPA 2003 s.228A.

10.21.2. Rate of interest – foreign currency loans

HM Revenue & Customs may set a different official rate in the case of foreign currency loans where the borrower normally lives in the foreign territory, has lived there at some time in the previous six years and the loan is made by reason of their employment *(ITEPA 2003 s.181(2))*. HMRC will only do this where interest rates in the territory concerned are lower than those in the UK.

10.21.3. Replacement loans

Where a beneficial loan is replaced by a loan made at arm's length the replacement loan will not automatically be a beneficial loan, even if, for example, the replacement loans have been made by a subsidiary of a commercial lender which has been set up for the purpose *(ITEPA 2003 s.186)*. The normal tests will apply in determining whether the loan is a beneficial loan.

Where an employee has left the employment through which they obtained the original loan and this loan is subsequently replaced through such an arrangement, ITEPA 2003 s.188(3) treats the replacement loan as a loan obtained by reason of his employment. This ensures that any subsequent waiver of the loan will be taxable.

A replacement loan will be treated as a loan obtained by reason of employment in order to prevent abuse of the averaging provisions in the following circumstances:

1. the original loan is replaced by another loan from the same employment; *or*
2. the original loan is replaced by a loan not from the employment and the second loan is subsequently replaced by another loan from the employment within the tax year or within 40 days from the end of the tax *(ITEPA 2003 s.186(1), (2))*.

In order for the anti-avoidance provisions to apply, the benefit of the second employment-related loan must be obtained from the same employer as, or an employer connected with, the employer through which the benefit of the original employment-related loan was obtained *(ITEPA 2003 s.186(4))*.

10.21.4. Exempt loans

The following types of loan are exempt from a benefit charge under this section:

- loans which are made in the normal course of an employer's business *(ITEPA 2003 s.176(2))*; and
    1. are available to potential customers for comparable purposes and on comparable terms (except for the rate charged) at the time the loan is made (e.g. cheap mortgages to bank employees). HM Revenue & Customs have stated that this criterion would not be met where, for example, the lending criteria are relaxed for employees or fees or charges in connection with the application are reduced or waived; and
    2. a substantial proportion of loans made at about the same time are made to the public (i.e. members of the public at large with whom the lender

deals at arm's length). The proportion is not fixed but it is accepted that this condition will be satisfied where the proportion of loans made to the public is greater than 50%, although a lower proportion may also qualify. A common-sense interpretation will be applied in determining the period of time to be treated as 'at about the same time'; and

3. the loan continues to be on terms comparable with loans to the public (i.e. loans made for the same or similar purposes) and any changes are made in ordinary course of business *(ITEPA 2003 s.176(6), (7))*.

(ITEPA 2003 s.176(3)&(4))

- loans made in the course of the lender's domestic or personal arrangements *(ITEPA 2003 s.174(5))*;
- qualifying beneficial loans, i.e. loans, the interest on which is tax deductible, either under ITEPA 2003 s.178, ITA 2007 s.383 or which is deductible from trading income or property income. These cover:
  1. loans made in order to purchase an interest in a trading or professional partnership or to make a contribution to capital or an advance to such an interest where the borrower is an active participant;
  2. loans to an individual to purchase ordinary shares in a close company or an employee-controlled company or to make a loan to a close company or company associated with a close company;
  3. loans to personal representatives of a deceased person before the grant of representation in order to enable them to pay IHT. The status of a qualifying loan lasts for one year from the date it is taken out;
  4. a loan to enable a loan under any of the above categories to be paid off;
  5. a loan the interest on which is deductible from the profits of a trade or profession carried on by the borrower which is treated as trading income or property income;
  6. a loan to enable an office holder to purchase machinery used in his work, e.g. an orchestral player who is required to purchase his or her own instrument;
  7. a loan to purchase a life annuity provided that the annuitant is at least 65 years of age and the loan is secured on their main residence.
- the loan represents an advance of deductible business expenses provided that:
  1. the amount advanced at any one time does not exceed £1,000; and
  2. the money advanced is spent within six months; and
  3. the employee is required to account to the employer at regular intervals for expenditure incurred.

  (SP7/79)

10.21.5. De minimis exemption

No benefit will arise if the total of non-qualifying loans did not exceed £10,000 at any time during the year *(ITEPA 2003 s.180)*. If the total value of non-qualifying loans exceeds £10,000 at any time during the year a benefit arises on the whole balance, not just the excess. This exemption will, for example, cover most season ticket loans.

It is very important to appreciate that a small increase in the amount advanced to an employee may in these circumstances give rise to a disproportionate benefit charge on the employee.

10.22. Scholarships

Scholarship income is exempt in the hands of the scholarship holder *(ITTOIA 2005 s.776)*, but a scholarship provided to a director or employee earning over £8,500, or member of their family, may be taxable under ITEPA 2003 s.212 if it is provided by reason of his employment unless:

1. a scholarship is awarded from a separate trust scheme;
2. the award is made to a person in full-time education or training; and
3. no more than 25% of the awards made by the trust during the tax year are made by reason of a person's employment.

(ITEPA 2003 s.213)

Where this exemption does not apply the amount of the benefit is the sum paid from the fund to the person holding the scholarship *(ITEPA 2003 s.214)*.

10.23. Relocation Packages and Guaranteed Selling Price Schemes

Where an employee sells his house to his employer the cost for the purpose of determining the cash equivalent *(ITEPA 2003 s.203(2)*&(3)) will be the sum of the price paid for the house by the employer and any other valuable consideration given for it plus any costs which would normally be met by a seller but are borne by someone other than the employee. Therefore, the payment or re-imbursement of costs by the employer which are not normally borne by the seller is ignored *(ITEPA 2003 s.326)*.

HM Revenue & Customs do not consider that payment of the proceeds before the transfer of the beneficial interest necessarily constitutes a beneficial loan, provided that the beneficial interest in the property is eventually transferred by the employer and the contract between the employee and the employer or relocation company is one of sale and not of loan. The benefit will not therefore end at the date of the transfer of the beneficial interest. Each case will be decided on its own facts, but the benefit will be taken to have come to an end when:

1. the employee has entered into a binding contract to dispose of the property; and
2. the employer has permanently surrendered possession of the property in accordance with the contract; and
3. the sale proceeds have been paid in full or in part.

Only costs incurred in connection with the transfer are covered by this concession since it is the facility to transfer the property to the employer or the relocation company which falls within ITEPA 2003 s.201. Costs incurred by the employer or relocation company in connection with a subsequent sale are not taxable under this section and, therefore, are not covered by the concession.

10.24. Medical Treatment and Medical Insurance

The provision of any sort of medical treatment or of private medical insurance is taxable unless it consists of providing medical treatment or private medical insurance for treatment outside the UK in cases where the employee is outside the UK for the purposes of his employment *(ITEPA 2003 s.317(1))*.

The provision of routine medical checks will not constitute a benefit, whether they are provided in-house or by an outside organisation, but a benefit will arise where an employer reimburses an employee for the cost of check-ups.

Where an employee is required to use a VDU as part of his duties no benefit will arise on the provision of eyesight tests or spectacles wholly for use at the VDU. Where the spectacles are for general use, but a special prescription is required for VDU a portion of the cost of the special prescription is allowable.

No benefit will arise on the provision of medical treatment for an injury or illness which is work-related, i.e. it is a risk normally associated with a particular trade or profession and is not a risk common to the population as a whole and which is intended to return the employee to the state of health they enjoyed before the illness or injury. An example would be treatment provided to sportsmen by their clubs.

Chapter 11. National Insurance Contributions

National Insurance Contributions and Employees

11.1. Earnings Period

11.1.1. General rules

Class 1 NIC are payable on an employee's earnings during an earnings period. This period will depend on the interval at which an employee is paid, and will generally, but not necessarily, be a week or a month (irrespective of the fact that months are of unequal length) *(SSCR 2001 regs. 2 & 3(1))*. Contributions for company directors are always calculated using an annual earnings period, regardless of when payments are made.

Unlike PAYE, contributions are not calculated on a cumulative basis. Therefore, contributions are calculated on any commission or bonus by reference to the earnings limits for the earnings period in which it is paid.

If extra payments are made at a regular interval shorter than the regular pay interval, the shorter interval will become the earnings period, unless HM Revenue & Customs direct that the longer or longest period be used on the grounds that the greater or greatest part of an employee's pay is paid at the longer interval *(SSCR 2001 reg. 3(2B))*, subject to the overriding provision that an earnings period cannot be less than seven days *(SSCR 2001 reg. 3(1))*. The direction will only be made if the greater part of an employee's earnings are paid at a period longer than that determined by using the normal rules, e.g. an employee is paid a relatively low weekly wage and a very substantial quarterly and/or annual bonus. A direction will, in general, only be made if it results in additional contributions of at least £125 per year. A direction may be made even if the extra payments are not intended as a method of avoiding contributions.

The first earnings period of a tax year starts on the first day of the tax year *(SSCR 2001 reg. 2)*. Therefore, for weekly-paid employees a year will occasionally contain 53 weeks, if they are paid on both 6 April and the following 5 April and employees paid on a four-weekly rather than monthly basis could similarly pay contributions on 56 weeks of earnings in a tax year.

11.1.2. Earnings period in unusual circumstances

HM Revenue & Customs' guidance CWG2 (2021) sets out the earnings period in the following unusual circumstances:

Interval of less than a week	All earnings paid in one tax week are aggregated and contributions are paid if the primary threshold is exceeded.
Irregular pay intervals of more than a week	The irregular earnings period equal to the period of payment is used each time. Exact percentage method must be used.
Employee works and is paid every other week/four weeks	A two-week/four-week earnings period is used.
Employee taken on for a particular job and is paid only once	Earnings period is duration of employment, unless this is less than seven days, in which case earnings period is seven days.

Payments made to employees under the Employment Rights Act 1996 where the payments represent earnings liable to contributions may have their own earnings period and are not aggregated with other payments made at the same time. Where payments are made under the provisions of the Employment Protection (Consolidation) Act 1978 the following rules apply:

1. guarantee payments paid for weeks where there is no work or medical suspension payments paid where an employee is suspended on medical grounds are subject to the normal earnings period rules;
2. the earnings period for awards of arrears in cases of orders for reinstatement or re-engagement or continuation of employment is the period for which arrears must be paid, or a week if longer;
3. the earnings period for pay due following a protective award is the 'protected period' stated in the award, or a week if longer.

Where arrears are paid, the earnings limits applicable are those for the date of payment, not the period to which payment relates.

11.1.3. Payment not made on usual day

If a payment is not made on the usual day, it is deemed to have been made for the earnings period in which the usual day falls *(SSCR 2001 reg. 7(1)(a), (2)(a))*, e.g. a weekly wage normally paid on a Friday is paid on a Wednesday, where Friday is Christmas Day.

Where the usual day is in one tax year, but the payment is actually made in another, e.g. a weekly wage paid early due to Easter, the payment is treated as having been made in the year in which it is paid *(SSCR 2001 reg. 7(3))*.

11.1.4. Payment of earnings of more than one period made in same earnings period

If two weeks' earnings are paid together, two earnings periods of a week are used. If the second week falls in a new tax year, the tax rates for the old tax year are used, but the earnings are not aggregated.

If two payments are received in an earnings period because of, for example, a permanent change in the date of payment, each payment has its own earnings period based on the regular interval.

11.1.5. Change in length of earnings period

Where the length of the earnings period is changed:

1. where the new earnings period is shorter, contributions on payments made after the change are calculated separately from contributions on payments made before the change;
2. where the new earnings period is longer, contributions on payments made after the change are calculated separately from contributions on payment made before the change unless payment has already been made at the old short interval in the first longer period. In this case, all payments in the first longer period are aggregated and total contributions payable for that period are adjusted to take account of amounts already paid. Where such a change involves entry into a contracted-out pension scheme, contributions on payments in the new earnings period are calculated at the contracted-out rate.

11.1.6. Change of normal payment date

Where there is a change in the normal payment date, but the payment interval remains unchanged, e.g. payment on 15th of the month changes to payment on 1st of the month, payment can be made as normal where the first payment on the new date falls in te following tax week or tax month from the last payment on the old date. Where both dates fall within the same tax week or tax month, the first payment on the new date is treated as an extra payment for that period, i.e. both payments need to be aggregated.

11.1.7. Extra payments made in earnings period

Where extra payments, e.g. overtime or commission, are made separately from the normal payment of wages and salaries, all payments made in an earnings period are aggregated.

11.1.8. Joiners and leavers

Where a new employee joins, the earnings period is the period at which the employee will be paid regularly. This will apply to the first payment, even if the employee has at that time only been employed for a few days.

Where an employee leaves payments are calculated in the usual manner.

If an employee receives accrued holiday pay on the day of leaving employment, the holiday pay is therefore aggregated with the normal pay for the last period and treated as paid in the same earnings period. Where an employee takes their accrued holiday entitlement after leaving work, i.e. the contract of service does not end until after the holiday period, the holiday pay is spread over the period of the holiday.

If an employee receives payments after leaving, contributions on regular payments, such as the final wages or salary payment, accrued holiday pay, week-in-hand payments or an expected bonus, contributions are calculated in the normal manner *(SSCR 2001 reg. 25 & Sch. 3)*, whereas contributions on a one-off payment, such as a retrospective bonus are, according to the official view, calculated using a weekly earnings period.

Where an employee receives two or more payments together and these are all regular payments, the earnings period rules will apply to each payment separately. Where some payments are regulqar payments and some are irregular payments, contributions are calculated on the total sum using the usual earnings periods. Where all payments are irregular sum, contributions are calculated on the total using a weekly earnings period.

Contributions on Statutory Maternity Pay (SMP) received after an employee's contract of service has ended are calculated using the weekly earnings period if it is paid in a lump sum, unless it is paid with the last payment of wages or salary, in which case the two payments are aggregated. If SMP is paid at the same regular interval as that at which the employee was previously paid, the period used during employment is used, otherwise the payment interval is the actual period between payments.

No contributions are payable on payments made after an employee dies.

11.2. Aggregation of Earnings

11.2.1. General principles

Where a taxpayer has more than one employment, they will pay class 1 contributions on his total earnings from all employments. In general, contributions will be calculated on each employment separately, but SSCBA 1992 Sch. 1 para. 1(1)(a) and SSCR 2001 regs. 14 & 15 require earnings from different employments to be aggregated where these are:

1. with the same employer;
2. with employers carrying on 'business in association with each other'. Employers are 'associated' for the purpose of these regulations if they are carrying on business in association, which involves the sharing of profits or losses, or to a large extent sharing resources such as accommodation,

equipment, personnel and customers, such that their fortunes are to some extent interdependent;
3. with employers, only one of which is deemed by regulation to be the secondary contributor;
4. with employers of whom none is the secondary contributor because some other person is deemed by regulation to be the secondary contributor.

11.2.2. Exceptions to requirement to aggregate earnings

Earnings from jobs with different employers are not aggregated and contributions are calculated on each jobs separately, ignoring the other, unless the employers carry on business in association with each other, i.e. if the respective businesses serve a common purpose, or, to a significant degree, share things such as accommodation, personnel, equipment or customers. In threse cases payments must be aggregated, unless it is 'not reasonably practicable' to do so. Guidance on the interpretation of the practicability test is given in the HMRC guidance *CWG2 (2021).*

- the onus is on the employer to show that aggregation is not reasonably practicable but in the case of disagreement between the employers and HMRC, a tribunal shall make a determination. This determination is not a once and for all decision and may change if circumstances change;
- the cost to the employer of aggregating the earnings, including not just financial cost, but also time and the effect on the business, is an important, but not decisive factor and this must be balanced against the loss of NIC and the benefit or pension entitlement of the employee. In *Mailier v Austin Rover Group (1989) (2 All ER 1087)* three principles were agreed:
    1. that 'reasonably practicable' is a narrower test than 'physically possible';
    2. that the risk of the loss of contributions must be balanced against the cost of removing the risk ; and
    3. that account must be taken of the likelihood of the risk arising. The view of HMRC is that aggregation is a known and recurring event, therefore employers can only rely on this to a very limited extent.

The following factors are taken into account:

1. whether the payroll software can, as a fact, aggregate earnings. An assumption that it cannot do so is insufficient;
2. whether the payroll software has been tailored by an internal IT department or can be upgraded internally;
3. whether the payroll system has been changed recently;
4. whether the provider of an outside system offers upgrading as part of the package;

5. whether it is possible to upgrade the system, the costs of doing so, or whether it would be necessary to buy a new system;
6. whether there is an internal IT team which could upgrade the system cheaply;
7. if work has to be carried out manually, the costs of carrying out the work;
8. whether the employer already has a manual support resource for payroll problems;
9. whether new staff would be required;
10. the number of employees affected;
11. total number of employees on payroll;
12. whether employees have similar pay periods;
13. whether there is a recurring need for aggregation or whether it is a one-off situation;
14. amount of NIC at stake and how this compares with the cost of compliance;
15. whether there has been a material change in the labour force since the decision not to aggregate;
16. Equal Opportunities legislation may be relevant if most of the employees affected are, say, female and their benefits would be affected.

11.3. Rate of Class 1 National Insurance Contributions

Primary class 1 contributions are payable at a rate of 12% by earners between the ages of 16 and 65 (for men) and 60 (for women) on earnings falling between the primary threshold (£184 p.w., £797 p.m. or £9,568 p.a. in 2021/22) and the upper earnings limit (UEL) (£967 p.w., £4,189 p.m. or £50,270 p.a. in 2021/22) and at a rate of 2% on earnings above the UEL.

Secondary class 1 contributions are payable by the employer on earnings above the secondary threshold (£170 p.w., £737 p.m. or £8,840 p.a.) at 13.8% (2021/22). For employees under 21 or apprentices under 25 the threshold is £967 p.w., £4,189 p.m. or £50,270 p.a. Employers are entitled an employment allowance of up to £3,000 p.a. which they can offset against their secondary contributions *(National Insurance Contributions Act 2014 s.1)*. where two or more companies are connected they receive a single allowance between them.

It is not possible to recover secondary contributions from an employee *(SSCBA 1992 Sch. 1 para. 3A)* (except in certain circumstances involving employment-related securities).

11.4. Class 1A Contributions

Class 1A contributions are payable by the secondary contributor at 13.8% (2021/22) on the cash equivalent of the benefit, i.e. the benefit charge on the employee, for the majority of benefits in kind. The amount is to be calculated to the nearest penny. In general the cash equivalent will be the same as the benefit charge on the employee since the exemptions to the class 1A charge contained in *SSCR 2001 reg. 40(2), (4)-(6))* are mirrored in exemptions elsewhere. The following exemptions from the class 1A charge should, however, be noted:

1. payments in kind upon which class 1 contributions are payable, e.g. cash and non-cash vouchers;
2. benefits covered by a PAYE dispensation;
3. benefits provided to lower paid employees e.g. accommodation benefit;
4. benefits included in a PAYE settlement agreement;
5. benefits otherwise not required to be entered on a form P11D or excluded from the class 1A charge;
6. childcare provision where this is provided by the employer or the employer contracts for places in private nurseries and the reimbursement of childcare expenses up to a limit of £50 per week;
7. fuel for use in an employee's own car;
8. payments to registered pension schemes liable to a benefit charge, but exempted from a class 1 liability under *SSCR 2001 Sch. 3 pt. VI, paras. 2(b), 3-5, 7, 10 & 11).*

Class 1A contributions are paid annually, whereas class 1 contributions are paid in respect of the earnings period of the employee.

Where an employee is given a cash alternative to the benefit, class 1A NIC is payable where the employee receives and retains the benefit. The liability is based on the amount chargeable on the employee. Therefore, if the cash alternative is greater than the value of the benefit using the normal rules, the liability is based on the amount of the cash alternative. Where an employee receives the cash, class 1 NIC is payable.

11.5. Calculation of Contributions

There are two methods of calculating the contributions:

1. Exact percentage method. This is the more accurate of the two methods.
2. Tables method. Contributions are calculated using one of a number of tables supplied by HM Revenue & Customs. The tables are issued annually and each table is applicable to employees in particular circumstances. Table A is for male employees between 16 and 64 and female employees between 16 and 59 who are in not contracted-out employment and do not have another employment where they pay NIC on earnings at or above the UEL. Table B is used for not contracted-out reduced rate contributions for married women and widows under 60. A number of other tables are also used in specific circumstances.

Example

David has a monthly earnings period and earns £4,500 per month. He has a company car which gives rise to a benefit charge of £3,000 p.a.

The monthly contributions payable are:

Primary Contributions

	£
(£4,189 - £797) x 12%	407.04
(£4,500 - £4,189) x 2%	6.22
	£413.26

Secondary Contributions

Class 1	£
(£4,500 - £737) x 13.8%	£519.29
Class 1A (annual)	
£3,000 x 13.8%	£414

11.6. Class 1A Charge Where Benefits Provided by Third Parties

Where a benefit is provided by a third party, the third party may under certain circumstances be liable to pay the class 1A liability if the benefit has not been facilitated or arranged by the employer. The third party must notify HM Revenue & Customs of its liability in writing *(SSCBA 1992 s.10ZA)*. Under SSCBA 1992 Sch. 1, para. 3A it is not permitted to recover a class 1A charge from an employee.

Where an employee concurrently holds two or more employments and a single benefit is provided in connection with more than one employment the class 1A charge is shared equally between the employers *(SSCR 2001 reg. 36)*.

Where an employee changes jobs, both employers are liable to pay the portion of the class 1A liability which relates to the period during which the employee was employed by them.

Non-cash vouchers provided to a lower paid employee by a third party are liable to a Class 1A charge *(SSCBA 1992 s.10ZB)*.

11.7. Earners over Pensionable Age

Where a payment which would normally be made after an employee's 60th or 65th birthday is made before the birthday no primary contributions are payable *(Social Security (Contributions) Regulations 2001 (SI 2001/1004 reg. 28)*.

Conversely, primary contributions are payable where a payment due before the birthday is actually made after the birthday *(SSCR 2001 reg. 29)*.

A pension will only be calculated on contributions paid up to 6 April preceding the relevant birthday.

Secondary contributions at the not contracted-out rate are due on payments to employees after their 60th or 65th birthday.

A certificate of age exception in respect of employees over pensionable age will be issued to an employee on application. Employers must continue to deduct primary contributions until the employee gives them this certificate and should deduct contributions at the standard rate, since they will be liable for any amounts under-deducted.

Contributions over-deducted may be refunded by the employer once a certificate is produced and this amount may be deducted from the employer's next payment to the employee, provided that this is in the same year. The employer is responsible for the custody of the certificate, but it must be returned to an employee if they leave.

11.8. Notional Payments of Class 1 Contributions

There is a notional payment where earnings exceed a lower earnings limit (£120 p.w., £520 p.m., £6,240 p.a. in 2021/22), but do not reach the primary threshold.

Although no payment is made, the notional payment preserves the earner's entitlement to benefits, such as the basic state pension. If the earnings exceed the lower earnings limit, but not the primary threshold, the earnings must be recorded, even though no contributions are payable.

National Insurance Contributions and the Self-Employed

11.9. Class 2 Contributions

11.9.1. Liability to Pay Contributions

Class 2 contributions are paid at a flat-rate of £3.05 per week by earners between the ages of 16 and 65 (for men) or 60 (for women). Class 2 contributions give entitlement to benefits, except unemployment benefit and the earnings-related element of the state pension scheme. There are slightly more than 52 weeks in a year. Therefore, every few years there will be a 53-week year in order to catch up. An earner will only cease paying class 2 contributions when they cease being ordinarily self-employed. Therefore, contributions are still payable even if they have no income in a particular week, e.g. holiday and illness *(Social Security (Categorisation of Earners) Regulations 1978 (SI 1978/1689 Sch. 2))*.

No class 2 contributions are payable if an earner is:

- not present in the UK in the contribution week for which the contribution is to be paid *(SSCR 2001 reg. 145(1)(c))*;
- has not been resident in the UK for at least 26 of the previous 52 contribution weeks *(SSCR 2001 reg. 145(1)(d))*;

- receiving sickness benefit, invalidity benefit or maternity allowance for the whole week;
- incapable of work for the whole week;
- in legal custody or imprisoned for the whole week;
- receiving unemployability supplement or invalid care allowance *(SSCR 2001 reg. 43(1))*.

The working week excludes a Sabbath (not necessarily Sunday) observed for religious reasons *(SSCR 2001 reg. 43(2))*.

11.9.2. Small Profits' Threshold

Class 2 contributions are not payable if an earner's self-employed earnings fall below a small profits' threshold (£6,515 in 2021/22) *(SSCBA 1992 s.11(4))*. This is calculated on the taxpayer's total actual earnings from all self-employed activities shown in the accounts during the tax year, i.e. the adjustment and basis period rules do not apply *(SSCR 2001 reg. 45(2))*. There is no deduction for class 2 or 4 contributions, but the following receipts are disregarded:

- receipts from employment as an employed earner shown in the accounts;
- receipts under the Welfare Reform Act 2007 s.60(1).

(SSCR 2001 reg. 45(2)(b)).

Class 2 contributions are paid on the basis of estimated earnings for the year, and will be repaid if it subsequently transpires that the earnings do not exceed the exemption limit.

A certificate is issued where exemption is granted, which will state the period covered by the exemption (normally a tax year or a period running to the following 5 April) *(SSCR 2001 reg. 44(4))*. The earner is obliged to present the certificate to any Officer of HMRC on request *(SSCR 2001 reg.44(6))*. If any of the conditions for issuing the certificate cease to be fulfilled the certificate ceases to be valid *(SSCR 2001 reg.44(5)(a))*. Certificates may be renewed annually provided the conditions continue to be fulfilled. Since the non-payment of contributions may affect an earner's entitlement to benefits they may continue to pay contributions notwithstanding the certificate *(SSCR 2001 reg. 46(b))*.

Retrospective claims may be made provided they are made in writing with supporting evidence by 31 January following the end of the tax year for which the exemption is to apply *(SSCR 2001 reg. 47(1), (2))*. Contributions paid during the period will be repaid to the earner, but any benefits claimed on the basis of these contributions must be repaid by the earner.

If an exemption certificate is issued and the taxpayer's earnings do in fact exceed the exemption limit for a tax year, contributions must be made retrospectively. These will be deemed to have been paid in the tax year to which they relate, provided that they are paid by the end of the following tax year. If they are paid after this date, they will be treated as having been paid in the year of actual payment, and must be paid at the highest of all the rates which have applied in any of the years between the year of liability and the year of payment *(SSCBA 1992 s.12(3))*.

Class 2 contributions paid in error in excess of the annual maximum, i.e. where a taxpayer is both an employed earner and a self-employed earner, will be repaid provided that they exceed a *de minimis* limit of 1/15 of a contribution at the primary percentage payable on earnings at the upper earnings limit for class 1 contributions *(SSCR 2001 reg.52A(4)(a))*. An application must be made within six years of the end of the tax year in which the contributions were paid.

11.10. Class 4 Contributions

11.10.1. Liability to pay contributions

Class 4 contributions are earnings-related and are payable on trading profits and gains *(SSCBA 1992 s.15(1))*. A deduction may be claimed for loss relief claimed under ITA 2007 ss.64, 72, 83 or 89. The losses to be offset are restricted to losses arising from activities, the profits or gains of which would be liable to class 4 contributions. Where loss relief has been claimed under ITA 2007 s.64 or s.72 and part of the loss has been offset against non-trading income, the portion offset against non-trading income may be carried forward and offset against future trading income for the purpose of calculating class 4 contributions *(SSCBA 1992 Sch. 2, para. 3 (4))*.

No deduction is permitted by SSCBA 1992 Sch. 2 para. 3(2) for personal reliefs, pension contributions, interest deductible under ITA 2007 s.24, and excess interest payments under ITA 2007 s.88 or s.94, although relief is given under SSCBA 1992 Sch. 2 para. 3(5) for interest payable under ITA 2007 s.383.

Contributions are payable at 9% on profits and gains between a lower limit and an upper limit (£9,568 and £50,270 respectively in 2021/22) and at a rate of 2% on profits in excess of the limit.

Examples

1. Susan has adjusted profits of £21,000 for the year ended 30 June 2021. Her class 4 contributions for 2021/22 are (£21,000 - £9,568) x 9% = £1,028.88.
2. Huw has adjusted profits of £55,000 for the year ended 30 September 2021. His class 4 contributions for 2021/22 are:

	£
(£50,270 - £9,568) x 9%	3,663.18
(£55,000 - £50,270) x 2%	94.60
	£3,757.78

The following are excepted from paying class 4 contributions:

- persons not resident in the UK during the year to which contributions relate *(SSCR 2001 reg. 91(b))*.
- persons under the age of 16 *(SSCR 2001 reg. 93(2),(6))* or over pensionable age *(SSCR 2001 reg. 91(a))* at the start of the tax year. Persons under the age of 16 must apply to HMRC for exception *(SSCR 2001 reg. 93(3))* and a certificate will be issued. An application must be made before the start of the tax year to which it relates or, if made after the start of the tax year, before contributions become due.
- divers and diving supervisors whose earnings are treated as trading income by virtue of ITTOIA 2005 s.15 *(SSCR 2001 reg. 92)*. Class 1 contributions are payable on these earnings.

11.10.2. Special Class 4 contributions

Special class 4 contributions are payable where an earner is deemed to be self-employed for the purpose of NIC, but has earnings in excess of the lower earnings limit, which are chargeable (but not necessarily charged) as employment income for the purpose of income tax, e.g. examiners, moderators and invigilators *(Social Security (Categorisation of Earners) Regulations 1978 (SI 1978/1689, Sch. 1, pt. II)*. These are calculated in the same manner as class 1 contributions *(SSCR 2001 reg. 105)* but are collected directly under the PAYE system. A notice is issued and the contributions are payable within 28 days of the notice unless an appeal is made *(SSCR 2001 reg. 106)*. The employer must record the amount of such earnings, the category letter and the contributor's National Insurance number *(SSCR 2001 reg. 104)*.

11.10.3. Exception from Class 4 contributions

An exception from class 4 contributions may be obtained in respect of earnings which are treated as being from an employed earner's employment for the purpose of NIC, but which are treated as trading income. These earnings will instead be liable to class 1 contributions and a certificate of exception will be issued *(SSCR 2001 regs. 94 & 95)*. An application must be made for exception from class 4 contributions and a certificate should be requested using form RD 901 before the start of the tax year, although late claims may be accepted *(SSCR 2001 reg. 94(2)&(3))*. If the certificate is issued erroneously, due to false information being provided or information being withheld, the certificate may be revoked and class 4 contributions will be payable *(SSCR 2001 reg. 97(4))*. Where a certificate is revoked, the contributions payable are calculated by HMRC and the earner must provide all necessary information, and the contributions will be payable within a period as directed by HMRC *(SSCR 2001 reg.98(a)&(b))*. Because the profits on which the class 1 contributions are payable are not known by the time the first instalment becomes payable on 31

July, a deferment may be granted where an application for exception from class 4 contributions is made before the start of the tax year *(SSCR 2001 reg. 95(4))*. The contributions will be collected in arrears.

11.11. Annual Maximum Contributions

Where a taxpayer has more than one employment, they will pay class 1 contributions in respect of his earnings from all employments. Similarly, where a taxpayer is both employed and self-employed, they will pay class 1 contributions in respect of his earnings from employment and class 2 and, if applicable, class 4 contributions in respect of his self-employed earnings. There is, however, a limit to the total NIC that an individual may pay in a tax year. There are, in fact, three separate limits which may apply in different situations:

1. where an individual has earnings from more than one employment, contributions are only payable on aggregate earnings up to the UEL;
2. where an individual has earnings from employment and self-employed earnings on which class 2 contributions, but not class 4 contributions are payable (i.e. the profits are below the lower limit), the total class 1 and class 2 contributions payable at the main rate may not exceed 53 weekly class 1 contributions at the main rate;
3. where an individual has earnings from employment and self-employed earnings on which both class 2 contributions and class 4 contributions are payable, the total class 1, class 2 and class 4 contributions may not exceed 53 weekly class 2 contributions plus the maximum class 4 contributions.

Example

Peter has a monthly earnings period and earns £4,150 per month and also has self-employed income with constant profits of £6,500 pa. The total NIC payable by Peter is restricted to:

Primary Class 1 contributions at main rate (£967 - £184) x 53 x 12%	£4,979.88

The contributions Peter will pay are:

Primary Class 1 contributions (£4,150 - £797) x 12 x 12%	4,828.32
Class 2 contributions £3.05 x 53	161.65
	£4,989.97

Contributions of £10.09 will therefore be refunded to Peter.

Elizabeth has trading profits of £48,000 and also employment income of £1,000 per month. The maximum contributions payable are:

Class 2 contributions £3.05 x 53	161.65
Class 4 contributions (£50,270 - £9,568) x 9%	3,663.18
	£3,824.83

The contributions paid by Elizabeth will be:

NATIONAL INSURANCE CONTRIBUTIONS

Primary Class 1 contributions (£1,000 - £797) x 12 x 12%	292.32
Class 2 contributions £3.05 x 53	161.65
Class 4 contributions (£48,000 - £9,568) x 9%	3,458.88
	£3,912.85

Class 4 contributions of £88.02 will be repaid to Elizabeth.

Chapter 12. Pensions

12.1. Introduction

The main features of the UK pensions regime are:

1. Each taxpayer is entitled to a single lifetime allowance, which for most taxpayers is £1,073,100 in 2021/22, on the amount of pension savings which qualify for tax relief. Benefits in excess of the limit taken in the form of pensions are taxed at 25%, or 55% if they are taken as a lump sum *(FA 2004 s.215(2))*.
2. Pension rights accrued at 6 April 2006 are protected by the regime.
3. The ability to enjoy tax relief in respect of contributions made (in the case of a defined contribution pension scheme) or pensions accrued (in respect of a defined benefit scheme) in any particular year by or on behalf of an individual is limited to an individual's annual allowance. For the tax year 2021/2022, the annual allowance is £40,000 for taxpayers earning up to £240,000. For individuals who have not flexibly accessed a money purchase arrangement this will taper at a rate of £1 for every £2 of income in excess of this amount until it falls to a minimum figure of £4,000 at an income level of £312,000. Provided that a taxpayer is a member of a registered pension scheme, any unused annual allowance may be carried forward for a maximum of three years *(FA 2004 ss.227, 228&228A)*. Contributions in excess of the annual limit plus any unused relief brought forward are taxed as the top slice of a taxpayer's income for the year *(FA 2004 s.227(4A))*. Contributions must be offset against the annual allowance of the current tax year and thereafter against the unused allowance of earlier years on a FIFO basis *(FA 2004 s.228A(6))*. It should, however, be noted that an individual may only obtain tax relief in respect of his own contributions (to a registered defined contribution scheme) insofar as they do not exceed the greater of £3,600 per annum (i.e. contributions of £2,880 grossed up by 100/80) or 100% of their relevant UK earnings (up to the annual allowance) that are subject to income tax for the tax year in question. If an individual has no relevant UK earnings, they may still qualify for tax relief on contributions to a registered pension scheme up to £3,600 per annum (see section **12.2** below).
4. Pension funds may offer members a tax-free lump sum of up to 25% of the value of the pension fund.
5. Members of registered pension schemes may draw retirement benefits whilst they are still working, if the rules of the scheme permit. At present, (other than in cases of ill-health) pensions may not generally be taken before the age of 55.

12.2. Scope of Regime

Pension schemes qualifying for relief under the regime are called *registered pension schemes (FA 2004 s.150(2))*. A registered pension scheme is a scheme registered with HM Revenue & Customs providing for benefits to be paid to members on death, retirement, the onset of serious ill-health or incapacity, the attainment of a given age or in similar circumstances *(FA 2004 s.150(1))*.

An employer or employers may establish a pension scheme to provide benefits to all employees of that or those employer(s) or any other employer, regardless of whether it may also provide benefits to other persons. These pension schemes are called *occupational pension schemes (FA 2004 s.150(5))*. An employer whose employees may benefit from an occupational pension scheme is termed a *sponsoring employer (FA 2004 s.150(6))*. An occupational pension scheme may have more than one employer "participating" in it.

There are, in principle, no restrictions on the type of individual who may join a registered pension scheme *(FA 2004 s.151)*. In practice, it may be difficult to obtain tax relief if an "active member" is not an employee of a sponsoring employer. A member is an active member if there are currently arrangements under the scheme for the accrual of benefits to, or in respect of, that member *(FA 2004 s.151(2))*. If a member is not an active member and is entitled to the present payment of benefits, that member is a pensioner member *(FA 2004 s.151(3))*. If a member has accrued rights under a scheme, but is not an active or a pensioner member, they are a deferred member *(FA 2004 s.151(4))*. A member who has rights under the scheme which are directly or indirectly attributable to pension credits is termed a pension credit member *(FA 2004 s.151(5))*.

The pension scheme may be a *money purchase arrangement*, a *defined benefit arrangement* or a *hybrid arrangement*, containing a mixture of money purchase and defined benefit arrangements. Under a money purchase scheme (sometimes referred to as a "defined contribution scheme"), contributions are paid into the scheme by and/or on behalf of a member, invested on behalf of that member, and the resulting "pensions pot" then used to fund the benefits when they come into payment. In contrast, under a defined benefit arrangement, a member's pension will be calculated by reference to a formula (typically 1/60 of the member's "final pensionable salary" for each year of pensionable service) and thus the member's pensions entitlement is not (directly) dependent upon the contribution rate(s) and/or investment return earned by the contributions.

Personal pension schemes are arrangements made between individuals and the pension provider, who will usually be an insurance company or similar organisation. Employers may make contributions to such schemes, but play no role in administering them. Employers may use such schemes to provide a 'group personal pension scheme' for their employees, but this is, in fact, just a collection of individual personal pension schemes, usually provided by the same provider. Money invested in personal pension schemes is invested by the provider and, upon retirement, the balance in the fund is used to purchase an annuity (and possibly a tax-free lump sum). The value of the pension will therefore depend on the stock market at the date of retirement.

12.3. Registration of Pension Schemes

Pension schemes must be registered with HM Revenue & Customs in order to qualify for tax relief. An application to register a pension scheme must contain all information which may reasonably be required, must be in a form specified by HMRC and must contain a declaration by the scheme administrator and any other declarations required by HMRC *(FA 2004 s.153(2))*. HMRC must register the pension scheme unless they believe that any information contained in the application is incorrect or any of the declarations are false *(FA 2004 s.153(4))*. If the scheme is approved as a registered scheme, HMRC will state a day on which the scheme is to take effect *(FA 2004 s.153(7))*. An annuity contract which does not provide for the immediate payment of benefits, but which secures benefits under a registered pension scheme, is treated as becoming a registered pension scheme on the day on which it is made *(FA 2004 s.153(8))*. The scheme administrator may appeal to the Tax Tribunal against a refusal to register a scheme within 30 days of the notification of the decision.

HMRC may withdraw the registration of a pension scheme if:

1. the scheme chargeable payments made during any 12-month period exceeds 25% of the aggregate of the sums paid and the market value of assets held by the scheme;
2. the scheme administrator fails to pay a substantial amount of tax, or interest on tax;
3. there is a significant failure by the scheme administrator to provide information to HMRC or if information or a declaration is materially false or inaccurate; or
4. there is no scheme administrator.

(FA 2004 ss.157&158)

The scheme administrator may appeal to the Tax Tribunal against a decision to de-register a scheme within 30 days of the notification of the decision. Schemes which were approved under the old regime are automatically treated as being registered under the new regime.

12.4. Payments by Registered Pension Schemes

A registered pension scheme may only make the following types of payments (known as "authorised member payments") to, or in respect of, persons who are, or who have been, members, i.e. surviving spouse and dependents:

1. pension payments or pension death benefits permitted under the pension scheme rules or pension death benefit rules of Finance Act 2004 *(FA 2004 ss.165 & 167)*. These include annuities and income withdrawals *(FA 2004 s.165(2))*;
2. lump sums payments or lump sum death benefits permitted under the pension scheme rules or pension death benefit rules of Finance Act 2004 *(FA 2004 ss.166&168)*;
3. recognised transfers *(FA 2004 s.169)*;
4. scheme administration member payments *(FA 2004 s.171)*;
5. payments under a pension sharing order *(FA 2004 s.164)*;
6. payments prescribed by regulations made by the Board of Inland Revenue (now HM Revenue & Customs).

12.5. Pension Payments

No pension payment may normally be made until the member reaches the normal minimum pension age of 55, unless the ill-health condition is met, which requires that:

(a) the scheme administrator has received evidence from a registered medical practitioner that the member is (and will continue to be) incapable of carrying on the member's occupation because of physical or mental impairment, and

(b) the member has in fact ceased to carry on the member's occupation.

(FA 2004 Sch. 28, pt. 1)

If the member dies within 10 years of becoming entitled to a pension, an annuity or alternatively secured pension may continue to be made to any other person until the end of the 10-year period, but no other payment may be made after the member's death.

12.6. Contributions

12.6.1. Member Contributions

A member of a registered pension scheme may claim tax relief on relievable pension contributions if:

- the member has earnings from relevant UK earnings (income from employment or self-employment) chargeable to UK income tax during the tax year; or
- the member is resident in the UK at some time in the tax year; or

- the member was resident in the UK at the time when they joined the scheme and has been resident in the UK at some time in the five tax years preceding the tax year in which relief is claimed; or
- the member, or the member's spouse, has general earnings from overseas Crown employment subject to UK tax.
  (FA 2004 s.189(1),(2))

The following contributions are not relievable pension contributions:

- contributions made after the member has reached the age of 75;
- contributions which are life assurance premium contributions. These are defined by FA 2004 s.195A as contributions where rights under a non-group life policy are (or later become) held for the purpose of the pension scheme and the contributions are treated as being paid in respect of premiums under the life policy;
- contributions made by the member's employer;
- amounts paid by HM Revenue & Customs under the Pension Schemes Act 1993 ss.42A(3) or 43 or the Pension Schemes (Northern Ireland) Act 1993 s.38A(3) or s.39 *(FA 2004 s.188(3))*; and
- a pension credit which increases the rights of the member under the pension scheme is only treated as a contribution on behalf of the member if it derives from a pension scheme which is not a registered pension scheme *(FA 2004 s.188(4))*. Any amounts recovered by an employer under the Pension Schemes Act 1993 s.8(3) or the Pension Schemes (Northern Ireland) Act 1993 s.4(3) recovery of minimum payments are treated as relevant pension contributions *(FA 2004 s.188(6))*.

Any other transfers of sums representing accrued rights under a pension scheme are not treated as relevant pension contributions *(FA 2004 s.188(5))*.

A member is entitled to relief on the greater of contributions on 100% of their relevant UK earnings (subject to the annual allowance), or on £3,600 *(FA 2004 s.190)*. If a member's earnings are less than £3,600 but is making a contribution of more than their level of earnings, they can only get tax relief on more than 100% of earnings (i.e. the difference between £3,600 and earnings) if the contribution is made by the relief at source method.

Tax relief for contributions is given at source at the basic rate *(FA 2004 s.192)* unless the pension scheme is permitted to operate a net pay arrangement *(FA 2004 s.191)*. Under the relief at source approach, the individual makes his relievable pension contribution after deducting a sum equivalent to the basic rate of tax, and the scheme administrator then claims back a sum equivalent to the basic rate of tax from HMRC. A higher rate tax payer can also obtain relief for the balance via his tax return *(FA 2004 s.192(4))*. A pension scheme may operate a net pay arrangement if it is an occupational pension scheme, the member is an employee of a sponsoring employer and relief for contributions made by all members of the scheme is given under a net pay arrangement *(FA 2004 s.191(3))*. Where a net pay arrangement is in operation the contribution is deducted from the member's employment income, so that relief is given through the PAYE system *(FA 2004 s.193)*. If it is not possible to give full relief by deduction from employment income, e.g. a member earns less than £3,600, that member may make a claim to deduct excess contributions from total income *(FA 2004 s.193(4),(6))*.

If full relief cannot be given either through relief at source or through a net pay arrangement, a member may claim relief through self-assessment *(FA 2004 s.194)*. FA 2004 s.195 allows the transfer of certain shares acquired under an HMRC-approved employee share scheme to be transferred to a registered pension scheme by a member.

12.6.2. Employers' Contributions

Employers may claim relief on contributions to registered pension schemes on behalf of their employees. Relief may be claimed by deduction from trading profits or as an expense of management *(CTA 2009 pt 16 ch. 2)*. Employers' contributions are not taxable on members as benefits in kind. This exemption is an excluded exemption under ITEPA 2003 s.228A, therefore it still applies where the employer's contributions are made under a salary sacrifice arrangement.

Where an employer's contribution in the current chargeable period is more than 210% of the contribution in the preceding chargeable period, relief for the excess contribution, provided that it is at least £500,000 *(FA 2004 s.197(1)-(3))*, may be spread over the current and immediately following periods, depending on the amount of the excess contribution.

Amount of Excess Contribution	**Fraction and Chargeable Period or Periods**
£500,000 or more, but less than £1,000,000	Half in the current chargeable period and half in the chargeable period immediately following
£1,000,000 or more, but less than £2,000,000	One third in the current chargeable period and one third in each of the two chargeable periods immediately following
£2,000,000 or more	One quarter in the current chargeable period and one quarter in each of the three chargeable periods immediately following

(FA 2004 s.197(4)&(5))

Example

A Ltd makes contributions to a registered pension scheme of £800,000 in year ended 31 March 2021 and £2,000,000 in year ended 31 March 2022. The excess contribution of £1,200,000 may be spread over three years with relief on £400,000 being claimed in each of the years ending 31 March 2022, 31 March 2023 and 31 March 2024.

If the current chargeable period is not the same length as the preceding chargeable period, the contribution of the preceding chargeable period must be adjusted by the fraction:

$$\frac{\text{Days in current chargeable period}}{\text{Days in preceding chargeable period}}$$

(FA 2004 s.197(8)&(9))

Example

B Ltd made a contribution of £600,000 in the nine months ended 31 March 2021 and a contribution of £1,500,000 in the year ended 31 March 2022.

The contribution in the earlier period is treated as being £799,270 (£600,000 x 365/274). The contribution paid in year ended 31 March 2022 is less than 210% of this figure, so there no relief is available for the excess to spread forward over subsequent periods.

Excess contributions may not be spread if they are paid to fund:

- an increase in the amount of pensions paid to pensioner members of the pension scheme to reflect increases in the cost of living or benefits which may accrue under a pension scheme to; or
- in respect of individuals who become members of the pension scheme in the current chargeable period as a result of future service as employees of the employer *(FA 2004 s.197(6)&(7))*.

If an employer permanently ceases trading in an accounting period to which a contribution has been spread forward, FA 2004 s.198 allows the deduction to be made in an earlier accounting period. The earliest such period is the period in which the contribution is paid. Employers therefore may make the choice in the light of their financial position.

An employer may also claim a similar deduction in respect of certain statutory payments, such as those under the Pensions Act 1995 s.75 or the Pensions (Northern Ireland) Order 1995 Art.75 *(FA 2004 s.199)*.

Employers are not permitted to deduct any payments other than contributions to registered pension schemes. This rule specifically overrides accounting standards in this area *(FA 2004 s.200)*.

Contributions paid by employers are not taxable on the employee as employment income *(FA 2004 s.201)*.

12.7. Pension Advice

No liability to income tax arises in respect of either the provision of, or reimbursement of the costs of, appropriate independent advice to an employee or former employee relating to the conversion or transfer of pension scheme benefits, where this advice is required under the *Pensions Scheme Act 2015 s.49 or s.52 (ITEPA 2003 s.308B).* This exemption is a special case exemption under ITEPA 2003 s.228A. Therefore it still applies where it is provided under a salary sacrifice arrangement.

No liability to income tax arises in respect of either the provision of, or reimbursement of the costs of, appropriate independent advice to an employee or former employee advice, provided that the value of that advice does not exceed £500 in a tax year. This exemption applies either where the advice is available to all employees or all employees at a particular location or is available to all employees who are less than five years below the normal pensionable age or meet the ill-health condition *(ITEPA 2003 s.308C).* This exemption is an excluded exemption under ITEPA 2003 s.228A. Therefore it still applies where it is provided under a salary sacrifice arrangement.

12.8. Purchase of Shares in Sponsoring Employer

An occupational pension scheme which is a registered pension scheme may purchase shares in a sponsoring employer, provide that the amount used to purchase is less than 5% of the net value of the fund at the date of the purchase. Subject to this limit there is, in principle, no limit on the percentage shareholding which the pension scheme may acquire, although the trustees must be satisfied that any particular investment is appropriate having regard to the interests of their beneficiaries as their general trust law duties. The shares may be listed or unlisted. Where there is more than one sponsoring employer up to 5% of the fund may be used to purchase shares in each of the sponsoring employers, subject to an overriding limit that less than 20% of the fund may be used for this purpose.

12.9. Loans to Employers

Registered occupational pension schemes may make loans to sponsoring employers if the following conditions are satisfied:

1. the loan does not exceed 50% of the value of the fund at the time of the loan;
2. the loan is secured by a charge which is of adequate value;
3. the interest payable is not less than the rate prescribed by HMRC;
4. the loan is repayable within five years of the date it is made, or the repayment date has been postponed to a date not later than five years after

the standard repayment date. The repayment may only be postponed once;
5. if any loans are made to a member or a connected party, they will be subject to a tax charge;
6. the amount repayable on each payment date is not less than:

$$\frac{\text{Amount of loan + total interest payable}}{\text{Total number of loan years}} \times \text{Number of loan years in period}$$

(FA 2004 s.179)

Where a loan does not satisfy all the conditions it will be treated as an unauthorised payment.

12.10. Unauthorised Payments Charge

Any payments made by a registered pension scheme other than those authorised by FA 2004 pt. 4 are subject to a tax charge of 40%. This charge applies to payments made to persons who are, or who have been, members or to a sponsoring employer *(FA 2004 s.208)*. The person liable to the charge is the member or sponsoring employer to whom the payment is made *(FA 2004 s.208(2))*. Where the payment represents 25% or more of the fund value at the date of the payment FA 2004 s.209 imposes an additional surcharge of 15%, bringing the total charge to 55% of the payment.

Where members can influence the investments of the scheme, if the scheme invests in 'taxable property', this will be treated as an unauthorised payment to the member whose arrangement acquires the property and the scheme administrator will be liable to a sanction charge on the income from the asset and any gain on its disposal. Broadly, taxable property covers residential property and most tangible moveable property, e.g. antiques or fine wine, whether situated in the UK or elsewhere *(FA 2004 ss.174A, 185A-185I, 273ZA and Sch. 29A)*. The provisions apply to property held directly or indirectly, except where the property is held through genuinely diverse commercial vehicles.

This is a complex area and advice should be sought before making any investments which may be treated as taxable property.

There are other charges that can arise with regard to pensions, and it is worth referring to HMRC's Registered Pension Schemes Manual.

Chapter 13. Capital Gains Tax and Chargeable Gains

13.1. Scope of Capital Gains Tax (CGT)

CGT is payable on chargeable gains realised by a chargeable person *(TCGA 1992 s.1)*. Chargeable persons include individuals, partnerships and trusts. Companies do not pay CGT, but instead pay corporation tax on their chargeable gains. Many of the rules relating to CGT apply to companies. However, aspects of the taxation of chargeable gains which relate solely to companies are covered in section **14.7-14.7.4**.

Chargeable gains may arise on the following types of disposal:

- sale of the whole, or part, of an asset;
- gift of the whole, or part, of an asset *(TCGA 1992 s.17)*;
- loss, or destruction, of an asset;
- receipt of a capital sum derived from an asset, even if the person paying the sum receives no assets in return, e.g. compensation or damages for injury or insurance proceeds *(TCGA 1992 s.22(1))*. All damages for infringement of copyright, injurious affection (diminution of value because of e.g. expropriation of neighbouring land for a road development) of land, and damage and destruction of assets are treated as falling within this section *(Powlson (HMIT) v Welbeck Securities Ltd (1987) (BTC 316))*, with the exception of compensation payable under the Agricultural Holdings Act 1986 s.60 to a tenant who is given a notice to quit, or statutory compensation payable under the Landlord and Tenant Act 1954 s.37, (as amended) paid after a lease has terminated;
- surrender, or non-exercise, of rights to an asset (e.g. granting a lease out of a freehold) *(TCGA 1992 s.22(1)(c))*;
- capital sums received as consideration for the use or exploitation of assets *(TCGA 1992 s.22(1)(d)) (Chaloner (HMIT) v Pellipar Investments Ltd (1965) (BTC 172))*;
- appropriation of an asset as trading stock;
- disposal of assets created by the person making the disposal, e.g. paintings or goodwill to the extent that they are not chargeable to income tax. Such assets may be represented by patents or copyrights.

13.2. Exemptions

Certain organisations are exempt from CGT, the main two being charities and pension funds. Gains on certain types of assets are exempt, some of the main ones being:

- disposals on death (legatees inherit the assets at the probate value on date of death *(TCGA 1992 s.274))*. Where no value has been agreed for IHT purposes, because for example, an asset qualifies for 100% business property relief, the base cost to the legatee will be the market value calculated in accordance with TCGA 1992 s.272;
- foreign currency for private use *(TCGA 1992 s.269)*. Foreign currency is a chargeable asset, and gains arising from currency speculation will be chargeable *(TCGA 1992 s.21(1)(b))*;
- motor vehicles which are commonly used as private motor vehicles *(TCGA 1992 s.263)*;
- gilt-edged securities;
- qualifying corporate bonds;
- damages or compensation for a wrong or injury inflicted on a taxpayer in his person in the course of his trade, profession or vocation *(TCGA 1992 s.51(2))*. This excludes financial damage, but includes compensation for other issues, such as embarrassment, or loss of dignity. ESC D33 para. 12 also extends the exemption to damages arising from claims for professional negligence, unfair discrimination, libel or slander relating to a trade, profession or employment, and to compensation received by a person other than the person who suffered the wrong or injury, such as financial support and compensation for emotional distress caused by the death of another person received by relatives of that deceased person;
- transfers to an employee benefit trust made by an individual, provided that they are exempt transfers for the purpose of inheritance tax *(TCGA 1992 s.239(1)(b)&(2); IHTA 1984 s.28)*. If the consideration received exceeds the cost of the asset, the gain is calculated using the actual proceeds rather than the market value of the asset *(TCGA 1992 s.17)*;
- investments held in personal equity plans and individual savings accounts;
- wasting chattels not qualifying for capital allowances *(TCGA 1992 s.45)*;
- tangible movable property disposed of for £6,000 or less *(TCGA 1992 s.262)* (see section **13.25**).

13.3. Residence

A taxpayer is liable to CGT if they are resident in the UK *(TCGA 1992 s.2(1))* (for company residence and chargeable gains see sections **1.1** and **14.7.1-14.7.5**). If a taxpayer is neither resident nor ordinarily resident, they are not liable to CGT on gains, even if they are realised on assets situated in the UK, unless the assets are being used in a trade, profession or vocation carried on in the UK through a UK branch or agency *(TCGA 1992 s.10)*. There are anti-avoidance rules to prevent a taxpayer avoiding CGT by realising gains whilst temporarily non-resident in the UK *(TCGA 1992 s.10A)*. Where a taxpayer is non-resident for five years or less, and was resident in the UK for at least four of the seven tax years before departure, gains realised after departure, but before the following 6 April will be taxable in the tax year of departure. Other gains realised whilst non-resident are taxable in the tax year of return. Gains on assets acquired whilst non-resident are excluded from these provisions *(TCGA 1992 s.10A(3))*. This rule also applies if a taxpayer is resident in the UK under UK tax law, but is treated as being non-resident under the provisions of a double tax treaty *(TCGA 1992 s.10A(3)(a)(ii))*.

Gains on assets situated outside the UK realised by taxpayers who are UK resident, but not domiciled in the UK are only taxable if, and to the extent that, the proceeds are remitted to the UK *(TCGA 1992 s.12)*, but this does not apply to foreign chargeable gains realised in the overseas portion of a split, regardless of the part of the year in which the proceeds are remitted *(TCGA 1992 s.12A)*. This will only apply to non-domiciled taxpayers who have been resident in the UK for at least seven out of the previous nine tax years if they pay an annual fee of £30,000, rising to £60,000 for taxpayers who have been resident in the UK for at least 12 of the previous 14 tax years and to all taxpayers who have been resident in the UK for at least 15 of the last 20 years *(TCGA 1992 s.12)*.

Where an asset ceases to be a chargeable asset by virtue of becoming situated outside the UK, the taxpayer is deemed to have sold the asset and to have immediately reacquired it at its market value at the time the asset becomes situated outside the UK *(TCGA 1992 s.25(1))*. Where an asset ceases to be a chargeable asset by virtue of the taxpayer ceasing to carry on a trade in the UK through a branch or agency, the taxpayer is deemed to have sold the asset, and to have immediately reacquired it at its market value at the time the taxpayer ceased to trade in the UK *(TCGA 1992 s.25(3))*.

13.4. Capital Losses

13.4.1. Interaction of capital losses with annual exemption

Individuals have an annual exemption from capital gains tax analogous to the income tax personal allowance (2021/22 £12,300) *(TCGA 1992 s.3)*. Unused income tax personal allowances may not be offset against capital gains. Each spouse or civil partner is treated as a separate person, and is entitled to his, or her, own annual exemption.

Losses incurred in a tax year must be offset against gains of the tax year, even if some, or all, of the annual exemption is thereby wasted *(TCGA 1992 s.2(2)(a))*. If losses exceed gains in a tax year, the excess losses are carried forward, and offset against the net gains of the next available year. Brought forward losses are not, however, offset if this would result in the annual exemption being wasted *(TCGA 1992 s.395(b))*. Losses arising in 1996/97 and subsequent years are offset in priority to losses arising before that year *(FA 1995 s.113(2)(a))*.

A loss arising in a tax year in which a taxpayer is not resident in the UK is not allowable, unless the loss arises on the disposal of an asset used in a trade carried on through a UK branch or agency *(TCGA 1992 ss.10 & 16(3))*. Losses arising to non-domiciliaries on assets not situated in the UK are only allowable if they make an irrevocable election under TCGA 1992 s.16ZA.

Example

Peter has had the following gains and losses since 6 April 2016.

Year	**Gains**	**Losses**
2019/20	£8,300	£4,000
2020/21	£2,400	£5,200
2021/22	£15,200	£2,400

The annual exemption was £12,000 in 2019/20 and £12,300 in 2020/21.

The net assessable gains are:

	2019/20	**2020/21**	**2021/22**
	£	**£**	**£**
Gains	8,300	2,400	15,200
Losses	(4,000)	(5,200)	(2,400)
	4,300	NIL	12,800
Losses b/f	NIL	NIL	(500)
	4,300	NIL	12,300
Annual Exemption	(4,300)	(NIL)	(12,300)
	£NIL	£NIL	£NIL
Losses c/f		£2,800	£2,300

Losses may not generally be carried back. The only exception is where losses are incurred in the year of death. These losses may be carried back against gains of the preceding three years *(TCGA 1992 s.62(2))*. The losses are offset against the latest year first, and are only offset insofar as they reduce the net gains to the level of the annual exemption *(TCGA 1992 s.3(5)(b))*.

TCGA 1992 s.16A denies relief for a loss if it arises directly or indirectly in consequence of, or otherwise in connection with any arrangements, the main purpose, or one of the main purposes, of which is to secure a tax advantage. This section does not apply where there has been a genuine economic transaction involving the sale of an asset at a loss. The straightforward use of a statutory relief does not of itself bring arrangements within this section. Equally, the existence of a tax advantage, such as obtaining a deduction for tax purposes, is not enough in itself to show that the arrangements have a main purpose of obtaining a tax advantage. In determining whether the obtaining of a tax advantage was one of the main purposes it will be relevant to consider whether, in the absence of the tax considerations, the transaction would have been made at all, or would have been made under the same terms and conditions, and, if so, whether the tax advantage would have been of the same amount. The use of marketed tax avoidance schemes will be taken as an indicator that tax avoidance was one of the main purposes of the arrangement.

13.4.2. Interaction of capital losses and capital allowances

A capital loss is reduced by any capital allowances which have been claimed, or could have been claimed on the assets *(TCGA 1992 s.41)*. This includes capital allowances claimed by or available to a transferor where an assets has been transferred at tax written down value. This will normally mean that no loss may be claimed on such disposals and that relief for the loss is given through the capital allowances computation. However, the case of *H and W Hire Ltd (unreported)*[6] suggest that losses may sometimes be available, particularly following trade incorporations. In this case H and W Hire operated as a partnership from 1994 to 1 January 2006, at which date the business was incorporated as H and W Hire Ltd. 61 items of plant with a total original cost of £3,346,000 were transferred into the company for a nominal sum of £100 each and at the date of incorporation the market value of these items was £1,327,000. With the exception of one item with a market value of £7,000, these items were sold by the company in the four accounting years to 31 December 2010 in arm's length sales for a total of £715,000. The transfer into the company generated a balancing allowance, but capital losses were precluded by s.41. For the purposes of capital allowances, H and W Hire Ltd had acquired the items at £100 each, and therefore the balancing charges on the subsequent sales meant that no capital allowances had been available and s.41 could not apply. Capital losses of £605,000 (market value of 60 items of £1,320,000 less sale proceeds of £715,000) could therefore be claimed.

Section 41 may also only apply where the expenditure taken into account in the disposal computation is the same as the qualifying expenditure for capital allowances, since its purpose is to deny both capital allowances and a capital loss **on the same expenditure**. This means that a capital loss would still have been available to H and W Hire Ltd, even if the transfer price had been far higher than £100 and capital allowances had been therefore available to the company, because the capital allowances would have been given by reference to the actual transfer value, whereas the value brought into the disposal computation was the market value.

[6] See article by Arthur Conway, *Harvesting Tax Losses* (*Taxation*, 5 June 2013)

13.5. Offset of Trading and Other Losses against Capital Gains

13.5.1. Trading losses

Under ITA 2007 s.71 or s.130 a taxpayer may offset a trading loss qualifying for relief against general income under ITA 2007 s.64 or an employment loss qualifying for relief against general income under ITA 2007 s.128 against the capital gains of the year. The conditions for claiming this relief are set out in TCGA 1992 ss.261B & 261C.

- In order to make this claim, the loss must first be offset against the taxpayer's general income under ITA 2007 s.64 or s.128, unless such a claim is not possible because the taxpayer has no income for the tax year *(TCGA 1992 s.261B(1),(2))*.
- The maximum gains against which the loss may be offset are the amount of the assessment which would be raised if the annual exemption and any relief under TCGA 1992 s.261B were ignored *(TCGA 1992 s.261C(2))*. The loss is treated in the same manner as a capital loss of the tax year, and is offset against the net gains of the year before the annual exemption. As well as wasting the income tax personal allowance, this claim may also waste some or all of the annual exemption.
- A claim must be made by 31 January in the second tax year following the year in which the loss is incurred *(TCGA 1992 s.261B(8))*.

Example

John has incurred a trading loss of £15,000 and has property income of £6,000 in 2021/22. He has also realised capital gains of £32,000, and incurred capital losses of £3,000 during the year. He has capital losses brought forward of £5,000.

John must first offset £6,000 of the loss against his property income, leaving £9,000 of the loss to be offset against his capital gains.

The maximum gains against which the loss could be offset are:

	£
Gains of tax year	32,000
Losses of tax year	(3,000)
Loss b/f	(5,000)
	£24,000

The loss claim would therefore be:

	£
Gains of tax year	32,000
Losses of tax year	(3,000)
	29,000
Losses TCGA 1992 s.261B	(9,000)
	20,000
Losses b/f	(5,000)

	15,000
Annual Exemption	(12,300)
Assessable gains	£2,700

A claim under TCGA 1992 s.261B should strictly be made in the same notice as a claim under ITA 2007 s.64, but HMRC have indicated that they will accept separate claims provided that the following conditions are satisfied:

- a claim under ITA 2007 s.64 has previously been made and the trader is entitled to make a claim under TCGA 1992 s.261B;
- the claim under TCGA 1992 s.261B is made within the time limit applicable to the claim under ITA 2007 s.64;
- after making the claim under ITA 2007 s.64, trading losses remain unrelieved;
- all other conditions for the relief are satisfied.

For members of LLPs and non-active or limited partners the amount of loss which may be claimed is restricted to contributions to the partnership plus any amount pledged in the event of insolvency, and may not exceed a maximum limit of £25,000 *(ITA 2007 pt. 4 ch. 3)*.

13.5.2. Post-cessation trading and post-employment expenses

If a taxpayer is entitled under ITA 2007 s.96 or s.125 to relief for expenses incurred within seven years of cessation in connection with a former trade or property against his general income, ITA 2007 s.101 or s.126 allow a further claim to be made to offset these expenses against the capital gains of the year. The conditions for claiming this relief are set out in TCGA 1992 ss.261D & 261E.

- In order to make this claim, the loss must first be offset against the taxpayer's general income under ITA 2007 s.96 or s.125 unless such a claim is not possible because the taxpayer has no income for the tax year *(TCGA 1992 s.261D(1),(2))*.
- The amount of the loss which may be offset against gains is the amount which would be chargeable to CGT if the following deductions were ignored:
  1. capital losses brought forward;
  2. annual exemption;
  3. loss claims under TCGA 1992 s.261B or s.261D.

Where a taxpayer has a choice of claims they may choose which should take priority, and, in general, a claim under ITA 2007 s.126 is likely to be more beneficial than a claim under TCGA 1992 s.261B.

It should be noted that, where there are losses brought forward and/or post-cessation trading or post-employment expenses, the maximum amount of gains available for relief under TCGA 1992 s.261D or s.263ZA will be different from the maximum amount of gains available for relief under TCGA 1992 s.261B, since the post-cessation payments are deducted in the latter calculation, but not in the former.

Where a taxpayer has more than one type of loss to offset, the order of set-off implied in the legislation is:

- capital losses of the year;
- deductions under TCGA 1992 s.263ZA;
- deductions under TCGA 1992 s.261D;
- loss claims under TCGA 1992 s.261B;
- annual exemption;
- capital losses brought forward.

Example

Anne has incurred expenditure of £10,000 in 2021/22 due to a claim for faulty work in connection with a trade which ceased in 2018/19. In 2021/22 she also incurred a trading loss of £25,000. In 2021/22 she also had other income of £7,000, capital gains of £30,000 and capital losses of £5,000. At 6 April 2021 she had brought forward capital losses of £4,000.

If she chooses to make a claim under TCGA 1992 s.261D, the position will be:

Offset of post-cessation expenditure against income:

	£
Other income	7,000
Post-cessation expenditure TCGA 1992 s.261D	(10,000)
Amount unrelieved	£(3,000)

The whole trading loss of £25,000 is therefore available to be offset against the gains of 2021/22.

a) Maximum amount of gains available for offset under TCGA 1992 s.261D:

	£
Capital gains of year	30,000
Capital losses of year	(5,000)
	£25,000

b) Maximum amount of gains available for offset under TCGA 1992 s.261B:

	£
Capital gains of year	30,000
Capital losses of year	(5,000)
	25,000
Capital losses b/f	(4,000)
Excess post-cessation expenditure	(3,000)
Maximum amount	£18,000

Chargeable gains of 2021/22:

	£
Capital gains of year	30,000
Capital losses of year	(5,000)
	25,000
Relief TCGA 1992 s.261D	(3,000)

Relief TCGA 1992 s.261B	(18,000)
	4,000
Annual Exemption (restricted)	(4,000)
	£NIL

Amounts carried forward

Capital losses brought forward £4,000

Trading loss £25,000 - £18,000 = £7,000

13.6. Capital Gains Tax Rate

Capital gains are treated as the top slice of income and in 2021/22 gains in the basic rate band are taxed at 10% and those in the higher rate band are taxed at 20% unless they are treated as upper rate gains, in which case the rates are 18% and 28% respectively *(TCGA 1992 s.4)*.

Upper rate gains are defined as gains arising on:

1. residential property or an interest in residential property;
2. non-resident CGT gains; and
3. gains relating to carried interest.
   (TCGA 1992 s. 2A)

Gains qualifying for entrepreneurs' relief (see section **13.33**) or investors' relief (see section **13.34**) are taxed at 10%. Where a taxpayer has some of their basic rate band available for capital gains, this band must first be allocated to gains qualifying for entrepreneurs' relief or investors' relief (*TCGA 1992 s.6A*). If there are no such gains, or some of the basic rate band remains after allocating these gains, a taxpayer may choose whether to allocate gains taxable at the lower rate or gains taxable at the upper rate to this band (*TCGA 1992 s.4BA*).

Example

Sarah has capital gains totalling £30,000 and taxable income of £33,000 in 2021/22. No business assets' disposal' relief is available. Her CGT liability will be:

	£
Capital gains	30,000
Less annual exemption	(12,300)
Assessable gains	£17,700
£4,700 (£37,700 - £33,000) x 10%	470
£13,000 (£17,700 - £4,700) x 20%	2,600
Tax liability	£3,070

13.7. Disposal Consideration

The disposal consideration will normally be the actual sale proceeds, but the market value (agreed with HMRC) is used in the following circumstances where:

- the disposal is not a bargain at arm's length;

- the disposal is to a connected person (see section **13.12**);
- the disposal consideration cannot be valued in monetary terms, e.g. a barter transaction.

(TCGA 1992 ss.17, & 18)

The market value is defined as the value for which an asset could be sold on the open market *(TCGA 1992 s.272(1))*, with no allowance being made for the fact that the whole of an asset might be placed on the market at the same time *(TCGA 1992 s.272(2))* (see section **13.19** for treatment of a series of disposals to connected persons).

In certain circumstances it is not necessary to agree the market value of an asset where hold-over relief is claimed (SP8/92) (see section **13.31.1**).

Where the consideration is in a currency other than sterling, the consideration is converted into sterling at the rate prevailing at the date of disposal *(Capcount Trading v Evans (HMIT) (1993) (BTC 3))*, and an exchange loss is not recoverable for the purpose of CGT *(Poseidon Inc. v Inspector of Taxes (1996) (SpC 82))*.

Where an asset is transferred at undervalue to an employee by an employer and the transfer was subject to a benefit charge, the employee is not treated as having acquired the asset for its full market value, but for the consideration actually given.

The following amounts are excluded from the disposal proceeds:

- amounts taken into account for the purpose of calculating income *(TCGA 1992 s.37(1))*, except amounts taken into account in calculating a balancing allowance or balancing charge *(TCGA 1992 s.37(2))*, or under ICTA 1988 ss.186 & 187 *(TCGA 1992 s.238(2))*;
- consideration for the disposal of trees (standing or felled and including saleable underwood) on woodlands managed on a commercial basis with a view to the realisation of profit *(TCGA 1992 s. 250)*.

Expenses connected with the sale, e.g. legal fees, accountant's or surveyor's fees, auctioneer's commission, SDLT, conveyancing costs, transfer fees, import duty, or costs of obtaining a valuation for CGT purposes, are deducted from the disposal consideration.

13.8. Date of Disposal

The date of the disposal is generally the date on which a contract is made, not the date of actual transfer of title, e.g. in a sale of property, the relevant date is the date of the exchange of contracts, rather than the date of completion *(TCGA 1992 s.28(1))*. Where a contract is conditional, the date of disposal is the date on which the condition is satisfied, and makes the contract binding *(TCGA 1992 s.28(2))*. The rule does not apply to situations where a contract is binding, but stipulates that certain matters must be carried out before disposal. Where an unconditional contract remains uncompleted there is no disposal.

In the case of capital sums derived from assets, the date of disposal is the date the sum is received *(TCGA 1992 s.22(2))*.

13.9. Allowable Costs

The allowable cost will be the sum of:

- the initial cost of the asset, or its value at 31 March 1982, if the asset was owned at that date. This includes any amounts paid in cash or in kind. This amount need not be the market value of the asset if the transaction is a *bona fide* arm's length transaction *(Stanton v Drayton Commercial Investment Co. Ltd (1983) (55 TC 286))*;
- incidental costs of acquisition, e.g. legal fees, accountant's or surveyor's fees, auctioneer's commission, stamp duty, conveyancing costs, transfer fees, import duty *(TCGA 1992 s.38(1)(a), & (2))*. The cost, or value, of personal work or labour *(Oram v Johnson (1980) (53 TC 319))* and amounts paid by a tenant in accordance with the terms of the lease are not allowable *(Emmerson v Computer Time International Ltd (1977) (50 TC 628))*. The cost of creating vacant possession before sale *(Chaney v Watkis (HMIT) (1986) (58 TC 707))* and the cost of establishing or defending title to an asset are allowable *(Passant v Jackson (HMIT) (1986) (59 TC 230))*;
- foreign taxes payable on a gain on disposal, to the extent that they are not relieved by discharge, or set-off, under a double tax agreement *(TCGA 1992 s.278)*;
- costs of valuing the asset for CGT purposes, e.g. value at 31 March 1982, but the costs of an appeal against a valuation are not allowable *(Couch (HMIT) v Caton's Administrators (1996) (BTC 114))*;
- costs of enhancing, or improving, the asset, e.g. building an extension to a house. These do not include any amounts which are an expense for the purpose of income tax *(TCGA 1992 s.39(1))*, or would be an expense if the asset were part of the fixed capital of a trade where profits are subject to income tax *(TCGA 1992 s.39(2))*. Insurance premiums *(TCGA 1992 s.205)*, payments of interest *(TCGA 1992 s.40)*, or expenditure met directly, or indirectly, by the Crown, or any government, public or local authority in the UK or elsewhere, *(TCGA 1992 s.50)* are not allowable;
- where capital allowances or renewals allowances have been claimed on an asset, any loss on disposal is reduced by the amount of any balancing allowance claimed on disposal *(TCGA 1992 s.41)*.

If the purchase price was denominated in a currency other than sterling, it is converted into sterling at the spot rate prevailing on the date of acquisition, even if the currency was acquired through an option contract, or forward exchange contract. A further gain or loss may therefore arise, on the difference between the sterling value of the purchase price translated at the spot rate and the sterling value translated at the forward rate, or rate specified in the option contract *(Capcount Trading v Evans (HMIT) (1993) (BTC 3))*.

13.10. Assets Owned at 31 March 1982

Where the disposal is of an asset which was owned at 31 March 1982, the value of the asset at that date is used in place of the actual acquisition cost.

Where a disposal is made of an asset which an individual making the disposal acquired between 1 April 1982 and 5 April 2008 and:

1. the disposal by which the individual acquired the asset ('the relevant disposal'), and any previous disposal made between these dates, were disposals to which any of the no gain/no loss provisions applied; and
2. the March 1982 value did not apply to the relevant disposal;

it will be assumed for the purposes of the current disposal that the March 1982 value was used in the relevant disposal and that any indexation allowance was computed on that value *(TCGA 1992 s.35A)*.

13.11. Married Couples and Civil Partners

Married couples and civil partners are treated as separate individuals for the purposes of CGT and each spouse is entitled to an annual exemption. Where assets are jointly held the gain will be apportioned in accordance with the beneficial interests held by the spouses. Where this is unclear, HMRC will generally accept that they hold equal shares *(IR Press Release 21 November 1990)*.

Assets are transferred between married couples/civil partners who are living together in accordance with TCGA 1992 s.288(3) on a no gain/no loss basis, i.e. the deemed proceeds for the spouse/civil partner making the transfer (the 'transferor spouse') is the allowable cost of the transferor spouse.[7] This rule also applies to the tax year in which a couple separate, but not after the end of that tax year. In subsequent years until the divorce, a husband and wife or civil partners will be connected persons (see section **13.12**). It is therefore possible to use an inter-spouse transfer to ensure that the annual exemption and/or the basic rate band of both spouses are utilised, although transfers between spouses before divorce may be attacked by HMRC if they believe they were

---

[7] If the transfer was before 6 April 2008 the taxable gain may be reduced by use of the indexation allowance up to the date of transfer *(TCGA 1992 s.58(1))* plus the accrued taper relief entitlement (but beware that certain assets that were business assets in the hands of the transferor spouse may be non-business assets in the hands of the transferee).

made purely for the purpose of tax avoidance and that beneficial ownership has not genuinely passed.

When a spouse disposes of an asset acquired from the other spouse/civil partner to a third party, the calculation of the gain depends on whether the transferor spouse owned the asset on 31 March 1982.

- If the transferor spouse did not own the asset on 31 March 1982, the base cost is the original cost of the asset to the transferor.
- If the transferor spouse owned the asset on 31 March 1982 the deemed proceeds are ignored and the transferee spouse is deemed to have owned the asset on that date *(TCGA 1992 s.55(6)(a))*. The gain or loss is therefore calculated in the normal way.

13.12. Disposal to Connected Parties

Where an asset is disposed of to a connected party, the disposal consideration will be the market value of the asset rather than the actual sale proceeds *(TCGA 1992 s.18(1)&(2))*.

Where an asset is sold to a connected person at a loss, the normal loss relief rules do not apply. The loss may only be offset against gains arising on future disposals to the same connected person whilst they are still connected *(TCGA 1992 s.18(3)&(4))*.

Connected persons are defined as:

- siblings, lineal ancestors and descendants of the taxpayer and their spouses, i.e. brothers and sisters of full and half-blood, brothers and sisters-in-law, parents, step-parents, grandparents, children, sons and daughters-in-law, grandchildren. Uncles, aunts, nephews, nieces and cousins are therefore not connected persons for this purpose;
- above relatives of spouse/civil partner, i.e. parents-in-law, brothers and sisters-in-law and stepchildren;
- spouses/civil partners of the relatives of the spouse/civil partner; *(TCGA 1992 s.286(2))*
- husband and wife or civil partners who separated in a previous tax year and who are not yet divorced *(TCGA 1992 s.286(2))*. Once they are divorced they are no longer connected persons by virtue of having been married or in a civil partnership, but may be connected if one of the other conditions applies;
- business partners;
- spouses/civil partners of business partners;
- relatives of business partners. *(TCGA s.286(4))*

This does not apply to the disposal of partnership assets 'under *bona fide* commercial transactions' between partners who would be unconnected, but for the fact that they are business partners *(TCGA 1992 s.286(4))*.

A trust is treated as being connected with the settlor and any person connected with the settlor at the time the settlement is made. The connection is, however, broken by the death of the settlor *(TCGA 1992 s.286(3))*.

A loss arising on the grant of an option to a connected person to buy or sell or enter into another transaction is only allowable if the subsequent disposal is made at arm's length to an unconnected person *(TCGA 1992 s.18(5))*.

If a vendor retains a right or otherwise places a restriction on property being transferred to a connected person, the market value used in the computation is reduced by the lower of the market value of the right or restriction and the amount by which the value of the property would increase if the right or restriction were extinguished *(TCGA 1992 s.18(6))*.

This does not apply where:

- the enforcement of the right or restriction would effectively destroy or substantially impair the asset without bringing any advantage to the person making the disposal or a connected person;
- the right or restriction is on option, or other right, to acquire the asset;
- the right or restriction is a right to extinguish the asset in the hands of the person giving the consideration by forfeiture or merger.

(TCGA 1992 s.18(7))

13.13. Valuation of Assets

Where an asset needs to be valued (either to obtain a March 1982 value or because the asset is being transferred to a connected person), the asset is valued at its open market value. Listed shares and securities are valued at the average of the lower and upper prices quoted.

13.14. Negligible Value Claim

Where the value of an asset has become negligible a taxpayer may make an election to this effect *(TCGA 1992 s.24(2)(a))*. Negligible is not defined in the legislation, but 'small' is defined as 5% of the acquisition cost of the asset, and it is the view of HMRC that negligible will therefore be considerably less than 5%. If a claim is accepted by HMRC, there is a deemed disposal of the asset, thus crystallising an allowable loss, and a re-acquisition at the negligible value. If the asset is subsequently sold, the allowable cost will be the negligible value, meaning that a gain may well arise if it regains some or all of its former value.

The disposal is deemed to have taken place at the date of the election, or may be back-dated to any date starting two years before the beginning of the tax year in which the claim is made, provided the value of the asset was also negligible at that time *(TCGA 1992 s.24(2)(b)(iv))*.

13.15. Value Shifting

There are anti-avoidance provisions to counteract the transfer of the economic benefit of an asset from one person to another, without an actual disposal taking place. A common example involves shares but the provisions also apply in certain other situations where:

- an asset is sold and actions have artificially reduced the value of the asset so as either to reduce the amount of the gain or increase the amount of the loss, and a tax-free benefit has been, or will be, conferred on the person making the disposal, or a person connected with him *(TCGA 1992 s.30)*;
- certain transactions involving leases *(TCGA 1992 s.29(4))*;
- the release or abrogation of rights or restrictions over an asset by the person entitled to enforce them *(TCGA 1992 s.29(6))*.

Under the value shifting provisions a disposal is deemed to have been made in these circumstances, even if no consideration passes. There will also be a deemed acquisition by the other party. In addition, where an asset is sold at a loss, the loss will not be allowable, insofar as it has been caused by value shifting transactions.

Where consideration passes the amount of the consideration used in the disposal computation will be adjusted by an appropriate amount in order to counteract the tax advantage.

13.16. Disposal by Way of Security

There is no disposal where property is transferred or conveyed by way of security (i.e. is used as collateral for a loan) *(TCGA 1992 s.26)*. If the borrower defaults on payment, so that the property is repossessed, there will be a disposal, but the vendor may elect for the gain to be limited to the net proceeds gained from the transaction, so that the original cost of the property is available to be used in any subsequent sale (ESC D18). If this election is not made, the cost of the property to be used in the reacquisition is the lower of:

1. the market value of the property; and
2. the outstanding amount of the debt *(TCGA 1992 s.251(3))*.

Where the cost on re-acquisition is the market value and the property is subsequently sold at a gain, the gain will be limited to the gain which would have arisen if the property had been acquired for the outstanding amount of the debt *(TCGA 1992 s.251(3))* (this does not apply if the property is sold at a loss).

13.17. Hire Purchase Transactions

Where an asset is acquired by means of hire purchase or a similar method involving the making of periodic payments for CGT purposes the purchaser is treated as having acquired the asset on the date they first obtain use and enjoyment of it. If the agreement is subsequently terminated without legal title having passed an adjustment may be made subsequently *(TCGA 1992 s.27).*

13.18. Appropriations to and from Trading Stock

Where a capital asset is appropriated as trading stock, a disposal at market value is deemed to have been made *(TCGA 1992 s.161(1))*. If the profits are treated as trading income the gain may be deferred by reducing the market value of the asset by the amount of the gain *(TCGA 1992 s.161(3))*. This will increase the taxable profit when the asset is sold. Therefore, this claim may or may not be beneficial depending on the trader's circumstances.

13.19. Series of Transactions

Where a disposal is made by way of a series of disposals, each disposal is treated as having disposed of a proportion of the total value of the asset provided that:

- there are two or more transactions by way of gift or otherwise *(TCGA 1992 s.19(3))*;
- the transactions occur within a period of six years of the last transaction *(TCGA 1992 s.19(3))*;
- the disposals are all made to a single person, or two or more persons with whom the vendor is connected *(TCGA 1992 s.19(1)(a))*;
- the original market value of the assets disposed of is less than the appropriate portion of the aggregate market value, at the time of the disposal, of all the assets disposed of in the transaction *(TCGA 1992 s.19(1)(b))*. The original market value is the market value of the latest asset being disposed of ignoring TCGA 1992 s.19 (i.e. valued as a single, self-standing asset) plus the value used for the purpose of CGT of all previous assets sold *(TCGA 1992 s.20(3)(a)&(b))*. The aggregate market value is the market value of all the assets which have so far been disposed of taken as a whole *(TCGA 1992 s.20(4)(a))*. Any assets acquired after the date of the first transaction are ignored and the number of assets to be aggregated cannot exceed the maximum number of assets which were held at any time between the dates of the first and the last transactions *(TCGA 1992 s.20(6))*.

Example

David owns a valuable set of three paintings and gifts one of them to each of his three children at different times. Each painting is worth significantly less singly than as part of the set. The values of the paintings are as follows:

Date of Disposal	Value of Single Painting at Date of Disposal	Value of Set at Date of Disposal
June 2020	£5,000	£45,000
Sept 2020	£7,000	£51,000
May 2021	£8,000	£60,000

At the time of the second disposal there will be no adjustment, assuming that the total value of the two paintings disposed of in June 2019 and September 2019 are worth no more than £12,000. At the time of the last disposal the values of the paintings will be adjusted as follows:

Date of Disposal	Value
June 2020	1/3 x £45,000 = £15,000
Sept 2020	1/3 x £51,000 = £17,000
May 2021	1/3 x £60,000 = £20,000

13.20. Options

An option is a distinct asset, so the granting of an option will give rise to a disposal for the purpose of CGT *(TCGA 1992 s.144(1))*. If the option is not exercised the whole of the consideration for the option, less any fees payable in connection with the grant, will be taxable *(Strange v Openshaw (HMIT) (1983) (BTC 209))*. The exercise of an option does not constitute a disposal, unless the grantor must sell an asset on the exercise of an option. In this case the consideration for the option is added to the consideration for the asset itself. Where the grantor must purchase an asset on the exercise of an option the consideration for the option is deducted from the cost of the asset *(TCGA 1992 s.144(2)&(3))*. Payments for the grant and the exercise of the option are therefore treated as a single transaction *(TCGA 1992 s.144(2))*. If the grantee receives a cash sum rather than an asset, the grantor deducts the payment made on the exercise of the option from the amount received on the grant of the option. The grantee will similarly deduct the payment made on the grant of the option from the sum paid on the exercise *(TCGA 1992 s.144A)*. The disposal of an option by a grantee is a normal disposal for the purposes of CGT.

The abandonment of an option does not constitute a disposal unless it is:

1. a quoted option to subscribe for shares; or
2. a traded or financial option; or
3. an option to acquire assets for use in a trade carried on by the option holder *(TCGA 92 s.144(4))*.

13.21. Debts

No gain arises on the disposal of a debt, other than a debt on a security, unless it:

1. is disposed of by someone other than the original creditor *(TCGA 1992 s.251(2)-(5))*; or
2. is a foreign currency bank debt which is not for private use *(TCGA 1992 s.252)*; or
3. is a loan to a trader which fulfils certain conditions *(TCGA 1992 ss.253 & 254)*. This does not include a loan on a security (see section **13.35**).

There is no clear definition of a debt on a security, but HMRC interpret TCGA 1992 s.132(3)(b) to mean that it must be loan stock or a similar security issued by a government, company or public or local authority. The courts have stated that the security must be marketable and have some degree of permanence.

The disposal of certain foreign currency bank debts is chargeable *(TCGA 1992 s.252(1))*.

13.22. Compensation

Strictly, the right to compensation or damages is a chargeable asset for the purposes of CGT *(Zim Properties Ltd v Proctor (HMIT) (1985) (BTC 42))*. However, ESC D33 treats damages and compensation as relating to the underlying asset. Compensation and damages will, therefore, only be taxable if the underlying asset is a chargeable asset. Any reliefs available in respect of the underlying asset (e.g. roll-over relief) will also be available for the compensation or damages. Compensation and damages are not taxable where there is no underlying asset. ESC D33 does not apply to payments under a warranty and indemnity included as part of a sale and purchase agreement.

13.23. Asset Derived from another Asset

Where an asset is derived from another asset, either through merger or division, the amounts allowable as a deduction are apportioned between the different assets *(TCGA 1992 s.43)*. There is no guidance on how this should be done.

13.24. Location of Assets

The location of assets may be relevant for a person not domiciled in the UK. The rules concerning location are:

- immovable property, or rights over such property, is located where it is situated. An interest by way of security is normally situated where the debt is situated;
- tangible movable property is situated where it is, in fact, situated;
- debts are situated in the UK if the creditor is resident in the UK;
- shares or debentures issued by a governmental or municipal authority, or by any body created by such an authority are situated in the country of the

authority concerned, unless the shares are in a company incorporated in the UK, in which case the shares are located in the UK;

- registered shares and securities are situated in the UK if the share register is kept in the UK;
- goodwill is situated where the trade, business or profession to which it relates is situated;
- patents, trademarks and registered designs, or rights under laws outside the UK which correspond to these, are situated where they are registered. If they are on more than one register, they are situated in each place. Licences or other rights in respect of above rights are situated in the UK if they, or any right derived from them, are exercisable in the UK;
- copyrights, design rights, franchises etc., or rights under laws outside the UK which correspond to these, are situated in the UK if they, or any right derived from them, are exercisable in the UK;
- a judgment debt is situated in the country of the judgment; *(TCGA 1992 s.275)*
- any intangible asset whose location is not covered by a specific rule is situated in the UK if it was subject to UK law, e.g. right to sue, at the time of its creation *(TCGA 1992 s.275A)*;
- where more than one person has an interest in an asset, for the purpose of determining whether the asset is located in the UK, it is assumed that the asset is wholly-owned by a person holding the interest in the asset *(TCGA 1992 s.275C)*.

13.25. Chattels and Wasting Assets

13.25.1. Definitions

A chattel is defined as tangible movable property, such as paintings, furniture or movable plant and machinery *(TCGA 1992 s.262(1))*. A wasting asset is an asset with a useful life of 50 years or less *(TCGA 1992 s.44(1))*. Freehold land is never a wasting asset *(TCGA 1992 s.44(1)(a))* and plant and machinery is always deemed to be a wasting asset *(TCGA 1992 s.44(1)(c))*. From the above it follows that a wasting chattel is tangible movable property with a useful life of 50 years or less. This will include plant and machinery, unless it is fixed.

The following are treated as machinery:

- antique clocks and watches;
- motor vehicles not usually used as private passenger vehicles *(TCGA 1992 s.263)*. These include taxi cabs, racing cars, single-seater sports cars, vans, lorries or commercial vehicles, motor cycles, scooters or motor cycle/sidecar combinations and railway engines and tramway engines;
- trawlers, fishing vehicles, tankers and other vessels powered by engines.

Vessels propelled by sails or oars are not treated as machinery, but may be wasting assets.

In addition to these three definitions, the tax treatment will depend on whether the asset qualified for capital allowances (the test is whether capital allowances could have been claimed rather than whether they were actually claimed), giving in total six different possibilities *(TCGA 1992 s. 45(2),& (3))*. The tax treatment of each category is summarised in tabular form on page 287.

13.25.2. Capital allowances are not available

Wasting chattels

Wasting chattels are exempt from CGT; therefore no gain and no allowable loss may arise *(TCGA 1992 s.45)*. This includes the situation where a taxpayer has elected to use the cash basis (see section **2.10**), the asset has been used for the purpose of the trade, profession or vocation at any time and any expenditure on the asset has been brought into account in calculating the profits of the trade, or would have been brought into account, if the cash basis had applied at the date of acquisition *(TCGA 1992 s.47A)*.

Other chattels

Other chattels are exempt provided that the gross proceeds (i.e. proceeds before incidental costs of disposal) do not exceed £6,000 *(TCGA 1992 s.262(1))*. This is to avoid the need to calculate gains on small, insignificant disposals. In the case of single, unrelated chattels, the £6,000 threshold applies to each item. Where the proceeds exceed £6,000, the gain will be the lower of the gain calculated in the usual way and the gain using the following formula:

5/3 x (Gross disposal proceeds - £6,000)
(TCGA 1992 s.262(2))

Where a taxpayer disposes of a set of chattels by way of a series of transactions at the same or different times, either with the same or connected persons, or persons acting in concert, the £6,000 threshold and the marginal relief formula will apply to the total consideration and gains *(TCGA 1992 s.262(4))*.

Where an asset is sold at a loss and the proceeds are less than £6,000, notional proceeds of £6,000 are used in the computation, rather than the actual proceeds *(TCGA 1992 s.262(3))*.

Wasting assets other than chattels

It is expected that a wasting asset will decline in value over its useful life. Therefore, the allowable cost must be written down in the computation *(TCGA 1992 s.46(1)(a))*. Any subsequent expenditure is treated similarly *(TCGA 1992 s.46(1)(b))*. The allowable cost will be:

$$\text{Cost/March 1982 value} \times \frac{\text{Useful life of asset at date of disposal}}{\text{Useful life of asset at date of acquisition / 31 March 1982}}$$

13.25.3. Capital allowances are available

Chattels (wasting and non-wasting)

These are treated in the same way as non-wasting chattels above, with the exception that no allowable loss may arise on the disposal. This is because tax relief has already been given for the loss through the capital allowances system.

Wasting assets other than chattels

The full cost or March 1982 value is included in the computation and is not written down *(TCGA 1992 s.47(1))*. No allowable loss may arise on the disposal. Where an asset has been used partly for the purpose of a trade there are provisions for apportionment *(TCGA 1992 s.47(2))*.

SUMMARY TABLE

	Not Eligible for Capital Allowances	**Eligible for Capital Allowances**
Wasting Chattel	Exempt	1. Gains exempt if **gross** proceeds £6,000 or less. 2. If proceeds exceed £6,000, gain restricted to maximum of 5/3 x (Gross proceeds - £6,000) 3. No loss may arise
Non-wasting Chattel	1. Gains exempt if **gross** proceeds £6,000 or less. 2. If proceeds exceed £6,000, gain restricted to maximum of 5/3 x (Gross proceeds - £6,000) 3. If proceeds are less than £6,000 and a loss arises, notional proceeds of £6,000 are used.	1. Gains exempt if **gross** proceeds £6,000 or less. 2. If proceeds exceed £6,000, gain restricted to maximum of 5/3 x (Gross proceeds - £6,000) 3. No loss may arise
Other Wasting Asset	Cost/1982 value written down	1. Cost/1982 value not written down 2. No loss may arise.

Example

Susan has made the following disposals of assets during the year ended 5 April 2022:

Date	Asset	Proceeds	Selling Expenses	Date of Acquisition	Acquisition Cost
30.4.21	Antique vase	£6,600	£300	Mar 1987	£2,500
15.6.21	Greyhound	£7,000	£200	Feb 1993	£3,200
13.7.21	Cutting Machine (Fixed) *	£4,000	---	July 2014 (10 yr life)	£5,400
30.8.21	Painting	£1,500	£150	May 1986	£7,000
31.3.22	Copyright	£20,000		31.3.2016 (30 yrs)	£18,000

* The machine was used for business purposes and capital allowances had been claimed.

Vase

	Cost
	£
Proceeds	6,600
Costs of Disposal	(300)
	6,300
Acquisition Cost	(2,500)
Gain	£3,800

The gain will be restricted to 5/3 x (£6,600 – £6,000) = £1,000

Greyhound

This is a wasting chattel and is therefore exempt.

Cutting Machine

Since capital allowances were claimed on the machine no allowable loss may arise.

Painting

	Cost
	£
Notional Proceeds	6,000
Cost	(7,000)
Loss	£(1,000)

Copyright

	Cost
	£
Proceeds	20,000
Acquisition Cost £18,000 x 24/30	(14,400)
Gain	£5,600

13.26. Part Disposals

13.26.1. General part disposal rule

Where there is a disposal of a part of an asset (e.g. two acres of land out of five), the allowable cost, i.e. cost or March 1982 value must be multiplied by the fraction A/A+B where:

- A is the value of part disposed of; and
- B is the value of the part retained

(TCGA 1992 s.42(2)).

The apportionment is made before any loss restriction by reference to any balancing allowance received in accordance with TCGA 1992 s.34, the no gain/no loss provisions relating to disposals between spouses under TCGA 1992 s.58 or roll-over relief on the disposal of business assets.

Where the part disposal is of land, HM Revenue & Customs recognise that there may be difficulties in establishing the value of the remaining land. Therefore, SP D1 permits the land sold and the land retained to be treated as separate assets and the attribution of part of the cost to the land sold to be made on any reasonable basis.

Example

Diane acquired four acres of land on 4 May 1999 at a cost of £50,000. She sold one acre of the land on 24 July 2021 for £60,000. The value of the remaining three acres at that date was £90,000.

		£
Proceeds		60,000
Allowable Cost £50,000 x	$\frac{60,000}{60,000 + 90,000}$	(20,000)
Gain		£40,000

13.26.2. Small part disposals of land

Where a taxpayer makes a small part-disposal of land they may claim that any gain arising should not be taxable immediately, but should instead be deducted from the allowable cost on a later disposal, thus producing a larger gain *(TCGA 1992 s.242).* The following conditions must be met:

- the land must be freehold or be held on a lease with more than 50 years to run *(TCGA 1992 s.242(7));*
- the disposal proceeds must not exceed 20% of the value of the whole piece of land and the total proceeds from all sales of land during the tax year must not exceed £20,000 (excluding land acquired by a local authority under a compulsory purchase order) *(TCGA 1992 s.242(3)(b));*
- if the land is acquired by a local authority under a compulsory purchase order the disposal proceeds must be no more than 5% of the value of the whole piece of land *(TCGA 1992 s.243(1)(a); IR Int. 157).*

13.27. Leases

13.27.1. Assignment of lease

An assignment of a lease is the sale of the remaining years of a lease by the lessee.

Two situations must be distinguished:

- assignment of a long lease, i.e. a lease with more than 50 years to run;
- assignment of a short lease, i.e. a lease with 50 years or less to run.

There are no special rules relating to the assignment of a long lease; however, a short lease is a wasting asset and the cost or March 1982 value must be written down. Unlike other assets, leases do not waste on a straight-line basis. The allowable cost must be written down using the following formula:

$$\frac{\text{\% relating to no. of years remaining at date of disposal}}{\text{\% relating to no. of years remaining at date of acquisition}}$$

(TCGA 1992 Sch.8 para. 1(4)(c))

Enhancement expenditure under *TCGA 1992 s.38(1)(b)* is similarly restricted.

Where the period is not a complete number of years the percentage taken is the percentage for the number of complete years remaining plus 1/12 of the difference between that percentage and the percentage for the next higher year for each additional remaining month, i.e. if there are 22 years and 4 months remaining on the lease the percentage will be:

Percentage 22 years	76.399
4/12 x (78.055* – 76.399)	0.552
	76.951

* Percentage for 23 years

14 or more odd days count as a complete month *(TCGA 1992 Sch. 8 para. 1(6))*.

Example

William acquired a 40-year lease on 30 September 2015 for £10,000. On 30 September 2021 he assigned the lease for £20,000.

		£
Proceeds		20,000
Allowable Cost £10,000 x	91.156 (34 yrs) / 95.457 (40 yrs)	(9,549)
Gain		£10,451

13.27.2. Grant of lease

A grant of a lease out of a freehold or superior leasehold interest is a part disposal and the allowable cost must be multiplied by the part disposal fraction set out in **13.26.1** *(TCGA 1992 Sch. 8 para. 2)*. In this case:

- A is the premium received on the grant of the lease. In the case of a short lease the A in the numerator will be after deducting any portion of the premium taxable as property income, the A in the denominator will be the full premium;
- B is the value of the reversionary interest; i.e. the value of the right to regain occupancy of the property after the lease has terminated.

(TCGA 1992 Sch. 8 para. 5(1))

Where a notional premium arises due to an obligation on the tenant to carry out certain works under the terms of the lease the amount taxed is treated as enhancement expenditure falling within TCGA 1992 s.38(1)(b).

A premium includes a sum payable:

- under the terms under which the lease is granted in lieu of rent *(TCGA 1992 Sch. 8 para. 3(2))*;
- by the tenant otherwise than as rent in consideration for a variation or waiver of the lease *(TCGA 1992 Sch. 8 para. 3(3))*;
- under the terms under which the lease is granted as consideration for the surrender of the lease *(TCGA 1992 Sch. 8 para. 3(2))*.

In the first two cases, where the landlord is the tenant under a superior lease, which is a short lease, the deemed premium is to be treated as enhancement expenditure *(TCGA 1992 Sch. 8 para. 3(5))*. In the third case the premium is to be treated as a completely separate transaction *(TCGA 1992 Sch. 8 para. 3(6))*.

Example

Bob acquired a property in October 2014 for £150,000 and in November 2021 he granted Sarah a 30-year lease for a premium of £40,000. The value of the reversionary interest is £300,000.

		£
Premium		40,000
Less: Assessable as property income		(16,800)
		23,200
Allowable Cost £150,000 x	£23,200 / £40,000 + £300,000	(10,235)
Gain		£12,965

13.27.3. Sub-lease granted out of short lease

Where a sub-lease is granted out of a short lease, the allowable cost is a portion of the premium paid on the grant of the original head lease *(TCGA 1992 Sch.8 para. 4(2)(a))*. This is calculated as:

$$\frac{\text{\% for remaining years on head-lease} - \text{\% for no. of years of sub-lease}}{\text{\% for total no. of years on head lease}}$$

Example

Stephen was granted a 20-year lease in September 2015, paying a premium of £20,000. In September 2021 he granted a 10-year sub-lease to Mary and received a premium of £15,000. The gain is:

	£
Proceeds	15,000
Cost: $\frac{61.617 \text{ (15 years)} - 46.695 \text{ (10 years)}}{72.770 \text{ (20 years)}}$ x £20,000	(4,101)
Gain	£10,899

Where the premium is less than the hypothetical premium which could have been charged if the same rent were demanded under the sub-lease as is payable under the head-lease, there is a further restriction. This is given by the fraction:

$$\frac{\text{Actual premium}}{\text{Hypothetical premium}}$$

(TCGA 1992 Sch. 8 para. 4(2)(b)).

In the previous example if Stephen had demanded a premium of £10,000 in exchange for a higher rent the gain would be:

	£
Proceeds	10,000
Cost: $\frac{£10,000}{£15,000}$ x £4,101	(2,734)
Gain	£7,266

Where the interest comprised in the sub-lease does not comprise the whole of the property there is a further reduction:

$$\frac{\text{Value of property comprised in sub-lease}}{\text{Value of property comprised in head-lease}}$$

(TCGA 1992 Sch. 8 para. 4(3))

13.27.4. Duration of lease

Where a lease includes provisions under which a landlord has the option to terminate the lease before the expiry date, the lease is treated as running to the earliest date on which the landlord could terminate the lease *(TCGA 1992 Sch. 8 para. 8)*. Where the terms of the lease make it unlikely that it will continue beyond a certain date, the lease is taken as running to that date. If a lease may be extended by giving notice to the tenant and this provision is included in the original lease, a lease is taken as running to the latest date to which the lease could be extended *(TCGA 1992 Sch. 8 para. 8(5))*.

13.27.5. Leases of property other than land

The assignment of leases of property other than land are treated as part disposals and are also subject to the provisions of TCGA 1992 Sch. 8 paras. 2, 3, 4, & 8 (premiums, grant of sub-leases out of short leases and duration of lease), although they do not waste in accordance with the table in TCGA 1992 Sch. 8 para. 1 *(TCGA 1992 Sch.8 para. 9(1))*.

Where a charge has been made under ITA 2007 pt 12A ch. 4 the amount is deductible from a gain arising on the disposal for which the sum paid is treated as consideration, but a gain may not be converted into a loss, nor may a loss be increased *(TCGA 1992 Sch. 8 para. 9(2))*.

13.27.6. Leases not treated as wasting assets

The following types of leases are not treated as wasting assets, notwithstanding that they have less than 50 years to run *(TCGA 1992 Sch. 8 paras. 1 & 2)*:

- a lease which was subject to a sub-lease not at a rack rent, i.e. a full market rent, when the lessee acquired it. It will become a wasting asset on the expiry of the sub-lease;
- the sub-lease continues to exist after the lessee takes the headlease;
- the value of the headlease when the sub-lease expires (estimated at the date the lease is acquired) is greater than the allowable expenditure.

13.27.7. Extension of leases

Where a lease is surrendered before its expiry and a new lease is granted for a longer period, ESC D39 provides that there is no disposal provided that:

- the disposal is at arm's length between unconnected parties or the parties are connected and HM Revenue & Customs are satisfied that the extension was made on arm's length terms;
- the transaction is not part of a larger transaction or series of transactions;
- no capital sum is paid by the lessee;
- the extent of the property concerned is not varied;
- the terms of the new lease, other than the duration and rent payable, have not been altered.

13.28. Loss or Destruction of Asset

Where an asset is lost or destroyed a disposal is deemed to have taken place *(TCGA 1992 s.24)*. If no compensation or damages are received, a loss equal to the allowable cost of the asset will arise. Where compensation or damages are received, this amount, plus any scrap proceeds from the disposal of the old asset, is included as consideration in the disposal computation.

In general law the destruction of a building is not a disposal, since the asset comprises the underlying land. Nevertheless, a taxpayer may make an election (but is not obliged to do so) to treat the building as a separate asset *(TCGA 1992 s.24(3))*. An election will not be worthwhile where full insurance proceeds are received to cover the loss, since the computation will produce a gain on the land.

Where compensation is used to purchase a replacement asset within one year from the date of receipt of the compensation (or such longer period as HMRC may allow) a claim may be made to roll over any gain against, i.e. deduct from the base cost of, the replacement asset *(TCGA 1992 s.23(4))*.

If some of the compensation proceeds are not reinvested, i.e. the compensation proceeds exceed the cost of the replacement asset, the excess amount will be chargeable immediately and may not be rolled over against the cost of the replacement asset.

Example

Cost of original asset	£50,000
Scrap proceeds	£1,000
Compensation received	£65,000
Cost of replacement asset	£70,000

The gain arising on the disposal will be:

	£
Compensation proceeds	65,000
Scrap proceeds	1,000
	66,000
Cost of old asset	(50,000)
Gain	£16,000

If a claim is made under TCGA 1922 s.23(4), the gain will be rolled over against the base cost of the replacement asset which will be £54,000, i.e. £70,000 less the gain of £16,000.

If the cost of the new asset had been £59,000, £7,000 of the gain, i.e. £66,000 less £59,000, would be chargeable and only the balance of £9,000 would be available to roll over against the cost of the replacement asset giving a base cost of £50,000.

Where the compensation proceeds from the destruction of a building are used to fund the construction or purchase of a new building elsewhere, both the old and new buildings are treated as distinct separate assets *(TCGA 1992 s.23(6))*. So, it will be necessary to apportion expenditure between the new building and the site.

13.29. Restoration of Assets

Where compensation or insurance is received in respect of a damaged asset there is a part disposal. In the part disposal, fraction A is the compensation or insurance proceeds and, if the asset has not been restored, B is the value of the asset in its damaged state. If the asset is restored, there is a part disposal of both the original cost and the restoration costs, and B in the part disposal fraction is the value of the asset after restoration.

Example

Cost of building – January 2001	£120,000
Compensation received – May 2021	£25,000
Restoration costs	£30,000
Value of building after restoration	£225,000

The gain will be:

	£
Proceeds	25,000
Cost (£25,000/(£25,000 + £225,000)) x (£120,000 + £30,000)	(15,000)
Gain	£10,000

If the proceeds are wholly applied in restoring the asset or if the proceeds not used to restore the asset are 'small' in relation to the overall proceeds and the value of the asset, there is no disposal if a claim is made under TCGA 1992 s.23(1). In this context HMRC will accept 'small' as being the greater of £3,000 and 5% of the value of the asset, although it is open to the taxpayer to argue for a different interpretation. Any amount not used for restoration of the asset is deducted from the cost of the asset *(TCGA 1992 s.23(2))*.

Example

Cost of asset – January 1999	£20,000
Compensation received – May 2021	£5,000
Restoration costs	£4,500

The cost of the asset after restoration will be £19,500, i.e. £20,000 less the excess compensation of £500.

If the asset were sold in June 2021 for £25,000 the gain would be:

	£
Proceeds	25,000
Cost – as above	(19,500)
Gain	£5,500

If the compensation not used in restoring the asset is not small there is a deemed part disposal *(TCGA 1992 s.23(3))*. The proceeds are the amount of the compensation proceeds not used for restoration, the allowable cost of the asset is increased by the restoration expenditure and the normal part-disposal fraction is used where:

- A is the amount of the compensation proceeds not used for restoration; and
- B is value of asset after restoration.

Example

Cost of asset (May 1999)	£150,000
Restoration costs (June 2005)	£40,000
Compensation proceeds	£60,000
Value of asset after restoration	£220,000

The gain arising is:

	£
Proceeds (£60,000 - £40,000)	20,000
Cost (£20,000/(£20,000 + £220,000)) x (£150,000 + £40,000)	(15,833)
Gain	£4,167

If the asset were subsequently sold for £250,000, the gain on disposal would be:

		£
Proceeds		250,000
Cost	150,000	
Less: Part disposal	(4,167)	
		(145,833)
Gain		£104,167

13.30. Replacement of Business Assets

13.30.1. Introduction

Businesses often need to replace business assets or move premises due to expansion, but it would be difficult for them to do so if part of the sale proceeds from selling the old asset, which are needed to finance the replacement, were lost due to the tax charge. In order to prevent this, the gain on the old asset may be 'rolled over', i.e. deducted from the cost of the new asset. The new asset will, therefore, have a lower base cost and a higher gain will arise on its eventual disposal. The gain can be deferred indefinitely, in theory, if the proceeds are always re-invested in a new asset.

If relief is available on a gain due to an extra-statutory concession, TCGA 1992 s.284A and s.284B make it clear that the deferred gain must be brought into charge on a subsequent disposal. If the benefit available under a concession is repudiated in a later period a deemed gain arises in the later period *(TCGA 1992 s.284A(3))*.

If roll-over relief is obtained through a concession, e.g. ESC D22, the deferred gain must be brought back into charge on the disposal of the replacement asset. It cannot be argued that it is not necessary to do this because the relief is non-statutory. If the deferred gain is repudiated, i.e. it is not brought back into charge by deducting it from the base cost of the replacement asset, it is chargeable in the period in which the replacement asset is sold *(TCGA 1992 s.284A(3))*. HMRC have made it clear that they will not invoke this section if the deferred gain is included in the self-assessment return of the period.

Any gain on the disposal of assets qualifying for this relief is likely to also qualify for business assets' disposal relief (see section **13.33**), provided all the conditions are satisfied and the lifetime limit of £1m has not already been exceeded and tax will therefore be payable on the gain at effective rate of 10%.

13.30.2. Categories of assets qualifying for relief

The old and new asset must both belong to one of the following categories although they need not both belong to the same category *(TCGA 1992 s.155)*:

1. land and buildings occupied and used wholly for the purposes of the trade. This category does not apply where the taxpayer is carrying on a trade of dealing in or developing land or, if they have an estate or interest in that land, of providing services to the occupier of the land *(TCGA 1992 s.156)*;
2. fixed plant and machinery;
3. goodwill;
4. ships, aircraft and hovercraft;
5. satellites, space stations and spacecraft;
6. milk, fish or potato quotas and ewe or suckler cow premium quotas;
7. payment entitlements under the basic payment scheme, i.e. the scheme of income support for farmers under Regulation (EU) No. 1307/2013 of the European Parliament and of the Council.

13.30.3. Use of assets in trade

The relief is available to taxpayers who are carrying on a trade, profession or vocation *(TCGA 1992 ss.152 & 158)* and, in order to obtain full relief, the old and new assets must both be used for the purpose of a trade carried on by the taxpayer, although they need not both be used in the same trade *(TCGA 1992 s.152(1))*. If the asset has only been so used for part of the period of ownership or, in the case of buildings only, only part of the asset has been so used an appropriate portion of the gain may be rolled over *(TCGA 1992 s.152(6)&(7))*. Periods before 1 April 1982 are ignored in making the apportionment. The new asset must not be purchased with a view to realising a gain on its disposal *(TCGA 1992 s.152(5))*. Relief is also not available where an asset is purchased for use in a business, but is sold before it is so used *(Temperley v Visibell Ltd (1973) (49 TC 129))*.

13.30.4. Time limits

The new asset must be purchased within a period commencing one year before and ending three years after the disposal *(TCGA 1992 s.152(3)&(4))*. HMRC will allow a claim made outside the normal time limit provided that the taxpayer had a firm intention to acquire a qualifying asset within the time limit, but was prevented from doing so by factors outside his control, and actually acquired the qualifying asset as soon as possible thereafter.

The new asset does not have to be taken into use immediately, but must be taken into use within a reasonable period of time. Where the new asset is used in a different trade from the old asset, HMRC accept that there will often be an interval between the cessation of the old business and the commencement of the new business and a claim is permissible provided that the interval does not exceed three years (*SP8/81*). In *Milton v Chivers (HMIT) (1995) (SpC 57)* it was held by the Special Commissioners that relief was not available when a taxpayer purchased a property in March 1990 intending to use it as a launderette, but changed his mind and opened a second-hand shop a year later. Where an asset is not ready for use when it is purchased, relief will be available provided that all reasonable steps are taken to bring it into use as soon as is practicable.

13.30.5. Provisional claim

A provisional claim may be made where an unconditional contract has been entered into to buy the new asset, but the purchase has not taken place *(TCGA 1992 s.153A*). In order to make a provisional claim:

- the whole or a specified part of the proceeds must be re-invested in the new assets;
- the reinvestment must take place within the specified time limits;
- the new assets must be within the classes of assets eligible for relief.

Any necessary adjustments may be made later by the repayment of tax even if the time limit has expired *(TCGA 1992 s.152(4))*. Under self-assessment a taxpayer may obtain the relief when they dispose of the old asset by declaring an intention to purchase a new asset. If the claim is not withdrawn and the proceeds are not reinvested, the claim will cease to be effective three years after

31 January in the year following the tax year in which the old assets are sold. Interest will run from the normal due date.

13.30.6. Partial re-investment of proceeds

If not all the proceeds are re-invested a portion of the gain is taxable immediately *(TCGA 1992 s.153)*. This portion is the lower of:

- the amount of the gain; and
- the proceeds (or portion of proceeds attributable to business use) not re-invested.

Example

Smith purchased a factory for £70,000 in May 1998. It was sold in March 2002 for £110,000, 10% of the factory having been let. In December 2001 a new factory was purchased for £95,000 and was used wholly for the purposes of their business. This factory was sold for £140,000 in August 2021.

Disposal March 2002:

	Business (90%)	**Non-business (10%)**
	£	**£**
Proceeds	99,000	11,000
Cost	(63,000)	(7,000)
	36,000	4,000
Taxable – lower of Proceeds not re-invested £4,000 (£99,000 - £95,000) Gain £36,000		
	(4,000)	
Gain rolled over	£32,000	

A total of £8,000, £4,000 relating to the non-business portion and the proceeds not re-invested of £4,000 was taxable in March 2002.

Disposal August 2021

	£	£
Proceeds		140,000
Cost	95,000	
Less: Gain rolled over	(32,000)	
		(63,000)
Gain		£77,000

13.30.7. Other points

A gain may be rolled over against the deemed cost of an asset, i.e. the market value of an asset received by way of a gift *(TCGA 1992 s.152(10))*. A gain arising on an asset disposed of by way of gift may be rolled over.

Where only part of an asset is sold, the gain on that part may not be rolled over against the cost of the remaining part of the asset *(Walton v Tippett (1996) (BTC 25))*.

Where the proceeds of a disposal are used to enhance existing assets, the gain may be rolled over against the enhancement expenditure, provided that the enhanced assets are only used for the purpose of the trade, and are immediately taken into use for the purpose of the trade after the completion of the enhancement *(ESC D22)*.

13.30.8. Held-over gains

If the replacement asset is a depreciating asset, the gain cannot be deferred indefinitely, but crystallises on the earliest of:

- the disposal of the replacement asset;
- the date the replacement asset ceases to be used in the trade (unless this is due to the death of the claimant *(ESC D45)*);
- 10 years after the acquisition of the replacement asset.

(TCGA 1992 s.154)

An asset is a depreciating asset if it is, or in the next 10 years will become, a wasting asset, i.e. it has an expected useful life of 60 years or less. This includes leased assets where the lease has less than 60 years to run. This rule exists because, if a taxpayer were allowed to roll a gain over against the cost of a wasting asset and this asset were subsequently scrapped, or sold for a very small sum, the original gain would never become taxable.

The gain may be transferred to a replacement non-depreciating asset if it is acquired before the gain crystallises *(TCGA 1992 s.154(4)&(5))*.

Any gain on the disposal of assets qualifying for this relief is likely to also qualify for entrepreneurs' relief (see section **13.33**), provided all the conditions are satisfied and the lifetime limit of £10m has not already been exceeded and tax will therefore be payable on the gain at effective rate of 10%.

Example

A building was sold on 1 April 2021, a piece of machinery is acquired in December 2021, and a hold-over election is made. A new building is acquired in 2024. Provided that the machine is still being used in the business at that date and the gain has not therefore already crystallised, the gain may now be rolled over against the cost of the new building.

13.30.9. Compulsory purchase

Where land is compulsorily purchased by any authority with the power to do so, and the consideration paid is less than the greater of £3,000 or 5% of the value of the total holding before the sale, any gain arising on the disposal may be deducted from the cost of the remaining land provided that the transferor did not take any steps to dispose of the remaining land or to make his willingness to do so known *(TCGA 1992 s.243)*. If the consideration exceeds the value of the remaining land there will be no allowable cost on a subsequent disposal of the remaining land *(TCGA 1992 s.244).*

Where land is compulsorily purchased and the transferor took no steps to dispose of the land or to make his willingness to do so known, and the sum received is greater than the above limits, the gain may be rolled over where the sum received is used to acquire other land, other than excluded land *(TCGA 1992 s.247(1)&(2)).* Excluded land is defined by TCGA 1992 s.248 as private residential property. For the purpose of making the claim the compulsory purchase is deemed to have been made at the time that the compensation payable is determined *(TCGA 1992 s.246).* Relief is available to a landlord where tenants exercise the right to buy the freehold under the Leasehold Reform Act 1967, Housing and Urban Development Act 1993 or the Housing Acts 1985-1996 (*SP 13/93*).

All the provisions concerning partial reinvestment, time limits and reinvestment in depreciating assets apply to compulsory purchase.

13.30.10. Exchange of joint interest in land

Where there has been an exchange of joint beneficial interests in land, so that each taxpayer becomes the sole owner of one or more pieces of land, roll-over relief is available on the exchange. The relief operates in the same manner as for compulsory purchase *(TCGA 1992 s.248A).* This does not apply where the land acquired is the taxpayer's main residence.

13.31. Gift Relief

13.31.1. Operation of relief

Where certain types of assets are transferred by way of a gift to a person who is resident in the UK, other than for a dual-resident person who is not liable to tax on the disposal by virtue of a double tax treaty, a joint election may be made by the donor and donee for the gain arising on the transfer to be deducted from the donee's acquisition cost *(TCGA 1992 s.165(1)(a)&(b)).*

The main types of transfers covered are:

- transfers of assets used in the donor's business *(TCGA 1992 s.165(2)(a));*
- shares or securities in a trading company or a holding company of a trading group, provided that these are not listed on a recognised stock exchange *(TCGA 1992 s.165(2)(b));*
- transfers which give rise to an immediate IHT charge, if a chargeable transfer were made at the time of the disposal *(TCGA 1992 s.260),* or is exempt due to being a transfer to a political party, a maintenance fund for historic buildings or is designated property under IHTA 1984 s.30;

- agricultural property (including short rotation coppices) which would be eligible for agricultural property relief if a chargeable transfer were made at the date of disposal, and it is not otherwise eligible as a business asset *(TCGA 1992 Sch.7 para. 1)*.

An election may only be made in respect of the appropriate portion of the gain where:

- in the case of a building, the asset has only satisfied the criteria for part of the period of ownership by the donor; or
- only part of the asset, e.g. part of a building, has satisfied the criteria.

(TCGA 1992 Sch.7 para. 5(1) & 6(1))

If consideration passes, e.g. the asset is sold at undervalue, a part of the gain is chargeable immediately. This is the lower of:

- amount of the gain;
- amount of consideration less original cost but before indexation allowance.

(TCGA 1992 s.165(4), (6)&(7))

As with roll-over relief, the gain is deducted from the donee's base cost.

It is not necessary to agree a valuation of an asset in many cases where hold-over relief is claimed *(SP 8/92)*. These are:

- a joint application is made by the transferor and transferee;
- a calculation incorporating informally estimated valuations if necessary and a statement that both parties have satisfied themselves that the value of the asset at the date of transfer was in excess of the allowable cost is sent to HM Revenue & Customs.

Once a claim is agreed on this basis it may not be withdrawn by a taxpayer and, if it subsequently emerges that any information was incorrect, or the statement by either the transferor or transferee was incomplete or incorrect, the CGT position of both of them will be reviewed in accordance with the statutory provisions *(SP 8/92 para. 8)*.

Example

John sold a property used in his business to his son, Peter, in October 2021 for £70,000 when its market value was £150,000. The property had been acquired in June 1998 for £65,000.

Disposal October 2021

	£	£
Market Value		150,000
Cost		(65,000)
		85,000
Gain chargeable October 2021		
Lower of:		
Actual proceeds	70,000	

Cost	(65,000)	
	£5,000	
and		
Total gain	£85,000	
		(5,000)
Gain eligible for gift relief		£80,000

Base cost of asset for Peter

	£
Market Value – October 2021	150,000
Gift Relief	(80,000)
Base Cost	£70,000

13.31.2. Crystallisation of Gain

Where the donee ceases to be resident in the UK within six years from the end of the tax year in which the gift was made *(TCGA 1992 s.168(4))* the held-over gain will crystallise and accrue to the donee on the date of emigration *(TCGA 1992 s.168(1))*. Where there has been a part disposal of the asset before emigration, the part of the gain which became chargeable on the part disposal is excluded from the gain becoming chargeable on emigration *(TCGA 1992 s.168(2))*. No gain/no loss disposals to a spouse are ignored *(TCGA 1992 s.168(3))*. These provisions do not apply where:

- the donee ceases to be resident in the UK due to his office or employment, all the duties of which are performed outside the UK; and
- within three years of that time the donee again becomes UK resident without having disposed of the asset *(TCGA 1992 s.168(5))*.

The donee is deemed to have disposed of the asset before emigration if they have disposed of it in circumstances which would have required the held-over gain to be deducted from the base cost of the asset, assuming that they had been resident in the UK at that date *(TCGA 92 s.168(6))*.

Where tax is not paid by the donee within 12 months of the due date it may be recovered from the donor, who may then recover the tax from the donee *(TCGA 1992 s.168(7), (9))*.

13.32. Transfer of Assets to a Limited Company

13.32.1. Operation of Relief

If an individual has been trading through an unincorporated business and subsequently transfers the business to a limited company, they make a disposal of chargeable assets. The gain arising on the transfer is deducted from the value of the shares received in the company *(TCGA 1992 s.162 (1)&(2))*.

In order to obtain the relief:

- the business must be transferred as a going concern, although there is no requirement for the business to continue as a going concern for a particular period after the transfer *(Gordon v IRC, IRC v Gordon (1991) (BTC 130))*;
- all the business assets (except possibly cash) must be transferred to the company. Relief is not precluded if some or all of the business's liabilities are not taken over by the company *(ESC D32)*. The assumption of responsibility for liabilities is not treated as consideration received by the transferor provided that the other conditions are satisfied;
- where the whole of the business of a partnership is transferred to a company each partner will be treated separately for the purpose of obtaining the relief *(ICAEW Tax Faculty Technical Release TAX 7/95)*.

Where the consideration for the transfer consists entirely of shares, the whole gain may be held over. Where there is a cash element the amount held over is:

$$\frac{\text{Value of Shares received from Company}}{\text{Total Consideration from Company}} \times \text{Total gains on assets}$$

(TCGA 1992 s.162 (3)&(4))

This relief will apply to all incorporations unless a taxpayer elects for the relief not to apply *(TCGA 1992 s.162A)*. Incorporations will generally qualify for entrepreneurs' relief and will therefore usually be taxable at 10%, but this relief may be applicable if, for example, a trader sells the shares within a year of incorporation and entrepreneurs' relief is therefore not available. The election must be made within two years of 31 January following the end of the tax year in which the business was transferred, although this time limit is reduced if the shares received are disposed of in the tax year of transfer or the following years. It is possible to avoid obtaining the relief by failing to transfer a non-cash asset into the company. In the case of a partnership, each partner may choose whether they wish to claim the relief.

Example

David transferred his business to a company in April 2002. The gain arising on the assets was £50,000 and the consideration comprised £80,000 in shares and £20,000 in cash. David sold the shares July 2021 for £110,000.

Gain held over April 2002

$$£50,000 \times \frac{£80,000}{£80,000 + £20,000} = £40,000$$

Gain July 2021

	£	£
Proceeds		110,000
Cost	80,000	
Gain held over	(40,000)	
		(40,000)
Gain		£70,000

13.32.2. Transfer of Goodwill

HMRC may challenge the value attributed to goodwill, where they feel that it has been overvalued. In such cases they will seek to reclassify the excess value as either employment income under ITEPA 2003 s.62, where they consider that the goodwill was overvalued in order to induce the individual to take up employment with the company, or as a distribution, where they consider that the excess value was received by the individual in his capacity as shareholder. They will allow 'inadvertent' distributions to be unwound by repayment of the excess to the company, if they consider that there was no intention to transfer the goodwill at overvalue and reasonable efforts were made to carry out the transaction at market value by using a professional valuation.

13.33. Business Asset Disposal Relief

13.33.1. Operation of relief

Business asset disposal relief (previously known as entrepreneurs' relief), reduces the CGT rate to 10% on all qualifying gains. Qualifying gains are treated as the lower tranche of a taxpayer's gains. Therefore, if the total of a taxpayer's taxable income and qualifying gains exceeds the higher rate threshold, all non-qualifying gains will be taxable at 20% or 28%. The relief applies to:

1. a material disposal of business assets, defined as a disposal of assets which have been owned by the individual throughout the period of two years ending on the date of the disposal *(TCGA 1992 s.169I(2)(a),(3))*. The period has been extended from one year to two years with effect from 6 April 2019. Goodwill will not qualify for the relief where the disposal is to a close company connected with the person making the disposal and immediately afterwards he, along with any connected person, owns 5% of the share capital or voting rights of the close company or of any company in a group company, unless sufficient shares are subsequently disposed of to another company within 28 days to reduce their interest to less than 5% of the share capital or voting rights *(TCGA 1992 s.169LA)*. The disposal must be of the whole or a part of the business, i.e. the business disposed of must be capable of being run as a going concern;
2. disposals of, or of interests in, assets in use for the purposes of the business at the time a business ceases to be carried on. The business with which the disposal is associated must have been owned by the individual throughout a period of two years ending on the date on which the business ceases to be carried on and the associated disposal must be made within three years from the date the business ceased *(TCGA 1992 s.169I(2)(b),(4))*.

The period has been extended from one year to two years with effect from 6 April 2019.;

3. a disposal of shares or securities in a company. The following conditions apply:
   a. the company must be the individual's personal company and must be a trading company or the holding company of a trading group;
   b. the individual must be an officer or employee of the company (or of one or more of the group companies).

These conditions must be satisfied throughout the period of two years ending on the date of disposal. The period has been extended from one year to two years with effect from 6 April 2019. A personal company is defined as a company in which:

1. the individual holds at least 5% of the ordinary share capital; and
2. that holding gives the individual at least 5% of the voting rights; and
3. that holding gives entitlement either to at least 5% of the amounts available to equity holders or to at least 5% of the assets available for distribution in a winding up *(TCGA 1992 s.169S(3))*.

Equity may also include loans other than normal commercial loans, in particular where the lender is entitled to more than a normal commercial rate of return.

Where two or more persons own shares jointly, they are treated as each holding the appropriate proportion of the holding and voting power, i.e. if a husband and wife jointly owned the entire share capital they are both assumed to each hold 50% of the shares and the voting power *(TCGA 1992 s.169S(4))*.

A holding company is defined as a company with one or more 51% subsidiaries and a trading company and trading group are defined as in TCGA 1992 s.165, subject to the modifications of TCGA 1992 Sch. 7ZA part 2 and trading activities are to be interpreted in accordance with TCGA 1992 Sch. 7ZA part 3 *(TCGA 1992 Sch. 7ZA para. 1)*. Part 2 sets out the circumstances in which a proportion of the activities of a joint venture company may be attributed to the company holding its shares and part 3 sets out how the activities of a company in its capacity as a member of a partnership are to be treated in determining a claimant's eligibility for entrepreneurs' relief.

Where a business is carried on as a partnership, the partnership assets are treated as belonging to the individual partners. The relief is also available where:

1. an individual carrying on a trade as a sole trader takes on a partner or partners and makes a disposal of assets;
2. an individual disposes of all of, or part of, his interest in the partnership. *(TCGA 1992 s.169H(8))*.

13.33.2. Transfer of assets to a company – transitional provision

Where assets are transferred to a limited company under circumstances where TCGA 1992 s.162 (see **13.32**) was available (even if the section was disapplied) and:

1. the company is the individual's personal company and is either a trading company or the holding company of a trading group; and
2. the individual is an officer or employee of the company or accompany which is a member of the trading group

relief will be available where the combined period of ownership of the assets in the unincorporated business and the shares is at least two years *(TCGA 1992 s.169I ss.7ZA&ZB)*

13.33.3. Associated disposals

Business asset disposal relief is also available on disposals of assets associated with relevant material disposals, i.e. disposals of assets which the claimant owns personally, but which are used by a partnership of which they are a member or by a company in which they are a shareholder. The material disposal must be made as part of a withdrawal from participation in the business of the partnership, company or group. The shares disposed of must constitute at least 5% of the ordinary share capital, carry at least 5% of voting rights of a company and beneficially entitle the holder to at least 5% of any distribution and assets on a winding up *(TCGA 1992 s.169K(1A)-(1D))*. Where the disposal is of an interest in a partnership, the individual must have an interest of at least 5% in the assets of the partnership, although, even if the interest is less than 5% at the date of disposal, this will still qualify if they held a 5% interest in the partnership for at least three of the eight years preceding the disposal *(TCGA 1992 s.169K(1AA))*.

No partnership or share purchase arrangement must exist at the date of disposal, although the material disposal of the partnership interest itself cannot be a partnership purchase arrangement and thereby deny relief for the associated disposal *(TCGA 1992 s.169K(1AA))*. Furthermore, where the associated disposal takes place before the material disposal of the interest in the partnership or company, any arrangements connected with the latter are not to be treated as partnership purchase arrangements or share purchase arrangements, thereby denying relief for the associated disposal *(TCGA 1992 s.169K(3AA)&(3BA))*. Arrangements are not to be treated as partnership purchase agreements or share purchase agreements if they were entered into before both the associated disposal and the material disposal and without regards to either of them *(TCGA 1992 s.169K(6A))*.

The assets (or interests therein) disposed of must have been owned for a period of three years ending on the earlier of the date of the disposal *(TCGA 1992 s.169K(4A))*. Where:

1. the assets disposed of were only used for the purpose of the business for part of the period that they were owned by the individual; or
2. only a part of the assets disposed of were used for the purpose of the business; or
3. the individual making the disposal was only involved with the business (whether as a sole trader, partner or employer or officer of a personal company) for part of the period that the assets disposed of were owned by the individual; or
4. the assets disposed of were rented to the business;

the relief will be restricted to a just and reasonable portion of the gain *(TCGA 1992 s.169P(1)-(4))*. In the first three cases the gain will be time-apportioned, whilst in the fourth case the amount of the gain qualifying for relief will depend on the extent to which the rent paid was less than a market rent *(TCGA 1992 s.169P(5))*.

The asset must have been used in the business for a period of at least one year ending on the earlier of the date of the disposal or the cessation of the business carried on by the partnership or company *(TCGA 1992 s.169K(4))*.

Where the disposal is not of shares or securities in a company, the relief is only available on the disposal of assets used for the purpose of the business and excludes shares and securities or other assets which are held as an investment *(TCGA 1992 s.169L)*.

13.33.4. Lifetime limit

A claim must be made for the relief and the claim must be made by 31 January following the end of the tax year in which the disposal is made *(TCGA 1992 s.169M)*. This relief is subject to a lifetime limit which was reduced from £10m to £1m with effect from 11 March 2020 *(TCGA 1992 s.169N(4))*.

Where there is a reorganisation of share capital within TCGA 1992 s.126 and the original shares and the new holding are treated as the same asset under TCGA 1992 s.127, it is possible that a disposal of the shares at the time of the reorganisation might qualify for relief, but that a later gain of the new holding might not do so, e.g. if the new holding no longer qualifies as the individual's personal company. TCGA 1992 s.169Q permits an election to be made to disapply TCGA 1992 s.127 on a reorganisation *(TCGA 1992 s.169Q(1)-(3))*. The election must be made by 31 January following the tax year in which the reorganisation took place *(TCGA 1992 s.169Q(4))*. Where there is a reorganisation and shares are exchanged for qualifying corporate bonds and any gain is deferred under TCGA 1992 s.116(10), relief may be claimed on the gain arising at the time of the reorganisation, provided that the deemed disposal satisfies all other conditions *(TCGA 1992 s.169R).*

13.34. Investors' Relief

The Finance Act 2016 introduced a new relief, which applies a 10% tax rate of CGT to gains arising on the disposal of qualifying shares in an unlisted trading company or the holding company of a trading group by individuals who are not officers or employees of the company. The shares must:

- be ordinary shares fully paid in cash which have been newly issued on or after 17 March 2016;
- have been issued at arm's length for genuine commercial reasons;
- have been held for at least three years.

Shares which have been held for less than three years, but which satisfy all the other conditions are termed 'potentially qualifying shares' *(TCGA 1992 s.169VB).*

There is a £10m lifetime limit, which is separate from the lifetime limit for business asset disposal relief/entrepreneurs' relief and was not reduced from 6 April 2020.

13.35. Losses on Loans to Traders

Debts, except debts on securities, are normally exempt assets. Therefore, no allowable loss may usually arise. An allowable loss may arise on a loan or guarantee made by an individual if:

- the money lent is used by the borrower wholly for the purposes of trade (not including that of lending money), or to set up a trade;
- the borrower is resident in UK;
- the debt is not debt on a security;
- the loan is not a discounted security.

(TCGA 1992 s.253(1))

To obtain relief:

- some or all of the principal must have become irrecoverable;
- the right to recover the amount must not have been assigned;
- the claimant and borrower must not have been married to each other at the time the loan was made, nor at any other time.

(TCGA 1992 s.253(3))

The taxpayer will be treated as having incurred an allowable loss equal to the irrecoverable amount and the loss is deemed to have arisen on the date the claim was made or at a specified time in the previous two years, provided that the loan was irrecoverable at that date *(TCGA 1992 s.253(3)&(3A); FA 1996 Sch.*

39, para. 8). Relief is only given for the amount of the lost principal, not lost interest *(TCGA 1992 s.253(3A))*.

Where all or some of the debt is subsequently recovered, i.e. a person receives money, or money's worth in consideration of their right to recovery, a gain will arise whether that person is the original lender or the right to recovery has been assigned to him *(TCGA 1992 s.253(5)&(9)*. The time limit for making a claim is 31 January in the sixth tax year after the guarantee payment is made.

13.36. Loan Guarantees

Relief is available for a payment under guarantee if:

- the guarantee was in respect of a qualifying loan. This is defined as in section **13.35** above, except that it may be a debt on a security;
- some of the principal or interest has become irrecoverable from the borrower;
- the claimant has not assigned the right to recover the amount in consequence of making payment;
- the claimant and borrower have not been married to each other at the time the loan was made, nor at any other time.

(TCGA 1992 s.253(4))

Where the loan was made before 24 January 2019 relief is only available if the borrower is UK resident *TCGA 1992 s.253(1)(b))*.

The taxpayer is deemed to have incurred a loss equal to the payment under the guarantee.

An individual can back-date the time of loss by up to two years. Unlike relief for losses on loans, relief is available both for lost amounts of principal and lost interest. If any part of the loan is subsequently recovered, the amount recovered is treated as a chargeable gain. The time limit for making a claim is 31 January in the sixth tax year after the guarantee payment is made.

Chapter 14. Corporation Tax

14.1. Scope of Corporation Tax

Corporation tax is payable by limited companies and by certain unincorporated organisations such as golf clubs. Companies which are resident in the UK pay corporation tax on their worldwide income. A company is resident in the UK if it is either:

- incorporated in the UK; or
- centrally managed and controlled in the UK.

(CTA 2009 s.14)

A company is resident where the real business of the company is carried on. 'Business' has a wider meaning than 'trade' and can include the purchase of stock or the holding of investments in a subsidiary company. In determining where central management and control is located, HMRC will look at the highest level of the company, for example where board meetings are held. There are no rigid guidelines and the factors taken into consideration, and their relative weightings, may vary in different cases. HMRC will look behind the legal position to determine the individuals who really control the company. For example, if the named directors are individuals resident in, say, the Cayman Islands and meetings take place there, but it is found that the named directors in practice act on the instructions of UK resident individuals ('shadow directors'), the company will be considered to be resident in the UK, although the decision in *Wood v Holden (HMIT) (2006) (STC 443)*, in which a Dutch-registered company was held[8] not to be UK resident, has established that there is a difference between exercising management and control and being able to influence those who do so.

The issue of central management and control arose in the case of *R v. Charlton, Cunningham and Wheeler (1996).* The company was advised to set up an offshore company incorporated in Jersey to shelter profits from UK corporation tax. However, the directors of the company were UK resident and board meetings were held in the UK; therefore, the company was UK resident. Following the decision in *News Datacom & Another v HM Revenue & Customs (2007) (SpC 561)* HMRC will try to build up a complete picture of how the business is run over a period of time, rather than looking at specific periods. It will not generally be the case that the company's residence status will change

---

[8] By the High Court and, subsequently, the Court of Appeal, overturning the Special Commissioners' decision.

if one board meeting takes place somewhere other than the jurisdiction in which the company claims to be resident.

14.1.1. Non-resident companies

Where a company is not UK resident it is not liable to corporation tax, unless it trades in the UK through a permanent establishment such as a branch or agency, in which case corporation tax is payable on the profits of the branch or permanent establishment, unless the profits are exempt under the terms of a double taxation treaty *(CTA 2009 s.5(2),(3))*.

14.2. Trading income

14.2.1. General

The rules concerning the taxation of trading income are broadly the same as for income tax. However, the following points should be noted:

- there is no disallowance of the private use element of motoring and other expenses, and full WDAs may be claimed on all company cars and other assets where there is an element of private use. The private use element is, instead, the subject of a benefit in kind charge on the employees;
- there are restrictions on claiming the annual investment allowance (AIA) which apply only to companies (see below);
- interest paid and received falls within the loan relationship regime (see section **14.3**), which has no equivalent in income tax; and
- gains and losses relating to intangible fixed assets fall within the intangible fixed assets (IFA) regime (see section **14.4**), which has no equivalent in income tax.

14.2.2. Annual investment allowance – restrictions applying to companies

CAA 2001 ss.51B–51H place a number of restrictions on claiming the AIA which apply only to companies.

- A company may only claim a single AIA, regardless of the number of qualifying activities which it carries on. The allowance can be allocated between the different activities as a company wishes *(CAA 2001 s.51B)*.
- Groups of companies may only claim a single AIA for a financial year, which may be allocated between the group companies as they see fit to the extent that the companies have incurred relevant AIA qualifying expenditure (i.e. AIA qualifying expenditure incurred by any company whose chargeable period ends in the financial year). This restriction applies where a parent undertaking controls another company at the end of that other company's chargeable period ending in the financial year *(CAA 2001 s.51C)*.
- Where two or more companies are controlled by the same person or are

related to one another (but are not part of the same group), they are only entitled to a single AIA, which may be allocated between the companies as they see fit to the extent that the companies have incurred relevant AIA qualifying expenditure (i.e. AIA qualifying expenditure incurred by any company whose chargeable period ends in the financial year) *(CAA 2001 s.51E)*.

- Where two or more groups are controlled by the same person or are related to one another, they are only entitled to a single AIA, which may be allocated between the companies as they see fit to the extent that the groups have incurred relevant AIA qualifying expenditure (i.e. AIA qualifying expenditure incurred by any company whose chargeable period ends in the financial year) *(CAA 2001 s.51D)*.

Control is defined by CAA 2001 s.574(2) in relation to companies which are corporate bodies, i.e. the ability to secure that the affairs of the company are carried in accordance with that person's wishes either through the holding of shares or powers conferred by the articles of association or other document. In relation to companies which are unincorporated bodies (C), control is defined as the power of a person (P) to ensure that the affairs of C are conducted in accordance with the wishes of P, whether through the possession of shares or voting power in relation to C or another body, or as a result of any powers conferred by the constitution of C or another body *(CAA 2001 s.51F)*.

Qualifying activities are related to one another if the activities are either carried on from the same premises *(CAA 2001 s.51G(5))* or if more than 50% of the turnover for each business is derived from activities sharing the same first-level NACE classification *(CAA 2001s s.51G(6),(7))*.

14.2.3. First-year tax credits

CAA 2001 Sch. A1 allows companies to claim a credit for a loss on a qualifying activity, the profits of which are chargeable to corporation tax, arising from claiming first year allowances under CAA 2001 s.45A (energy-saving plant) or s.45H (environmentally beneficial plant or machinery). However, these will be withdrawn for expenditure from 1 April 2020 onwards. This does not include additional VAT liabilities treated as qualifying expenditure under CAA 2001 s.236. The credit may either be paid to the company or used to discharge outstanding corporation tax liabilities *(CAA 2001 Sch. A1 para. 18)*. A first–year tax credit is not treated as income of the company for any purpose *(CAA 2001 Sch. A1 para. 23)*. The maximum credit which may be claimed is:

1. the surrenderable loss (the lower of loss incurred in carrying on the qualifying activity and the amount of the first year allowance claimed) multiplied by the corporation tax rate(s) applicable to the chargeable period; and

2. the **greater** of £250,000 and the total of the company's PAYE and NIC liabilities for payment periods ending in the chargeable period. The total of the PAYE and NIC liabilities disregards any deduction which a company is required to make in respect of child tax credit, working tax credit, statutory sick pay or statutory maternity pay.

(CAA 2001 Sch. A1 paras. 1-3, 17)

Any loss in respect of which a first-year tax credit is claimed must be deducted from any loss carried forward for offset against the profits of future chargeable period *(CAA 2001 Sch. A1 paras. 19-20)*.

A claim must be made for first-year tax credit in a company's return and these must be separately shown and identified *(CAA 2001 s.262(2B))*.

A first-year tax credit may only be claimed on property income other than a furnished holiday lettings business or an overseas property business if it is carried on on a commercial basis *(CAA 2001 Sch. A1 paras. 5, 6)*.

A first-year tax credit may not be claimed if a company is an 'excluded company' at any time during the period. An excluded company is a company which, at any time during the period, is entitled to make a claim under:

- CTA 2010 ss.642-649 (co-operative housing association);
- CTA 2010 ss.651-657 (self-build society);
- CTA 2010 ss.472-477 (charitable companies).

(CAA 2001 Sch. A1 para. 1(4))

The unrelieved loss, where the qualifying activity is an activity other than a life assurance business or a furnished holiday lettings business is the loss reduced by:

1. any relief which has been claimed, or which could have been claimed, under CTA 2010 s.37(3)(a) (offset of loss against total profits of same chargeable period); or
2. any relief which has been claimed, or which could have been claimed, under CTA 2010 s.37(3)(b) or s.42(2)(4) (offset of loss against total profits of earlier chargeable periods); or
3. any loss surrendered, or which could have been surrendered to another group company or consortium member under CTA 2010 s.99; or
4. any amount set off against the loss under CTA 2010 ss.92-96 (write-off against government investment).

(CAA 2001 Sch. A1 para. 11(2),(4))

The loss available for the credit may not be increased by:

1. losses brought forward from earlier chargeable periods under CTA 2010 s.45(4); or
2. losses carried back from a later chargeable period under CTA 2010

s.37(3)(b) or s.42(2)(4); or

3. losses incurred on a leasing contract to which CTA 2010 s.53 applies.

(CAA 2001 Sch. A1 para. 11(3))

Where the qualifying activity is a letting business, other than a furnished holiday lettings business the amount of the loss must be reduced by:

1. any relief which has been claimed, or which could have been claimed, under CTA 2010 s.62(1)-(3) (offset of loss against total profits of same chargeable period); or
2. any loss surrendered, or which could have been surrendered to another group company or consortium member under CTA 2010 s.99; or
3. any loss surrendered under a tax credit provision contained in CTA 2009 ss. 1151-1158 (tax credits for remediation of contaminated land); or
4. any amount set off against the loss under CTA 2010 ss.92-96 (write-off against government investment).

The loss available for the credit may not be increased by losses brought forward from earlier chargeable periods under CTA 2010 s.62(4),(5) *(CAA 2001 Sch. A1 para. 12).*

Where the qualifying activity is an overseas property business, other than a furnished holiday lettings business, the amount of the loss must be reduced by any amount set off against the loss under CTA 2010 ss.92-96 (write-off against government investment), but the loss available for the credit may not be increased by losses brought forward from earlier chargeable periods under CTA 2010 s.66(1)-(3) *(CAA 2001 Sch. A1 para. 13).*

All or part of the first-year tax credit may be clawed back where the item of plant and machinery which gave rise to the credit is disposed of within a period of four years from the end of the chargeable period in which it is acquired and the disposal proceeds are less than the amount of the credit originally claimed *(CAA 2001 Sch. A1 paras. 24-26).*

14.2.4. Expenditure on plant and machinery in designated assisted areas

An ECA of 100% may be claimed by companies on expenditure incurred on plant and machinery acquired for use in 'designated assisted areas' by the later of eight years of the date that an area is first so designated by a Treasury order and 31 March 2021. The conditions for claiming this allowance are:

1. the company is within the charge to corporation tax; and
2. the expenditure is incurred for the purposes of a qualifying activity under CAA 2001 s.15(1)(a) or 15(1)(f); and
3. the business for which the expenditure has been incurred is not of a kind previously carried on by the company, is an expansion of the business

previously carried or is the start-up of an activity which represents a fundamental change in a product or production process; and

4. the plant or machinery is unused; and
5. the expenditure is not incurred on plant and machinery intended to perform the same or similar function as other plant and machinery on which qualifying expenditure has previously been incurred and which has been superseded by the new plant or machinery.

Where the expenditure has significantly enhanced the function of plant or machinery on which expenditure has previously been incurred, an ECA may be claimed on that part of the expenditure which may fairly be attributed to the enhancement.

(CAA 2001 s.45K)

14.2.5. Super-deductions and other temporary first-year allowances

FA 2021 allows companies, but not sole traders or partnerships, to claim enhanced first-year allowances on the following expenditure:

1. The expenditure must be incurred between 1 April 2021 and 31 March 2023 by a company within the charge to corporation tax, unless it is incurred as a result of a contract entered into before 3 March 2021, in which case it is treated as being incurred on the date the contract was entered into;
2. The expenditure must be on plant and machinery which is new and not second-hand;
3. It does not fall within any of the exclusions in CAA2001 s.46(2), the principal exclusion being cars.

(FA 2021 s.2(2)&(3))

The amount of the deduction available is:

1. In the case of special rate expenditure 50% (termed an SR allowance);
2. In the case of expenditure on plant and machinery for use partly in a ring-fence trade and partly in another qualifying activity 100%;
3. In all other cases 130% (termed a super-deduction).

(FA 2021 s.2(1))

These allowances will be reduced where the expenditure is incurred in a chargeable accounting period ending after 31 March 2023.

It is not possible to claim an AIA and a super-deduction or SR allowance on the same expenditure. It will generally be more advantageous to claim a super-deduction in preference to the AIA, but the decision whether to claim the AIA or a SR allowance is more complex and will depend whether a balancing might arise on disposal.

Where a disposal is made of expenditure in respect of which a super-deduction or an SR allowance has been claimed, a balancing charge will arise. For disposals in chargeable accounting periods ending on or before 31 March 2023, the charge will be 130% of the disposal proceeds, where a super-dedution has ben claimed, and 50% of the disposal disposal proceeds, where an SR llowance has been claimed *(FA 2021 ss.12&13)*.

14.3. Loan relationships

Loan relationships and the tax treatment of intangibles are complex areas of law. The next two sections therefore provide an overview rather than a comprehensive guide.

14.3.1. Definition of loan relationship

A loan relationship exists when a company is a debtor or creditor in respect of a debt which either:

- arose through the lending of money in any currency, whether or not the debt is secured; or
- is a debt on a security.

(CTA 2009 ss.302 & 303)

Trade debtors and trade creditors do not, therefore, fall within the loan relationship rules since a trade debt arises from the sale of goods; however, the rules cover interest paid or received, whether net or gross, such as bank overdraft interest, bank deposit interest, building society interest and debenture interest.

14.3.2. Scope of loan relationship rules

All receipts and payments under a loan relationship are covered by the rules, including exchange gains and losses arising on a loan relationship *(CTA 2009 s.307(3) & s.328(1))*. Payments falling within the loan relationship rules include charges and expenses incurred directly in:

- bringing the loan relationship into existence, e.g. arrangement fees;
- giving effect to transactions under the loan relationship;
- making payments under the loan relationship;
- taking steps to ensure receipts under the relationship.

(CTA 2009 s.307(4))

The rules also cover such payments relating to abortive loan relationships and loan relationships which the company might still enter into *(CTA 2009 s.329(1)&(2))*.

14.3.3. Accounting for loan relationships

In determining the profit or loss of an accounting period a company may use any method which is in accordance with generally accepted accounting practice (GAAP) *(CTA 2009 s.307(2))*. If a method has been used in the accounts which is not in accordance with GAAP, the profit or loss must be re-computed using such a method *(CTA 2009 s.309)*. An amount is recognised in determining the profit or loss of the period if it has been recognised in the period in either the profit and loss account, income statement, statement of comprehensive income, statement of total recognised income and expense, statement of changes in equity, statement of income and retained earnings, statement of comprehensive income or any other statement of items brought into account in computing the company's profit and losses for the period, unless they relate to the correction of fundamental errors *(CTA 2009 s.308)*.

A company may use different methods for different loan relationships, or indeed for the same loan relationship in different accounting periods or different parts of the same accounting period. In the latter case, there is a deemed disposal and re-acquisition of the loan relationship at the date of the change, and the loan relationship before the change is therefore deemed to be distinct from the loan relationship after the change. Both the deemed disposal and the deemed acquisition are taken to be at the fair value of the relationship at that time *(FA 1996 s.90(4))*. In the period when a change is made, the difference between the amounts which would have been brought into account, on the assumption that there is a disposal and re-acquisition of the loan relationship at fair value at the date of the change and the amounts which have actually been brought into account, is treated as a net debit or credit *(FA 1996 s.90(3))*.

14.3.4. Basis of taxation

The basis on which the loan relationships are taxed depends on whether they arose for a trading or a non-trading purpose. Receipts and payments relating to trading loan relationships such as bank overdraft interest or debenture interest payable are included in trading profits on an accruals basis *(CTA 2009 s.297)*. A company is unlikely to receive any income under a trading loan relationship unless it is a bank or other financial institution.

All profits, gains and losses arising under non-trading loan relationships are aggregated and if there is a net profit, this is taxed as a non-trading profit *(CTA 2009 s.301)*. Where there is a net loss, relief is available in a similar manner to trading losses (see section **14.14**) *(CTA 2009 ss. 456-462)*.

14.3.5. Loan relationships between connected parties

Where a loan relationship is between connected parties, only an amortised cost method of accounting may be used (the amount at which the loan relationship is measured at initial recognition, less principal repayments and plus or minus any unamortised original premium or discount) *(CTA 2009 s.349(2))*. Two parties are connected if, at the time the loan relationship arises:

- one party is a company which is controlled by the other company; or
- both parties are companies which are controlled by the same person.

(CTA 2009 s.348(6) & s.466)

Control is defined by CTA 2009 s.472 as the power of a person to secure that the affairs of the company are conducted in accordance with his wishes either:

1. by means of the holding of shares or the possession of voting power in or in relation to the company or any other company; or
2. by virtue of any powers conferred by the articles of association or other document regulating the company or any other company.

14.4. Intangible Fixed Assets

14.4.1. Scope of provisions

The intangible fixed assets legislation is contained in CTA 2009 pt. 8 and applies to intangible fixed assets acquired or created on or after 1 April 2002 *(CTA 2009 s.882(1), s.889(1) & s.905(8))*. These provisions cover all assets treated as intangible fixed asset under GAAP, including internally-generated assets, except for the following:

- rights over intangible fixed assets *(CTA 2009 s.805);*
- websites, which had previously been treated as tangible assets under FRS 15, but which were not treated as intangible assets following the adoption of international standards *(CTA 2009 s.804);*
- oil licences *(CTA 2009 s.809);*
- financial assets *(CTA 2009 s.806);*
- rights in companies, trusts etc. *(CTA 2009 s.807);*
- intangible fixed assets held for a non-commercial purposes *(CTA 2009 s.803)*.

Assets which come within these provisions include:

- patents, unless an election has been made for the 'patent box' provisions to apply (see section **14.4.12**);
- licences;
- goodwill;
- know-how.

Assets held under finance leases are generally treated as if the assets were owned by the lessor, i.e. the lessor must account for the cost of the asset of the asset under the IFA regime and is entitled to any deductions under these provisions *(Corporation Tax (Finance Leasing of Intangible Assets) Regulations 2002 SI2002/1967 reg. 3)*. A lessor is, however, not entitled to:

1. elect for a writing down allowance on a fixed rate basis (see section **14.4.3**);

2. claim roll-over relief when an intangible fixed asset is disposed of and the proceeds are re-invested.

(Corporation Tax (Finance Leasing of Intangible Assets) Regulations 2002 (SI2002/1967) reg. 4)

Up to 30 June 2020 the provisions only applied where an asset was acquired from a related party, if:

- the asset was acquired from a firm (i.e. company, partnership or LLP) in relation to which the asset was a chargeable intangible asset immediately before the acquisition; or
- the asset was acquired from an intermediary who acquired the asset before commencement from a party who was unrelated both at the time of the acquisition of the asset by the intermediary and at the time of the acquisition of the asset by the company from the intermediary; or
- where the asset was created after commencement, whether by the person from whom it was acquired or by another person.

(CTA 2009 s.882(3)-(5))

From 1 July 2020, any asset acquired from a related party will be within the intangible assets regime *(CTA 2009 s.882(1C))*.

Two parties are related in the following four cases where a person (either a natural person or a legal entity) is a related part of a company:

1. one party controls the other as defined by CTA 2010 s.1124, or has a 'major interest' (defined as an interest of at least 40%) in the other;
2. both parties are under the control of the same single person;
3. the company is a close company and the person is a participator, or an associate of a participator, in the company; or
4. the other person is a company and both companies are in the same group.

Assets not falling within the legislation are termed **existing assets**, meaning that they were already existing when the regime began *(CTA 2009 s.881)*. These "existing assets" provisions do not apply to assets acquired following a reorganisation under TCGA 1992 s.139 or s.140A *(CTA 2009 s.892)*.

An asset is treated as having been created or acquired on the date that the expenditure is incurred *(CTA 2009 s.883)*. Expenditure is treated as having been incurred when it is recognised for accounting purposes in the profit and loss account, statement of total recognised gains and losses or statement of changes of equity or other similar statement, or which would have been so recognised if accounts had been drawn up in accordance with GAAP *(CTA 2009 s.716 & s.905)*. This excludes the correction of fundamental errors. If only part of the expenditure was incurred on or after 1 April 2002, that part is treated as a separate asset and the provisions apply to that part and expenditure must be allocated on a just and reasonable basis *(CTA 2009 s.883(5)&(7))*. Internally generated goodwill is regarded as having been created before 1 April 2002, if the business in question was carried on at any time before that date by the company or a related party, e.g. if a sole trader commenced trading before 1 April 2002, but incorporated on or after that date *(CTA 2009 s.884)*. Internally generated assets are only treated as having been created after commencement if they were held at any time before that date by the company or a related party *(CTA 2009 s.885(7))*.

The provisions only apply to royalties in relation to expenditure recognised for accounting purposes after commencement, regardless of when the associated intangible asset was acquired *(CTA 2009 s.896)*.

14.4.2. Treatment of gains and losses

Gains and losses arising in relation to an intangible fixed asset held for the purpose of the trade or a property business are treated as trading receipts or expenses in the calculation of taxable profit *(CTA 2009 ss.747 & 748)*. Gains and losses arising on intangible fixed assets not held for the purposes of the trade are aggregated and an aggregate gain is taxed separately from trading profits *(CTA 2009 ss.751 & 752)*.

An aggregate loss may be relieved in one or more of the following ways:

- offset against total profits for the period;
- carried forward to be offset against non-trading gains of future periods;
- surrendered by means of group relief.

(CTA 2009 s.753)

Companies may elect to apply a tax rate of 10% rate of corporation tax to all income from qualifying patents and other qualifying intellectual property rights, whether they are paid separately as royalties or are embedded within the price of products (see **14.4.12**).

14.4.3. Deductible expenditure

The following expenditure and losses are deductible:

- expenditure on intangible fixed assets charged to profit and loss account as incurred *(CTA 2009 s.728)*;
- abortive expenditure on intangible fixed assets *(CTA 2009 s.727)*;
- amortisation or impairment write-down of intangible fixed assets charged in the accounts *(CTA 2009 s.729 & s.742)*. This is subject to certain exclusions contained in *Finance Act 2019 Sch. 9*.

  In general the tax loss will be equal to the accounting loss, but this may not be the case if the tax value is not equal to the accounting value, if, for example, roll-over relief (see **14.4.7** below) has been claimed for tax purposes. In this case the deductible amount is

$$\text{Accounting loss} \times \frac{\text{Tax value}}{\text{Accounting value}}$$

- reversal of accounting gains recognised in previous period *(CTA 2009 s.732)*. If the amount of the gain previous taxed was not the same as the accounting gain the deductible loss is adjusted as above.

Where an intangible fixed asset is capitalised and not amortised in the accounts, a writing down allowance of 4% p.a. straight line may be claimed *(CTA 2009 ss.730, 731 & 743)*. This allowance may also be claimed instead of the accounting charge, where an asset is being amortised.

The following income and gains are taxable:

- receipts relating to intangible fixed assets which are recognised in the profit and loss account in the period in which they arise are taxable on an accruals basis *(CTA 2009 s.721)*;
- revaluations, up to a maximum of the expenditure and losses for which a deduction has previously been claimed *(CTA 2009 s.723)*. If the tax value of an asset is not equal to the accounting value the taxable portion of the revaluation is given by:

$$\text{Accounting gain} \times \frac{\text{Tax value}}{\text{Accounting value}}$$

  A gain on revaluation is not taxable where an asset is being written down at a fixed rate *(CTA 2009 s.723(6))*;
- negative goodwill arising on the acquisition of a business written back in the accounts *(CTA 2009 s.724)*; and
- reversal of accounting loss recognised in a previous period *(CTA 2009 s.725)*. This is limited to a maximum of:

$$\text{Accounting gain} \times \frac{\text{Loss recognised for tax}}{\text{Accounting loss}}$$

14.4.4. Bad debts

A deduction is available where a debt which has been brought into account is either estimated to be bad or is released as part of a statutory insolvency agreement. Any gain arising in the latter case is ignored *(CTA 2009 s.869)*.

14.4.5. Realisation of intangible fixed assets

An intangible fixed asset is deemed to have been realised when it ceases to be recognised in the company's balance sheet *(CTA 2009 s.734)*. A part-realisation may occur when the accounting value of the intangible fixed asset is reduced *(CTA 2009 s.737)*. The gain or loss on realisation is calculated:

- if an asset has been shown in the balance sheet the gain or loss is the difference between the realisation proceeds and the cost, in the case of assets which have not been written down, or the tax written down value, in the case of assets which have been written down *(CTA 2009 ss.735 & 736)*;

- if an asset has never been shown in the balance sheet the gain is equal to the realisation proceeds *(CTA 2009 s.738)*;
- in the case of abortive expenditure a loss equal to the amount of the expenditure arises *(CTA 2009 s.740)*.

Where there is a part-realisation, the cost or tax written down value with which the proceeds must be compared is given by:

$$\text{Cost or tax written down value} \times \frac{\text{Reduction in accounting value}}{\text{Previous accounting value}}$$

(CTA 2009 s.737)

Example

Hughes Ltd has an accounting date of 31 March. Goodwill amounting to £250,000 on the acquisition of a business was acquired on 1 April 2020. For tax purposes this was reduced to £150,000 through claiming reinvestment relief and the goodwill is being written off over five years. On 31 March 2022 part of this business was sold and the proceeds apportioned to goodwill were £80,000. The accounting value of the remaining goodwill is £100,000.

The amortisation charge in the accounts for the years ended 31 March 2021 and 2022 was £50,000 (£250,000/5), giving a net book value of £150,000 (£250,000 – (2 x £50,000) at 31 March 2022 (before taking the disposal into account).

A tax deduction of £30,000 has been claimed in each of these periods, given a tax written down value at 31 March 2022 of £90,000 (£150,000 – (2 x £30,000)).

The reduction in the accounting value as a result of the disposal is:

£60,000 (£150,000 - £90,000).

The tax written down value of the part of the goodwill disposed of is therefore:

$$£90{,}000 \times \frac{£150{,}000 - £100{,}000}{£150{,}000} = £30{,}000$$

A taxable gain therefore arises of £50,000 (£80,000 - £30,000)

14.4.6. Change of accounting basis

Any adjustment to the value of intangible fixed assets arising from a change in accounting basis will be brought into account for tax purposes *(CTA 2009 s.871)*.

The maximum charge which may arise is equal to the excess of total deductions previously given over the total gains previously brought into account *(CTA 2009 s.872(5))*.

Where the tax value is not equal to the accounting value the adjustment brought into account is given by:

$$\text{Accounting difference} \times \frac{\text{Tax value}}{\text{Accounting value}}$$

(CTA 2009 s.872)

An adjustment will not be made where an election has been made for an asset to be written down at a fixed rate where it is not being amortised in the accounts *(CTA 2009 s.872(1))* or if, in the accounting period of the change, either:

- an accounting gain or loss relating to a previous period is being reversed; or
- there is a revaluation, either above cost or which restores previous losses.

(CTA 2009 s.878)

14.4.7. Rollover relief

Where the proceeds of the disposal of an intangible fixed asset are reinvested in other intangible fixed assets, the cost of the new assets may be reduced by the taxable gain arising on the disposal of the old asset, provided that all of the proceeds have been reinvested. Where a portion of the proceeds have not been reinvested, that portion is taxable and the cost of the new asset may only be reduced by the amount of any remaining gain *(CTA 2009 s.758)*. This is very similar to rollover relief on the disposal of tangible assets. In order to qualify for relief the old asset must have been used for a business or commercial purpose throughout the period of ownership *(CTA 2009 s.755(1))*. Where an asset has been so used for a substantial part, but not all, of the period of ownership the portion of the gain relating to this period qualifies for relief, provided that the asset is a chargeable intangible asset at the date of disposal *(CTA 2009 s.755(5)-(7))*.

The expenditure on the new asset must satisfy three conditions:

- The expenditure must have been incurred in the period commencing one year before and ending three years after the disposal of the old asset.
- The expenditure must have been capitalised in the accounts.
- The expenditure must be on chargeable intangible assets.

(CTA 2009 s.756)

A claim for relief must specify the old asset and the expenditure on the new asset or assets to which the claim relates *(CTA 2009 s.757)*. Rollover relief may be restricted where a transaction has involved related parties *(CTA 2009 s.850)*. Rollover relief is not available on deemed disposals and re-acquisitions *(CTA 2009 s.763)*.

14.4.8. Groups

A group of companies may be treated as a single company for the purpose of these provisions. A group is defined for this purpose in the same manner as a capital gains tax group (see section **14.15.10**) *(CTA 2009 ss.765-769)*.

Where an intangible fixed asset is transferred between two group members, the transfer is not treated as a realisation by the transferor company. The transferee company is deemed to have held the asset at all times when it was held by the transferor company, and done all things which were done by the transferor company *(CTA 2009 ss.775 & 776).* The transfer pricing regime does not apply to such transfers.

Rollover relief is available where one member of a group realises a gain on an intangible fixed asset and another group member incurs expenditure on intangible fixed assets, provided that these assets were not acquired from another member of the group and sections 775 & 776 apply *(CTA 2009 ss.777-779).* Where payment is made for group rollover relief, this payment is ignored for the purpose of calculating profits or losses for the purpose of corporation tax provided that it does not exceed the amount of the relief *(CTA 2009 s.799).*

If a transfer is made under sections 775 & 776 and the transferee company subsequently leaves the group within six years of the transfer, the transferee is deemed to have realised and immediately reacquired the asset at its market value on the date of the original transfer *(CTA 2009 ss.780-798).* Deductions for subsequent amortisation charges etc. will therefore be recalculated based on the market value.

This charge does not apply if the transferee and transferor companies leave the group at the same time or if the transferee company ceases to be a group member solely because the principal company becomes a member of another group *(CTA 2009 ss.785 & 786).* An election may be made for the charge to be re-allocated to other members of the group, e.g. to other members with a lower marginal rate of tax *(CTA 2009 ss.792-794).*

Example

A patent with a cost of £50,000 was acquired by company A on 1 January 2018 and is being written off over ten years. On 1 January 2020 the patent was transferred to company B (a group company) when the market value of the patent was £56,000. On 31 December 2021 company B left the group.

Company A claimed a deduction of £5,000 (£50,000/10) in the years ended 31 December 2018 and 2019.

On 1 January 2020 the patent is transferred at £40,000 (£50,000 – (2 x £5,000)) and company B claims a deduction of £5,000 in the years ended 31 December 2020 and 2021.

On 31 December 2021 company B is deemed to have realised the patent acquired on 1 January 2020 for £56,000 and immediately reacquired it for that amount. A gain of £16,000 (£56,000 - £40,000) will therefore arise in that period and the deduction in the years ended 31 December 2020 and 2021 will be revised to £7,000 (£56,000/8).

14.4.9. Computer software

Software acquired with the related hardware is excluded for these provisions, except in relation to any royalties arising if it is treated for accounting purposes as part of the hardware *(CTA 2009 s.813).* Software not acquired with hardware is subject to these provisions and such expenditure does not qualify for capital allowances. However, it is possible to make an election that these provisions will not apply except in relation to:

- receipts recognised as they accrue, e.g. royalties; or
- any loss resulting from an adjustment to the value of such receipts; or
- realisation proceeds not taken into account under the Capital Allowances Act 2001.

The election is irrevocable and must be made within two years from the end of the accounting period in which the expenditure is incurred.
(CTA 2009 s.815 & s.903)

14.4.10. Transactions with related parties

Where an intangible fixed asset is transferred between a firm (i.e. company, partnership or LLP) and a related party, it is deemed to have been transferred at market value *(CTA 2009 s.845)*. A related party is a party which holds a 'major interest' in the company, i.e. holds at least 40% of the shares, votes or other powers through which the company is controlled *(CTA 2009 ss.836 & 837)*. CTA 2009 s.845 outlines four situations where these provisions will apply.

1. A firm (P) controls, or has a major interest in another firm (C), or C controls or has a major interest in P.
2. Both P and C are controlled by the same person.
3. C is a close company and P is a participator.
4. Both P and C are companies in the same group.

14.4.11. Anti-avoidance

Any arrangements entered into by a company will be disregarded, if one of the main objects is either:

1. to obtain a deduction or greater deduction than it would otherwise be entitled to; or
2. to avoid bringing a gain into account or to reduce the amount of the gain being brought into account.

(CTA 2009 s.864)

14.4.12. Patent box

The 'patent box' provisions which are contained in CTA 2010 ss.357A-357GE allow companies to make an election for income from the sale of patented items, licensed-in patent rights and compensation for the infringement of patent rights to be taxed at a preferential rate of 10% *(CTA 2010 s.357A& ss.357CA-357CE)*. The election will continue in force until the company revokes it. The provisions are very complex and this section only provides a brief overview.

A patent must either have been granted with the UK patent office, the European patent office or the patent office of certain other countries and the company must have actively developed the patent or a product incorporating the patent and if the company holding the patent is a member of a group it must have played an active role in developing the patent. Companies may take a 'formulaic' approach to the calculation of the patent box profit by calculating turnover which is derived from patents as a proportion of total turnover and then applying this proportion to expenses and thus to profits *(CTA 2010 s.357C)*. Companies may use an alternative method based on actual data if it gives a better result. A 10% mark-up on all routine expenses, such as wages and salaries, legal and professional expenses and capital allowances is assumed and this 'routine profit' is apportioned between the patent box profit and other profits and is deducted from the former, giving the 'qualifying residual profit' (QRP) *(CTA 2010 s.357CI)*. Where the QRP is less than £1m it is possible to elect for a 'small claims treatment' and deduct 25% of the QRP to account for the 'brand' element *(CTA 2010 s.357CM)*, but where the QRP is greater than £1m or a company feels that the brand element is less than 25% of the profits a 'notional marketing royalty' must be calculated, which is what the company would pay to a third party to exploit the brand and this must be based on OECD transfer pricing principles *(CTA 2010 s.357CO)*.

Patent box losses can only be offset against patent box profits and such losses arising in one trade may be offset against patent box profits of another trade or of another company in the same group. Any patent box losses not set off in this way must be carried forward to be offset against patent box profits of future periods *(CTA 2010 ss.357E-357EC)*.

14.5. Derivative Contracts

14.5.1. General

Derivative contracts are taxed under CTA 2009 pt. 7 ch. 7. This schedule applies to:

- 'relevant contracts', which cover options, futures and contracts for differences which are treated as derivative contracts by FRS 13;
- certain options, futures and contracts not covered by FRS 13, where these are treated as financial assets by the financial reporting standard;
- options, futures and contracts not otherwise within the scope of this schedule whose subject matter is commodities and contracts for differences whose subject matter is intangible fixed assets.

(CTA 2009 ss.576-578)

The legislation does not apply to options, futures or contracts for differences whose subject matter is:

1. intangible fixed assets (except for contracts for differences);
2. shares in a company, subject to a number of exceptions where the return on the shares is in the nature of interest.

(CTA 2009 ss.589-591)

14.5.2. Taxation of profits and losses

Profits and losses from derivative contracts (including exchange gains and losses) are recognised and related contracts are brought into account for tax purposes in the period in which they are recognised in the company's accounts, provided that the accounts are drawn up according to GAAP *(CTA 2009 s.595(2))*. If accounts are not drawn up in accordance with GAAP, the amounts are brought into account on the assumption that "correct accounts" are drawn up *(CTA 2009 s.599)*.

Relief is also available for the following charges and expenses:

- expenses incurred in bringing the contract into existence;
- expenses incurred in giving effect to any of its transactions;
- expenses incurred in making payments under any derivative contract or under a related transaction; and
- expenses incurred in taking steps for ensuring the receipt of payments under a derivative contract or in respect of a related transaction.

(CTA 2009 s.595(4))

Relief is also available for charges and expenses incurred in relation to a derivative contract which the company has not yet entered into *(CTA 2009 s.607)*.

14.5.3. Related transactions

A related transaction is any disposal or acquisition of rights under a derivative contract and includes any rights or liabilities transferred or extinguished by any sale, gift, surrender or release and those where the contract is discharged by performance in accordance with its terms *(CTA 2009 s.596)*.

14.5.4. Derivatives for unallowable purposes

No relief is available for charges, expenses and losses incurred on derivatives for unallowable purposes, and any income or gains arising from such contracts are ignored. These are defined as derivative contracts otherwise than for business or other commercial purposes, in respect of activities which are not within the charge to corporation tax or where the main purpose, or one of the main purposes, is tax avoidance *(CTA 2009 ss.590-592)*.

14.5.5. Capitalised expenditure

Where expenditure is capitalised in the company's accounts in accordance with GAAP, any gains or losses are brought into account in the same manner as if the expenditure had not been capitalised (*CTA 2009 s.604*). A deduction is not available under this section for expenditure and losses for which relief is available under CTA 2009 pt. 8 (Intangible Fixed Assets).

14.5.6. Transactions with related parties

Where there is a transfer of value to a connected company, which is not within the charge to corporation tax as the result of the expiry of an option, which until its expiry was a derivative of the transferor company, it is assumed that, had there not been a connection between the two companies, the option would not have been allowed to expire and would have been exercised on the date of expiry. Any gain which would have arisen on this assumption is taxable *(CTA 2009 s.695)*.

Where derivative contracts are not on arm's length terms, any exchange gains or losses are ignored to the extent that profits or losses on the contract are ignored under the transfer pricing legislation. Where the terms are adjusted under these provisions, a similar adjustment is made in computing the exchange gain or loss under this section *(CTA 2009 s.694)*.

Derivative contracts may be transferred between members of a group (defined as for capital gains tax) at no gain/no loss, provided that both companies are within the charge to tax *(CTA 2009 ss.625-627)*. Where the transferee company leaves the group within six years of the intra-group transfer the transferee company is deemed on the date of the transfer to have assigned its rights and liabilities under the contract and immediately reacquired them at their market value at that date *(CTA 2009 ss.630-632)*.

14.6. Property Income

Property income is calculated in the same manner as income tax except that interest on a loan to purchase a property falls within the loan relationship rules rather than property income and the methods of loss relief are different (see section **14.14.8**).

14.7. Chargeable Gains

Unlike income tax, corporation tax covers both income of a revenue nature and gains of a capital nature. The rules for the computation of the gains are similar to those for unincorporated businesses, but there are a number of differences and these are set out in sections **14.7.1** to **14.7.5** below.

14.7.1. Indexation Allowance

An indexation allowance is available on the cost of the asset to eliminate the inflationary element of any gain arising from April 1982 to December 2017. The indexation allowance is calculated by multiplying the allowable cost by the following fraction:

$$\frac{A - B}{B}$$

Where:

A is the RPI at date of disposal (or December 2017, if earlier), and
B is the RPI at date of acquisition (or March 1982 if later)

(TCGA 1992 s.54)

The legislation stipulates that the allowance must be rounded to three decimal places. Expenditure may only be indexed from the date on which it is incurred. Where expenditure has been incurred on an asset at different times, the indexation allowance must be calculated separately on each portion of the expenditure.

Example

In April 2021 Williams Ltd sold a property for £200,000 and incurred estate agent's fees of £1,500 and legal expenses of £1,800. The property was purchased in May 1987 (RPI 101.9) for £60,000, and in August 1991 (RPI 134.1) they built an extension at a cost of £10,000. The RPI for December 2017 was 278.1.

	£	£
Proceeds	200,000	
Less: Legal Fees	(1,800)	
Agent's Fees	(1,500)	
		196,700
Allowable Cost		
May 1987	60,000	
August 1991	10,000	
		(70,000)
Unindexed Gain		126,700
Indexation		
May 1987 $\frac{278.1 - 101.9}{101.9}$ (1.729)	103,740	
August 1991 $\frac{278.1 - 134.1}{134.1}$ (1.074)	10,740	
		(114,480)
Indexed Gain		£12,220

14.7.2. Indexation and Losses

An indexation allowance may not create or increase a loss, but will merely reduce the unindexed gain to nil. If there is an unindexed loss, no indexation allowance is available *(FA 1994 s.93(1))*.

14.7.3. Assets Owned at 31 March 1982

Computation of gains and losses

Where an asset was owned at 31 March 1982 two CGT calculations are performed. The allowable cost in the first of these is the actual acquisition cost plus subsequent improvements, and in the second the market value of the asset at 31 March 1982 (in many cases this value may be the subject of protracted negotiation with HM Revenue & Customs) plus improvements after that date *(TCGA 1992 s.35(1)&(2))*. In both calculations the indexation allowance will be calculated on the higher of actual cost and the March 1982 value.

- Where both calculations produce gains, the smaller gain is taken *(TCGA 1992 s.35(3)(a))*.
- Where both calculations produce losses, the smaller loss is taken *(TCGA 1992 s.35(3)(b))*.
- Where one calculation produces a gain, and the other a loss, there is no gain and no loss *(TCGA 1992 s.35(4))*.

Where capital allowances have been claimed on an asset after 31 March 1982 the re-basing value is the March 1982 less capital allowances given after that date *(TCGA 1992 Sch. 3 para. 3)*.

Example

Hughes Ltd has made the following disposals:

April 2021	Sold a property for £1,250,000, incurring costs of £12,000. The property had been purchased on 1 March 1975 for £150,000. In July 1976 an extension was built at a cost of £25,000, and in September 1986 (RPI 98.3) another extension was built at a cost of £60,000. The value of the property at 31 March 1982 (RPI 79.44) was £300,000.
April 2021	Sold an asset for £600,000. The asset had been purchased in May 1978 for £140,000 and the value at 31 March 1982 (RPI 79.44) was £180,000.
May 2021	Sold another asset for £900,000. The asset had been purchased in December 1980 for £250,000 and the value at 31 March 1982 (RPI 79.44) was £235,000.
	The RPI at December 2017 was 278.1

Property

	Cost	Cost	1982 Value	1982 Value
	£	£	£	£
Proceeds		1,250,000		1,250,000
Costs of Disposal		(12,000)		(12,000)
		1,238,000		1,238,000
Acquisition Cost	150,000			
March 1982 value			300,000	
Bathroom – July 1976	25,000			
Kitchen – September 1986	60,000		60,000	
		(235,000)		(360,000)
		1,003,000		878,000

Indexation				
March 1982				
278.1 - 79.44 (2.501 x £300,000) / 79.44	750,300		750,300	
Sept 1986				
278.1 - 98.30 (1.829 x £60,000) / 98.30	109,740		109,740	
		(860,040)		(860,040)
Gain		£142,960		£17,960

The gain will be the smaller of the two gains, i.e. £17,960.

Asset 1

	Cost	1982 Value
	£	£
Proceeds	600,000	400,000
Acquisition Cost/March 1982 value	(140,000)	(180,000)
	460,000	420,000
Indexation		
March 1982		
278.1 – 79.44 (2.501 x £180,000) / 79.44	(450,180)	(450,180)
Gain	£9,820	£NIL

There is no gain and no loss.

Asset 2

	Cost	1982 Value
	£	£
Proceeds	900,000	900,000
Acquisition Cost/March 1982 value	(250,000)	(235,000)
	650,000	665,000
Indexation		
March 1982		
278.1 - 79.44 (2.501 x £250,000) / 79.44	(625,250)	(625,250)
Gain	£24,750	£39,750

Note that in this case the indexation allowance is calculated on the original cost, being higher than the March 1982 value.

The gain is the lower of the two, i.e. £24,750.

March 1982 value election

Where a company has made an irrevocable election that the gain or loss on all disposals of assets held at 31 March 1982 should be calculated solely by reference to the March 1982 value *(TCGA 1992 s.35(2),(5))*, only one calculation is therefore performed. This has the following consequences:

- if the March 1982 value should produce a higher gain than a calculation based on cost, this will be the gain which will be tapered;
- conversely, if the March 1982 value should produce a higher loss than a calculation based on cost, this will be the allowable loss;
- if the March 1982 value is lower than the original cost, as in the final example above, the indexation allowance will be calculated on the March 1982 value, giving a higher gain. The computation in the last disposal in the above example would therefore be:

	£
Proceeds	900,000
March 1982 value	(235,000)
	665,000
Indexation	
March 1982	
$\frac{278.1 - 79.44}{79.44}$ (2.501 x £235,000)	(587,735)
Gain	£77,265

In most cases the election will not make any difference to the final result. The election is most likely to be of benefit where a business is likely to dispose of old assets, such as buildings, where it is unlikely to be possible to establish an accurate figure based on actual cost. Any extra tax payable on the disposal is likely to be outweighed by the savings in time, effort and professional fees.

Assets held at 31 March 1982 – roll-over relief

Where an asset was acquired between 6 April 1982 and 5 April 1988 and a gain arising on the disposal of an asset held on 31 March 1982 has been rolled over against the cost of that asset, on a subsequent disposal of that asset the rolled-over gain is halved (*TCGA 1992 Sch. 4 para 1-4*).

Example

Smith sold an asset in April 2021 for £270,000. The asset had been acquired in July 1986 (RPI 97.52) for £80,000 and a gain of £20,000 was rolled-over against the cost. The RPI for December 2017 was 278.1.

	£	£	£
Proceeds			270,000
Cost		80,000	
Gain rolled over	20,000		
Less: 50%	(10,000)		
		(10,000)	
			(70,000)
			200,000

Indexation	
278.1 – 97.52 / 97.52 1.852 x £70,000	(129,640)
	£70,360

14.7.4. Assets Owned at 6 April 1965

General rule

CGT was introduced in the 1965/66 tax year and, where an asset is sold which was owned on that date, three calculations must be performed:

1. The allowable cost is the actual cost of the asset and the indexed gain is time-apportioned between the period up to 5 April 1965 and the period from 6 April 1965. Any asset acquired before 6 April 1945 is deemed to have been acquired on that date. Only the gain relating to the period from 6 April 1965 onwards is taxable *(TCGA 1992 Sch.2, para. 16)*. Where there has been enhancement expenditure the overall gain must be apportioned between each element on the basis of their respective values and time-apportionment is applied to each element separately *(TCGA 1992 Sch. 2 para. 16(4))*.

Example

Hughes Ltd bought a property for £2,000 in February 1943 and built an extension for £3,000 in April 1969. It sold the property in April 2020 for £250,000. The RPI at December 2017 was 278.1. The value of the property at 31 March 1982 was £70,000. The gain would be:

	£
Proceeds	250,000
Cost – 1943	(2,000)
Enhancement – April 1969	(3,000)
Unindexed gain	245,000
Indexation	
278.1 - 79.44 / 79.44 (2.501 x £70,000)	(175,070)
	£69,930
Allocation of gain	
Cost – £69,930 x (£2,000/(£2,000 + £3,000)	£27,972
Enhancement – £69,930 x (£3,000/(£2,000 + £3,000)	£41,958
Time-apportionment	
Cost – £27,972 x 56/76 =	20,611
Enhancement	41,958
	£62,569

If the cost is disproportionately small in comparison with the value of the asset immediately before enhancement expenditure was incurred the portion of the gain which is attributable to the extra expenditure is calculated on the available facts, and the remaining part is treated as expenditure incurred when the asset was acquired *(TCGA 1992 Sch. 2, para. 16(5))*.

2. The allowable cost is the budget day value (BDV) of the asset, i.e. the market value of the asset at 6 April 1965. An election to use the BDV must be made within two years from the end of the tax year in which the disposal takes place *(TCGA 1992 Sch. 2, para. 17)*.
3. The allowable cost is the March 1982 value.

If all three calculations produce a gain, the taxable gain is the lowest of the three. Where one or more of the calculations produces a loss, there is a two-step procedure to be followed to determine the gain or allowable loss:

1. the result based on original cost is compared with the result based on BDV. If both results show a gain the smaller gain is taken. If one result shows a gain and the other a loss there is no gain/no loss. If both results show a loss the smaller of the loss using BDV and the loss using cost **before** time-apportionment is taken;
2. the result from step 1 is compared with the result using the March 1982 value. If both results show a gain the smaller gain is taken. If one result shows a gain and the other a loss there is no gain/no loss. If both results show a loss the smaller loss is taken.

Land with development value

Where land held on 6 April 1965, and which has been materially developed[9] after 17 December 1973, is sold for more than its current use value[10] it is treated as having sold and reacquired the land at its market value at that date *(TCGA 1992 Sch.2 para. 9-15)*. There are a number of exceptions to the definition of material development contained in *TCGA 1992 Sch.2 para. 13*:

- work for the maintenance, improvement or enlargement of a building, provided the cubic size of the building is increased by no more than 1/10;
- the rebuilding of a building which existed at that time, or which had been destroyed or demolished within the previous ten years, provided that the cubic size of the new building is no more than 1/10 greater than that of the old building;
- the use of any land or building for agricultural purposes or the construction of buildings for agricultural use;
- the use or development of land or buildings for the purpose of displaying an advertisement, announcement or direction of any kind;

---

[9] Meaning making any change in the state, nature or use of the asset.

[10] Meaning the value on the assumption than no further development of the land is permitted other than development for which the taxpayer has obtained planning permission.

- the development or use of land for the purposes of car parking, provided that the duration of use did not exceed three years;
- the change of use from the use current at the relevant time to any other use within the same class. If the land was unoccupied at the relevant time, the purpose for which the land was last used is taken;
- where different parts of land or a building were used by one person for different purposes, any increase in the proportion of the building used for a particular purpose is excluded provided that the cubic size of the building (or area in the case of land) is increased by no more than 1/10;
- the change back to normal use, where land was being used temporarily for another purpose at the relevant time;
- where land was unoccupied at the relevant time, the resumption of use for the same purpose as that for which it was being last used.

Classes of use:

Class A Use as a dwelling house for the purpose of any activities which are not carried on wholly or mainly for profit, except for uses falling within classes B, C or E;

Class B Use as an office or retail shop;

Class C Use as a hotel, boarding house or guest house, or as premises licensed for the sale of intoxicating liquors for consumption on the premises;

Class D Use for the purpose of any activities which are not carried on wholly or mainly for profit, except use as a dwelling house or for the purposes of agriculture or forestry or any purpose falling with classes B, C or E;

Class E Use for any of the following purposes:

a) The carrying on of any process for, or incidental to, any of the following purposes:
   i) the making of any articles, or part of any article, or the production of any substance;
   ii) the altering, repairing, ornamenting, finishing, cleaning, washing, packing or canning or adapting for sale, or breaking up or demolishing of any article;
   iii) without prejudice to the above, the getting, dressing or treatment of minerals;
   iv) being a process carried on in the course of a trade or business other than agriculture or forestry, but excluding any process carried on at a dwelling house or retail shop.

b) Storage purposes (whether or not involving use as a warehouse or repository) other than storage purposes ancillary to a purpose falling within classes B or C.

14.7.5. Rollover Relief

The following categories of assets contained in TCGA 1992 s.155 are excluded because they fall within the intangible fixed assets regime.

i) goodwill; and
ii) milk, fish or potato quotas or ewe or suckler cow premium quotas.

14.8. Dividends Received

Dividends received from other UK companies are not charged to corporation tax provided that:

1. the payer is resident in, and only in, the UK, or in a territory with which the UK has a double taxation agreement which contains a non-discrimination provision; and
2. the amount does not exceeds a normal commercial rate, although such situations will generally be dealt with using the transfer pricing rules; and
3. the amount does not qualify for a tax deduction in a territory outside the UK; and
4. the payment is not part of a tax advantage scheme.

(CTA 2009 ss.931B & 931C)

A distribution which represents the repayment of share capital in a winding up is not treated as a distribution for the purposes of the Corporation Tax Acts *(CTA 2010 s.1030)*. However, a distribution made out of a reserve arising from a reduction in share capital is treated as being made out of the profits available for distribution *(CTA 2010 s.1027A(2))*.

14.9. Payments to Charities

Payments by a company to charities made under the gift aid scheme are deductible from total income (see section **1.3**). These payments are made gross *(CTA 2010 s.189)*. There are restrictions on the associated benefits received by the company or a person associated with the company as a result of the payment (see section **1.4.1**) *(CTA 2010 ss.195-198)*.

From 1 April 2014 Community Amateur Sports Clubs (CASCs) have been included within the definition of charities. Therefore, relief is available for payments to CASCs *(CTA 2010 s.202(aa))*. Where a company is owned by a CASC, this relief is restricted by the amount of any 'inflated member-related expenditure'. This is defined as employment expenditure incurred in respect of employment by the company of a member of the CASC on other than arm's length terms or the provision of goods and services to the club by a member of the club or a member-controlled body on other than arm's length terms unless the effect of such arrangements is beneficial to the company, rather than the third party *(CTA 2010 s.202B&C)*. The relief is restricted by the total amount of such expenditure, not just the excess over the amounts which would have been paid if the arrangements had been entered into on an arm's length basis.

14.10. Distributions

14.10.1. General

Any payment of a dividend by a company is treated as a distribution out of the assets of the company, including a capital dividend *(CTA 2010 s.1000(1)A)* except:

1. a repayment of capital, e.g. repayment of redeemable share capital;
2. a payment which is equal in amount or value to any consideration received by the company for the distribution *(CTA 2010 s.1000(1)B)*; or
3. the issue of bonus redeemable share capital or securities in respect of shares in, or securities of, the company is treated as a distribution, except insofar as it is made for new consideration *(CTA 2010 s.1000(1)C)*.

A distribution is treated as being out of the assets of a company if the cost falls on the company *(CTA 2010 s.1173(3),(4))*. Therefore, a bonus issue of shares, or the bonus element of a rights issue, is not treated as a distribution, because the company does not incur a cost in making the issue.

Interest on a loan may be treated as a distribution, insofar as it represents more than reasonable commercial return for the use of the principal *(CTA 2010 s.1000(1)E)*.

14.10.2. Stock dividends

A stock dividend is the issue of share capital in lieu of a dividend or as bonus shares, where there is a right to the shares under the terms of issue of the original shares *(CTA 2010 s.1049(1),(2))*.

14.11. Chargeable Accounting Periods

Corporation tax is payable on the profits of a company's chargeable accounting period (CAP). A company's first CAP commences on the date that it commences trading and every subsequent CAP commences immediately after the previous CAP has ended *(CTA 2009 s.9(1))*. A CAP will end on the earliest of the following dates:

- 12 months after the date of commencement;
- the date to which the company draws up accounts;
- the date on which winding up proceedings commence;
- the date the company becomes, or ceases to be, resident in the UK;
- the date the company ceases to be in administration;
- the date on which the company ceases to be within the charge to

corporation tax.
(CTA 2009 s.10(1))

A company's CAP will therefore normally coincide with its accounting period. Where a company changes its accounting date by drawing up accounts for a short period, the CAP will again coincide with the accounting period. Where a company changes its accounting date by drawing up accounts for a long period, the accounting period will be divided into two CAPs, the first comprising the first 12 months and the second CAP comprising the balance. In this case income, gains and charges must be allocated between the CAPs:

- trading income, property income and profits from non-trading loan relationships are time-apportioned on the basis of the number of days in the respective periods;
- other income, such as patent royalties, chargeable gains and charges on income, is included in the period in which the income or gain is realised or the charge is incurred;
- capital allowances are calculated separately for each period. WDAs for short CAPs must be reduced *pro rata*.

(CTA 2009 s.52)

14.12. Computation of Tax Liability

14.12.1. Rates of corporation tax

Corporation tax rates and limits are set for a financial year *(CTA 2009 s.8)*. A financial year runs to 31 March and is designated by the calendar year in which it commences. The financial year (FY) 2021 therefore started on 1 April 2021 and will run to 31 March 2022 *(CTA 2010 s.1119)*. Unless a company has an accounting date of 31 March, its CAP will generally straddle two financial years. In contrast to income tax, there is no equivalent of the basis period rules and the profits of a CAP are time-apportioned between the two financial years and taxed accordingly. If a company draws up accounts to 30 September 2021, the profits of the first six months will be taxed at the rates applicable to FY2021 and the last six months at the rates applicable to FY2021. The corporation tax rate is 19% for both FY20 and FY21, so an apportionment is not currently necessary, in practice.

Example

Hughes Ltd has no associated companies and draws up accounts to 31 December each year. Its results for the year ended 31 December 2021 are as follows:

Trading income	£250,000
Income from non-trading loan relationships	£60,000
Property income	£40,000
Dividends received from other UK companies (net)	£72,000
Charges on income (gross)	£6,000

Hughes Ltd's corporation tax liability will be:

	£
Trading income	250,000
Income from non-trading loan relationships	60,000
Property income	40,000
Charitable donations	(6,000)
Total taxable profits	£344,000
Tax @ 19%	£65,360

14.13. Corporation Tax – Interaction with Income Tax

14.13.1. Introduction

Income tax will interact with corporation tax because, although companies do not pay income tax, they will make payments, such as debenture interest and patent royalties, from which tax must be deducted at source and this tax must be paid to HM Revenue & Customs. Tax must be deducted at source on payments where the recipient is liable to income tax, whilst payments to recipients liable to corporation tax are made gross.

14.13.2. Accounting for income tax

Each quarter a company must account for income tax withheld on payments during the period on a form CT6l(Z). The following types of payments are covered by these provisions:

- payments of yearly interest *(ITA 2007 s.874(2));*
- payments in respect of building society securities *(ITA 2007 s.889(4));*
- certain payments of UK public revenue dividends *(ITA 2007 s.892(2));*
- annual payments made by persons other than individuals *(ITA 2007 s.901(4*));
- patent royalties *(ITA 2007 s.903(7*));
- royalty payments where the owner lives abroad *(ITA 2007 s.906(5));*
- proceeds of sale of patent rights paid to non-UK residents *(ITA 2007 s.910(2));*
- chargeable payments connected with exempt distributions *(ITA 2007 s.928(2));*
- directions for deduction from payments to non-UK residents *(ITA 2007 s.944(2)).*

Returns must normally be made for the quarters ending on 31 March, 30 June, 30 September and 31 December of each year, but in addition a company must also complete a return on its accounting date if it does not coincide with one of the above dates *(ITA 2007 s.947).* A company with an accounting date of 30 April will therefore have to complete a return five times a year. The relevant date for including a transaction in a return is the date of receipt or payment *(ITA 2007 s.949(1));* in the case of interest this contrasts with the accruals or mark method used to calculate the income or expenditure to be included in the corporation tax computation.

Where a payment falling within ITA 2007 s.946 is made during an accounting period, the form CT61(Z) must be returned within 14 days of the end of the accounting period *(ITA 2007 s.949(3))*. Tax suffered on amounts received is offset against tax withheld on payments and any amount payable must be paid with the return *(ITA 2007 s.949(4))*.

14.14. Losses and Corporation Tax

14.14.1. Introduction

Companies may obtain relief for trading losses in one or more of the following ways:

- carry forward for offset against trading profits of future CAPs *(CTA 2010 s.45)*;
- offset against the total profits of the same CAP *(CTA 2010 s.37(3)(a))*;
- offset against the total profits of earlier CAPs *(CTA 2010 s.37(3)(b))*;
- surrender to another group company *(CTA 2010 s.99)*. (This will be covered in detail in section **14.15**).

14.14.2. Offset against future profits

Losses may be carried forward and offset against the profits of subsequent CAPs. Losses incurred before 1 April 2017 may only be offset against the trading profits of the later period *(CTA 2010 s.45)*. However, companies may now specify the amount of loss offset. No election is necessary, although it is possible to make a claim to disapply this.

Losses incurred on or after 1 April 2017 may be offset against either the trading profits or the total profits of the later period, provided that:

- the company continues to carry on the trade in all subsequent accounting periods up to, and including, the period in which the loss is offset;
- the trade did not become small or negligible in the loss-making period and the company was not debarred from surrendering the loss to another group company *(CTA 2010 ss.45A&B)*.
- the trade is carried on on a commercial basis in both the loss-making period and the period in which the loss is offset.

Any loss remaining may again be carried forward, subject to the same restrictions *(CTA 2010 ss.45C-45E)*. The time limit for making a claim under this section is two years from the end of the later period.

For losses incurred on or after 1 April 2017 it has been possible to make a claim specifying the amount of loss which is to be offset against the profits *(CTA 2010 s.45-45B)*.

It will now be necessary to stipulate the amount of brought forward losses to be deducted in the corporation tax return.

Where a CAP straddles 1 April 2017 it is necessary to split into two periods for the purpose of carrying forward losses and the total trading losses must be apportioned between the two periods. This will generally be done on a time basis, although an alternative basis may be used, provided that that produces a just and reasonable result.

If a company carries on more than one trade the income and expenses must be apportioned between the various trades. The activities of a company are only likely to be considered to be different trades if:

- they are quite different in nature, so that they can be seen to be quite separate; and
- they are separately organised and managed right up to board level.

14.14.3. Offset against total profits of the period

The trading loss is offset against the total profits of the period before charges *(CTA 2010 s.37(3)(a))*. Unrelieved gift aid donations are lost. The time limit for claiming this loss relief is two years from the end of the loss-making period *(CTA 2010 s.37(7))*.

14.14.4. Offset against total profits of earlier periods

Trading losses incurred in chargeable accounting periods ending between 1 April 2020 and 31 March 2022 may be carried back and offset against the total profits of CAPs falling wholly or partly in the previous 36 months *(CTA 2010 s.37(3)(b))*. This is a temporary extension contained in FA 2021 Sch. 2 and the normal carry-back period is 12 months. Where only a part of a CAP falls within the 12 month period, the loss may be offset against the appropriate portion of the total profits. It is only possible to carry back a loss if it is first offset against the total profits of the same CAP. The time limit for making a claim to carry a loss back is two years from the end of the loss-making period *(CTA 2010 s.37(7))*. Any loss which cannot be offset against the profits of the current period or carried back must be carried forward.

Example

Richards Ltd has had the following recent results:

	Y/e 30.6.18	y/e 30.6.19	y/e 30.6.20	9m/e 31.3.21	Y/e 31.3.22	Y/e 31.3.23
Trading profit/(loss)	£30,000	£15,000	£25,000	£20,000	£(100,000)	£50,000
Property income				£5,000	£5,000	£5,000
Chargeable gains				£8,000	£3,000	£4,000
Charitable donations	£(2,000)	£(2,000)	£(2,000)	£(2,000)	£(2,000)	£(2,000)

The corporation tax computations for the above periods will be as follows:

	Y/e 30.6.18	Y/e 30.6.19	Y/e 30.6 20	9me 31.3.21	Y/e 31.3.22	Y/e 31.3.23
	£	£	£	£	£	£
Adjusted profit/(loss)	30,000	15,000	25,000	20,000	NIL	50,000
Loss relief s.45(4)(b)						(11,500)
						38,500
Property income				5,000	5,000	5,000
Chargeable gains				8,000	3,000	4,000
	30,000	15,000	25,000	33,000	8,000	47,500
Loss relief s.37(3)(a)					(8,000)	
	30,000	15,000	25,000	33,000	NIL	47,500
Loss relief s.37(3)(b)	(7,500)	(15,000)	(25,000)	(33,000)		
	22,500	NIL	NIL	NIL	NIL	47,500
Charitable donations	(2,000)	NIL	NIL	NIL	NIL	(2,000)
	£20,500	£NIL	£NIL	£NIL	£NIL	£45,500

Loss memorandum:

	£
Trading loss y/e 31.3.22	100,000
s. 37(3)(a)y/e 31.3.22	(8,000)
	92,000
s. 37(3)(b) 9m/e31.3.21	(33,000)
	59,000
s. 37(3)(b) y/e30.6.20	(25,000)
	34,000
s. 37(3)(b) y/e30.6.19	(15,000)
	19,000
s. 37(3)(b)y/e 30.6.18 £30,000 x 3/12	(7,500)
	11,500
s.45(4)(b) y/e 31.3.23	(11,500)
	£NIL

A claim, or claims, may only be made under this section for losses totalling £2,000,000 for each of the chargeable accounting periods falling in the two-year period. However, only claims for up to a total of £200,000 (a 'de-minimis' claim) may be made before 31 March 2022 in respect of the chargeable accounting period falling between 1 April 2021 and 31 March 2022. *(FA 2021 Sch. 2 paras 5&6)*. Where a company is a member of a group, both limits apply to the total loss claimed under this section by all group companies *(FA 2021 Sch. 2 paras. 9&10)*.

14.14.5. Terminal Loss

Trading losses incurred in the final 12 months of trading may be carried back against the profits of CAPs falling wholly or partly in the preceding three years *(CTA 2010 s.39)*.

14.14.6. Losses on-trading loan relationships, foreign exchange and financial instruments

The excess of aggregate receipts over aggregate payments arising from the above transactions is taxed a non-trading profit. Where a loss is incurred, i.e. the aggregate payments exceed the aggregate receipts, relief may be obtained in one or more of the following ways:

- carry forward for offset against total profits (for losses incurred on or after 1 April 2017 only) or non-trading profits (i.e. chargeable profits less trading profits) of future CAPs *(CTA 2009 s.457);*
- offset against the total profits of the same CAP *(CTA 2009 s.461);*
- offset against profits of CAPs falling wholly or partly in the previous 12 months *(CTA 2009 s.462)*.

Unlike the loss relief provisions for trading losses, a company may choose how much of the loss to relieve in the current period, how much to carry back and how much to carry forward.

14.14.7. Losses on Miscellaneous Transactions

Where losses arise on transactions not covered by specific provisions, they may be offset against gains from similar transactions in the same CAP. A net loss may be carried forward to be offset against net gains from similar transactions in future CAPs *(CTA 2010 s.91).*

14.14.8. Property Losses

A property loss may first be offset against other income of the same CAP and then carried forward to be offset against income from all sources in future CAPs *(CTA 2010 s.62).*

14.14.9. Capital Losses

Capital losses may only be carried forward and offset against chargeable gains of future periods *(TCGA 1992 s.8(1)).*

14.14.10. Excess Management Charges

Where the expenses of an investment company exceed its income and gains for a CAP, the excess may either be carried forward and offset against the income of future CAPs (*CTA 2009 s.1223*) or surrendered to another group company or member of the consortium *(CTA 2010 s.99 (1)(f)).*

14.14.11. Anti-avoidance: trades carried on on an uncommercial basis

Where a trade of farming or market gardening is being carried on and there has been a trading loss in the current CAP and each of the five preceding CAPs, the loss may only be carried forward to be offset against future profits from the same trade *(CTA 2010 s.48).* This does not apply where the trade of farming or market gardening is anciliary to a larger undertaking.

14.14.12. Anti-avoidance: change in ownership

Where there is a change in ownership and:

- within a period starting three years before the change and ending three years after the change there is a major change in the nature of the trade or the way in which it is conducted; or
- after the change in ownership, activities which had become negligible at the date of the change are subsequently revived,

trading losses arising in accounting periods before the change may not be carried forward to be offset against profits arising in accounting periods after the change, and trading losses arising in accounting periods after the change may not be carried back to be offset against profits arising in accounting periods before the change *(CTA 2010 ss.673 & 674).*

A major change will be a change of either a qualitative or a quantitative nature and each case will be decided on its own particular facts. However, the sorts of changes which are covered by these provisions are changes in:

- the types of goods or services dealt in;
- customers or outlets;
- markets.

(CTA 2010 s.673(4))

These provisions do not include changes in order to maintain or approve efficiency or to keep pace with changing technology, e.g. internet trading *(SP10/91 para. 2(7)).*

In determining where these sections apply HM Revenue & Customs will look at a three year period which includes the date of the change and it does not matter whether the change is a gradual one or whether it clearly occurs at a particular time *(SP10/91 para. 2(4)*). All of the factors will be evaluated as a whole, although, on occasion, a change in one factor may be decisive *(SP10/91 para. 2(5)).*

SP 10/91 gives the following examples where a change does not, in itself, constitute a major change:

- a company moves its manufacturing operations from three obsolescent factories to one new factory (improving efficiency);
- a company manufacturing kitchen utensils replaces enamel by plastic, or a company manufacturing timepieces replaces mechanical by electronic components (keeping pace with technology);
- a company operating a dealership in one make of car switches to operating a dealership in another make of car satisfying the same market (not a major change in the type of property dealt in);
- a company manufacturing both filament and fluorescent lamps (of which filament lamps form the greater part of the output) concentrates solely on filament lamps (a rationalisation of product range without a major change in the type of property dealt in);
- a company whose business consist of making and holding investments in UK quoted shares and securities changes its portfolio of quoted shares and securities (not a major change in investments held).

The following changes would be regarded as major changes:

- a company operating a dealership in saloon cars switches to operating a dealership in tractors (a major change in type of property dealt in);
- a company owning a public house switches to operating a discotheque in

the same, but converted, premises (a major change in the services or facilities provided);
- a company fattening pigs for their owners switches to buying pigs for fattening and resale (a major change in the nature of the trade, being a change from providing a service to being a primary producer);
- a company switches from investing in quoted shares to investing in real property for rent (a change in the nature of investment held).

(SP10/91 para. 10)

14.14.13. Transfer of Losses on Transfer of Trade

Where a trade is transferred from one company to another, trading losses of the transferor company may be transferred to the transferee company where:

1. at any time within the two years after the transfer at least 75% of the shares are held by the same persons as they belonged to at some time in the year before the transfer; and
2. during that period the trade was at all times carried on by a company within the charge to corporation tax.

It is not necessary for there to be 75% common ownership during the whole period, simply at some point both before and after the transfer *(CTA 2010 s.941(1))*.

The restriction on the carry forward of losses under CTA 2010 ss.673 & 674 (see section **14.14.12**) does not apply where there is a company reconstruction under CTA 2010 pt. 22, ch.1. Where the transferee company only takes over a part of the trade of the transferor company or takes over the trade of the transferee company as only part of its own trade, the trade taken over is regarded as a separate trade and an apportionment of total profits may be required to establish the profits against which the loss may be offset, or the amount of the loss available for offset *(CTA 2010 ss.951 & 952)*.

14.15. Groups and Consortia

14.15.1. Introduction

There are three situations to which provisions for groups and consortia apply. These are:

- related 51% group company;
- group relief, surrender of losses between group companies;
- chargeable gains and transfer of assets between group companies.

The definition of a group is different in each case and there are three different types of group:

- related 51% group companies;
- 75% group;
- chargeable gains group.

14.15.2. Related 51% group companies

A company is a related 51% group company of another company if:

- one company is a 51% subsidiary of the other; or
- both companies are a 51% subsidiary of a third company.

A company is a 51% subsidiary of another company if the other company holds, directly or indirectly, more than 50% of its ordinary share capital.

The number of related 51% group companies is relevant in determining whether corporation tax must be paid in instalments.

14.15.3. Group relief – definition of group

The above losses may be surrendered to a UK resident member of a 75% group. In order for two companies to be members of a 75% group, one company must be a 75% subsidiary of the other, or both companies must be 75% subsidiaries of a third company. A company will be a 75% subsidiary of another company if:

- one company holds over 75% of the share capital of the second; and
- one company is entitled to over 75% of the income of the second company on a distribution; and
- one company is entitled to more than 75% of the assets of the second company on a winding up. Assets payable to a loan creditor are disregarded only if the loan is a normal commercial loan.

(CTA 2010 s.151(4), s.166 & s.1154(3))

Shareholdings where a profit on disposal would be treated as a trading receipt are disregarded in determining a company's interest in a second company *(CTA 2010 s.151(3))*.

Where one company has an indirect interest, the different interests are multiplied. For example, where A has an 80% interest in B and B has an 80% interest in C, A and C cannot be part of the same 75% group, since A only has a 64% interest in C. Where A has a 90% interest in B, and B has a 90% interest in C, A has an 81% interest in C and all three companies may be part of the same 75% group.

A group may contain non-UK-resident companies, i.e. where A Ltd and B Ltd are both subsidiaries of C Inc. (resident in the US); however, losses may only be surrendered between UK members of a group.

14.15.4. Group relief – losses available for group relief

The group relief provisions enable the following types of losses to be surrendered to another group company:

- trading losses (excluding losses of foreign trades and certain trades not carried on with a view to a gain and farming where loss relief is restricted by CTA 2010 s.37(5),(6) or s.44 and losses from farming and market gardening where relief is restricted by CTA 2010 s.48) *(CTA 2010 s.100(2));*

- excess capital allowances;
- property losses;
- deficit on non-trading loan relationships;
- non-trading loss on intangible fixed assets;
- excess charges on income;
- excess management expenses of investment companies.

(CTA 2010 s.99 (1))

Capital losses are not available for group relief.

14.15.5. Group relief – surrender of losses

The surrendering company may surrender trading losses, excess capital allowances and deficits on non-trading loan relationships in preference to claiming another method of relief *(CTA 2010 s.99(3))*. Charges on income, property losses, management expenses and a non-trading loss on intangible fixed assets may only be surrendered to the extent that they exceed in aggregate the company's gross profits for the period. Gross profits are defined as the profits for the period without deduction of any losses or allowances mentioned in CTA 2010 s.99(1) (see section **14.15.4**) or losses carried back from later periods or carried forward from earlier periods *(CTA 2010 s.105(5))*. Losses are deemed to have been surrendered in the following order:

- qualifying charitable donations;
- property losses;
- excess management expenses;
- losses on intangible fixed assets.

(CTA 2010 s.105 (4)).

A company need only surrender a specified amount of the loss *(FA 1998 Sch. 18 para. 69(1))*. This will enable a company to leave sufficient profits within the charge to tax to make use of the small companies' rate band. The claimant company may, however, only offset a loss surrendered to the extent of any remaining profits if it were to claim any relief available for losses of the current period or losses brought forward from previous periods. This includes deficits on non-trading loan relationships and excess charges on income. It is not necessary for the claimant company actually to claim these reliefs; it may be merely a notional offset which restricts the group relief available.

Example

A Ltd has three wholly-owned subsidiaries — B Ltd, C Ltd and D Ltd. They have the following results for the year ended 31 March 2022:

	A Ltd	B Ltd	C Ltd	D Ltd
Trading profit/(loss)	£40,000	£(60,000)	£100,000	£500,000
Chargeable gains	£10,000	£20,000	£20,000	£30,000
Profit/(loss) from non-trading loan relationships	£(5,000)	£30,000		£40,000

B Ltd is not obliged to offset the trading loss against its chargeable gains and profit from non-trading loan relationships, but may surrender the entire £60,000. This would leave £50,000. The loss could be surrendered in its entirety to C Ltd or D Ltd, but only £45,000 of the loss could be surrendered to A Ltd, even if A Ltd were to decide to carry the loss from non-trading loan relationships forward.

From 1 April 2017 it has been possible to carry forward losses for group relief. However, brought forward losses may only be surrendered to the extent that the surrendering company cannot offset them against its own profits.

Example

E Ltd and F Ltd have the following results for the years ended 31 March 2021 and 31 March 2022.

	E Ltd y/e 31.3.21	E Ltd y/e 31.3.22	F Ltd y/e 31.3.21	F Ltd y/e 31.3.22
Trading profit/(loss)	£(150,000)	£20,000	£60,000	£100,000

E Ltd may surrender £60,000 of its loss in y/e 31 March 2021 to F Ltd, but can only surrender £70,000 to F Ltd in y/e 31 March 2022, since it must first use £20,000 of the loss against its own profits for that year. *(CTA 2010 ss.188AA-FD)*

14.15.6. Group relief – non co-terminous accounting periods

Where the surrendering company and the claimant company do not have the same accounting date the amount of the loss which may be surrender is the lower of:

1. the unrelieved part of the profits of the claimant company for the overlapping period, i.e. after deducting any previously claimed group relief for the overlapping period; and
2. the unused part of the loss of the surrendering company for the overlapping period, i.e. after deducting previous surrenders relating to the overlapping period.

(CTA 2010 ss.138-140)

Example

A Ltd has an accounting date of 31 December and B Ltd, its wholly-owned subsidiary, an accounting date of 31 March. A Ltd incurred a loss of £100,000 in the year ended 31 December 2021. B Ltd's profits were £120,000 for the year ended 31 March 2021 and £150,000 for the year ended 31 March 2022. B Ltd claimed group relief of £40,000 from its fellow subsidiary C Ltd for the year ended 31 March 2021. The amounts which B Ltd may claim from A Ltd are:

Year ended 31 March 2021

Lower of:

Loss of A Ltd £(100,000) x 3/12	£(25,000)
Profits of B Ltd (£120,000 - £40,000) x 3/12	£20,000

Year ended 31 March 2022

Lower of:

Loss of A Ltd £(100,000) x 9/12	£(75,000)
Profits of B Ltd £150,000 x 9/12	£112,500

B Ltd may therefore claim group relief from A Ltd of £20,000 in the year ended 31 March 2021 and £75,000 in the year ended 31 March 2022.

14.15.7. Group relief – arrangements exist for company to leave group

Where arrangements exist for a company to become a member of another group, or for control of a company to pass to another person, without control of other group companies similarly passing or for the trade of a company to pass to another company outside the group, that company may not participate in group relief arrangements in respect of losses incurred or profits earned after these arrangements come into existence *(CTA 2010 ss.154-156)*. The definition of arrangements is wide and can include any sort of formal or informal arrangements whereby a group company might be sold and applies even if the proposed disposal is on normal commercial terms. SP3/93 states that if an agreement provides for the creation of option rights exercisable at some time in the future, 'arrangements' come into existence when the agreement is entered into *(SP3/93 para. 5)*. An arrangement through 'option arrangements' may exist, even if the agreement is not enforceable *(SP3/93 para. 10)*. Where a company is proposing to dispose of another group company, simply entering into negotiations with another party does not constitute 'arrangements' within this section *(SP3/93 para. 6)*. Where the disposal requires the approval of shareholders, operations leading towards disposal will not constitute 'arrangement' until that approval is given, or until the directors become aware that approval will be given *(SP3/93 para. 7)*. If, after negotiations with several potential purchasers, a holder of shares or securities concentrates on a particular purchaser, this will not constitute arrangements, but arrangements may exist if there is an understanding between the parties in the nature of an option *(SP3/93 para. 8)*. Where a reconstruction requires the approval of shareholders under company law, operations leading towards disposal will not constitute 'arrangement' until that approval is given, or until the directors become aware that approval will be given *(SP3/93 para. 9)*.

14.15.8. Group relief – payment for losses surrendered

A claimant company may make a payment to the surrendering company in respect of the loss claimed. A payment up to a maximum of the amount of the loss surrendered (not merely up to the amount of tax saved) is outside the scope of corporation tax for the receiving company and is not treated as a distribution or charge on income of the paying company *(CTA 2010 s.183).*

14.15.9. Group relief – time limit for claim

Group relief will be claimed in the tax return of the claimant company *(FA 1998 Sch. 18 para. 67(1))*, but the surrendering company must also give its consent in its own tax return *(FA 1998 Sch. 18 para. 70(1))*. A group relief claim may not be amended, but it may be withdrawn and a new claim substituted, which amounts to the same although the wording of the paperwork will be different *(FA 1998 Sch. 18 para. 73)*. The time limit for making a claim is one year from the filing date for the corporation tax return or 30 days after HM Revenue & Customs has completed its enquiries into a return, if later *(FA 1998 Sch. 18 para. 74(1))*.

14.15.10. Chargeable gains groups — definition of group

A chargeable gains group consists of:

- a principal company; and
- its 75% subsidiaries; and
- where any 75% subsidiary itself has a 75% subsidiary, the second tier subsidiary and so on *(TCGA 1992 s.170(3)(a))*; provided that the principal company has at least an effective 51% holding in the subsidiary *(TCGA 1992 s.170(3)(b))*.

A principal company cannot be itself a 75% subsidiary of another company *(TCGA 1992 s.170(4))*, unless it is prevented from being a part of the same group as the company holding the 75% by virtue of TCGA 1992 s.170(3)(b) *(TCGA 1992 s.170(5))*.

A company is a 75% subsidiary of another company if at least 75% of its ordinary share capital is held by the other company (TCGA 1992 s.170(2)(c)). A company is an effective 51% subsidiary if the principal company is entitled to more than 50% of any distribution to equity holders and to more than 50% of the assets in a winding up *(TCGA 1992 s.170(7))*.

Example

1. If A owns 80% of B and B owns 70% of C, A and B will form a capital gains group; however, C will not be part of the group since B owns less than 75% of C.
2. If A owns 80% of B, B owns 75% of C, C owns 75% of D and D owns 75% of E, A, B and C will form a capital gains group since A has an effective interest of 60% in C. D and E will not form part of this group, since A only has an effective interest of

45% in D and 31.75% in E. B, C, D and E cannot form a second capital gains group with B as the principal company, since B is a 75% subsidiary of A. However D and E can form a separate group, since D cannot be part of the same group as C.

Capital gains groups may include non-UK-resident companies, but transfers may only be made to a UK branch or agency of such companies, so that the gain on the eventual disposal of any asset will still be subject to UK corporation tax *(TCGA 1992 s.171(1A))*.

14.15.11. Chargeable gains groups — transfer of assets

Assets may be transferred between companies within a chargeable gains group on a no gain/no loss basis, i.e. no chargeable gain or allowable loss will arise in the transferor company and the transferee company will acquire the asset at the base cost to the transferor *(TCGA 1992 s.171(1))*. Where a company wishes to dispose of an asset which is pregnant with gain, shortly before sale it may transfer the asset to a company with available capital losses which can be used to shelter all or part of the gain. Alternatively, it can ensure that the gain arises in the group company with the lowest marginal rate of corporation tax.

It is also possible to make an irrevocable election to transfer a gain or loss, or part thereof, to another member of the group *(TCGA 1992 s.171A)*. The election must be made jointly by both companies. The time limit for making the election is two years after the end of the CAP in which the disposal took place. Any payment in consideration of the transfer up to the amount of the gain or loss transferred is ignored for the purposes of corporation tax *(TCGA 1992 s.171B(6))*.

14.15.12. Chargeable gains groups — company leaving group

Where a company leaves a group, any gains and losses which, but for the no gain/no loss provisions, would have accrued on assets transferred into the company in the preceding six years are deemed to crystalise at the date the company leaves the group *(TCGA 1992 s.179(1),(1A))*. If the asset is subsequently sold by the company, the base cost will be the market value of the asset on the date that it was acquired. This does not apply to a transfer where:

1. the transferee and transferor companies leave the group at the same time; and
2. one company is a 75% subsidiary and an effective 51% subsidiary of the other or both companies are 75% subsidiaries and effective 51% subsidiaries of a third company; and
3. the original no gain/no loss transfer was between the two companies leaving the group *(TCGA 1992 s.179(2),(2A))*.

However, *Johnston Publishing (North) Ltd v HMRC (2008) (EWCA Civ 858)* has confirmed that this exception only applies if the two companies were members of the same group both at the time of the transfer and the time the companies leave the group.

14.15.13. Chargeable gains groups — roll-over relief - groups

Roll-over relief is available in cases where the disposal is made by one group company and the new asset is acquired by another group company, provided that both the acquisition and the disposal are made either by UK resident companies or a permanent establishment of a non-resident company *(TCGA 1992 s.175(1), (1A))*.

14.15.14. Chargeable gains groups — appropriation of capital asset as trading stock

Where an asset is transferred which is used as a capital asset in the transferor company, but is appropriated as trading stock by the transferee company, the asset is deemed to have been appropriated from trading stock by the transferor company immediately before the transfer *(TCGA 1992 s.173(1))*. This will give rise to a chargeable gain in the transferor company. An election may be made for the resultant gain or loss to be set against the value of the asset transferred. This will increase the trading profit in the transferee company (or reduce the profit in the case of a loss). These provisions do not apply where there is a reconstruction or re-organisation, one group company receives shares and relief is available under TCGA 1992 ss.126 & 127.

14.15.15. Chargeable gains groups — transfer out of stock for use as capital asset

Where an asset is transferred which is trading stock in the transferor company, but is appropriated as a capital asset by the transferee company, the asset is deemed to have been appropriated as a capital asset at its market value by the transferor company immediately before the transfer *(TCGA 1992 s.173(2))*. The asset will therefore be deemed to have passed at its market value at that date and any increase in its value since acquisition will be treated as a trading receipt and any subsequent gain will give rise to a chargeable gain in the transferee company. These provisions do not apply where there is a reconstruction or re-organisation, one group company receives shares and relief is available under TCGA 1992 ss.126 and 127.

14.15.16. Chargeable gains groups — pre-entry losses

Where a company purchases a company with realised capital losses, brought-forward capital losses in such a company may not be used to offset gains elsewhere in the group, but may only be used to offset future chargeable gains arising on assets which were:

- owned by the target company at the date on which it joined the group; or
- acquired by the target company after it joined the group, provided that the asset was acquired from outside the group and has only been used for the purpose of a trade it was carrying on at the date that the company joined the group.

(TCGA 1992 Sch. 7A para. 1)

Where a pre-entry loss is available for offset, it must be offset in priority to other losses *(TCGA 1992 Sch. 7A para. 6(1)(c))* and a pre-entry loss of the current year is offset in priority to a pre-entry loss brought forward from a previous period.

14.15.17. Chargeable gains groups — pre-entry gains

If a company joins a group part-way through an accounting period, chargeable gains realised before the date the company joined may only be offset by losses realised before that date or on the disposal of assets held by the company at that date *(TCGA 1992 Sch. 7AA).*

14.15.18. Chargeable gains groups — depreciatory transactions

Assets may be transferred between group companies at no gain/no loss regardless of the consideration which passes between them. If an asset is transferred from one group company to another at either undervalue or overvalue, this transaction will reduce the value of the shares of one of the parties to the transaction. Where such shares are subsequently sold at a loss, the allowable loss will be reduced to the extent that it is attributable to a depreciatory transaction *(TCGA 1992 s.176).*

14.15.19. Consortia

A consortium-owned company is a company which is not a 75% subsidiary of any company where at least 75% of its share capital is owned by companies, all of which hold at least 5% and all of which are entitled to at least 5% of income on a distribution and 5% of any assets on a winding up *(CTA 2010 s.153).*

The types of losses which may be surrendered are those mentioned in CTA 2010 s.99 (1) in relation to groups.

Consortium loss relief may be surrendered as follows:

- a consortium member may claim a portion of the loss of the consortium-owned company (which may be a trading company or a holding company) equal to its holding in the company;
- a consortium member may claim a portion of the loss of a trading company which is a 90% subsidiary of the consortium-owned company equal to its holding in the company;
- a consortium member may surrender a loss to the consortium-owned

company, a trading company which is a 90% subsidiary of the consortium-owned company, for offset against a portion of the consortium-owned company's profits equal to its holding in the company.

(CTA 2010 s.132(1)-(3), s.133(1),(2) & s.153(3))

A consortium relief claim may not be made if a profit on the sale of the shares in the consortium-owned company would be treated as a trading receipt *(CTA 2010 s.132(4),(5)&s.133(3),(4))*. Where the shareholding in the consortium-owned company changes during the period, the portion of the loss which may be claimed or the portion of the profits against which a loss may be offset, is calculated using a weighted average of the holdings during the period (*SPC6*). Where a consortium member is also a member of a group, the consortium-owned company may surrender a portion of its loss to another member of the group of which the consortium company is a member and a member of the group may surrender a loss for offset against a portion of the consortium-owned company's profits *(CTA 2010 s.133(1),(2))*. All members of the consortium must consent to such a claim.

14.16. Close Companies

14.16.1. General

A company is a 'close company' if it is controlled by:

- five or fewer participators together with their associates; or
- any number of participators, together with their associates, who are also directors.

(CTA 2010 s.439 (1))

The definitions of these terms are widely drawn.

14.16.2. Control

Control is defined as:

- possessing or being entitled to acquire over 50% of the company's share capital or voting rights; or
- being entitled to receive over 50% of a company's profits by way of distribution; or
- being entitled to receive over 50% of a company's assets on a winding up.

(CTA 2010 s.450 (1),(2))

14.16.3. Director

A director is:

- anyone occupying such a position, whether or not they are actually called a director;
- any person in accordance with whose instructions the directors are accustomed to acting (shadow directors);
- a manager of the company who beneficially owns, directly or indirectly,

alone or with associates, at least 20% of the share capital.
(CTA 2010 s.452 (1),(2))

14.16.4. Participator

A participator includes a number of persons other than shareholders, such as persons who are entitled to acquire share capital or voting rights and loan creditors in respect of money borrowed (except a bank lending in the ordinary course of business) *(CTA 2010 s.453)*.

14.16.5. Associates

A participator's holding will be aggregated with those of their associates. Associates are:

- the participator's spouse or civil partner;
- the participator's brothers and sisters;
- the participators parents and remoter lineal ancestors and children and remoter lineal descendants; uncles, aunts and in-laws are excluded (but see example below);
- the participator's business partners;
- trustees of a settlement of which the participator or their relatives are the settlor;
- trustees of a settlement where the participator is interested in shares or obligations of the company under the terms of the settlement;
- personal representatives of the deceased, where the participator is interested in shares or obligations of the company under the terms of a will.

(CTA 2010 s.448)

The holdings of the participators and associates will be aggregated in such a manner as to produce the lowest number of participators.

Example

The shareholders of Bowen Ltd are:

A	10%
B - wife of A	8%
C-sister of B	5%
D	2%
E-son of D	3%
F-wife of E	1%
G	8%
H	8%
I	8%
Other shareholders < 1%	47%

None of the shareholders are associated with each other except as stated.

If A is taken as the main participator, B is associated with A, but C, A's sister-in-law, is not. Similarly, if D is taken as a main participator, E is associated with D, but F, D's daughter-in-law, is not. If, however, B is taken as a main participator, both A and C are associated with B. Similarly, both D and F are associated with E. The company is therefore controlled by five participators.

B	8	
A – husband of B	10	
C - sister of B	5	
		23
E	3	
D – father of E	2	
F – wife of E	1	
		6
G		8
H		8
I		8
Total		53%

Two companies are associated if:

- one company controls the other;
- they are both controlled by the same person or company.

(CTA 2010 s.449)

14.16.6. Exemptions from close company status

There are a number of exemptions which mean that a company will not be a close company even if the above conditions are satisfied. These include the following:

- the company is not resident in the UK *(CTA 2010 s.442);*
- the company is controlled by one or more non-close companies. This means that subsidiary companies are not close companies unless the holding company is itself close *(CTA 2010 s.444(2)(a));*
- the company could only be regarded as being under the control of five or fewer participators by including a non-close company *(CTA 2010 s.444 (2)(b));*
- the company's shares have been both listed and dealt on a recognised stock exchange in the preceding 12 months and at least 35% of the shares are held beneficially by the public *(CTA 2010 s.446(1)*). This exemption does not apply if the five principal members, together with their associates, hold over 85% of the voting rights *(CTA 2010 s.446(2)*). The five principal members are the five members who, again along with associates, have the largest shareholdings. Any aggregate holding of 5% or less is, however, ignored and if two or more shareholders tie for fifth place they are all included *(CTA 2010 s.446(3),(4))*. Broadly speaking the public includes any non-close company and any other shareholder other than the five principal members, directors and their associates.

14.16.7. Consequences of being a close company – loans to participators

Where a loan is made by the company to one of its participators, or an associate, the company must pay a tax charge to HM Revenue & Customs equal to the percentage of the loan or advance that correspondes to the dividend upper rate (32.5%).

The definition of a loan for the purpose of these provisions includes:

- an advance of money;
- an overdrawn current account;
- debts owed to the company;
- debts incurred by a participator personally and assigned to the company.

(CTA 2010 s.455 (1), (2), (4))

This section also applies where a loan is made to a third party other than in the course of business and a participator, or associate, indirectly benefits from the loan *(CTA 2010 s.459)*. The tax is due nine months after the end of the period in which the loan is made *(CTA 2010 s.455(3))*. If the loan, or a part of it, is repaid before the due date, tax is not payable on the portion repaid. However, this is subject to anti-avoidance rules to prevent 'bed and breakfasting' of amounts above a *de minimis* level of £5,000. Where:

(a) within any period of 30 days:
   (i) the qualifying amount of repayments made to a close company in respect of one or more chargeable payments made by the company to a person totals £5,000 or more; and
   (ii) the available amount of the the relevant chargeable payments made by the company to the person or an associate of the person totals £5,000 or more; and

(b) the relevant chargeable payments are made in an accounting period subsequent to that in which the chargeable payments mentioned in (a)(i) were made;

the qualifying amount of the repayments, so far as not exceeding the available amount of the relevant chargeable payments, is to be treated as a repayment of the relevant chargeable payments.

(CTA 2010 s.464C(1))

The new chargeable payments may be in the same accounting period as the repayments, but must be in a later period than the original chargeable payments. References to repayments include conversion of outstanding balances into dividends or bonuses.

Example

K Ltd has an accounting date of 31 December and at 31 December 2021 a loan of £20,000 was outstanding to X, a participator. On 8 August 2020 X repaid £8,000 of the loan, but on 22 August 2021 K Ltd advanced a further £6,000 to X. Without the above anti-avoidance provisions the repayment of £8,000 would reduce the amount on which K Ltd had to pay tax on 1 October 2020 to £12,000 and the further advance of £6,000 would be treated as having been made in the year ended 31 December 2021. However, since the advance of £6,000 is made within 30 days of the repayment of £8,000 it is matched against the repayment and K Ltd must pay tax on £18,000 on 1 October 2021.

The matching rule also applies where a repayment is made under arrangements which result in a further amount being paid to the participator. The repayment is treated, as far as possible, as a repayment of the new payment. This applies if the amount outstanding before the repayment is £15,000 or more and the available amount of the chargeable payments made to the participator, or associate, under the arrangements totals £5,000 or more *(CTA 2010 s.464C(3))*.

If a loan is repaid, released or written off after the due date the amount relating to this portion will be refunded. The company must make a claim under this section within six years of the end of the period in which the loan is repaid, released or written off *(CTA 2010 s.458(1)-(3))*, but where the repayment, release or write-off is made after the date on which the tax has been paid, no repayment or relief will be given before nine months after the end of the period in which the repayment, release or write-off occurred *(CTA 2010 s.458(4),(5))*.

Any loan released or written off is treated as a dividend in the hands of the participator *(CTA 2010 s.463)*.

Where a loan taxable under this section is written off, in full or in part, no relief is available to the company under the loan relationship rules *(CTA 2009 s.321A)*.

Where a benefit arises directly or indirectly to a participator or an associate as a result of tax avoidance arrangements to which the company is a party, and no charge to tax arises either on the company under CTA 2010 s.455 or on the participator or associate, the company must pay corporation tax on the value of the benefit at a rate which corresponds to the dividend upper rate *(CTA 2010 s.464A)*. This tax is refunded if the participator or associate makes a payment to the company in respect of the benefit and no consideration is given in return for this payment. The company must claim the refund within four years of the end of the financial year in which the payment to the company is made by the participator or associate *(CTA 2010 s.464B)*.

Debts resulting from the supply of goods in the normal course of business are not treated as a debt, unless the credit term given either exceeds six months or is longer than the credit term the company would normally give its customers *(CTA 2010 s.456(2))*. The tax charge on the company is in addition to any benefit charge on the participator under ITEPA 2003 pt. 3 Chapter 7, if they are also an employee.

Certain loans are, however, excluded:

- the loan is made in the ordinary course of business and at a commercial rate of interest. It is not sufficient for the loan to simply be at a commercial rate of interest;
- loans to directors and employees provided that:
  - the loan does not exceed £15,000; and
  - the borrower is a full-time director or employee; and
  - the borrower, with associates, would not be entitled to more than 5% of the assets of the company on a winding up.

(CTA 2010 s. 456 (3)-(7))

14.16.8. Consequences of being a close company — benefits in kind provided to participators

Where a benefit in kind (e.g. car or accommodation) is provided to a participator and the benefit is not taxable as employment income (generally because the participator is not an employee or director of the company), an amount equal to the benefit charge is treated as a dividend. The cost of providing the benefit is disallowable in the company's tax computation *(CTA 2010 ss.1064 & 1065)*.

14.17. Companies with Investment Business

A company with investment business is a company whose main business is the making of investments *(CTA 2009 s.1218(1))*. This may consist of either property or financial investments. This income will not be treated as trading income; therefore, the expenses of management and capital allowances will be deducted from the investment income *(CTA 2009 s.1219(1))*, provided that the expenses relate to the holding of investments which are held for a business or commercial purpose of the company and are held for purposes which are within the charge to UK corporation tax *(CTA 2009 s.1219(2))*. A deduction is not available under this section where a deduction is available under another section *(CTA 2009 s.1219(3)(b))*. Expenses of a capital nature are not deductible except for capital allowances which cannot be offset against income for the period under CAA 2001 s.253(2) and expenses where a deduction is specifically permitted under the Taxes Acts *(CTA 2009 s.1219(3)(a), & s.1233)*. Where these exceed the investment income, the excess management expenses, capital allowances, deficits on non-trading loan relationships and excess trade charges may be carried forward to be offset against income of future periods *(CTA 2009 s.1223)*. These are also available for group relief (see section **14.15.4**). Where accounts are drawn up in accordance with GAAP and an accounting period coincides with a CAP, a deduction for expenses may be claimed in the period in which it is charged in the accounts *(CTA 2009 s.1225(1))*. Where an expense relates to more than one CAP, it must be apportioned between those periods in a reasonable manner *(CTA 2009 s.1225(2),(3))*. If accounts are not drawn up in accordance with GAAP, expenses are deductible in the CAP in which they would have been deductible on the assumption that accounts had been drawn up in accordance with GAAP *(CTA 2009 s.1226)*.

Where there is a change in ownership of an investment company, and

- within three years of the change the total of the share and loan capital is either doubled or increased by at least £lm; or
- there is a major change in the nature of the business and/or the way it is conducted in the period commencing three years and ending three years after the change (a change in the shares held in a portfolio will not count as a major change); or
- the business has become negligible before the change in ownership and subsequently revives,

any losses incurred before the change may not be carried forward to be offset against income arising after the change *(CTA 2010 ss.677-691)*.

14.18. Close Investment-holding Companies

A close investment-holding company (CIC) is a close company which is neither a trading company nor a member of a trading group which coordinates the administration of trading companies. Companies which deal in land or shares or which let property on a commercial basis are treated as trading companies for this purpose.

14.19. Demergers

14.19.1. General

There are two methods of demerging, the 'direct' and 'indirect' methods. In the direct method the distributing company distributes its shares in a 75% subsidiary to its own shareholders, thereby breaking the group relationship. In the indirect method, the distributing company transfers either a trade or shares in a 75% subsidiary to a third company, which issues shares to the shareholders of the distributing company.

A distribution by the direct method is exempt from the normal distribution provisions if:

1. it consists of a transfer to all or any of its members by a company of shares

in one or more companies which are its 75% subsidiaries;

2. the shares are not redeemable and constitute the whole or substantially the whole (defined as 90% or more) of the distributing company's holding of the ordinary share capital of the subsidiary and confer the whole or substantially the whole of the distributing company's voting rights in the subsidiary. Relief will not, however, be denied solely because there is concurrently a transfer or issue of other shares or securities of a kind which does qualify for relief. The condition of "substantially the whole" will be treated as being satisfied, even if the shareholders give some consideration;
3. the distributing company must be a trading company or the holding company of a trading group after the distribution, unless the demerger involves the transfer of the trade or the shares in two or more 75% subsidiaries of the distributing company and the distributing company is thereafter dissolved without there being any net assets of the company remaining for distribution in a winding up or otherwise.

(CTA 2010 s.1076 & s.1082)

By concession, a distributing company will be treated as having complied with these conditions if it retains sufficient funds to cover the winding up and the negligible amount of share capital remaining *(ESC C11).*

A distribution by the indirect method is also exempt, provided that:

1. where a trade is transferred, the distributing company retains no interest, or only a minor interest in that trade. The term "interest" is construed widely, but in general involves retaining influence or control over the trade or the assets by, for example, being a major supplier. The term "minor" is interpreted as being the opposite of "substantially the whole", i.e. 10% or less;
2. where shares in a subsidiary are transferred they constitute the whole or substantially the whole (defined as 90% or more) of the distributing company's holding of the ordinary share capital of the subsidiary and confer the whole or substantially the whole of the distributing company's voting rights in the subsidiary;
3. the only or main activity of the transferee company, or companies, after the distribution must be the carrying on of the trade or the holding of shares transferred to it;
4. the shares issued by the transferee company must not be redeemable and must constitute the whole or substantially the whole of its issued share capital and must confer the whole or substantially the whole of the voting rights in that company;
5. the distributing company must, after the distribution, be a trading company or the holding company of a trading group unless there are two

or more transferee companies, each of which has a trade or shares in a separate 75% subsidiary of the distributing company transferred to it and the distributing company is thereafter dissolved without there being any net assets of the company remaining for distribution in a winding up or otherwise.

(CTA 2010 s.1077 & s.1083)

A trade is transferred between companies by transferring a parcel of assets necessary for carrying on that trade, and it is not essential that the distributing company carried on the same trade. The trade transferred may, for example, only be a part of the trade carried on by the distributing company, or the assets may have been brought together for the first time from one or more trades carried on by the distributing company or the group of which it is a member. Assets may also be included which had not previously been used in a trade or held by a trading company, such as property. What matters is that there is a division of trading activities and that the assets transferred should be transferred to be used in a trade by the transferee company and should be so used. Relief will not be denied simply because a minor asset unconnected with the trade is also transferred *(SP13/80).*

The demerger must be made wholly or mainly for the purpose of benefiting some, or all, of the trading activities which were previously carried on by the single company and which, after the demerger, will be carried on by two or more companies or groups *(CTA 2010 s.1081 (3))*, and must not form part of a scheme or arrangement, or have as one of its main purposes:

1. the avoidance of tax;
2. the making of a 'chargeable payment';
3. the acquisition by any person or persons other than members of the distributing company of control of that company, of any other relevant company or of any company which belongs to the same group as any such company. The concurrent sale of another group company will not necessarily be a bar to obtaining relief, but relief will be denied if the sale is part of a scheme or arrangement of which the distribution was a part; or
4. the cessation of a trade, or its sale after the distribution.

(CTA 2010 s1081 (4)-(7))

A chargeable payment is defined as any payment made within five years of an exempt distribution otherwise than for *bona fide* commercial reasons or which forms part of a scheme or arrangement the main purpose, or one of the main purposes of which, is the avoidance of tax and which:

1. a company concerned in an exempt distribution makes directly or indirectly to a member of that company or of any other company concerned in that distribution; and

2. is made in connection with, or with any transaction affecting, the shares in that or any such company; and
3. is not a distribution or exempt distribution or made to another company which belongs to the same group as the company making the payment.

(CTA 2010 ss.1028,1088 & 1089)

14.19.2. Approval

A company wishing to undertake a demerger may apply to HM Revenue & Customs for clearance. The application must give full details of the demerger and HMRC may request further details within 30 days and the company has a further 30 days to supply these. HMRC must give a decision within 30 days of the receipt of the application. The approval may be void if the company fails to give full details *(CTA 2010 ss.1091-1094)*.

The following details are required in an application, preferably in the order given below, and the information should be expanded as necessary, with additional information being given at the end.

1. ***Companies***

   The name of each 'relevant company' showing:
   a) whether it is a 'distributing', 'subsidiary' or 'transferee' company;
   b) its tax district and reference;
   c) whether it is resident in the UK;
   d) status, i.e. holding company or trading company or some other type of company, such as investment company.

2. ***Groups***

   Where appropriate a statement or diagram showing the shareholding interest of each group company in other group companies. A group for this purpose is the largest 51% group to which the distributing company belongs.

3. ***Purpose and benefits***

   A statement of the reasons for the demerger, the trading activities to be divided, the trading benefits expected and any other benefits expected to accrue, whether or not to the company concerned. If this can be stated more clearly after giving a statement of the proposed transactions, the item may be included after item 4.

4. ***Transactions***

   A detailed description of the proposed transactions including:
   a) *Share Capital*

      Particulars (class, amount and voting rights) of **all shares** of the companies in (1) above, issued (or to be issued) in the course of the demerger showing the shares to be transferred and/or issued (or exchanged) in the demerger and to which the shareholders (or classes of shareholders) or companies are entitled. Particulars of any changes to be made in shareholders' rights or loan capital arrangements in connection with the demerger should also be given.

b) *Transfer of trade (as distinct from trading subsidiary)*
   Particulars of the transfer, including all trading and other assets and liabilities to be transferred and retained. (Approximate statements of affairs for the distributing and transferee companies before and after the demerger would be helpful). Particulars of any interest in the trade to be retained by the distributing company or its group should also be given.

c) *Prior transactions*
   Particulars of any prior transactions or arrangement within a group in preparation for the demerger. The description should make clear why it is considered that all the relevant conditions are satisfied.

5. ***CTA 2010 s.1081 conditions***
   Confirmation, together with all relevant information, that the distribution is not part of a scheme or arrangement etc. falling within the above section. A statement should also be given of the circumstances, if any, in which it is envisaged that control of a 'relevant company' listed in (1) above might be acquired by someone other than members of the 'distributing company' or a trade carried on by one of those companies before or after the demerger might cease or be sold. Such circumstances might exist, but not as part of a scheme or arrangement or otherwise to cause any of the qualifying conditions to be failed.

6. ***Balance sheet and profit and loss account***
   The latest available balance sheet and profit and loss accounts of the existing companies listed in (1) above and, in the case of a group, the consolidated balance sheet and profit and loss account, together with any material relevant changes between the balance sheet date and the proposed demerger.

14.20. Purchase of Own Shares

14.20.1. General

Companies may repurchase their shares out of distributable profits or proceeds of a new issue. Payments to shareholders are normally treated as distributions, if the shareholder is an individual. Where the shareholder is a company, it will give rise to a chargeable gain *(SP 4/89)*.

Payments on the repurchase, redemption or repayment of its own shares by an unquoted company which is either a trading company or the holding company of a trading group are not treated as distributions if either:

- the repurchase etc. is for the benefit of a trade carried on by the company or any of its 75% subsidiaries; or
- the proceeds are to be applied in meeting an inheritance tax liability.

(CTA 2010 s.1033)

14.20.2. Repurchase for Benefit of Trade

The repurchase, redemption or repayment must be for the benefit of a trade carried on by the company or any of its 75% subsidiaries and must not form part of a scheme or arrangement, one of the main purposes of which is to enable the owner of the shares to participate in the profits of the company without receiving a dividend or the avoidance of tax *(CTA 2010 s. 1033(2))*. The company may be required to make a declaration in writing that no such scheme or arrangement exists and must supply any information required in order to enable an officer to decide whether the payment is for the benefit of the trade. If required to do so, the company must comply within 60 days *(CTA 2010 s.1046 (2))*.

SP2/82 gives the following examples of where such a payment may benefit the trade:

1. Buying out a dissident shareholder.
2. The proprietor of the company is retiring to make way for new management.
3. A shareholder has died and the beneficiaries or personal representatives do not wish to keep the shares.

A payment is less likely to be considered to meet this condition if the shareholder is merely reducing their proportionate share by 25% or more.

14.20.3. Payment of Inheritance Tax Liability

Where the proceeds of the repayment are used for the payment of an inheritance tax liability, the whole or substantially the whole of the sum must be used for that purpose within two years of the death *(CTA 2010 s.1033 (3))*. The payment will be treated as a distribution if the liability could have been paid from other funds without incurring undue hardship *(CTA 2010 s.1033(4))*.

Vendor

The shareholder or vendor must satisfy the following conditions:

- They must be resident in the UK in the year of the payment. If the payment is made to a personal representative, the deceased must have been resident in the UK at the date of death *(CTA 2010 s.1034)*;

- They must have owned the shares for five years at the date of sale. If they acquired the shares as a beneficiary under a will the minimum period is three years and the period of ownership will include the period during which the shares were held by the deceased *(CTA 2010 s.1035(1) & s.1036);*
- If the vendor has acquired shares of the same class at different times the shares disposed of are assumed to be of the earliest acquisition and any previous disposals of the same class of share are assumed to be disposals of later acquisitions *(CTA 2010 s.1035(2));*
- If the vendor owns shares in the company after the repurchase, their interest (or the interest of themselves and their associates) after the repurchase, expressed as a fraction of the total share capital of the company, must be no more than 75% of their interest before the repurchase *(CTA 2010 s.1037).* If a vendor had a 20% interest before the repurchase, it is not, therefore, sufficient to sell one quarter of the interest, since, after the repurchase, the interest will be 15/95 or 15.8%. This condition is not satisfied if the share of a distribution of profits available for distribution to which a vendor is entitled immediately after the repurchase is more than 75% of their entitlement immediately before the repurchase. If they were entitled to a fixed amount before the repurchase, they are treated as being entitled to that same fixed amount after the purchase *(CTA 2010 s.1038);*
- If the vendor has an interest in the shares of a group, their interest in each group company, expressed as a fraction, must be totalled and divided by the number of group companies, including companies in which the vendor holds no shares *(CTA 2010 s.1040).*

'Profits available for distribution' is defined as the profits so available under CA 2006 s.830(2) plus £100 and plus any fixed, periodic distribution to which a person is entitled *(CTA 2010 s.1038 (3)-(5)).* In calculating the interest of a vendor, the interest of associates must be included *(CTA 2010 s.1037(2)).* This rule may be relaxed in certain cases where a vendor agrees to the purchase in order that another vendor may satisfy the condition *(CTA 2010 s.1043).*

A payment will not be exempt under these provisions, if it is only made as part of a scheme or arrangement which is designed to give, or is likely to give the vendor, or any of their associates, interests in any company, such that, if they had those interests immediately after the purchase, any of the conditions in CTA 2010 ss.1037-1042 would not be satisfied, or if the vendor remains connected with the company *(CTA 2010 s.1042, ss.1062& 1063).*

A company wishing to redeem shares may apply to HM Revenue & Customs in writing for approval. The company must give full details and HMRC have 30 days in which to request further information. HM Revenue & Customs have 30 days from the receipt of the application, or the further information requested, to give a decision. If the company fails to give full information the approval may be void *(CTA 2010 ss.1045 & 1046)*.

Chapter 15. Incorporation, Disincorporation and Choice of Business Medium

15.1. Introduction

When a taxpayer starts a business, one of the most important decisions is the choice of business medium. He can operate either as a sole trader (or as a partnership, if the business is to be run by more than one person) or as a limited company. If they decide to operate the business initially as a sole trader they may later decide to incorporate the business. Conversely, if they decide to operate the business initially as a limited company, they may later wish to disincorporate the business. Note: In this chapter the term 'spouse' has been used in order to avoid confusion with a partner in a partnership. The comments apply equally to civil partners or unmarried couples.

15.2. Incorporation

15.2.1. Cessation

There will be a cessation of the unincorporated business and the closing year basis period rules *(ITTOIA 2005 s.202(1))* will apply (see section **5.2**). The date of cessation should be chosen carefully to avoid a large assessment in the tax year of cessation (see section **5.3**). It is also necessary to take the cashflow consequences of cessation into account. For example, if a sole trader has an accounting date of 30 June, there is a delay of 19 months between the end of the accounting period and the balancing payment of the related tax liability. If an unincorporated business were to incorporate on 1 April 2021, the basis period for 2020/21 would run from 1 July 2019 to 31 March 2021, i.e. 21 months. There will therefore be a large balancing payment on 31 January 2022 and, from 1 April 2021, the sole trader will not be generating any gross income out of which to fund the tax liability; their income will solely consist of remuneration and dividends received from the company.

15.2.2. Transfer of assets

A balancing charge or allowance may arise on the transfer of assets to the company. The disposal value to be brought into the final computation of the unincorporated business in respect of plant and machinery will be either the actual proceeds or the market value at the date of incorporation. The taxpayer may make an election under CAA 2001 s.266 to transfer assets at tax written down value (see section **3.10.2**). A similar election may be made on the transfer of an industrial building under CAA 2001 s.569.

15.2.3. Transfer of trading stock

Trading stock and professional work-in-progress are generally deemed to be transferred at market value *(ITTOIA 2005 s.177)*, but an election may be made to use the greater of the sale proceeds and book value *(ITTOIA 2005 s.178(1)-(4))*. Professional work-in-progress may be transferred on a similar basis, provided that the excess of market value or sale proceeds over cost is treated as a post-cessation receipt *(ITTOIA 2005 s.184(2))*. HM Revenue & Customs will normally accept the value attributed to work-in-progress, unless it is clearly 'illusory, colourable or fraudulent' *(ICAEW Guidance note Tax 7/95)*.

15.2.4. Losses

A loss arising in the last 12 months of the unincorporated business may be carried back under ITA 2007 s.89 (see section **6.4**).

Unrelieved trading losses at the date of cessation may be relieved against income received by the taxpayer from his company, i.e. remuneration and dividends (see section **6.3**).

15.2.5. Transfer of chargeable assets

Chargeable gains will arise on the transfer of chargeable assets to the company, but gift relief *(TCGA 1992 s.165)* or incorporation relief *(TCGA 1992 s.162)* may be claimed on the transfer (see sections **13.31** and **13.32**). The advantages of claiming relief under TCGA 1992 s.165 are that it is not necessary to transfer all non-cash assets into the company, and that the company issues shares in exchange for the assets. A company can therefore be set up with minimal share capital. The disadvantage of claiming gift relief is that the gains arising on the transfer of the assets are deducted from their base cost in the company, which will therefore be no higher than the original cost to the unincorporated business. Where relief is obtained under TCGA 1992 s.162 (which is automatic unless the taxpayer opts for this section not to apply under TCGA 1992 s.162A) the gains on the transfer of the assets are deducted from the base cost of the shares received by the sole trader or partners. Therefore, the base cost of the assets on a subsequent disposal by the company will be their market value at the date of incorporation. Conversely, where relief is claimed under TCGA 1992 s.165, the base cost of the shares will be the total original base costs of the assets which were transferred into the company, whereas, if relief is claimed under TCGA 1992 s.162 the base cost of the shares will be their nominal value.

If the sole trader owns the business premises from which the business operates, they will generally wish to retain personal ownership after incorporation. This will, therefore, mean that it is not possible to claim relief under TCGA 1992 s.162.

15.2.6. Transfer of goodwill

No stamp duty is payable on the transfer of goodwill and entrepreneurs' relief may be available to reduce any gain arising on disposal (see section **13.33**), which will reduce CGT to 10%. It may therefore be advisable to transfer goodwill to the company for its full market value.

HM Revenue & Customs take the view that there are three types of goodwill, although they are not separable. Personal goodwill, i.e. the reputation and skills of an individual, is not capable of sale and much of the goodwill of a sole trader looking to incorporate will be of this type. It can be exploited, but, if there is more than one shareholder, it may be advisable for the company to enter into a restrictive covenant with an individual with particular skills to prevent the exploitation of the personal goodwill elsewhere. Any payment made by the company in return for the restrictive covenant is taxable as employment income. Inherent goodwill attaches to the location of the business and can only be transferred with the property. Free goodwill is not fixed to any attribute of the business and may derive, for example, from a transferable customer list or brand names. Free goodwill may be transferred independently of the transfer of any other asset.

The goodwill acquired by the company will not qualify for relief because it has been acquired from a connected party *(CTA 2009 pt. 8)*.

15.2.7. Stamp Duty Land Tax

Stamp duty land tax is payable on the market value transfer of land (except in Scotland) and buildings, even if no consideration is given *(FA 2003 s.53)*, provided that the value exceeds the threshold of £150,000.

15.2.8. Inheritance tax

Business assets owned by a sole trader qualify for 100% business property relief. The availability of relief after incorporation should be considered. For example, if a business property is retained by the sole trader it will attract relief only if they control the company and relief will only be at a rate of 50%.

15.2.9. Value Added Tax

The transfer of assets to the company is treated as a supply immediately before the cessation of trade unless it is treated as the transfer of a business as a going concern *(VATA 1994 s.49)*. If the conditions are satisfied, the transfer is treated as being neither a supply of goods nor of services and it is generally possible for the company to take over the unincorporated business's VAT registration. The company will, therefore, take over the VAT liabilities and obligations of the unincorporated business, i.e. it must file any outstanding returns on behalf of the unincorporated business and is liable to any VAT penalties which the unincorporated business may have incurred.

15.2.10. Notification of incorporation

The issue of shares in the company upon incorporation does not need to be notified to HM Revenue & Customs. Further allotments of shares do not need to be reported if the following conditions are satisfied:

1. the additional shares are acquired by a person to whom some of the initial subscriber shares have been transferred or the person is a director or prospective director of the company; and
2. the shares are acquired at nominal value; and
3. the shares are not acquired by reason of or in connection with another employment (whether that is the only employment or one of a number of employments).

15.3. Disincorporation

15.3.1. Methods of disincorporation

If a taxpayer wishes to disincorporate and operate as a sole trader or partnership, this may be done either through a members' voluntary liquidation (MVL) or through dissolution. An MVL is only permitted if the company is solvent and the directors must make a statutory declaration of solvency, i.e. that the company will be able to pay its liabilities within 12 months of the commencement of winding-up. Whichever route is chosen, the first step must be to pass a resolution winding up the company. Under a MVL the liquidator will pay the liabilities and make a capital distribution of the surplus under TCGA 1992 s.122. Where a company is dissolved, the company's trade and assets are transferred to an unincorporated business. This transfer may be challenged by a shareholder who feels that this is prejudicial to their interests. Liabilities may be settled either by the company or, with the agreement of the relevant creditors, by a successor business. The company will then be dissolved under CA 1985 s.652. Where a company is dissolved, it is not possible to distribute its share capital or non-distributable reserves.

15.3.2. Chargeable accounting periods and payment of tax

Under CTA 2009 s.12(7) passing a winding-up resolution will bring a chargeable accounting period of the company to an end. A new chargeable accounting period will commence immediately after the resolution is passed and the company will remain liable to corporation tax until it has been wound up. Corporation tax on the profits arising up to the date the resolution is passed will therefore be payable nine months after that date.

15.3.3. Capital allowances

A balancing adjustment will arise on the transfer of plant and machinery to the shareholders, unless an election is made under CAA 2001 s.266 for the transfer to take place at tax written down value. Similarly, an election may be made to transfer industrial buildings at tax written down value under CAA 2001 s.569. In both cases, the election must be made within two years of the transfer of the trade. Whilst the value of any assets used in any transfer must reflect their market value, there is some scope for allocating values in a tax-efficient manner. If any of the assets qualify for allowances under CAA 2001 s.28 (thermal insulation of industrial buildings) it will be advantageous to allocate as much of any sale proceeds to these as possible, since the disposal value is always deemed to be nil. No balancing charge will therefore arise on the disposal of these assets.

15.3.4. Transfer of trading stock

Trading stock will normally be transferred at market value, but an election may be made to use the greater of the sale proceeds and book value *(CTA 2009 s.167)*. Professional work-in-progress may be transferred on a similar basis, provided that the excess of market value or sale proceeds over cost is treated as a post-cessation receipt *(ITTOIA 2005 pt 2 ch. 12)*. HMRC will normally accept the value attributed to work-in-progress, unless it is clearly 'illusory, colourable or fraudulent' *(ICAEW Guidance note Tax 7/95)* (see section **15.2.3**).

15.3.5. Losses

Trading losses of the company may not be carried forward to be offset against future profits of the unincorporated business. Trading losses may be offset against other income of the same chargeable accounting period or the total profits of the preceding chargeable accounting period *(CTA 2010 pt 4 ch. 2)*. A trading loss of the final 12 months of trading, which may include part of the penultimate chargeable accounting period, may be carried back and offset against the trading profits of the preceding 36 months. The loss is offset against the profits of the latest period first.

It is not possible to offset trading losses against chargeable gains arising after a company ceases trading, therefore it is advisable, if possible, to sell any assets on which a gain may arise to the shareholders before the cessation of trade.

15.3.6. Chargeable gains

Disposals of assets to shareholders will take place at market value, which may be the subject of protracted negotiations with HM Revenue & Customs. If any gain has been rolled over or held over the disposal will crystallise this gain and it may be advisable to dispose of assets before the cessation of trade. The date of transfer for the purpose of chargeable gains is the date of the contract. Therefore, payment may be deferred until the winding up. If any of the company's assets have a negligible value, it may be worth considering a negligible value claim under TCGA 1992 s.24 (see section **13.14**), since the date of the deemed disposal may be back-dated by up to two years. A capital loss may therefore arise in a chargeable accounting period in which it may be possible to obtain relief.

If disincorporation involves the liquidation of two or more group companies and if a capital loss arises in one company and a chargeable gain in another, an election may be made under TCGA 1992 s.171A for a deemed transfer of one of the assets to have been made immediately before sale. In this way the gain and the loss will arise in the same company. The election must be made within two years of the end of the chargeable accounting period in which the deemed transfer is to take place.

15.4. Disincorporation Relief

Disincorporation relief applies where a businesses transfers its business to some of all its shareholders. The following conditions must apply for the relief to apply:

i) the business must be transferred as a going concern;
ii) the business must be transferred to individuals. This includes an individual acting as a member of a partnership, but not as a member of a limited liability partnership;
iii) the individuals must have held shares in the company throughout a period of 12 months ending on the transfer date;
iv) all assets, except possibly cash, must be transferred;
v) the total market value of the assets transferred must not exceed £100,000.

(FA 2013 s.58)

A claim, which is irrevocable, for this relief to apply must be made jointly by the company and all of the shareholders to whom the business is transferred within two years of the date of the date of transfer *(FA 2013 s.59)*.

The effect of the relief is that the consideration for pre-FA 2002 goodwill and interests in land which are not held as trading stock is deemed to be the lower of allowable cost and market value at the date of the transfer *(TCGA 1992 s.162C)*. The consideration for post-FA 2002 goodwill is deemed to be the lower of its tax written down value and its market value at the date of the transfer *(CTA 2009 s.849A(2))*. Where the goodwill has not been written down in the balance sheet the deemed consideration will be the lower of cost and market value *(CTA 2009 s.849A(3))* and if the goodwill has not been shown in the balance sheet the consideration is deemed to be nil *(CTA 2009 s.849A(4))*.

15.4.1. Loans to participators

The company being wound up will almost invariably be a close company. If it has made a loan to a participator and the loan is written off when the company is wound up, the corporation tax charge under CTA 2010 s.455 (1) arising when the loan was made will not be recoverable. In addition, the grossed up value of the loan will be treated as a benefit in kind in the hands of the participator. It is advisable to ensure that such loans are repaid before winding up.

15.4.2. Value Added Tax

The transfer of assets by the company is treated as a supply immediately before the cessation of trade unless it is treated as the transfer of a business as a going concern *(VATA 1994 s.49)*. If the conditions are satisfied, the transfer is treated as being neither a supply of goods nor of services and it is generally possible for the unincorporated business to take over the company's VAT registration. The unincorporated business will therefore take over the VAT liabilities and obligations of the company, i.e. it must file any outstanding returns on behalf of the company and is liable to any VAT penalties which the company may have incurred.

15.4.3. Pre-sale dividends and capital distributions

A pre-sale dividend will reduce the value of the company on liquidation and will be treated as an income distribution. The consequences to the shareholders will be that there is no income tax liability to the extent that the dividends are taxable at the starting rate or basic rate, but dividends taxable at the higher rate are taxed at 32.5% of the net dividend declared and distributions taxable at the additional rate are taxed at 38.1%. Distributions made in the course of a liquidation are treated as capital and are subject to CGT. Under the entrepreneurs' relief regime, pre-sale distributions are therefore unattractive, since the shares will, in practice, invariably be business assets and, provided that they have been held for at least one year, any gain will be taxable at an effective rate not exceeding 10%. No SDLT will generally arise where land and buildings of the company are distributed to the shareholders on the winding up *(FA 2003 s.54)*.

15.5. Choice of Business Medium

15.5.1. Advantages of Company

- A company may enhance the image of a business and give an impression of greater substance, particularly if it registers voluntarily for VAT.
- The owner(s) acquire the protection of limited liability. The 'veil of incorporation' may only be lifted in certain circumstances involving fraudulent conduct, making the directors personally liable.
- It may be easier for a company to raise loan finance.
- It is easier to dispose of shares than individual assets if the taxpayer wishes to sell all, or part, of the business.

- Retained profits are only subject to corporation tax, unless the personal service company rules (IR 35 provisions) apply *(ITEPA 2003 ss.53-61)* (see section **8.8**). Profits will be taxed at a rate of no more than 19%.
- More generous pension provision can be made through a company than is possible by an unincorporated business.
- Benefits in kind can be structured in a tax-efficient manner. Certain benefits may be exempt, such as the provision of a computer or a mobile phone or the payment of a mileage allowance or training costs.

15.5.2. Disadvantages of company

- A company must make statutory returns to Companies House.
- There are greater disclosure requirements for a company than for an unincorporated business, although, provided that the profits do not exceed the threshold for a small company, these are not extensive.
- Trading losses may only be offset against the company's profits and not against the other income of the taxpayer.
- There are no provisions to carry back losses in the opening years of trading.
- It is not possible claim a deduction for remuneration paid to a spouse or civil partner in excess of a reasonable payment for the duties performed. Any excess will be disallowed in the company's tax computation, whilst the spouse or civil partner will be taxed under PAYE on the full salary received. This restriction also applies to sole traders, but this can be circumvented by forming a partnership (see **Chapter 17**). HM Revenue & Customs have also attacked the payment of dividends to a non-working spouse or civil partner in *Arctic Systems (Jones v Garnett) (2007) (UKHL35),* in which the payment of such dividends were held to fall within the anti-avoidance settlement provisions of ITTOIA 2005 ss.624-627. This was a highly contentious case, which was eventually decided in favour of the taxpayer in the House of Lords.
- The rates of NIC payable on salaries are higher than those payable on the profits of unincorporated businesses. Class 4 contributions are payable on business profits at a maximum of 9%, whereas primary class 1 contributions may be payable by the employee at 12% and secondary contributions by the company at 13.8%.
- A company must pay tax on profits sooner than the self-employed. A company must pay tax nine months after the end of the chargeable accounting period, whereas an unincorporated business can create a period of up to 22 months between the end of an accounting period and the payment of the related tax.
- There is a potential double tax charge on disposal of company assets; first a chargeable gain in the company's tax computation, and a subsequent tax

charge when the proceeds are extracted from the company through either remuneration or a dividend.

15.6. Comparison of Tax Treatment of Companies and Sole Traders

15.6.1. Overall tax burden

The calculation of the overall tax burden of trading as a sole trader as compared to trading as a company is complex and many variables must be taken into consideration. Nevertheless, the overall tax burden of a small business will generally be lower when trading through a limited company, although detailed projections should be drawn up in all cases based on the taxpayer's circumstances and estimated profits.

15.6.2. Remuneration

- An unincorporated business pays tax and national insurance on adjusted business profits, not just drawings.
- A taxpayer is an employee of a company and is paid a salary.
- Only salary paid to the taxpayer by the company is taxed as employment income, unless the personal service company rules apply (see section **8.8**). The salary paid is tax deductible in the company's tax computation.
- Retained profits are only liable to corporation tax, unless the personal service company rules apply.
- Remuneration may be by means of a dividend, although the dividend received will depend on the relative shareholdings rather than the extent of work performed. No NIC is payable on a dividend.
- HM Revenue & Customs may challenge a salary paid to a spouse or civil partner by a company on the grounds that it is excessive.
- If a spouse or civil partner is an active partner in a partnership, his or her partnership share will not be challenged by HMRC. The spouse or civil partner may therefore receive half the partnership profits whilst performing significantly less than half the work.
- A company may make more generous pension contributions on behalf of employee.
- A company must comply with minimum wage requirements, if there is a contract of employment.

15.6.3. Computation of profits

A sole trader is subject to the opening year basis period rules *(ITTOIA 2005 ss.199-201)*.

If it is envisaged trading as a partnership it may be worth operating as sole trader for the first couple of years with a spouse or civil partner as a salaried employee, making them a partner after that period. In this way it may be possible to minimise profits in the opening years of the business.

15.6.4. Private use of assets

Private use of assets by the proprietor(s) of an unincorporated business is disallowed in the tax computation.

Private use of assets by an employee gives rise to a benefit in kind, which may be either more or less beneficial, depending on the nature of benefit.

15.6.5. Loss relief

Loss relief is available under ITA 2007 s.72 to an unincorporated business in first four years, and ITA 2007 ss.64 & 72 allow trading losses of a sole trader to be offset against other income.

Trading losses of a company can only be offset against a company's other income.

15.6.6. Tax rates

A company's profits are taxed at 19%, whereas if the taxable profits and assessable gains of a sole trader, or partner, exceed £50,000, the excess is taxed at 40% and, if they exceed £150,000, the excess is taxed at 45%.

Sole traders and partners have an annual capital gains tax exemption on the sale of assets by an unincorporated business, but a company does not have an annual exemption.

There is a potential double charge on extracting profits from a company, with tax payable on the profits in the company and again on the distribution of the profits to the shareholders.

15.6.7. National insurance

Higher rates of NIC are payable on salary both by an employee and by the company, but an employee has better Social Security benefits and gains entitlement to the State Second Pension.

15.6.8. Payment of expenses

It is easier for the self-employed to deduct business expenses than an employee.

Payment of expenses by the company on behalf of an employee may give rise to a benefit in kind.

15.6.9. Cash flow

Sole traders and partners pay tax on a current year basis but use a preceding year basis to calculate payments on account.

A company pays tax nine months after the end of a chargeable accounting period.

Tax and NIC on salary is paid under PAYE.

15.6.10. Other points

Tax planning should envisage possible changes of circumstances.

Winding up a company and disincorporation is more complex than winding up an unincorporated business.

Example

Peter expects to make profits of £60,000 before tax and NIC.

Compare the consequences of:

- trading as a sole trader and
- trading as a company, paying a salary of £20,000 and the largest possible dividend not giving rise to a loss of capital.

Trading as sole trader

	£
Trading income	60,000
Personal Allowance	(12,570)
Taxable income	£47,430
£37,500 x 20%	7,500
£9,930 x 40%	3,972
	£11,472
Class 2 NIC 52 x £3.05	162
Class 4 NIC (£50,270 - £9,568) x 9% + (£60,000 - £50,270) x 2%	3,868
Total NIC	£4,030
Total tax and NIC (£11,500 + £4,007)	£15,502
Net income (£60,000 - £15,507)	£44,498

Trading as a limited company

Corporation tax

	£
Trading income	60,000
Salary	(20,000)
Employer's NIC (£20,000 - £8,840) x 13.8%	(1,540)
Chargeable profits	£38,460
Tax	
£38,460 x 19%	£7,307
Maximum dividend £38,460 - £7,307	£31,153

	Non-savings (£)	Dividends (£)	Total (£)
Employment income	20,000		20,000
Dividend		31,153	31,153
	20,000	31,153	51,153
Personal allowance	(12,570)		(12,570)
Taxable income	£7,430	£31,153	£38,583

Non-savings income	
£7,430 x 20%	1,486
Dividend	
£2,000 x 0%	0
£28,070 x 7.5%	2,105
£1,083 x 32.5%	352
	£3,943
Class 1 NIC	
(£20,000 - £9,568) x 12%	£1,252
Total tax and NIC (£3,943 + £1,252)	£5,195
Net income	
Salary	20,000
Dividend	31,153
	51,153
Less: Tax and NIC	(5,195)
	£45,958

Peter's net income is £1,460 higher if he trades through a limited company.

15.7. Salary vs Dividends

- Salary reduces a company's profits and potential gain on the disposal of shares.
- Salary qualifies as employee's relevant UK earnings and therefore gives entitlement to pay contributions into a registered pension scheme (see section **12.6**).
- NIC is payable by an employee and the company on salary.
- Dividends are paid out of taxed profits.
- No NIC is payable on dividends.
- Dividends in excess of the dividend allowance and any available personal allowance are taxed on the shareholder at 7.5% if they are in the basic rate band, 32.5% if they are in the higher rate, and at 38.1%, if they are in the additional rate band.
- The timing of the payment of a dividend should seek to ensure the maximum benefit for a shareholder.
- A dividend paid reflects the size of the shareholding, rather than the amount of work performed.

Example

A company makes profits (before remuneration) of £30,000 in the year ended 31 March 2022.

Compare the tax consequences of:

- paying the entire profits as salary; and
- paying a salary of £8,840 and the balance as a dividend.

Company

If the salary only route is taken, the salary paid will be the amount, which together with the employer's NIC, will total £30,000. The employer's NIC is given by (£30,000 - £8,840) x 13.8/113.8 = £2,566. The salary will be £27,434 (£30,000 - £2,566).

	Salary (£)	**Salary and Dividends (£)**
Profit	30,000	30,000
Salary	(27,434)	(8,840)
Employer's NIC	(2,566)	NIL
	£NIL	£21,160
Tax		
£21,160 x 19%		£4,020
Maximum distribution		£17,140
£21,160 - £4,020		

Director

Salary

	Non-savings (£)	**Dividends (£)**	**Total (£)**
Employment income	27,434		27,434
Personal Allowance	(12,570)		(12,570)
Taxable income	£14,864		£14,864
Salary and dividends			
Employment income	8,840		8,840
Dividend		17,140	17,140
	8,840	17,140	25,980
Personal allowance	(8,840)	(3,730)	(12,570)
	£NIL	£13,410	£13,410

	Salary	**Salary and dividend**
Non-savings income		
£14,864 x 20%	2,973	
Dividends		
£2,000 x 0%		0
£11,410 x 7.5%		856
	£2,973	£856
Class 1 NIC (£27,434 - £9,568) x 12%	£2,144	
Disposable income		
Salary	27,434	8,840
Dividend		17,140
	27,434	25,980
Tax	(2,973)	(856)
Employee's NIC	(2,144)	NIL
	£22,317	£25,124

The saving by paying a combination of salary and dividends is £2,807.

Chapter 16. Special Classes of Taxpayers

16.1. Construction Industry Scheme

16.1.1. Introduction

The construction industry scheme (CIS) provisions apply to any body or person carrying on a business which includes construction operations or any person whose average expenditure on construction operations in the previous three periods of account has exceeded £1,000,000 (or, if they were not carrying on the business at the start of the three-year period, their expenditure on construction operations since they started carrying on the business has exceeded £3,000,000) *(FA 2004 s.59(1))*. Where the person is a company the expenditure on construction must be aggregated with the expenditure of any other company in which they hold more than 50% of the shares (*Income Tax (Construction Industry Scheme) Regulations (SI2005/2045) para. 22)*.

The CIS applies to any payments made under a construction contract to the sub-contractor, any person nominated by either the contractor or sub-contractor or any person nominated by a sub-contractor under another contract relating to the construction operations *(FA 2004 s.60(1))* unless one of the following exceptions applies:

1. the payment is treated as earnings under ITEPA 2003 pt. 2 Chapter 7 *(FA 2004 s.60(3))*;
2. the person to whom the payment is made and the person for whose labour the payment is made are registered for gross payment *(FA 2004 s.60(4))*. If the payment is made to a nominee the person making the nomination must also be so registered. If the person to whom the payments are made is registered for gross payment as a partner in a firm, gross payments may only be made under contracts with the firm, or where the person has been nominated, contracts with the person making the nomination *(FA 2004 s.60(5))*. If the person to whom payments are made is registered for gross payment other than as a partner in a firm, payments made under contracts with the firm may not be made gross *(FA 2004 s.60(6))*;
3. the total payments under the contract (excluding the direct cost of materials) will not exceed, or are not likely to exceed £1,000 (*Income Tax (Construction Industry Scheme) Regulations (SI 2005/2045) para. 18)*;
4. the payment is made in relation to property owned by the body or person making the payment, or agricultural property of which that body or person is a tenant (*Income Tax (Construction Industry Scheme) Regulations (SI 2005/2045) para. 19)*;

5. the payment is a reverse premium as defined by FA 1999 Sch. 6 para. 5 *(Income Tax (Construction Industry Scheme) Regulations (SI 2005/2045) para. 20)*;
6. the payment is made by the governing body or head teacher of a maintained school as the agent of a local education authority under section 49(5)(b) of the School Standards and Framework Act 1998 *(Income Tax (Construction Industry Scheme) Regulations (SI 2005/2045) para. 21)*;
7. the payment is made under a private finance transaction, i.e. the resources are provided partly by one or more public bodies and partly by one or more private persons, the transaction is designed wholly or mainly for the purpose of assisting a public body to discharge a function or is ancillary to the function of a public body and the public body makes payments by instalments at annual or more frequent intervals *(Income Tax (Construction Industry Scheme) Regulations (SI 2005/2045) para. 23)*;
8. the payment is made by any body of persons or trust established for charitable purposes only *(Income Tax (Construction Industry Scheme) Regulations (SI 2005/2045) para. 24)*.

Where a sub-contractor or nominee is not registered for gross payment, the contractor must deduct 20% from so much of any payment which does not represent the direct cost to any other person of materials used or to be used in the construction operations *(FA 2004 s.61(1))*. If the person to whom the payment is made does not possess a registration card or certificate 30% must be deducted *(FA 2004 s.61(3)(a))*. The sum deducted from the payment must be paid to HM Revenue & Customs *(FA 2004 s.62(1)(a))*.

16.1.2. Registration for Gross Payment

An individual or firm may register for gross payment by making an application to HM Revenue & Customs. HMRC must register an individual or a firm for gross payment if the applicant has satisfied them that they meet the requirements under FA 2004 s.64 and Sch. 11 *(FA 2004 s.63)*. These requirements are:

1. the individual, firm or company must be carrying on a business in the UK consisting of, or including, the carrying out of construction operations or the provision of labour for such operations and this business is to a substantial extent carried out through a bank *(FA 2004 Sch. 11 paras. 2 & 6)*;
2. the individual, firm or company is likely to receive turnover from construction operations in excess of the prescribed threshold. For individuals that threshold is £30,000 *(FA 2004 Sch. 11 para. 3)*. For partnerships the threshold is the lower of £30,000 multiplied by the number of partners and £200,000 *(FA 2004 Sch. 11 para. 7)*. For companies the threshold is the lower of £30,000 multiplied by the number of relevant

persons and £200,000 *(FA 2004 Sch. 11 para. 11(1)&(2))*. A relevant person is a director of the company and the beneficial owner of shares in a close company *(FA 2004 Sch. 11 para. 11(3))*. Where the number of partners or relevant persons has fluctuated during the period, the threshold is multiplied by the maximum number of partners or relevant persons at any one time during the period *(Income Tax (Construction Industry Scheme) Regulations SI2005/2045 para. 30)*;

3. the individual, firm or company must have complied with its obligations under the taxes acts, and all requests for information by HMRC during the 12 months ending on the date of application *(FA 2004 Sch. 11 paras. 4(1), 8(1) & 12(1) & para. 14)* and there must be an expectation that they will continue to do so *(FA 2004 Sch. 11 paras. 4(7), 8(4) & 12(7))*. An application will not be accepted if the tax affairs have been put in order just before the application is made. Individuals and companies are also required to have paid any social security contribution due *(FA 2004 Sch. 11 paras. 4(6) & 12(4))*. An exception is made for non-compliance provided that there was a reasonable excuse and the individual, firm or company complied within a reasonable period after the excuse ceased *(FA 2004 Sch. 11 paras. 4(4), 8(3) & 12(3))* or if the non-compliance was of a minor nature *(FA 2004 Sch. 11 paras. 4(3), 8(2) & 12(3))*.

Where there is a change in control of a company registered for gross payment, HMRC may request information in connection with the change *(FA 2004 s.65)*.

HMRC may cancel registration if the individual, firm or company fails either the turnover or compliance tests, if they make an incorrect return or supply incorrect information, or if they fail to comply with any provision of the scheme *(FA 2004 s.66(3))*. If false returns or information have been supplied fraudulently or a person has knowingly failed to comply with provisions of the scheme, cancellation will take effect immediately *(FA 2004 s.69(4))*.

Otherwise cancellation will take effect 90 days from the date of the notice *(Income Tax (Construction Industry Scheme) Regulations SI 2005/2045 para. 26)*. A person may appeal to a tribunal against either a decision to refuse registration or the cancellation of their registration within 30 days of being notified of the decision. Contractors must confirm whether a sub-contractor who they are proposing to pay is registered for gross payment *(FA 2004 s.69)*.

16.2. Farmers and Market Gardeners

16.2.1. Introduction

Farming and market gardening, and the commercial occupation of land in the UK with a view to the realisation of profits, are treated as trades *(ITTOIA 2005 ss.9 & 10)*. The two trades of farming and market gardening are distinct, and therefore losses of one trade may not be offset against profits of the other, but a market gardening business which is incidental to a farming business is unlikely to be considered a separate trade. 'Farming' is defined as 'the occupation of land wholly or mainly for the purpose of husbandry, which includes arable and dairy farming and livestock breeding, but does not include market gardening'. The definition also includes the growing of hops and the breeding and rearing of horses *(ITA 2007 s.996(1),(2))*. An intensive enterprise, in which livestock or fish are kept and reared separate from the land and fed entirely on purchased feed, is not farming *(Jones v Nuttall (1926) (10 TC 346))*, although the averaging provisions (see **16.2.2**) have been extended to such activities by ITTOIA 2005 s.221.

'Farm land' is construed accordingly, but any dwellings or domestic offices are excluded. In certain contexts, such as the restriction of loss reliefs, farming may include activities outside the UK.

Where farm land is let for a period of 365 days or more, the tenant will be the occupier and the person farming the land for tax purposes. Land is often let for grazing for a period of less than 365 days, with no right of renewal and the owner generally remains in occupation of the land and is treated as farming for tax purposes.

'Market garden land' is defined as 'land in the UK occupied as a garden or nursery for the growing of produce for sale', and 'market gardening' is to be defined in accordance with this definition *(ITA 2007 s.996(5))*. Market garden land will only be considered as such if the operation is conducted predominantly on a commercial basis, but this will not be applied rigidly where a taxpayer sells fruit and vegetables as part of a wider business, e.g. a farm shop on the premises selling farm produce *(Lowe v JW Ashmore (1971) (46 TC 597))*.

The cultivation of 'short rotation coppice' (defined as 'a perennial crop of tree species planted at high density, the stems of which are harvested at ground level at intervals of less than ten years' *(ITA 2007 s.996 (6))* is treated as farming and not exploitation of commercial woodland *(ITA 2007 s.996(4))* and profits are therefore taxable as trading income. The consequences of this treatment are:

- the initial spraying, fencing, planting etc. of the land are treated as capital expenditure;
- the trees are treated as part of the land for CGT purposes and the initial cost expenditure may be treated as an allowable cost provided that it is reflected in the state of the land at the date of disposal. The cost may also be used to shelter other gains *(ESC D22)*;

- revenue costs, e.g. weeding and disease prevention must be matched against income from sale, and must therefore be carried forward in the valuation of the coppice or in some other way. Indirect costs should in general be treated similarly, although it is also acceptable to include them in the general farming account;
- set-aside payments are not regarded as income from the coppice.

Where more than one person, or body of persons, operates more than one farm the results must be aggregated *(ITTOIA 2005 s.9(2))*. Where a sole trader becomes a partnership or vice versa, or the composition of a partnership changes, the cessation and commencement rules will apply, subject to an election under ITTOIA 2005 s.860(1)&(2). Where a farmer ceases to operate one farm and commences at another farm, this will not normally be treated as a cessation and recommencement, but special rules may apply where there is a significant period between the cessation and recommencement.

16.2.2. Fluctuating profits

Where, in two consecutive years of assessment, the assessable profits of one year are less than 70% of the other, the profits of the two years may be averaged. The averaged profits are then compared with the following or the previous year of assessment, which may give rise to another averaging claim *(ITTOIA 2005 ss.221-224)*.

Example

The assessable profits of Giles have been:

2018/19	£25,000
2019/20	£30,000
2020/21	£10,000
2021/22	£12,000

No averaging claim may be made initially in respect of 2018/19 and 2019/20, although an averaging claim may be made in respect of 2019/20 and 2020/21, giving profits of £20,000 in each year. The assessment of £25,000 in 2018/19 is now compared with the revised assessment of £20,000 in 2019/20. The smaller figure is 80% of the larger, so no averaging claim is possible, but in 2020/21 and 2021/22, the £20,000 of the earlier year is compared with the £12,000 of the later year. A second averaging claim may therefore be made in respect of these years. The assessments, subject to any further averaging claims, are therefore:

2018/19		£25,000
2019/20	$\frac{£30,000 + £10,000}{2}$	£20,000
2020/21	$\frac{£20,000 + £12,000}{2}$	£16,000

2021/22	$\frac{£20,000 + £12,000}{2}$	£16,000

Where the profits of one year are greater than 70% of the other, but less than 75%, a form of marginal averaging may be used. The profits of both years are adjusted by an amount given by the following formula:
Profits of higher year: H – (3(H – L) – ¾H)
Profits of lower year: L + (3(H – L) – ¾H)

Where:
H = profits of higher year, and
L = profits of lower year.

Example

MacDonald's recent assessable profits have been as follows:

2020/21	£40,000
2021/22	£29,000

The adjusted profits after averaging are:

2020/21	£40,000 – (3 x (£40,000 – £29,000) – ¾ x £40,000)	£37,000
2021/22	£29,000 + (3 x (£40,000 – £29,000) – ¾ x £40,000)	£32,000

In the case of a farming partnership, an averaging claim is made by individual partners in respect of their profit shares.

An averaging claim is related to the later of the two years *(TMA 1970 Sch. 1B, para. 3)*, and the profits of the earlier year are adjusted by the difference between the profits previously returned, and the profits after the latest averaging claim *(TMA 1970 Sch. 1B, para. 3(3))*. Both amounts are calculated after taking into account all reliefs and allowances. Effect is given to the change in profits of the earlier year in the later year, either by increasing the tax liability of the later year or notionally increasing the payments on account made in the later year to leave a lower balancing payment *(TMA 1970 s.59B)*. Where more than one averaging claim is made in respect of the profits of a particular year, any increase or decrease in respect of an earlier claim is ignored in any subsequent claim *(TMA 1970 Sch. 1B, para. 3(6))*.

The averaging claim must be made by 31 January in the second tax year following the end of the tax year in which the profits of the later year are taxed *(ITTOIA 2005 s.225)*.

An averaging claim may not be made for either the first or final year of trading. Where the results of one year show a loss, this is treated as nil for the purposes of averaging. An averaging claim is also likely to change the national insurance liabilities for the years involved.

From 2017/18 it has been possible to make an averaging claim over a five year period where either:

1. the profits of the last of the five years is less than 75% of the average profits of the first four years, or vice versa; or
2. the profits of one or more, but not all, of the five years in £Nil.

(ITTOIA 2005 s.222A(1), (2))

An averaging claim under this section may still be made if an averaging claim has already been made in respect of one or more of the first four years *(ITTOIA 2005 s.222A(3))*, but not if an averaging claim has been made in respect of a tax year later than the last of the five years *(ITTOIA 2005 s.222A(4))*. A claim may not be made in respect of the year of commencement or cessation *(ITTOIA 2005 s.222A(5))*. A claim must be made by 31 January in the second tax year following the last of the five years *(ITTOIA 2005 s.222A(6))*.

Example

Richard has had the following profits since 2016/17.

2017/18	£20,000
2018/19	£25,000
2019/20	£30,000
2020/21	£15,000
2021/22	£15,000

Richard may made a claim to average the profits of 2019/20 and 2020/21 at £22,500, but regardless of whether he does so, he may make a five year averaging claim, since the average profit of the first four years is £22,500 and the 2021/22 profits are less than 75% of that figure. If he makes this claim the profits of each of the five years will be £21,000 ((£20,000 + £25,000 + £30,000 + £15,000 + £15,000)/5).

16.2.3. Grants, subsidies and compensation

Grants will generally reduce the expenditure which may be claimed as an expense or which is included in the capital allowances computation.

A subsidy is normally treated as a trading receipt.

The treatment of compensation will depend on the circumstances. Compensation for the 'loss of profits' is treated as a trading receipt. Where this relates to the compulsory slaughter of animals, e.g. foot and mouth disease, by concession the receipt is spread equally over the three years following the year of receipt *(ITTOIA 2005 ss.225ZA-225ZF)*. The profit on compensation should be calculated by deducting the value of slaughtered animals, calculated in the following manner:

1. animals born or bought before the start of the accounting period in which the compensation is received, the valuation of the animal at the start of the accounting period;
2. animals born in the same period, 75% of the compensation;
3. animals purchased in the same period, the purchase price.

Where a farmer has taken out private insurance, compensation in respect of the slaughtered animals is treated in the same manner as the statutory compensation and compensation for any consequential loss is treated as a trading receipt.

Compensation relating to the compulsory purchase of land or insurance money receivable in relation to the loss or destruction of an asset is chargeable to CGT *(TCGA 1992 s.21)*, but roll-over relief is available in both cases.

Payments under a statutory scheme of compensation for temporary losses are treated as income of the trade, particularly if:

- the payment is fixed by reference to the farmer's former income;
- there is no disposal of a capital asset by the farmer;
- there is no goodwill;
- an obligation is entered into to conduct the farming business in a certain manner for a specified number of years;
- the payment is in consideration of the farmer undertaking to carry out his business in a certain manner for a specified period *(White v G. & M. Davis (1979) (CMLR 620); IRC v Biggar (1982) ((53 TC 254))*.

Payments under the Arable Area scheme are treated as a trading receipt. The receipt should be apportioned between sales and trading stock, in proportion to the amount of the crop for the year which has been sold and the amount which remains as trading stock. Therefore, if at 31 December 2019 three-quarters of the crop for the year has been sold, £7,500 of a receipt of £10,000 will be added to sales and £2,500 will be added to closing trading stock.

HM Revenue & Customs have stated that they would accept a receipt in respect of the following being included in the accounts either at the date of receipt or at the end of the retention period, provided that the basis is applied consistently:

- Suckler Cow premium quotas;
- Beef Special Premium Scheme;
- Sheep Annual Premium Scheme;
- Hill Livestock Compensatory Allowances; and
- Extensification Payments.

Other bases may also be accepted, provided that they do not contravene tax statutes. A change may be made, if the need to change outweighs the requirement for accounts to be produced on a consistent basis.

16.2.4. Levies

A milk production superlevy is allowable, but the purchase of an additional milk quota to ensure that it is not subject to the levy is capital expenditure.

16.2.5. Cultivations, unexhausted manures and growing crops

Expenditure on the above items and the cost of seeds constitutes work-in-progress. HM Revenue & Customs accept that where the valuation from one year to another does not vary greatly, a detailed valuation is not required. If a detailed valuation is performed it is done on a 'waygoing' basis, i.e. the basis which would be used if the payment for relinquishing a tenancy were to be calculated.

16.2.6. Deadstock

Items such as corn, fertiliser etc. should be valued at the lower of cost and net realisable value. Deadstock may be valued at 85% of market value by concession.

16.2.7. Livestock

Livestock are treated in the same way as other stock and work-in-progress, unless an election for the herd basis is made *(ITTOIA 2005 s.30(1))*. For the purpose of grants and subsidies, livestock is valued on a percentage of deemed cost, where records do not allow the actual cost to be readily determined. If a grant or subsidy has been brought into account in full in a period there is no effect on the valuation, but if that is not the case but the grant or subsidy that has been applied for the application has had a material effect on the market value of the animal, the grant or subsidy should be added to the deemed cost of the animal. Where grants or subsidies have been accounted for, even though an application has not yet been made, the anticipated subsidy should be brought into account in calculating the market value of an animal.

16.2.8. Herd basis

Where a farmer keeps a 'production herd' (animals of the same species, irrespective of breed), wholly or mainly for the sake of selling the products which can be obtained from them when alive, they may make an election to use the herd basis *(ITTOIA 2005 s.112(1),(2), s.124(6))*. The product obtained from the animal must be offspring or products which can be obtained without slaughtering the animal, i.e. milk or eggs *(ITTOIA 2005 s.112(2)(b))*. An election covers all herds of the same species kept for the same purpose, i.e. all dairy cattle herds, even if they are of different breeds, even if the farmer only owns one animal of the species. However, separate elections must be made for dairy and beef herds *(ITTOIA 2005 s.113(2))*. A farmer may elect for the herd basis to apply to one species, and for a herd of another species to be treated as trading stock. An election covers all herds owned by the same farmer even if they are kept on different farms. An election does not usually include immature animals unless the land on which animals are kept is of such a nature that animals which die, or which cease to be a part of the herd, can only be replaced by animals bred and reared on that land, or where the relevant animals are bred in the herd and are necessarily maintained to replace animals which die or cease to be a part of the herd. Immature animals may only be included in an election to the extent that they are necessary to maintain the size of the herd *(ITTOIA 2005 s.112(3)-(6))*.

An election must be made by:

- 31 January in the second tax year following the tax year in which the accounting period in which a farmer first keeps a production herd of the class to which the election is to apply ends, i.e. if a farmer first keeps a production herd in the year ended 30 September 2021 the time limit is 31 January 2024 *(ITTOIA 2005 s.124(2)(a))*; or
- if the tax year in which a farmer first keeps a production herd of the class to which the election is to apply is the first tax year of assessment the time limit is 31 January in the third tax year following the tax year *(ITTOIA 2005 s.124(2)(b))*.

An election is irrevocable *(ITTOIA 2005 s.124(5))* so, even if a farmer ceases to keep a production herd, the election will apply to a subsequent herd. An election will lapse if a farmer ceases trading and there is an interval of at least five years before resumption. In this case, it is necessary to make a new election *(ITTOIA 2005 s.125(1),(2))*. Where a farm is sold the purchaser must make a new election if one is not already in force.

In the case of a farming partnership new partners must make an election in respect of their share of a herd.

Where an election is made the initial cost of the herd is treated as capital expenditure, and the value of the herd is ignored for the purpose of calculating profits and losses *(ITTOIA 2005 s.114)*. The cost of acquiring additional mature animals is also capital *(ITTOIA 2005 s.115(1),(2))*. Where immature animals are acquired to be reared and added to the herd once they are mature, or animals are reared from birth, the costs of acquisition and rearing are initially a trading expense, but once the animal is mature those costs must be transferred to the valuation of the herd from the profit and loss account *(ITTOIA 2005 s.115(3),(4))*. The cost of rearing an animal may be estimated either by taking an approximate monthly rearing cost or a percentage of the market value of the animal. Where there are no detailed records the deemed cost of a calf, lamb or foal born to one of the herd is deemed to be 60% of its market value.

The cost of the replacement of animals is generally treated as a trading expense *(ITTOIA 2005 s.116(1),(2),(4))* and proceeds from the sale of the animals being replaced are treated as a trading receipt, but there are exceptions where the replacement animal is of superior or inferior quality or the animal was compulsorily slaughtered. Where a replacement is of higher quality the trading expense is limited to the amount which would have been necessary to acquire an animal of comparable quality *(ITTOIA 2005 s.116(5))*. If the animal is of lower quality and the animal it replaces was slaughtered, the deduction is limited to the replacement cost *(ITTOIA 2005 s.117)*. An animal will be considered a replacement if there is a causal connection between the disposal of the previous animal and the acquisition of the new one, but it is not simply sufficient that the herd is being restored to its previous position. Replacement animals must generally be purchased within 12 months of the disposal, although a longer period may be allowed in certain cases. If animals are sold without being replaced, but they do not form a substantial part of the herd, the profit, i.e. the difference between the proceeds and the acquisition plus rearing costs, is treated as a trading receipt *(ITTOIA 2005 s.118)*. 'Substantial' is generally taken as 20% *(ITTOIA 2005 s.120(7))*, although a lesser percentage may be substantial, depending on the circumstances. If a whole herd is replaced and another herd of the same class is acquired the replacement rules apply to the number of animals in the smaller of the two herds *(ITTOIA 2005 s.120(1),(2),(6))*. Any additional animals purchased are treated as additions to the herd and are therefore capital, whereas if the replacement herd is smaller, the profit on animals not replaced is treated in the same way as animals sold without replacement.

Where a substantial part of a herd is sold without replacement, a profit or loss is disregarded *(ITTOIA 2005 s.119)*. HM Revenue & Customs will generally accept disposals of 20% of a herd or more to be substantial. The rules concerning replacement apply also to animals which are either slaughtered or die of natural causes, and the proceeds from the sale of carcasses are treated in the same way as the proceeds from the sale of live animals *(ITTOIA 2005 s.113(3),(4))*.

If a herd basis election has not been made and a herd is compulsorily slaughtered due to a disease and compensation is received, an election may be made on the basis that the period in which compensation is received is the first relevant period *(ITTOIA 2005 s.126)*, i.e. for a sole trader or a partnership, by 12 months after the fixed filing date for the first period of assessment for which the farming profits or losses are computed by reference to the period in which the compensation becomes due, and for a company, by two years from the end of the first accounting period for which the computation of farming profits or losses is, or would be, apart from the election, affected by the compensation receipt. In each case, the election takes effect from the period in which the compensation becomes due.

16.2.9. Grant of grazing rights etc.

A payment received in consideration for the grant of grazing rights is taxable as property income *(Bennion (HMIT) v Roper (1970) (46 TC 613))*. Where a farmer let grass parks for grazing, the profits were held to be his trading income since, despite the tenancy, he still occupied the land for the purpose of husbandry *(IRC v Forsyth Grant (1943) (25 TC 369))*.

16.2.10. Orchards.

The initial cost of planting and preparing the orchard is capital *(CIR v Pilcher (1949) (31 TC 314))*. However, all subsequent expenditure on cultivation and production is allowable as a revenue expense *(Vallambrosa Rubber Co Ltd v Farmer (1910) (5 TC 529))*.

16.2.11. Farmhouse rent and farm cottages.

The portion of any rent which relates to the farmhouse is disallowable. The exact proportion will depend on the facts of the case. Where a cottage is provided rent-free for a farm employee, related expenditure of a revenue nature is allowable.

16.2.12. Quotas.

A quota is normally a capital asset. Therefore, expenditure of the acquisition of a quota is disallowable and the sale of a quota may give rise to a capital gain. Roll-over relief is available on any gain arising. Compensation for the permanent loss of a quota is treated as a capital receipt. Quotas acquired by farming companies fall within the intangible fixed assets regime (see section **14.4**), which supersedes the above rules.

16.2.13. Stud farms.

The profits of a run on a commercial basis are treated as trading income, regardless of its commercial viability, but profits from the breeding of race horses for recreational purposes, e.g. prize money, is not taxable *(Wernher v IRC (1942) (1 KB 399))*. Except where the herd basis is used, mares and stallions should be treated as stock and valued individually at the beginning and end of each year. For stallions (but not mares) the cost may be written off in equal instalments until the animal reaches the age of 10, unless the value of the animal increases, or falls at a significantly slower rate, due to successful progeny, or the method gives an unreasonable result or a better method is available.

Stud or nomination fees paid by the owner of the mare should be treated either as:

1. a prepayment;
2. increasing the value of the mare by the amount of the fee, whilst she is carrying the foal; or

3. stock valuation of the embryo or foetus;

unless the mare has already given birth, or is known not to have conceived or to have aborted the foal. Once the foal is born, it should be included in the stock valuation at cost.

If the occupier of a stud farm races animals which they have bred themself, when animals are transferred to training, the stud farm accounts should be credited with the market value of the animal at that date *(Sharkey v Wernher (1955) (36 TC 275))*. When animals are returned to stud, the stud farm accounts should be debited with their market value at that date. If an animal, which has not been bred by the stud farm, is later brought into stud, the stud farm accounts should similarly be debited with their market value on that date.

16.2.14. Loss relief

In order to make a claim under *ITA 2007 s.64*, it must be shown that in the period in question, the business had been carried on on a commercial basis and with a view to, and reasonable expectation of, the realisation of profits *(ITA 2007 s.66)*. The onus is on the taxpayer to show that the business is not being carried on in an uncommercial manner. This does not just apply to 'hobby farming', but to all operations which are not conducted on a sufficiently commercial basis. Relief for a loss, including related capital allowances incurred in the trade of farming or market gardening may generally only be claimed under ITA 2007 s.64 if there has been a profit in at least one of the five preceding years *(ITA 2007 s.67(2))*. This applies even where the trade is carried on outside the UK. This does not apply if it is anticipated that profits will arise in a future period, if the activities are undertaken by a competent farmer or market gardener, and at the start of the five-year period the activities could not reasonably have been expected to have shown a profit by the end of the year in respect of which a claim is being made *(ITA 2007 s.77(3))*.

The rule also does not apply to farming and market gardening activities undertaken as part of a larger trade. Where one trade ceases and a new trade commences, the five-year period is calculated separately for each trade. If there is a change in the persons carrying on the trade, the restrictions apply to both persons carrying on the trade as if there were no change. A husband and wife are treated as a single person.

For stud farms, due to the nature of the business, the five-year period is extended to 11 years.

16.3. Authors, Artists and Composers

16.3.1. Relief for fluctuating profits

Self-employed writers, artists, sculptors etc. may make a claim to average the profits derived from the creation of literary, musical or artistic works *(ITTOIA*

2005 ss.221-225). The claim is made in the same manner as the similar claim made by farmers (see section **16.2.2**).

16.3.2. Awards and bursaries

A literary award, prize or bursary is taxable as a professional receipt if it is an incident in the exercise of an author's profession or vocation. It is not necessary for the author to have applied for the bursary or entered the competition personally or for the author to undertake to complete a particular piece of work during the currency of the award, or to refund the award in the event that they fail to do so, for the award to be taxable. An award which is unsolicited and which is awarded as a mark of honour, distinction or public esteem in a particular field is not taxable.

16.3.3. Royalties to person other than author

Copyright royalties received by a person other than the author etc. are treated as earned income, even if they do not form part of the receipts of a trade or represent post-cessation expenditure.

16.4. Actors, Musicians and Entertainers

16.4.1. Employed or self-employed

Actors, dancers, singers and other entertainers may be engaged under contracts for services or contracts of service and may therefore be either employed or self-employed. They will frequently be engaged under standard contracts which incorporate a number of terms which typically feature in contracts of employment, such as minimum rates of pay, overtime, agreed subsistence allowances, holiday pay and agreed disciplinary procedures. These terms may often be persuasive in determining that the entertainer is to be treated as an employee, as in the case of *Fall v Hitchen (1973) (49 TC 433)*. However, in 1993 two actors, Samuel West and Alec McCowen, successfully argued before the Special Commissioners that they were self-employed, even though they derived their income from standard Equity contracts. In the former case Mr Hitchen was engaged for a period of approximately six months 'to rehearse, understudy, play and dance as and where required by the Manager.' He could therefore have been asked to perform a number of roles during the six-month period. In contrast, Messrs West and McCowen were engaged to play a specific role for the run of the play, or a shorter fixed period and had other media commitments which ran consecutively or concurrently with the contracts in question. This type of contract is more frequently encountered nowadays, and entertainers will frequently have periods when they are not earning between such contracts.

The employment status of orchestral musicians will depend on the type of work which they undertake and the constitution of the orchestra. Musicians working for many orchestras, e.g. BBC Symphony Orchestra are employees, but the major London orchestras, e.g. the London Symphony Orchestra, are self-governing bodies. The players are shareholders and are treated as being self-employed. If a musician is paid separately for each performance, they are treated as self-employed. If musicians are engaged under a 'first call' or 'guarantee' contract, whereby the orchestra has a right to call on their services, but limits this demand, so that they may undertake other work, they will generally be treated as employed earners for the purpose of NIC.

Musicians engaged at musicals, pantomimes and other theatrical performances are covered by the same guidance as actors.

16.4.2. Expenses

Certain types of expenditure may be disallowable on the grounds that they have not been incurred 'wholly and exclusively' for business purposes. Common examples might be clothing and medical expenses.

16.4.3. Clothing

Expenditure on clothing will often be disallowable following the decision in *Mallalieu v Drummond (1983) (2 AC 386, BTC 380)*. However, expenditure on 'costume' used in a performance which is not 'part of an everyday wardrobe' is allowable. Actors' costumes will generally be supplied by the theatre company, and the types of clothing which HM Revenue & Customs envisage falling within this category are a lounge suit purchased by a self-employed television interviewer and an evening gown purchased by a film actress solely for the purpose of attending the première of her latest film. There is, however, considerable uncertainty in this area and the cost of a dinner jacket purchased by an orchestral musician has been disallowed.

16.4.4. Medical expenses

Health-related medical and surgical expenses will generally be disallowed, unless, in exceptional cases, it can be shown that they were incurred solely for business purposes and that there was no private benefit. An example given by HM Revenue & Customs is that of a radio performer who starts to do TV work and who is advised that his or her irregular teeth are holding him or her back. The costs of dental treatment may be allowable if it can be established that the individual had been content with his or her appearance and were incurred solely for the purpose of the TV work. Again, there is considerable uncertainty and the cost of dental treatment incurred by a professional bassoonist in order to enable him to continue playing his instrument has been disallowed.

16.5. Entertainers – other workers

Behind-camera workers, such as cameramen, producers, electricians are treated as self-employed for both tax and NIC purposes if their jobs (called 'grades' in the industry) are itemised on a 'grading list' published by HM Revenue & Customs. Engagements in a grade outside the list are generally treated as employment, although special arrangements may occasionally be made for certain engagements to be paid gross where these are either very short, or an individual can show that they are in business on their own account, e.g. *Hall v Lorimer (1994) (66 TC 349).*

16.6. Builders

16.6.1. Mortgage

Where a builder sells a property and takes a mortgage in respect of part, or the whole of, the purchase price, the trading receipt will be the money received plus the value of the mortgage. Normally the mortgage will be valued at face value, but if it is a second mortgage, or if it, exceptionally, fails to provide full security for the debt after taking account of the current and future vacant possession value of the property, the current and future creditworthiness of the mortgagor and any other factors which expose repayment of the debt to risk, its value may be less than its face value.

16.6.2. Retentions

Retentions will typically be treated in the accounts in one of two ways:

1. retentions are included in turnover and a provision is made of the cost of remedial work and any bad or doubtful debts; or
2. recognition of retentions is deferred until their receipt becomes virtually certain.

HM Revenue & Customs will accept either of these methods, unless an unreasonably conservative view has been taken.

16.6.3. Premiums

See section **7.4**.

16.6.4. Ground rents

Where a builder grants a lease, the reversionary interest should be brought into account as stock-in-trade at the lower of cost and net realisable value and any subsequent sale should be treated as giving rise to a trading receipt. The cost of the reversionary interest is calculated as **c/(b+c)** x **a** where:

a is total expenses, including cost of land and development and incidental expenditure;

b is the total consideration for the grant of the lease; and

c is the market value of the reversionary interest (including the right to receive ground rents) at the time of the grant.

In the case of improved ground rents, where the land covered by the lease is only part of the holding and the holding is not fully developed, the market value should assume that the holding is fully developed. In such cases the head lessor has a right to recover head ground rent out of any part of the building and the value of the reversionary interest is small, and less than the cost of creation, until the development reaches the stage where the improved ground rents receivable exceed the ground rent payable on the whole holding. Up to this point the amount brought into the computation will, therefore, normally be the actual market value, and not the cost.

The effect of taxation provisions should be ignored, e.g. that part of the consideration for the lease is not treated as a trading receipt *(ITTOIA 2005 s.158)*.

16.6.5. Rent

Rent received from a property held as trading stock should be treated as property income. If a builder or property dealer purchases a property, such as a block of flats, and buys out tenants over a period, with a view to selling the whole block, the expenses relating to let flats should be separated from the expenses relating to vacant flats. The latter have ceased to be part of the trade and may only be deducted from property income.

16.6.6. Property not acquired as trading stock

If property is not acquired for trading purposes, any profit on disposal will not be treated as a trading profit unless its development and preparation for sale indicate that the transactions are operations in the nature of a trade, or there are grounds for regarding the property as having been brought into a new or existing trade.

16.6.7. Compensation under town and country planning acts

Compensation under these acts for events such as compulsory purchase, the refusal or revocation of planning permission should be treated as a trading receipt on the date when the amount of the compensation payable is determined where the land in question is held as trading stock.

16.6.8. Private street works

Where a building is erected on land fronting onto a private street, the owner of the land must pay a sum to the local authority representing the estimated cost of the street works. If the amount paid exceeds the actual cost of the street works, the excess is repaid, together with interest at a rate fixed by the Treasury. Where the actual cost exceeds the amount paid, the interest is appropriated by the local authority and applied towards that cost.

The amount paid is treated as a trading expense if the land is held as stock-in-trade at the date the payment is made and should be taken into account in any subsequent valuation of the land. Where the estimated cost is merely secured to the local authority, no deduction is allowed until the payment is made. Any refund should be credited in the trader's accounts at the time of receipt and the value of stock should be adjusted. If a further amount needs to be paid, this amount is allowable as a trading expense at the date it is paid.

16.6.9. Own occupation

Where a house is built by a builder for his own occupation, it does not become stock-in-trade and the costs of construction should be disallowed, but the principle of *Sharkey v Wernher (1955) (36 TC 275)* (now enacted in ITTOIA 2005 s.172B) does not apply. If a house is built and offered for sale in the ordinary course of business, but is subsequently occupied by the builder, this principle does apply and the transfer should be treated as a sale at market value.

16.7. Care Providers

16.7.1. Childminders

HM Revenue & Customs reached an agreement with the Professional Association for Childcare and Early Years (PACEY) concerning the deduction of expenses, and childminders may calculate their profits in accordance with this agreement, regardless of whether they are members of PACEY. However, they may also calculate their profits on the statutory basis, if they wish. Reasonable expenses which are directly attributable to childminding are deductible and the cash book and attendance register produced by PACEY are acceptable means of recording revenue and expenditure. No receipts are required for items costing less than £10.

Childminders may deduct a proportion of their household expenses in accordance with the following table. The deductible percentage depends on the number of hours worked, not the number of children cared for.

Hours Worked	% of Heating and Lighting costs	% of Water Rates, Council Tax and Rent
10	8%	2%
15	12%	4%
20	17%	5%
25	21%	6%
30	25%	7%
35	29%	9%
40	33%	10%

Wear and Tear Allowance – Furniture

A wear and tear allowance of 10% of childminding income may be claimed. This will also cover household items not exclusively used for childminding. Where this allowance is claimed, no deduction is available when an item is replaced. Reasonable costs of cleaning household items may be deducted, where the need for cleaning is a result of childminding activities.

Food and Drink

Reasonable estimates of the costs of food and drink provided for the children are deductible.

Car Expenses

Childminders may claim using the authorised mileage rates for the Fixed Profit Car Scheme (45p per mile for the first 10,000 miles per year and 25p thereafter), where appropriate. The actual cost of motoring may be claimed instead.

Other Expenses

The following expenses are also allowable:

1. toys;
2. outings;
3. books;
4. safety equipment;
5. stationery;
6. travel costs;
7. PACEY subscription;
8. public liability insurance;
9. actual cost of telephone calls relating to childminding activities.

Grants

Grants received by childminders to help them start up their business or to meet capital or running costs are treated using normal principles. A grant received before commencement of the trade is not a trading receipt, but may reduce the amount of pre-trading expenditure which may be claimed.

16.7.2. Foster carers

Profits received by a foster carer are exempt if they do not exceed an exempt amount. If the profits exceed this amount, the assessable profit may be calculated in either of the following ways:

1. total receipts less actual expenses and capital allowances; or
2. the excess of the total receipts over the exempt amount, without any separate relief for expenses or capital allowances.

Foster carers do not have to use the same basis consistently; they can choose whichever basis is more beneficial each year. Where a carer changes from an actual basis to an exempt basis, for the purposes of capital allowances **only** there is a deemed cessation of trade.

The exempt amount comprises a fixed annual amount (£10,000 in 2021/22) plus a weekly amount for each child cared for (£200 p.w. for children under 11, £250 p.w. for children 11 or over). Part of a week counts as a week for this purpose. Where a child, who herself has a child, is cared for, an exempt amount may be claimed for both the parent and the child, even though only the parent has technically been placed in care. Where foster carers care for children with a disability or other special needs, relief may be claimed for expenditure which is clearly not of a type covered by normal maintenance. If the carer's expenses are exceptional by degree, rather than by type, there may be no practical way of calculating the additional expenditure. In such cases the actual expenditure should be recorded and regularly recurring expenses may be sampled.

Example

Sarah provides foster care in 2021/22 for a 7-year old throughout the year and a 13-year old for 20 weeks during the year. She received £30,000 during the year and incurred expenses of £22,000. Her assessable profits are the lower of:

1. £30,000 - £22,000 = £8,000
2.

	£	£
Receipts		30,000
Less: annual amount	10,000	
Child 1 (52 x £200)	10,400	
Child 2 (20 x £250)	5,000	
		(25,400)
		£4,600

The assessable profit will therefore be £4,600.

16.7.3. Adult carers and adult placement schemes

The normal rules apply to carers looking after one or more adult on a full-time basis. However, simplified rules apply to individuals, or couples, looking after a maximum of three adults in their own home to relieve them of the burden of keeping detailed records. In these cases the minimum weekly expenses which will be accepted are £400 p.w. for the first adult and £250 p.w. for the second and third adults HMRC have not updated this information since August 2008 and the limits have not increased since that time. Alternatively, a record of expenses may be kept for a period of time in order to agree an acceptable level of expenditure. This agreement will remain in force whilst the carer's circumstances remain broadly the same.

Since each adult will normally be provided with their own room, carers may also claim exemption under the rent-a-room scheme (see section **7.12**), but this will not normally be beneficial. Where care is provided for more than three adults, carers are required to keep records of receipts and expenditure.

16.7.4. Respite carers

Where a respite carer provides care for no more than a total of 182 days in the year (calculated by adding up the number of days care per adult per year), the profits are not taxable. Where respite care is provided for more than 182 days per year, the rules in the previous section relating to care for up to three adults apply.

16.7.5. Capital gains – principal private residence relief

Since carers are treated as carrying on a business, there will be some loss of relief when a house is sold. However, in most cases, letting relief will be available and there will be no capital gains tax consequences of providing care.

16.8. Barristers

A barrister cannot be treated as commencing business during the first six months of their pupillage. Thereafter, the date of commencement will be a matter of fact, but is likely to be the date on which they are in a position to accept, and instruct their clerk to obtain, briefs. Barristers may use the cash basis in the first seven years following holding themselves out for business *(BIM74020)*.

The costs of pin-striped suits and black dresses are not deductible *(Mallalieu v Drummond (1983) (2 AC 386, BTC 380))*, but the cost of replacing gowns, wigs and frock coats by Queen's Counsel are deductible.

16.9. Bookmakers

Contributions paid to the Horserace Betting Levy Board are deductible in computing taxable profits.

16.10. Breweries and Licensed Premises

16.10.1. Types of houses

The treatment of the following types of premises must be distinguished for tax purposes:

1. tied houses;
2. managed houses; and
3. unlicensed properties let to tenants and licensed properties without tie.

The results of managed houses should be included in the profits of the brewery.

16.10.2. Allowable expenditure

The costs of attempting to enhance the potential of retail outlets, e.g. securing a relaxation of the licensing laws, may exceptionally be deductible, if it is part of a continuing campaign to promote trade *(Cooper v Rhymney Breweries (1965) (42 TC 509))*.

16.10.3. Disallowable expenditure

The following expenditure is disallowable:

1. expenses of applications (whether successful or not) for the removal of existing licences, including payments for 'call of licence' or compensation payments to tenants of tied houses *(Southwell v Savill Bros Ltd (1901)(4 TC 430); (Mose v Stedeford (1934) (18 TC 457))*; and
2. payments to Guarantee Fund Trustees.

16.10.4. Tied houses – rent

Rents receivable from tied houses should be treated as trading income, not income from property. Rent paid is an allowable deduction. Although, strictly, rent receivable is taxable on an accruals basis and rent paid on a cash basis, this will not normally be considered to be material, provided that the treatment is consistent. A deduction for rent waived may not be claimed if it does not arise wholly and exclusively from the normal trading relationship between the brewery and the tied tenant.

16.10.5. Tied houses – allowable deductions

Expenditure of a revenue nature incurred by a brewery directly in connection with tied houses will be deductible. This may include:

1. repairs and maintenance;
2. fire and licence insurance premiums;
3. expenses of defending licences;
4. rates and taxes;
5. licence duties;
6. Compensation Fund Charge;
7. losses on loans to tied tenants (see section **2.22**)
8. premiums to provide 'death in service' benefits for tied tenants under the Licensed House Tenants' Pension Fund Scheme.

16.10.6. Tied houses – disallowable deductions

The following expenditure is disallowable:

1. compensation to outgoing tenants for not requiring any payment for 'goodwill' from their successors;
2. payments to existing tenants for accepting new agreements prohibiting them from requiring any payments for 'goodwill' from their successors;
3. compensation paid to tied tenants for surrender of their tenancies when tied houses are taken into the management of the brewery group *(Watneys London Ltd (and another) v Pike (1982) (57 TC 372))*.

16.10.7. Licensed premises – legal expenses

The legal expenses relating to an application for the grant of a new licence are not deductible, but the expenses relating to the renewal of an existing licence are deductible. If a licence is transferred from one trader to another, the expenses are not deductible. Legal expenses relating to the removal of a licence are not deductible.

16.10.8. Licensed premises – rent payable

The portion of rent payable which relates to domestic accommodation must be disallowed. There is a widespread belief that an agreement exists between HMRC and breweries that 10% represents a reasonable disallowance, but this is untrue, and each case must be determined on its own facts.

16.10.9. Public house tenants – compensation received

Most licensed premises are held on annual, renewable tenancies. These are treated as a single tenancy for the purpose of capital gains tax. Provided that the contractual period of notice is given, tenants have no security of tenure and no right to compensation for loss of the tenancy, but most brewers will pay compensation in accordance with a code of practice drawn up in the industry. The compensation may consist of a 'basic' element and an 'additional' element, payable where the tenant surrenders the tenancy before the end of the expiry period. The additional element is within the scope of capital gains tax, but the basic element is not.

16.11. Doctors and Dentists

16.11.1. Fees received by hospital staff

Fees received by hospital medical and dental staff for professional services outside their normal contract of employment are assessable as trading income.

16.11.2. Allowances received

Allowances paid in addition to capitation payments (payments made on the basis of the number of patients registered with the practice), such as supervision fees for the training of an assistant or an inducement payment to work in an unattractive area, are assessable as trading income.

16.11.3. Reimbursement of rent

Medical practitioners receive reimbursement of rent and general rates on practice accommodation and sums reimbursed are treated as practice income. Where the doctor owns the premises, the reimbursement is based on a notional commercial rent. If the premises are used partly for professional and partly for private purposes the reimbursement is based on the District Valuer's apportionment of the gross rateable value between the professional and private parts of the premises. Doctors contracted to the NHS may sell their premises to the General Practitioners' Finance Corporation and lease them back at a rent based on the cost of the premises. If the rent exceeds a commercial rent, the allowable deduction could, in theory, be restricted under CTA 2010 pt. 19 ch. 1. However, since the rent is substantially reimbursed, no restriction is made.

16.11.4. Cremation fees donated to charity

Where a doctor arranges for a cremation fee to be paid directly to a medical charity, the tax treatment depends on whether the fee would be treated as trading income. If it would be so treated, the full cremation fee is assessable. Where the fee is not treated as trading income, by concession, it may be ignored, provided that it is assigned in advance and is paid directly to the charity.

16.11.5. Remuneration withheld for breach of terms

Remuneration withheld from a doctor or dentist under regulations under the National Health Service Acts for breach of terms of service is an allowable deduction.

16.11.6. Part-time hospital doctors

Receipts from an office which a doctor or dentist may hold in addition to practising his profession, e.g. where a General Practitioner holds a part-time appointment in the NHS, are strictly taxable as employment income, although they are in practice often taxed as trading income. There are no guidelines as to when receipts will be taxed as trading income, but it is understood that they will be taxed in this manner where they only form an insubstantial part of their total receipts from the profession. Termination payments are, however, not taxed as trading income.

16.11.7. Expenses

Where hospital medical- and dental-staff use their own equipment in connection with professional services outside the scope of their contract capital allowances may be claimed and the full cost of maintenance is deductible, provided that the use of such equipment for their employment is insubstantial.

A hospital doctor in the NHS is reimbursed on a mileage basis for the use of a car on official journeys, and in the case of a part-time hospital doctor, the allowance includes travelling up to a distance of 10 miles each way between the consulting room or residence and the hospital. These payments are to be treated as employment income.

The costs incurred by self-employed doctors in achieving revalidation under the General Medical Council are deductible.

16.11.8. Dentists – successions

Where a principal dentist leaves a practice in one location and moves to a practice in another location, this is treated as a cessation of business in the old location and a recommencement in the new location. Where associate dentists move location, there will generally be no cessation and recommencement because they usually have no equipment, premises or patients of their own. Occasionally, associate dentists may work on terms which are similar to those of a principal dentist and the correct treatment should be determined on the facts of the individual case.

16.12. Motor Dealers – Valuation of Used Vehicle Stocks

Motor dealers will generally only pay trade value for used cars, except where they acquire them in part exchange for a new car, in which case they may pay more than the trade value as an inducement for the customer to purchase the new car. The used car should be valued at trade value in the dealer's accounts, with the excess being treated as a discount on the price of the new car.

16.13. Fishermen

16.13.1. Grants

Four types of grant are payable under the Fishing Vessels (Financial Assistance) Scheme 1983.

Decommissioning grant

A decommissioning grant is payable where a vessel is scrapped, permanently transferred to a country outside the EU or transferred to a use other than fishing. Since the vessel permanently ceases to be used in the trade, the grant is treated as disposal proceeds in the capital allowances computation. If the grant exceeds the original cost of the vessel a capital gain may arise.

Laying-up grant

A laying-up grant represents compensation for loss of profits for temporarily laying up a vessel and is taxable as a trading receipt.

Exploratory voyage grant

A grant to assist with the costs of an exploratory voyage where the receipts from the catch are less than the costs of the voyage is normally treated as a trading receipt.

Joint venture grant

The treatment of a joint venture grant which involves the temporary or permanent transfer of a vessel to a third country depends on the particular circumstances of the joint venture.

16.14. Franchising

16.14.1. Franchiser

The initial lump sum receipt will normally be treated as a trading receipt. When the franchiser is a company this receipt will fall within the intangible fixed assets regime (see section **14.4**), but this will not affect the treatment of the receipt.

16.14.2. Franchisee

The initial payment will be treated as capital, even if it is paid by instalments over a number of years, but the annual fees are a deductible expense. If the franchisee is a company the payments will fall within the intangible fixed assets regime and these provisions override the above treatment (see section **14.4**).

16.15. Solicitors

16.15.1. Part-time offices

Receipts from an office which a solicitor may hold in addition to practising his profession, e.g. a company registrar, are strictly taxable as employment income, although they are in practice often taxed as trading income. There are no guidelines as to when receipts will be taxed as trading income, but it is understood that they will be taxed in this manner where they only form an insubstantial part of their total receipts from the profession. Termination payments are, however, not taxed as trading income.

16.15.2. Interest

Solicitors may receive interest from clients' money placed on deposit. The money may be placed either in a designated clients' deposit account or in an undesignated deposit account. In the former case the client is entitled to the money and the solicitor will simply pass on the interest, which will be paid net or gross, depending on the status of the client. The interest is therefore not taxable. In the latter case the interest, which is paid gross, arises to the solicitor. The solicitor owes his clients an amount corresponding to the amount deposited and must account for the interest arising thereon. Interest paid by the solicitor to clients is assessable on the clients and the solicitor must deduct tax if the interest is both yearly and paid to a client whose usual place of abode is overseas. The solicitor is taxed on the net interest retained in the year. If the interest in the year exceeds the interest received, the excess will be a deduction from trading profits.

No liability arises where a solicitor receives mortgage interest etc. on behalf of a client resident in the UK.

16.15.3. Temporary loans and guarantees

A solicitor may make a temporary loan to facilitate legal transactions, e.g. a bridging loan for a house purchase. In such cases they may themself borrow temporarily to do so. Provided that the loan is made to remove an obstacle to the progress of professional legal work, any interest received or paid is treated as a professional receipt or expense. A loss on a temporary guarantee given for a similar purpose is allowable *(Jennings v Barfield (1962) (40 TC 365))*.

Interest received on loans made for other purposes should be treated as investment income, e.g. a loan to a speculative builder, even if the loan may help to generate future business. Any interest payable on borrowings to facilitate such a loan, or any losses in relation to it, is disallowable.

16.16. Sub-postmasters

The remuneration of a sub-postmaster is strictly employment income. However, when a retail trade is carried on from the same premises, the remuneration is in practice treated as part of the trading profits, unless the trade is negligible or the sub-postmaster requests the statutory basis of assessment. If the trade is carried on by a company, the salary is the income of the sub-postmaster, but it may be treated as the income of the company, provided that they are required to, and does, hand over his salary to the company. This practice only applies for tax purposes and class 1 national insurance contributions are payable on the salary.

Introductory payments made by a sub-postmaster to the Post Office are capital and not wholly and exclusively for the purpose of the retail trade carried on from the same premises *(Dhendra v Richardson (1997) (SpC 134))*.

16.17. Clubs, Societies and other Mutual Organisations

16.17.1. Profits from mutual trading

The profits of a club, society or other similar organisation where ownership rests with the general membership arising from mutual transactions, i.e. transactions between members, are not liable to tax. Similarly, losses arising from mutual trading are not allowable. This is because the surplus does not arise from carrying on a trade, since the activities lack the necessary element of commerciality and also because the surplus belongs to the same members whose income has generated it, the surplus being returned to the members in the event of the club etc. being wound up. In order to be exempt there must be:

1. complete identity, as a class, between the contributors to the surplus and the participators therein; and
2. arrangements to ensure that the surplus ultimately is returned to the contributors and no arrangements whereby it may go to anyone else; and

3. a reasonable relationship between the amount a person contributes to the surplus and amount distributed to them on winding up; and
4. arrangements which entitle the contributors to the common fund to control it, e.g. an elected committee for which all members are entitled to stand.

Where ownership of the club rests other than with the general membership, the surplus is not exempt from tax under the mutual trading rule and the question of whether it is carrying on a trade must be determined using normal principles. In order to be non-taxable all members must be eligible to participate in any surplus; the rules must not permit any profits to be paid to non-members (*English and Scottish Joint CWS Ltd v Assam Agricultural Income Tax Commr (1948) (2 All ER 395))* and the fund must be controlled by the members. If the organisation is an unincorporated association, the right of all members to participate in a surplus is protected by general law, but this is not the case if an organisation is constituted as a company, and the rules must explicitly allow all members to participate.

16.17.2. Profits from dealing with non-members

A surplus generated from dealing with non-members will be taxable and, where clubs organise events which are open both to members and non-members, e.g. an open golf tournament, the income and expenditure from such events must be apportioned between services provided to members and services provided to non-members. The method of apportionment will depend on the type of income. For example, where programme production or catering has been the responsibility of the club, income should be apportioned between sales to members and sales to non-members. If these activities have been contracted out, any franchise fee receivable is treated as trading income.

Where the same prices are charged to both members and non-members, expenses may be apportioned by reference to income from the two sources, where that is known or can be measured with reasonable accuracy. If different prices are charged to members and non-members, the apportionment must be weighted according to the specific circumstances. For example, in a members' golf club the weighting may be based on the total number of rounds played and the proportion of those rounds which generate taxable income. Where an expense can be attributed solely to a specific category of income it should be matched with that income. Where a facility such as a bar is used by both members and non-members, HM Revenue & Customs do not expect detailed records to be kept to determine the split between usage by members and non-members and a split determined over a representative period will suffice.

Visitors' fees paid by members on behalf of non-members will be treated as part of the members' surplus. However, in contrast, it was held in *Carlisle and Silloth Golf Club v Smith (1913) (6 TC 198*) that visitors' fees charged to non-members were taxable. If visitors are designated as 'temporary members' the fees will still be taxable unless their rights (including voting rights) are similar to those of full members. In this respect the rights enjoyed by 'junior members' or 'associate members' must be carefully considered. In *Westbourne Supporters of Glentoran Football Club v Brennan (HMIT) (1995) (SpC 22),* a supporters' club was held to be a mutual organisation notwithstanding the fact that 'associate members' did not have voting rights, because there was no real difference in the relationship between the club and the two classes of members.

Income from fund-raising activities must be carefully examined in order to make any necessary apportionment. Examples include:

- sale of merchandise. Most over-the-counter trade is likely to be with members, but a significant proportion of mail order sales may be to non-members;
- profits from lotteries and raffles etc. The treatment will depend on whether tickets are sold solely to members or not;
- sponsorship income will be taxable unless it has been provided personally by a member (i.e. not through the member's company or partnership);
- receipts from the sale of hospitality boxes to non-members are taxable;
- receipts from advertising are taxable;
- receipts from gaming machines are not taxable if they are only accessible by members, otherwise an apportionment must be made on the basis of usage;
- car-parking receipts will not be taxable if the facilities are only available to members, otherwise an apportionment must be made on the basis of usage;
- television income is taxable;
- grant income (see section **2.11.8**);
- donations are not taxable, provided that it is a genuine donation.

16.17.3. Clubs incorporated as limited company or industrial or provident society

Where a club is incorporated as a limited company, it is not liable to corporation tax, provided that the company is simply a means of enabling members to conduct a social club. A company will be treated as satisfying this where all the following conditions are met:

1. no dividends are paid, or, if the other conditions are satisfied, this condition will also be satisfied unless there is a marked inequality of shareholdings and the dividends are substantial;

2. the share capital is all of one class and every member, other than a member with restricted rights, is a shareholder;
3. the intention is that the members and shareholders should be an identical body; and
4. there is, in practice, substantial identity between members and shareholders.

If a club is registered under the *Industrial and Provident Societies Act 1965* (or the equivalent act in Northern Ireland) the members of the club are required to be the club's shareholders and no member is allowed to hold a large amount of share capital.

16.17.4. Interest paid or received

Interest received by a club is taxable. Where a club pays interest, e.g. on a loan from a brewery, it may have to account for tax under ITA 2007 pt. 15, ch. 15.

16.17.5. Commission income

Commission received from proprietors of gaming machines etc. is not taxable.

16.17.6. Distributions

Distributions by mutual concerns to their members are taxable in a member's hands where:

1. a deduction has been allowed in calculating the profits of the member's trade for a payment to the mutual concern for the purpose of its mutual business;
2. the mutual concern has been, or is being, wound up or dissolved;
3. a person who is carrying on the trade, or was doing so at the time of the payment, receives money, or money's worth, representing the concern's assets; and
4. the assets represent profits of the mutual business conducted by the concern *(ITTOIA 2005 s.104(1))*.

If the recipient is carrying on a trade at the date of receipt, the dividend will be treated as a profit of the trade *(ITTOIA 2005 s.104(2))*, otherwise it is treated as a post-cessation receipt *(ITTOIA 2005 s.104(3))*.

Distributions made by companies which are unincorporated associations fall within CTA 2010 s.1000, notwithstanding that the amount is derived from a mutual surplus and is distributed to a participator therein *(CTA 2010 s.1070)*. Where such a company, substantially the whole of whose activities have been of a social or recreational nature, is dissolved, it may elect that the distribution of its assets to its members be treated as capital receipts in the hands of the members *(ESC C15)*.

16.17.7. Payments by companies to community amateur sports clubs (CASCs)

From 1 April 2014 CASCs are included within the definition of charities, therefore companies may obtain tax relief for donations to them (see section **14.9**) *(CTA 2010 s.202(aa))*.

16.18. Charities

16.18.1. Trading income

Trading income of a charity is not taxable where either:

1. it is carried out in furtherance of one of the primary purposes of the charity, e.g. a conference organised by an educational charity; or
2. the work in connection with the trade is carried mainly by beneficiaries of the charity.

(ITA 2007 s.525(1))

Where a trade is carried out partly in furtherance of a charity's primary purposes and partly otherwise, or where a trade is carried out partly by its beneficiaries and partly otherwise, the two parts of the trade must be treated as a separate trades *(ITA 2007 s.525(2),(3))*. Trading income which would otherwise be chargeable will also be exempt if it is applied for charitable purposes and

1. does not exceed £5,000; or
2. where the income exceeds £5,000, but does not exceed £50,000, it forms 25% or less of the charity's total income for the tax year.

(ITA 2007 s.523(4),(5) & s.528)

16.18.2. Gifts

Gifts from individuals or companies are not taxable, insofar as they are applied for charitable purposes. If the gifts have been made under the Gift Aid scheme, the gifts are treated as having been made net of basic rate tax of 20% and this tax can be reclaimed by the charity *(ITA 2007 ss.521 & 522)*.

16.18.3. Investment income

Property and savings investment income received by charities are not taxable *(ITA 2007 ss.531 & 532)*.

16.18.4. Payments from other charities

Receipts from other charities within the UK are not taxable, insofar as they are applied for charitable purposes, provided:

1. they are not made for full consideration in money or money's worth; and
2. they are not charged to income tax except under this section; and
3. they are not exempt under any of the provision of ITA 2007 pt. 10.

If the payments have been made net of basic rate tax of 20%, this tax can be reclaimed by the charity.
(ITA 2007 s.523)

16.18.5. Fund-raising events and lotteries

The profits of fund-raising events are not taxable provided that they arise from a VAT-exempt event and are applied for the purposes of the charity *(ITA 2007 s.529)*. The profits of lotteries are not taxable, provided that they are promoted and conducted in accordance with the *Lotteries and Amusements Act (1976) s.3 or s.5* (or the equivalent act in Northern Ireland) and the profits are applied for the purposes of the charity *(ITA 2007 s.530)*.

16.18.6. Exemption for transactions in deposits

Profits or gains from the disposal of exempt deposit rights, i.e. transactions in certificates of deposit and deposit rights where there is no certificate, but the person entitled to the rights can call for the issue of a certificate, are not taxable provided that the gains are applied for the purposes of the charity *(ITA 2007 s.534)*.

16.18.7. Restriction on exemptions

Where a charity incurs non-charitable expenditure, part of its income will be taxable. The taxable amount is the lower of:

1. the non-charitable expenditure for the year; and
2. the total of the charity's income and gains which would otherwise be exempt under ITA 2007 pt. 10 or TCGA 1992 s.261.

(ITA 2007 s.540)

Where part of a charity's income is taxable, the trustees may specify the part which is to be taxable and, where HM Revenue & Customs so requires, a specification must be made within 30 days of the requirement being made. If the trustees fail to do so, HMRC may determine the part of the income which is to be taxable *(ITA 2007 s.542)*.

16.18.8. Profit-shedding through Gift Aid

Where a charity carries on a trade through a subsidiary company, the profits of the company will not be exempt under ITA 2007 pt. 10. In order to avoid paying tax on the profits the company may pass the profit for the year to the charitable trust by making a donation under the Gift Aid scheme *(CTA 2010 s.189)*. The condition that a payment must not be subject to a condition of repayment does not apply if the amount of the initial payment is the estimated profits of the company which would otherwise be taxable and there is a subsequent adjustment to this amount. The repayment must be made no later than 12 months after the end of the accounting period to which it relates *(CTA 2010 s.192)*. From 1 April 2014 Community Amateur Sports Clubs (CASCs) have been included within the definition of a charity (see section **16.17.7**). Therefore, where a CASC owns a company, the company may shed its profits to the CASC.

A gift aid payment from a subsidiary is, in law, a distribution and a company must therefore have sufficient distributable reserves to cover the payment. If the taxable profit is greater than the accounting profit and there are no distributable reserves brought forward it will not be possible to pay all the taxable profits to the charity and a tax liability on the the excess will therefore arise.

16.19. Credit Unions

Credit unions are incorporated as industrial and provident societies and are therefore liable to corporation tax. The following specific provisions should, however, be noted:

1. The activities of making loans to members or placing on deposit or otherwise investing surplus funds are not regarded as the carrying on of a trade *(CTA 2009 s.40(1))*.
2. Interest received on loans made to its members are not chargeable to tax *(CTA 2009 s.397(1))*.
3. Dividends and other forms of share interest are not treated as a distribution and no deduction may be made either as a trading expense or as a non-trading loan relationship debit for any dividend, share or loan interest, annuity or other annual payment *(CTA 2009 s.133 & s.397(3))*.
4. A credit union is not treated as an investment company under CTA 2009 s.1218(2) in respect of the deduction of management expenses or for the purpose of plant and machinery allowances.

16.20. Housing Associations

The following reliefs are available to approved co-operative housing associations:

1. Rents receivable from members are not taxable.
2. Yearly interest paid in respect of let property is disregarded for tax purposes. However, a deduction is available for interest paid in respect of unlet property. The total interest paid by the association must therefore be apportioned between interest attributable to let properties and interest attributable to unlet properties and the apportionment may be made using any reasonable method, e.g. by reference to the approximate capital expenditure on the respective properties or to the actual rent receivable in respect of let properties and notional rent receivable on unlet properties.
3. Chargeable gains arising on the disposal of any property which is, or has been, occupied by a tenant of the association are exempt.

(CTA 2010 ss.642 & 643)

Investment income is chargeable to corporation tax and any interest is subject to the loan relationship rules.

An association may be disqualified from relief if there is letting by the association, or its members, to non-members *(CTA 2010 s.647(2),(3))*. If the requirements of this section have been substantially complied with the association will not lose its exemption entirely, but the rent receivable from non-members will be taxable and any interest in respect of the property let to non-members is deductible under the loan relationship regime. Where a member of the housing association dies, his rights under the lease pass to his personal representative. For a period of six months after his death, occupation by non-members under the terms of his will or the intestacy rules will be treated as occupation by a member *(CTA 2010 s.647(4))*.

16.21. Self-build Societies

A self-build society is exempt from corporation tax on rents received from and on gains on disposals to its members, provided that the society exists for the purpose of building or improving dwellings, mainly by use of its members' own labours, for eventual sale to its members for their occupation *(CTA 2010 ss.651 & 652)*. The society must be registered under the Housing Associations Act 1985 (or the equivalent in Northern Ireland).

Chapter 17. Partnerships

17.1. Definitions

A partnership is defined as 'the relationship which subsists between persons carrying on business in common with a view to profit' *(Partnership Act 1890 s.1)*. The term "business" includes all trades, professions and vocations. In England and Wales a partnership, in contrast to a company, is not a distinct legal person. Therefore, there is no distinction in law between a partnership and its member partners. In Scotland, however, a partnership is a distinct legal person. Even if a partnership has no separate legal existence, a partner is bound by the partnership agreement and all partners are jointly and severally liable for any acts or omissions of any partner. Partners also have unlimited liability for partnership debts, although they may sue other non-paying partners for their share.

In order for a partnership to exist there must be an agreement between the partners, although this may be oral or implied through their conduct, and does not necessarily have to be in writing. The most important factor is the behaviour of the partners towards each other. The existence of an agreement is persuasive, but not conclusive, evidence of the existence of a partnership.

Within a partnership the usual status of a partner is that of a full equity partner who shares in profits and losses and who has unlimited liability for partnership debts. There are two special classes of partner.

Salaried Partner

A salaried partner receives a fixed amount of the partnership profits in the manner of a salary. Therefore, whether they are a genuine partner is a matter of fact and depends on, *inter alia*, his ability to enter into contracts which bind the other partners, the extent of his liability for partnership debts and his participation in the management of the partnership. If the facts demonstrate that the salaried partner is not in fact a partner, the salary will be treated as an expense of the partnership, whereas, if the salaried partner is to be treated as a partner, his salary is an appropriation of profit.

Sleeping Partner

A sleeping partner provides capital for the partnership, but takes no active part in the management of the partnership. The sleeping partner's profit share is treated as an appropriation of profit; however, it is not treated as earned income.

17.2. Limited Partnerships

Under the Limited Partnerships Act 1907 certain partners of specially registered partnerships may limit their liability for partnership debts, to the amount which they originally contributed in the manner of the shareholder of a company. There must, however, be at least one partner (the 'general partner') who retains unlimited liability. A limited partnership must fulfil the following conditions:

- it must be registered with the Registrar of Companies *(Limited Partnerships Act 1907 s.5)* giving the firm's name, nature and principal place of business, full name of each partner, the starting date and planned description;
- a statement that the firm is limited, with amounts contributed by the limited partners *(Limited Partnerships Act 1907 s.8)*;
- at least one partner must have unlimited liability. This may be a corporate partner;
- limited partners must not take any part in the running of the business and must not have the power to enter into contracts binding the partnership.

The profit of the partnership is shared according to the normal rules (although no class 4 NIC is payable on the profit share of limited partners since it is treated as unearned income), but there are special rules relating to loss relief and other claims by limited partners.

A limited partner is defined as an individual who:

- is a limited partner in a limited partnership registered under the Limited Partnerships Act 1907;
- is a partner in a firm, but is not entitled to take part in the management of the trade and is entitled to have any liabilities (or liabilities beyond a certain limit) for debts or obligations to be met or reimbursed by another person; or
- carries on a trade jointly with other persons, under the law of a territory outside the UK and who is not entitled to take part in the management of the trade and, under that law, is entitled to have any liabilities (or liabilities beyond a certain limit) for debts or obligations to be met or reimbursed by another person.

(ITA 2007 s.103A)

A non-active partner is defined as an individual who carries on a trade as a partner in a firm at a time during the year, other than as a limited partner, who devotes a significant amount of time, defined as an average of less than 10 hours a week, to personal activities connected with the trade during the relevant period. The relevant period is defined as the basis period, unless this period is of less than six months duration, in which case it is either the first six months or the last six months of trading. If relief is given on the assumption that an individual will devote a significant amount of time, but that individual does not, in fact, do so, the relief is withdrawn by making an assessment *(ITA 2007 s.103B)*.

17.3. Limited Liability Partnerships

The Limited Liability Partnerships Act 2000 permits the formation of Limited Liability Partnerships (LLPs) which limit the liability of partnerships under the following conditions:

- the firm must be registered as an LLP and must comply with a disclosure regime;
- an LLP is treated as a corporate body, i.e. it is a distinct legal person with full legal capacity;
- the liability of members is limited to their actual and pledged contributions;
- financial statements must be disclosed in the same manner as for limited companies;
- similar rules to those applying to company directors relating to wrongful trading etc. apply to members.

The main tax features of LLPs are:

- the LLP is treated as a partnership for the purposes of income tax and CGT *(ITTOIA 2005 s.863)*;
- the loss relief rules applying to limited partnerships under the Limited Partnerships Act 1907 apply to non-active members of LLPs, except that relief is restricted to the amount subscribed plus any further amount pledged in the case of insolvency. There are anti-avoidance rules to prevent the premature withdrawal of capital *(ITA 2007 ss.107&108)*. A non-active member of an LLP is defined as an individual who devotes less than 10 hours per week on average to the business of the partnership *(ITA 2007 s.112)*;
- the LLP is treated as a partnership for the purpose of CGT *(TCGA 1992 s.59A)*, except that the insolvency rules relating to companies apply in the case of an insolvent partnership;
- on insolvency any gain on which a partner has claimed roll-over relief will become chargeable *(TCGA 1992 s.156A)*;
- class 4 NICs are payable on members' profits shares from the LLP *(SSCBA 1992 s.15(3A))*.

Salaried partners of LLPs will be treated as employees and their rights and duties will be treated as rights and duties under a contract of employment during periods where all the following conditions are satisfied:

1. it is reasonable to assume that at least 80% of the total amount payable by the LLP in respect of the partner's performance is either:
   i) fixed; or
   ii) varied, but the variations are determined without reference to the overall profits or losses of the LLP; or

iii) not affected in practice by the overall amount of the profits and losses of the LLP;

2. the mutual rights and duties of the LLP and its members do not give the partner significant influence over the affairs of the LLP;
3. the partner's contribution to the LLP is less than 25% of the disguised salary, i.e. the amount falling within 1. above, which it is reasonable to assume that the partner will receive during the tax year in respect of services to the partnership. The amount of the contribution is the amount the partner has contributed as capital, including profits calculated under GAAP, less any amounts they have either previously drawn out or received back, is entitled to withdraw or receive back at a time that they are a member of the LLP, or is, or may be, entitled to require another person to reimburse to him. The entitlement to withdrawal, receipt or reimbursement may be direct or indirect. A partner's contribution includes amounts which the partner has undertaken to contribute to the capital of the LLP, whether the undertaking is legally enforceable or not, provided that the contribution is made by the later of 5 July 2014 or two months after becoming a member of the LLP.

(ITTOIA 2005 ss.863A-863G)

In determining whether ITTOIA 2005 s.863A(2) applies, any arrangements are to disregarded, the main purpose, or one of the main purposes, of which is to prevent this section from applying *(ITTOIA 2005 s.863G(1))*. In particular:

1. if an individual personally performs services to an LLP under arrangements involving a member of the LLP who is not an individual; and
2. the main purpose, or one of the main purposes of these arrangements, is to prevent ITTOIA 2005 s.863A(2) from applying; and
3. an amount becomes payable to the member of the LLP in relation to the performance of these services which would fall within ITTOIA 2005 s.863A(2) if the amount had arisen directly to the individual under a contract of service to the LLP,

the individual will be treated as a member of the LLP and the amount will be treated as employment income of the individual *(ITTOIA s.863G(2)-(4))*.

Any amounts treated as employment income under ITTOIA 2005 s.863A(2) are allowable as a deduction in calculating the profits of the LLP (*ITTOIA 2005 s.94AA)*.

17.4. Allocation of Profits

The profits from professional activities of a partnership as a whole are to be calculated by the normal rules as if it were an individual resident in the UK *(ITTOIA 2005 s.848)*, and are shared amongst the partners in accordance with the partnership agreement *(ITTOIA 2005 s.850(1))*. If there is no agreement or the agreement is silent on this matter, the profits are shared equally between all the partners. Other income of the partnership is treated separately and is treated as if it arose from a distinct trade. A profit-sharing agreement will state the shares in which profits are to be shared, but may also contain the following features:

- **Partnership salary**
  This is not to be confused with salaries paid to employees or a salaried partner. It is a prior allocation of profit to a partner as remuneration for specific responsibilities, e.g. a human resources partner, and is not a deductible expense.
- **Interest on capital accounts or current accounts**
  Partners will maintain an account with the partnership which contains capital contributed and profit shares not withdrawn. These may be split between current and capital accounts and the agreement may contain restrictions on the partners' ability to make withdrawals from a capital account. Different partners may have contributed different amounts of capital and may withdraw different amounts of their profit shares. Therefore, the profit-sharing agreement may provide for profit to be shared in the form of interest on the balance on the partners' capital accounts, current accounts or both.
- **Interest on drawings**
  Conversely, different partners may make different levels of drawings, and so interest may be charged to partners on their drawings during the year, i.e. this will reduce a partner's profit share.
- **Profit share**
  Any remaining profit after deducting salaries and interest is shared in an agreed proportion. If total salaries and interest exceed the profit for the year this figure is a loss, although it is a purely notional loss for the purpose of profit sharing and is not available for loss relief of any kind.

Example

Peter and Paul have been trading in partnership since 1999 sharing profits and losses equally. On 1 July 2019 they agreed to take Mary into partnership and the profit sharing agreement was changed to:

	Salary	**Profit Share**
Peter	£5,000	1/2
Paul	£10,000	1/4
Mary	£10,000	1/4

Peter decides to retire on 30 June 2021. His overlap profits on commencement were £8,000.

The adjusted trading profits have been:

y/e 30.6.19	£45,000
y/e 30.6.20	£30,000
y/e 30.6.21	£50,000

The profit shares of the partners will be:

Y/e 30.6.19

	Peter	Paul		Total
Profit share	£22,500	£22,500		£45,000

Y/e 30.6.20

	Peter	Paul	Mary	Total
	£	£	£	£
Salary	5,000	10,000	10,000	25,000
Profit share	2,500	1,250	1,250	5,000
	£7,500	£11,250	£11,250	£30,000

Y/e 30.6.21

	Peter	Paul	Mary	Total
	£	£	£	£
Salary	5,000	10,000	10,000	25,000
Profit share	12,500	6,250	6,250	25,000
	£17,500	£16,250	£16,250	£50,000

17.5. Assessment of Partnerships

Partners are taxed on their profit share on the same basis as if they were sole traders. This has the following consequences:

- a partner will normally be taxed on the current year basis;
- when a new partnership commences, the commencement rules will apply to the profit shares of all partners;
- when a partnership ceases, the cessation rules will apply to the profit shares of all partners;
- when a new partner joins a partnership or a partner leaves the partnership or dies, the commencement rules or cessation rules will apply only to the new partner or the partner leaving. The existing or continuing partners continue to be taxed on the current year basis;
- a change in the personal representative of a deceased partner or the trustees of a trust carrying on a business in partnership is not treated as a change *(ITTOIA 2005 s.258(1),(2))*;
- each partner has his own overlap profits and will deduct them in the year that they cease to be a partner.

These rules also apply where a sole trader becomes a partnership or vice versa.

Example

Using the profit shares in the previous example the assessments are:

2019/20

	Peter	Paul	Mary
Basis period y/e 30.6.19	£22,500	£22,500	
Basis period 1.7.19 – 5.4.20			
£11,250 x 279/365			£8,599

2020/21

	Peter	Paul	Mary
Basis period y/e 30.6.20	£7,500	£11,250	£11,250

Mary's overlap profits are £8,599

2021/22

	Peter	Paul	Mary
Basis period y/e 30.6.21	17,500	16,250	16,250
Less: Overlap profits	(8,000)		
	£9,500	£16,250	£16,250

17.6. Other Income of Partnership

Non-trading income arising in the business period e.g. interest or dividends is shared amongst partners in their profit sharing ratio *(ITTOIA 2005 s.851(1),(2))*.

17.7. Non-trading Partnerships

Profits and losses arising to a partnership not carrying on a trade are shared amongst partners on the basis of the profit-sharing agreement for the period *(ITTOIA 2005 s.847(2),(3))*.

17.8. Post-cessation Receipts

The rules relating to post-cessation expenses and receipts (see section **2.45**) apply on the cessation of membership of a partnership by a partner *(ITTOIA 2005 s.246(2)-(4))*.

17.9. Losses

Losses are divided amongst partners in a similar manner to profits, and each partner may choose how to claim relief for their profit share. This includes loss relief under ITA 2007 ss.72-74 when they first join the partnership and relief under ITA 2007 ss.89-92 when they leave. The amount of loss relief is restricted to the total amount of the loss incurred by the partnership in the period. Therefore, if the partnership makes a loss, but due to the profit sharing arrangements one of more of the partners has a profit, this profit is shared amongst the remaining partners in proportion to the loss allocated.

Example

Tom, Jerry and Spike have been in partnership for many years, sharing profits and losses as follows:

	Salary	Share
Tom	£5,000	1/2
Jerry	£10,500	1/4
Spike	£13,500	1/4

The loss for the year ended 31 December 2021 was £19,000. The loss available to each partner is:

	Tom	Jerry	Spike	Total
Salary	5,000	10,500	13,500	29,000
Profit share	(24,000)	(12,000)	(12,000)	(48,000)
	(19,000)	(1,500)	1,500	(19,000)
Profit re-allocated	1,390	110	(1,500)	
	£(17,610)	£(1,390)	£NIL	£(19,000)

Profit re-allocated to Tom: £1,500 x 19,000/20,500 = £1,390
Profit re-allocated to Jerry £1,500 x 1,500/20,500 = £110

17.10. Notional Losses

If the partnership as a whole makes a profit, but due to the profit-sharing arrangement one or more partners show a loss, this loss is re-allocated to the remaining partners in proportion to the profit allocated to them.

Example

Continuing the previous example, assuming the profit for the year ended 31 December 2021 were £11,000. The partners' profit shares would be:

	Tom	Jerry	Spike	Total
Salary	5,000	10,500	13,500	29,000
Loss share	(9,000)	(4,500)	(4,500)	(18,000)
	(4,000)	6,000	9,000	11,000
Profit re-allocated	4,000	(1,600)	(2,400)	
	£NIL	£4,400	£6,600	£11,000

Loss re-allocated to Jerry £4,000 x 6,000/15,000 = £1,600
Loss re-allocated to Spike: £4,000 x 9,000/15,000 = £2,400

17.11. Mergers and Amalgamations

Where a merger of partnerships results in a business which is different in nature from either or any of the previous businesses carried on by the constituent partnerships, there is a cessation of the old partnerships and a commencement of the new merged partnership *(SP 9/86 para. 2)*.

Where the business of the merged partnership is similar to those of the old partnerships, it is a question of fact whether there is a cessation and commencement in the case of each individual partner.

Where there is a demerger and the activities of the new partnerships are similar to those of the old partnership, the partners of the old partnership who continue as a partner of one of the new partnerships are taxed on a continuing basis. If one or more of the new partnerships carry on a different business, there will be a cessation and commencement for the partners of that partnership or those partnerships.

17.12. Restriction on Loss Relief for Limited and Non-Active Partners

The loss on which a limited or non-active partner or partner in an LLP may claim relief by offset against other income and capital gains, i.e. claims under *ITA 2007 ss.64,72 & 89* and *TCGA 1992 s.261B* is restricted to the lower of the amount of their actual and pledged capital contributions at the end of the basis period in which the loss was incurred *(ITA 2007 ss.104 & 110)* and £25,000 *(ITA 2007 s.103C)*. This does not affect the carry-forward of losses under ITA 2007 s.83 or the giving of sideways relief against profits from the same trade *(ITA 2007 s.103C(7))*. Any capital contributed to an LLP in a period in which a partner does not devote a significant amount of time to the trade (interpreted as less than an average of 10 hours per week) is to be disregarded if the main purpose, or one of the main purposes of making the contribution is to obtain a tax reduction through relief under the above sections (*ITA 2007 s.113A)*. For this purpose, an amount of money or an asset is not treated as having been contributed towards the capital of a firm or LLP until it is paid or transferred to the firm or LLP *(FA 2007 Sch. 4 para. 2)*.

This applies to limited partners under the Limited Partnerships Act 1907, any partner in an LLP *(Limited Liability Partnerships Act 2000)* and any participant in a joint venture arrangement whose liability is restricted by contract, agreement, guarantee or the laws of other countries and states. Any remaining loss may be carried forward to be offset against future profits arising from the partnership.

17.13. Partnership Property Income

Property income arising to a partnership which is incidental to its professional income is assessable on the same basis as trading income. The letting of jointly-owned properties does not itself create a partnership, and in this case the income will be treated as the partners' personal income rather than partnership income. If the facts indicate that there is a partnership, and the income from letting jointly owned properties is substantial enough to constitute a separate business, the income will be treated as partnership income*)*. If a property business is carried on in combination with another business the property income is assessable using the same basis period rules which apply for trading income *(ITTOIA 2005 ss.854 & 855)*. If the activities have been arranged so that there are two separate businesses the property income would be taxable on a tax year basis *(ITTOIA 2005 s.847(2))*.

17.14. Corporate Partners

Where one or more of the partners is a limited company, the profits of the partnership are computed as if the partnership were a company, in order to find the profit share of the corporate partner *(CTA 2009 s.1259)*, i.e. interest etc. will be dealt with under the loan relationship rules. Initially distributions are ignored, and there is no adjustment for charges on income and no deduction is made for losses brought forward from earlier periods. Loss relief is limited to the capital contributed by the company *(CTA 2009 s.56 & s.59)*. Where there is a change in persons carrying on the trade, and there is a corporate partner both before and after the change, but the corporate partner after the change was not a member before the change, there is a transfer of trade *(CTA 2009 s.1261(5))*. If there is at least one common corporate partner to both the old and the new partnership there is no transfer, but a continuation.

A company's profit share is based on its entitlement during its accounting period, which may not coincide with that of the partnership, and corporation tax is charged on that share as if it was derived from a trade carried on by the company alone during its accounting period.

Example

Wilson Ltd has an accounting date of 30 September and is a partner in a partnership with a 31 March accounting date. Their share of the partnership profits is as follows:

Y/e 31.3.21	£20,000
Y/e 31.3.22	£30,000

The partnership profits subject to corporation tax in the year ended 30 September 2021 are therefore (181/365 x £20,000) + (184/365 x £30,000) = £25,041.

If the partnership is managed and controlled abroad, but the corporate partner is UK-resident, assessments will be made on the company as if the partnership were resident in the UK *(CTA 2009 s.1259 (4))*.

Although the profits are computed as if the partnership were a company, this does not extend to making the partnership a connected person under CTA 2009 s.348, nor to making it a participator or associate under CTA 2010 s.454 and the partnership is therefore not connected with any of its members which provide loans to the partnership.

Subject to any exclusions in ITA 2007 ss.875-888, yearly interest paid by, or on behalf of a partnership in which a company is a member is paid under deduction of tax *(ITA 2007 ss.874 & 875)*.

17.15. Partnerships and Capital Gains Tax

17.15.1. General principles

The treatment of capital gains by partnerships is covered in Statement of Practice D12. Transactions between partners and third parties will be at arm's length, whereas certain transactions between partners will not be *(TCGA 1992 ss.17, 286(4))*. A partner is connected with any other of the existing partners and their spouses and relatives, except if the disposal is made as a *bona fide* commercial arrangement *(TCGA 1992 s.286(4))*. Where there is a disposal to a person who is connected for reasons other than because they are a partner, the exception will, in practice, be applied if the terms of disposal are such as they would have been if the parties had not been connected.

Gains on the disposal of partnership assets are assessed on the partners individually since each partner is deemed to own a part of the asset. The partnership agreement may stipulate a ratio for sharing gains which is different from the ratio for sharing profits, but if the agreement is silent on the matter the profit sharing ratio is used.

17.15.2. Distribution of assets in kind amongst partners

Where a partner receives an asset in kind from the partnership they are not treated as making a disposal, but the deemed proceeds will be the market value of his share less the amount of the gain attributable to him. The other partners are treated as making a disposal of their share.

Example

Sarah, Elizabeth and Helen are in partnership sharing profits and gains equally. Elizabeth and Helen transfer partnership assets with a market value of £100,000 to Sarah. The assets had cost £70,000 in 1999. A gain of £10,000 (1/3 x (£100,000 - £70,000)) will be attributable to each of Elizabeth and Helen. The deemed acquisition cost of the asset for Sarah will be £90,000, i.e. the market value of £100,000 less the gain of £10,000 attributable to her. If a loss had arisen on the transfer this would have been added to the market value.

17.15.3. Change in partnership profit sharing ratios

Where there is a change in partnership profit sharing ratios, or a partner joins or leaves the partnership, a partner reducing his profit share or leaving the partnership is treated as disposing of some, or all, of his share of the asset(s), and a partner increasing his profit share or joining the partnership is treated as making a corresponding acquisition.

Where assets have not been revalued in the accounts and no payments are made between partners outside the partnership, the disposal will be on a no gain/no loss basis.

Example

Stephen and David have been in partnership since 2000 sharing profits equally. They take Paul into partnership in June 2021, sharing the profits in the ratio of 2:2:1. No payments are made outside the accounts. The acquisition cost of chargeable assets in the accounts at the date of admission is £150,000. Stephen and David are each treated as making a disposal of £15,000 (10% x £150,000) to Paul, who acquires a share in the partnership assets of £30,000. The base cost of Stephen and Paul's remaining shares in the assets is £60,000.

Where there is a part disposal, the portion of the original cost or March 1982 value which is included is not calculated using the part disposal formula, but a fractional share is taken *(SP 1/89).*

17.15.4. Adjustment through the accounts

Where a partnership asset is revalued in the accounts, the revaluation does not in itself give rise to a charge, but if there is a subsequent reduction in a partner's share in asset surpluses they are treated as realising a gain of the appropriate fraction of the increase of the value of the asset. A partner whose share in asset surpluses increases will carry forward a base cost of the appropriate fraction of the revised value of the asset.

Example

Up to August 2021 William, Mary and John shared profits and losses equally. In September 2021 the profit shares were changed to William ½, Mary and John ¼ each. An asset acquired in 1992 for £120,000 was revalued to £360,000 in the accounts. Mary and John are both treated as making a disposal of £30,000 to William, i.e. 1/12 x £360,000 and William's share of the asset will be £100,000, i.e. (1/3 x £120,000) + (2 x £30,000).

17.15.5. Payments outside the accounts

Where payments are made outside the partnership accounts, these are included as part of the disposal consideration.

Example

Claire, Joanne and Zoë have been in partnership since 2001 sharing profits equally, but in 2021 Zoë leaves the partnership. The assets in the balance sheet have never been revalued and are valued at £300,000 at the date Zoë leaves. Claire and Joanne each pay Zoë a sum of £50,000 in addition to repaying the balance on her capital account. Since the reduction in Zoë's profit share would normally take place on a no gain/no loss basis, the consideration must be increased by the £100,000 which she receives from the other partners. Zoë therefore makes a gain of £100,000.

17.15.6. Transfer between persons not at arm's length

A charge to tax may arise where there is a disposal which is not at arm's length since market value is used in the computation instead of deemed or actual consideration. This will arise, for example, where there is a transaction between the partners which is not a *bona fide* commercial transaction. If the connection between the parties is other than that of both being partners, and the terms are such that those which would have existed between unconnected parties, this rule will not apply.

17.15.7. Disposals – annuity payments

The capitalised value of an annuity may be included as consideration for a disposal *(TCGA 1992 s.37(3))*; however, it will not be included to the extent that it represents 'reasonable recognition' of a partner's past contribution. Where a partner has been a partner for 10 years or more before retirement, including any period spent as partner of a firm which has subsequently merged with the current firm, the maximum annuity which is regarded as reasonable recognition is calculated as in the example in section **17.15.5** above. Where the period is less than 10 years, the average profits must be reduced to the following fractions:

Complete number of years	Fraction
1 to 5	1/60 for each year
6	8/60
7	16/60
8	24/60
9	32/60

If the capitalised value of the annuity is to be treated as consideration received by the retiring partner, it will be treated as capital expenditure by the other partners.

A lump sum payment to a retiring partner must be included as consideration paid for the purpose of 'reasonable recognition'. This will be the case where the aggregate of the annuity and 1/9 of the lump sum does not exceed the above fraction *(SP 1/79)*. However, the lump sum is still regarded as consideration.

17.15.8. Shares acquired in stages

If a partner acquires his share in the partnership in stages, the acquisition costs are pooled (provided the first acquisition was after 5 April 1965). If one or more of the acquisitions was before that date disposals are matched with acquisitions on a first in first out basis, unless this produces an unreasonable result.

17.15.9. Roll-over relief

Partners may claim roll-over relief on the disposal of business assets which are either owned by the partnership or which are owned outside the partnership. Roll-over relief is also available on a merger where assets are taken over by the merged partnership and payment is made outside the accounts or there has been a previous revaluation *(TCGA 1992 s.152)*. The relief will be restricted if the deemed consideration for the replacement assets is less than the deemed consideration for the old assets.

If assets are distributed to a partner on dissolution of a partnership, an increase in a partner's share is treated as a new asset for the purpose of roll-over relief.

Example

Andy and Richard have been in partnership sharing profit in the ratio 3:2. In 2021 the partnership is dissolved with each partner pursuing a business interest as a sole trader. The partnership owned two shops and each of them took over one of them. Andy disposed of a 3/5 share of the shop transferred to Richard and acquired a 2/5 in the shop transferred to him and vice versa in the case of Richard.

17.16. Roll-over and Gift Relief - LLPs

Where, as a result of claiming business asset roll-over relief *(TCGA 1992 ss.152-154)*, or gift relief *(TCGA 1992 s.165)* a limited liability partnership (LLP) member postpones a chargeable gain through his acquisition of a share in a LLP, there is the potential for that gain to fall out of charge in the future by reason of the LLP ceasing to be transparent. For example, if the LLP ceases trading the asset will vest in the liquidator, who will calculate any gain without reference to any previous roll-over or gift relief claims by partners. Each member who has postponed a gain is deemed to have a chargeable gain accruing to them immediately before the LLP ceases to be transparent. The gain is equal to the amount of the postponed gain or gains which has not then come back into charge *(TCGA 1992 s.156A)*. Gains which accrue to a member in consequence of this special provision qualify for entrepreneurs' relief.

Index